OPEN AND DISTA
LEARNING TODAY

Fred Lockwood here presents a comprehensive account of research and development activities in open, distance and flexible learning from acknowledged experts from around the world. The use of open, distance and flexible learning materials is expanding dramatically, not just in schools, further and higher education, but also in industry, commerce and the social services. Most higher education institutions now have an open learning unit or educational development centre, and many major commercial and industrial organisations have formed units to develop their own teaching and training materials. Internationally, growth is even more impressive, with new open universities planned for Singapore, Bangladesh and India, while those in Malaysia, Thailand, Australia and South Africa continue to expand. But current and future practice must be based on research evidence rather than intuition. With contributions from all leading names in the field, this book will be a key sourcebook for teachers, trainers and students.

Fred Lockwood is a Senior Lecturer within The Open University Institute of Educational Technology. He is an active researcher and consultant, and has published widely in the field of open and distance learning.

ROUTLEDGE STUDIES IN DISTANCE
EDUCATION
Series editor: Desmond Keegan

THEORETICAL PRINCIPLES OF DISTANCE EDUCATION
Edited by Desmond Keegan

DISTANCE EDUCATION: NEW PERSPECTIVES
Edited by Keith Harry, Magnus John and Desmond Keegan

COLLABORATION IN DISTANCE EDUCATION
Edited by Louise Moran and Ian Mugridge

OTTO PETERS ON DISTANCE EDUCATION
Edited by Desmond Keegan

THEORY AND PRACTICE IN DISTANCE EDUCATION
Börje Holmberg

TECHNOLOGY, OPEN LEARNING AND DISTANCE EDUCATION
A.W. (Tony) Bates

OPEN AND DISTANCE LEARNING TODAY

Edited by
Fred Lockwood

London and New York

First published 1995
by Routledge

11 New Fetter Lane, London, EC4P 4EE

Transferred to Digital Printing 2004

©1995 Fred Lockwood, selection and editorial matter

Typeset in Times by Melanie Bayley

British Cataloguing in Publication Data
A catalogue record for this book is available from the British Library.

Library of Congress Cataloguing in Publication Data
A catalogue record for this book has been requested.

ISBN 0–415–12758–0 (hbk)
ISBN 0–415–12759–9 (pbk)

CONTENTS

Part III Information Technology

Part IV Learner Use of Media

Part V Course Design and Assessment

Part VIII Evaluation and Quality

CONTRIBUTORS

Pirkko Aalto, a psychologist, has worked as Education Coordinator at the Turku University Centre for Extension Studies, Finland, since 1990. She has experience in health care, as a video producer and adult educator.

Tony Bates is Executive Director, Strategic Planning, Research and Information Technology at the Open Learning Agency (OLA) in British Columbia, where he has worked since 1990. Prior to that, he was Professor of Educational Media Research at The Open University, UK, where he worked for twenty years, and was one of the founding members of staff. His research groups at The Open University, UK, and OLA have published over 300 papers in the area of distance education and the use of technology for teaching. He is the author of five books and has worked as a consultant in over thirty countries.

Liz Burge is an Associate Professor in Adult Education in the Faculty of Education at the University of New Brunswick, Canada. She teaches graduate courses and continues to run workshops in adult and distance education, conduct research and development projects and link reflective practice to theory development.

Judith Calder is Head of the Student Research Centre at the Institute of Educational Technology at The Open University, UK, and has written about course and programme evaluation in open and distance learning systems. She has directed and undertaken an extensive number of different types of research and evaluation programmes in the open and distance learning field. Her research interests include adult learning strategies and change processes, and evaluation for open and distance learning systems.

Ellie Chambers is Senior Lecturer in Educational Technology and Chair of the Humanities Higher Education Research Group at The Open University, UK. She has twenty years' experience of working with colleagues in the Arts Faculty, as a pedagogic adviser and course evaluator.

John Dekkers is Professor and Head of the Distance Education Centre, Central Queensland University, Rockhampton, Australia. He has been involved in curriculum development and evaluation projects in science, mathematics and distance education in Australia and consultancies in America and South East Asia establishing open and distance learning systems. He is the author/co-author of three books and over 300 publications in the field of open and distance education. His research and development interests include communications technology for distance education and open learning programmes, school science and mathematics enrolment trends as well as student learning styles, while his current major research interests are in multimedia use and student support networks for open learning.

Terry Evans is Professor, and Head of the Graduate School of Education, at Deakin University in Australia where he has been actively involved in the development and teaching of the Master of Distance Education course. He has been a researcher of distance education in Australia and the UK. Some of his research has concerned students' experiences of off-campus study and, in this regard, he has recently published *Understanding Learners in Open and Distance Education* (Kogan Page; 1994).

David Harris is a Senior Lecturer in Social Sciences at the College of St Mark and St John in Plymouth, UK. He has worked for The Open University, UK, researched it for his PhD, and has since published several pieces about the OU and distance education. His interests include social theory and cultural studies and their connections with education.

James Hartley is Professor of Applied Psychology at the University of Keele. He has published extensively in the area of written communication and is widely recognised as an international expert in this field. Professor Hartley is a Fellow of both the British and the American Psychological Association.

David Hawkridge is Professor of Applied Educational Sciences in the Institute of Educational Technology at The Open University, UK, and was Director of the Institute from 1970 to 1988. His teaching and research interests include applications of information technology in distance education.

Merja Jalava has worked as Education Coordinator at the Turku University Centre for Extension Studies in, Finland, since 1986. He is responsible for the planning of distance education, and is an adult educator at the Finnish Open University and in professional continuing education.

Desmond Keegan is manager of the European Virtual Classroom for Vocational Training Project at the Audio Visual Centre, University College Dublin, Ireland, and editor of the Routledge 'Studies in Distance Education' series.

Neale Kemp has worked in the printing and publishing industry for over twenty years in the areas of typesetting, graphic design, education and management. He was previously Manager of the University Publishing Unit at the Central Queensland University, Australia, where he was instrumental in establishing a sophisticated distance education computer-publishing network. Having completed a Master's degree researching the effect of typography upon student learning through instructional print materials, he is presently establishing a typography and print production consultancy in Canada.

Adrian Kirkwood has experience of all phases of course development and currently works in the Programme on Learner Use of Media within The Open University's Institute of Educational Technology, UK. He undertakes research and evaluation studies related to access and applications of media and information technologies, both within The Open University and outside. He has published widely and co-authored *Personal Computers for Distance Education* (Paul Chapman; 1992).

Badri Koul is Pro-Vice-Chancellor within the Indira Gandhi National Open University (IGNOU) in New Delhi, India. He has worked at Udaipur University, CIEFL in Hyderabad and at IGNOU since 1986. His major contributions to the field have been the conceptualisation, development and implementation of Post-Graduate Diploma in Distance Education and MA programmes in Distance Education at IGNOU.

Jack Koumi has degrees in mathematics and psychology, and for six years was a university lecturer and teacher trainer. For twenty-two years, from 1970 to 1992, he worked for the BBC Open University Production Centre, producing audio and video programmes. Additionally, since 1981, half his time has been spent training producers and scriptwriters of educational media. He has undertaken over forty such training and consultancy projects, in sixteen different countries. He has published many papers on production and management of educational media and now works full time in the field, as a freelance trainer/ consultant.

Colin Latchem is Associate Professor and Head of the Teaching Learning Group at Curtin University, Perth, Western Australia. He has a background in teacher education and educational technology, and has undertaken numerous consultancies. In recent years, he has edited a book on interactive multimedia and has written extensively on videoconferencing and other telecommunications applications in distance education.

Paul Lefrere is Lecturer in Educational Technology in the Centre for Information Technology in Education at The Open University, UK, and is a member of the Information Design Association. His research interests are in effective communication and in systems for communication. He uses desk-top publishing software and specialised graphics software extensively.

Roger Lewis is BP Professor of Learning Development at the University of Humberside, UK. He has previously worked in most major national UK open learning institutions, including the National Extension

College, The Open University and The Open College. He has taken most of his own qualifications by open learning.

Fred Lockwood is Senior Lecturer in Educational Technology at The Open University, UK, and is heavily involved in developing open learning material both at The Open University and as a consultant to other open and distance teaching centres. He is Series Editor of the Open and Distance Learning Series published by Kogan Page.

Richard Lowe has developed flexible learning materials for academic, industrial and government organisations. He is an active researcher in the field of pictorial comprehension with a particular interest in explanatory illustrations such as technical diagrams. His development work includes designing instructional illustrations for interactive multimedia applications.

Michael Macdonald-Ross has worked at The Open University, UK, since 1969 where he is Reader in Textual Communication and leads the Institute of Educational Technology's Programme for Texts and Readers. He has held the Special Award of the US–UK Educational Commission (Fulbright) and has been Visiting Scholar at Stanford University, California, and consultant to the UN Development Programme of the World Bank and the World Health Organization.

Robin Mason is Head of the Centre for Information Technology in Education at The Open University, UK. Her primary research area is the design and evaluation of telecommunications-based teaching and learning. She has worked on a number of European-funded projects involving telecommunications technologies and her recent book entitled *Using Communications Media in Open and Flexible Learning* distils her experience in this area.

Michael Moore is Academic Director of The American Center for Study of Distance Education at The Pennsylvania State University, USA, and founding editor of *The American Journal of Distance Education*. He spent nine years in The Open University, UK, seven in East Africa, three in Canada, and was Vice President of ICDE from 1988 to 1992.

Alistair Morgan is Senior Lecturer in Educational Technology in the Institute of Educational Technology at The Open University, UK. He has wide experience of research in student learning and developing student-centred pedagogies in open and distance learning.

Hilary Perraton trained as an administrator at the London County Council and has worked on educational policy and on distance education at the National Extension College, International Extension College and Commonwealth Secretariat. He is currently Educational Planner for Distance Education at the University of the West Indies.

Jay Reid trained as a primary school teacher and taught until appointed Director of a Teachers' Centre in 1985. In 1987 he joined Auckland College of Education and in 1992 was appointed Northern Regional Manager of The Open Polytechnic of New Zealand. For many years he has been a passionate advocate of open and distance learning and is interested in how technology may be applied to improve both teaching and learning.

Bernadette Robinson is currently Director of Professional Development at the International Extension College, UK. Formerly of The Open University, UK, she has extensive international experience of open and distance learning as a consultant and trainer. Her research and writing are on the use of telecommunications, teacher education, learner support and quality.

Alexander Romiszowski is Technical Director, Training Systems Institute, and Research Professor, Instructional Design, Development, and Evaluation at Syracuse University. His research and development interests include instructional design, distance education and new technologies, particularly multimedia and telecommunications and their application to adult education/training. He has worked as consultant to many private and public organisations and in United Nations projects in Spain, Italy, India, Hungary and Brazil. Prior to Syracuse, he taught instructional technology in universities in England, Brazil and Canada. He has published extensively in the field, including the 'trilogy': *Designing Instructional Systems, Producing Instructional System* and *Developing Auto-Instructional Materials.*

Alan Tait has worked in the field of student support in open and distance learning for The Open University, UK, since 1974, both at its headquarters in Walton Hall and since 1978 in the Regional Centre in Cambridge where he is a Senior Counsellor. He has worked for the OU in continental Europe and internationally as a consultant.

Mary Thorpe is Director of the Institute of Educational Technology at The Open University, UK. She has been engaged in teaching research and devellopment at the OU for twenty years. Her publications include *Evaluating Open and Distance Learning* (Longman; 1993) and the edited reader *Culture and Processes of Adult Learning* (Routledge; 1993).

Martin Valcke received his PhD in educational computing at the University of Gent, Belgium, where he conducted research on microworlds and programming environments. He is now Senior Lecturer and Research Manager in the Centre for Educational Technology and Innovation at the Open universiteit in the Netherlands.

Tom Vincent, MBE, is Senior Lecturer in Educational Technology at The Open University, UK. He has directed the 'Information Technology for Blind People' project since 1979 and is co-author of several books including *Learning Difficulties and Computers: Access to the Curriculum.*

Guillaume Vuist received an MS in cognitive science from the University of Nijmegen, where he was engaged in the field of knowledge acquisition and user interface design. Now working at the Open universiteit of the Netherlands for his PhD where he is researching the application of knowledge-based systems in the context of distance education.

Peter Whalley is Research Fellow in the Institute of Educational Technology at The Open University, UK. His main research topic is the development and evaluation of multimedia teaching materials for distance education. Other interests include the development of simple direct-manipulation authoring environments that allow young children to create dynamic multimedia documents describing their school work.

Alan Woodley is a Senior Research Fellow in Institute of Educational Technology at The Open University, UK, where he carries out research into the characteristics of OU students, their progress and subsequent outcomes. He is particularly interested in issues of access and equal opportunities and is currently working on the evaluation of the OU's 'Living in a Changing Society' access modules.

Bob Zimmer works in the Institute of Educational Technology at The Open University, UK. He believes that participants in courses of all kinds want to experience community and find clarity. His work centres on making sure that they can.

Preface

Sir John Daniel

Vice-Chancellor
The Open University

In the summer of 1970 a first cohort of 25,000 students were admitted to a new university. They took a risk in joining The Open University. It was an untried institution whose radical innovations of open admission and multimedia distance learning had provoked hostility among politicians and scepticism in educational circles. Now, a generation later, we can see that those intrepid students actually pioneered the most important educational innovation of their time. From its uncertain beginnings, The Open University has become the UK's largest university and now plays a central role in the credit transfer and award validation mechanisms that knit British higher education and training together. Moreover, over the last twenty-five years the success of The Open University has inspired the creation of similar projects in dozens of countries around the world.

Now a second revolution is under way. Spurred by continuing growth in the demand for education, especially among adults, teaching and training institutions of all types are exploring and adopting the methods of open and distance learning. They are encouraged by the convergence of computers, telecommunications and television, which will turn our homes into environments for learning as rich as our schools and colleges.

This is a handbook for successful revolutionaries. Between these covers the world's foremost experts have distilled the lessons of the first generation of open and distance learning. They give the keys to successful practices, they describe the wheels that do not need to be reinvented, and they show new ways of accessing knowledge and skills that can liberate millions of human beings.

Part I

TRENDS AND DIRECTIONS

1

THE BIG BANG THEORY IN DISTANCE EDUCATION

David Hawkridge

INTRODUCTION

Join any group of distance educators today and the chances are you will hear talk of exponential expansion of distance education when the information superhighways come into being, within a decade. This might be called the Big Bang theory of distance education. You will hear enthusiastic talk about two-way communication (at last) between teacher and student, replacing the old one-way systems of print, radio and television. At last, students everywhere will be able to explore massive knowledge stores. You may also hear gloomy comments about limited access, costs and the dangers of technological determinism. You may even hear critics who seriously decry the commodification of knowledge represented by distance education. And, of course, there will be those cautious optimists who advocate slow but steady advance, but not at any price. Who is right?

This chapter outlines the reasons for thinking that distance education can expand exponentially. It examines the differences between old and new media for distance education, especially their capacities to sustain two-way communication that aids learning. It assesses the doubts expressed about access, costs and other negative aspects now looming. It looks briefly into the dangers of domination by multinational capitalist interests. Finally, it summarises The Open University's attempts to create a Big Bang for its own students.

IS THE BIG BANG COMING IN DISTANCE EDUCATION?

When the London Stock Exchange switched overnight from paper to computers, this electronic transformation was called the Big Bang. The name doubtless reflected the megalomaniacal aspirations of stockbrokers and systems analysts who, god-like, wished to create a new universe in a single moment. It also reflected fears that the whole project would explode, severely damaging one of the largest financial markets on earth. In fact, the Big Bang worked.

Some people think that distance education's Big Bang is due shortly, because of changes in telecommunications. Nearly twenty years ago, James Martin, of IBM's Systems Research Institute, wrote an upbeat analysis of telecommunications (Martin, 1977). He foresaw many changes including optical fibre cables going into homes, cheap electronic mail and television news with worldwide satellite coverage. He made other forecasts that were wrong, but for the late 1990s he predicted that, 'The wideband, rapidly-switched communication networks ... [will] form an infrastructure vital to the running of industry. Nations which do not have this expensive infrastructure [will] find that their industrial productivity and hence economic strength is falling far behind the nations with advanced telecommunications.' Today, these networks have the grand title of electronic information superhighways.

Vice-President Al Gore, speaking to the International Telecommunications Union in Buenos Aires, ensured maximum publicity for US attempts to build these superhighways (Gore, 1994). He proposed the creation of a Global Information Infrastructure (GII), which would, among other things, 'help educate our children', to say nothing of adults. In the US, this 'network of networks' would provide telephone and interactive digital video to almost every American. With President Clinton, Gore called for the network to be extended into every classroom, library, hospital and clinic in the US by the year 2000. Every user, worldwide, would be able to reach 'thousands of different sources of information – video programming, electronic newspapers, computer bulletin boards – from every country, in every language.' Gore envisaged a Global Digital Library, via Internet, that would allow millions of students, scholars and business people to find the information they need. Was his speech a fantasy, or a far-sighted vision? Recent multi-billion dollar deals in the US give a foretaste of superhighways to come. Internet is growing at 10 per cent per month and may have 100 million users within a few years (Bildt, 1994).

Not everyone thinks this vision is correct. Syfret (1994) doubts whether progress towards the GII will be as fast in Europe as in the US because of problems of investment and payback. Digital superhighways can carry all kinds of traffic. He says that it is conceivable that 'one or two of these, like videophony or home shopping, will be so profitable in their own right that they alone can carry the burden of highway construction', but other kinds of traffic will incur their own specific investment costs, and will be expected to run profitably too. On the other hand, he quotes George Gilder, a Canadian, who foresees a million-fold increase in the cost-effectiveness of computers and their networks, resulting in the death of broadcast television and other 'mass media' and the birth of interactive systems that suit individuals' needs. Digital videocompression is a revolutionary technology that will allow instant access video-on-demand. Videos held in a massive computer store will be available through the telephone network or cable, or via satellite, says Forrest (1994).

Other countries besides the US are certainly trying to create these superhighways, some with an eye for education (for a European discussion, see Eraut, 1991). Sweden, for example, is creating a national infrastructure for information, with new digital networks being constructed all over the country. Its government wants everyone to be able to retrieve information and communicate with each other quickly, easily, safely and cheaply by electronic means. 'It is a matter of saving lives, creating jobs, revealing opportunities for each of us to obtain access to the best education offered in the world,' said Carl Bildt, Prime Minister. He chairs a cabinet-level commission on information technology with the task of sweeping away barriers and providing about one billion Swedish crowns (about £865 million) for research and development in this field (Bildt, 1994).

In the United Kingdom, BT (formerly British Telecom) may be stalled on the superhighway (Bell, 1994). A report by Parliament's Trade and Industry Committee on fibre-optic networks recommended that the government should keep them under urgent review, but it did not give the go-ahead to BT to build such a national network, and actually prevented BT from offering any television services before 2002. Instead, the US-owned cable companies received some encouragement. Despite these recommendations, Bell reported authoritative sources as saying that the UK is at the forefront in creating a superhighway, with faster investment than in the US. Cable is being laid at an incredible 280 miles a week. Numbers of cable connections are projected to pass satellite dish installations by the year 2000, although another competing system, involving digital television, radio, telephone and data transmissions via satellite may be about to be born that could remove the need for cable (BBC, 1994).

The question of which companies would provide a service that included education was not addressed, let alone answered, by the Parliamentary Committee's report. It is just as well that SuperJANET, the British universities' superhighway for education and research, will soon offer advanced distance learning, remote library access, instant document delivery, electronic journals and interactive browsing. BT carries the network, paid for by the government, and plans to offer wide access to it within the UK and abroad (Yeomans, 1994).

These political and technological developments certainly hold out the possibility of a Big Bang in distance education, perhaps not on a single day but more likely over a period of 5–15 years, in which institutions switch from essentially a paper-based system to one that is electronic. It is hardly surprising to hear that 600 US universities and colleges, plus 100 corporate associates, are busily planning a National Learning Infrastructure Initiative which could remove constraints of time and place from much of US higher education (Graves, 1994). The Big Bang is not so much a theory as a vision supported by much reasoning and speculation about the benefits for students of such a revolutionary change. In particular, exponential expansion seems possible, given sufficient students, because the superhighways could overcome many of the difficulties of supporting these students while they study. Indeed, they could transform the way the students are taught. One advocate of a Big Bang is Duning (1993). She suggests that fundamental changes are approaching with lightning speed, fostered by those who believe in distance education through telecommunications, rather than by educators. She cites the rapid expansion of electronic networks, belonging to multi-site companies and other organisations in the US, and used for video teleconferencing for training staff. IBM's Interactive Satellite Television Network is a prime example, serving an average of 18,000 employees each working day. Says Duning, 'With the classroom doors flung open by satellite … the effects on interactive teaching are likely to be profound.'

While some people think about the Big Bang, others are ready for it. Mapp (1994) mentions plans to create a virtual campus in a British university – unnamed – with most learning materials and transactions available through an electronic network. At least one already exists in the USA:

For Immediate Release

16 July 1994

Contact: Robert Donnelly

donnelly@coyote.csusm.edu

Dr William Painter

wpainter@bigcat.missouri.edu

Virtual Online University is For Real!

The Virtual Online University, Inc. (VOU) announces beginning classes on the Internet in September 1994. VOU was founded in April 1994, and incorporated as a non-profit educational organisation in June to provide a novel approach to alternative education by offering fully online, accredited distance learning using the Internet. The goal of VOU is to provide low-cost, high-quality education and training.

Current offerings include an accredited Liberal Arts degree program, emphasising numeracy, literacy and critical thinking as components of its interdisciplinary approach to distance education. Future offerings will include post-graduate programs, anticipated to begin during the second half of 1995. VOU has temporary space at (telnet) falcon.cit.cornell.edu 8888 and is seeking permanent server space prior to beginning classes in September.

According to Dr William Painter, Executive Director, VOU will "... target two primary audiences: first, current college and university students in traditional education paths who wish to broaden their opportunities with online education; and second is the non-traditional, learning-disenfranchised person, that is, individuals who have limited access to traditional education due to financial restrictions, physical challenges, being part of at-risk populations, or with responsibilities which preclude pursuing traditional educational paths."

The corporate mission statement of Virtual Online University is:

• to provide low-cost, high-quality education;

• to offer distance education using interactive, interdisciplinary methods outside of traditional learning paths;

• to assist traditional and non-traditional learners in furthering their educational objectives;

• to form working relationships within business and industry to provide students with valuable hands-on experience to supplement a liberal arts education;

• to conduct research and provide a practical forum for investigation of online environments and applications in distance education, telecommunications and electronic delivery systems.

Virtual Online University operates within a Virtual Education Environment using Multiuser Object-Oriented environment database software (a MOO). Some MOOs are programmed as virtual cities and research centers, others as educational environments. VOU will use various MOOs as online virtual campuses, including a 'traditionally designed' university campus and one designed as an orbiting space station in Geosynchronous Earth Orbit. Others are currently in planning, including an undersea environment.

HOW DO OLD AND NEW MEDIA FOR
DISTANCE EDUCATION DIFFER?

Whether or not a MOO successfully provides an undersea teaching environment in the Virtual Online University must be a matter of doubt. There is a rumour abroad that old media are used for good new teaching methods, while new media are used for bad old ones. It is certainly true that methods of using older media such as print, television, videocassettes, radio and audiocassettes are now highly developed. There are plenty of examples of high-quality teaching materials based on these media: in 1994 The Open University received an 'excellent' rating for its distance teaching in management, chemistry and geography when these were assessed by the national Quality Assessment Unit. Methods of using newer media such as

7

computers, teleconferencing and interactive television are so far rather underdeveloped. Bad, old programmed learning is still possible on the new computers. Many teachers resort to bad, old methods on new interactive television. Bad old 'full frontal teaching' and talking-head lectures go out over new videoconferencing channels. Even IBM's two-way video distance learning system for staff and customers uses a lecturer-plus-visuals format (Scott, 1993). There is widespread ignorance concerning how best to exploit the new media, despite analysis and evaluation by Laurillard (1994) and many others.

The greatest difference, however, between the old and new media is in their capacities to sustain two-way communication that aids learning. Two-way communication between teacher and student(s) is replacing the old one-way systems of print, radio and television. Laurillard (1993), in her analysis of teaching in higher education through media, emphasises the power of two-way communication systems to enhance reflection and understanding. She points out that academic learning is mediated rather than experiential: it deals with other people's conceptions of how the world is understood. Reflection, in particular, is difficult to foster in distance education without two-way communication, therefore the new media have something valuable to offer. Laurillard raises warning signals about them, however, because she sees each as having disadvantages as well as being of benefit to learners.

A second substantial difference between old and new media is that through the latter students are able to explore massive knowledge stores – the databases. If this were simply a matter of being able to search bibliographies, that would be an advance on many 1994 distance education courses, which expect students to do no more than read what is sent to them. It is more than this: students on the superhighway can search whole libraries, obtain electronic copies, consult distant experts, and so on. This can radically change their approach to learning, and their teachers' approach to teaching. Of course, it is easy to exaggerate what is immediately available. Students will repeatedly end up in cul de sacs simply because digitisation has not proceeded fast enough in a particular back street off the highway. On the other hand, it is also easy to be unaware of the pace of change in this field. For example, new educational television programmes in several countries will be entirely digitised within a few years, print production is already digitised, and so on. With digitisation, creation of massive knowledge stores is feasible.

DOUBTS ABOUT ACCESS, COSTS AND OTHER NEGATIVE ASPECTS

Quite rightly, people have serious doubts about limited access and high costs. Despite Mr Gore's democratic vision, market forces seem likely to oblige telecommunications companies to install the superhighways first where heavy traffic is guaranteed and tolls can be collected. The power of governments to ensure that remote communities or disadvantaged minorities can get onto the superhighways is not absolute. True, transmissions by satellite as well as cable may result in more even coverage than by cable alone. But costs, and prices, in rural districts are likely to be higher than in towns. High prices will place access to the superhighways beyond the reach of people on low incomes, or will force them to spend on this access, money they can ill afford. Even after getting on to the road, so to speak, such people may not be able to afford to stop at the garages, because entry to the knowledge stores will be too expensive and their products will cost too much. These are the dangers of technological determinism, of technology driving society rather than vice versa. The Big Bang in distance education could leave many aspiring students out in the cold, unable any longer to buy the cheap, old, good teaching contained in books and distance education units.

Some critics seriously decry the commodification of knowledge represented by distance education, which turns out knowledge products for sale to mass markets of students. The Big Bang would clearly add to the dangers of domination of distance education institutions by multinational interests, who own the superhighways without exception. Think of capitalism, the market and the profit motive: the costs of producing digitised materials may rise, requiring greater investment on which the shareholders will want a quick and substantial return. Every day, Rupert Murdoch and his ilk are buying into the means of production and distribution of knowledge. Is it too fanciful to think of large national open universities being denationalised within a decade? Will they be sold off, privatised? With their large enrolments, steady demand and efficiencies of scale, would they become rather profitable, given a powerful launch on to the superhighways?

IS THE OPEN UNIVERSITY HEADING FOR A BIG BANG?

Bates (1993) suggests that The Open University is slow to change its technology. The fact is that using the new technology for teaching is not a matter of any interest to a considerable majority among present OU academic staff, who prefer to stick to their reading and writing. The OU's experience with computer-mediated communication in half a dozen courses is well-documented (e.g. Mason and Kaye, 1989; Mason, 1992). These courses usually have a small, vociferous and enthusiastic group of users, and a majority of non-users, among staff as well as students.

In 1993–4 the university was examining opportunities for offering electronic services and systems to students and tutors throughout the UK, with priority perhaps for those who are housebound, disabled, overseas or rurally located. The students would choose to register for electronic versions of some courses. They would opt for tutorial support via e-mail and teleconferencing and their tutor would not necessarily be nearby. Correspondence tuition would initially be handled on paper, while systems for marking and commenting upon assignments submitted online were set up and evaluated.

The OU could capitalise on the experience and enthusiasm of some thousands of OU students (and their tutors) who have already used online services, mainly computer-conferencing. They are quite keen to maximise the use of equipment and software they already have. In implementing a pilot system, no value judgements need be made about the relative merits of face-to-face and online tutoring, only an assumption that some students may prefer one form of support over the other for some courses, in some circumstances.

Improvements are needed quickly, however, if the OU wants to keep its students happy. The conferencing system should be changed from CoSy to a well-supported commercial product such as First Class or Lotus Notes. CoSy was once a sensible choice, but there are now far better systems on the market. Students and staff need a transparent integrated interface to all online services available through the OU system, including conferencing, e-mail, Internet and OU administrative services such as course information, student records, registration, summer school allocation, fee payments and so on. Students need low-cost access from other European countries and elsewhere in the world, possibly via Internet and national academic networks. Tutors need training, probably through an online course about designing and tutoring online courses.

In 1994 the first 'virtual summer school' was held at the OU, replacing a compulsory week-long period of residential study and laboratory work for a dozen students taking a psychology course. Linked to the tutor and each other via e-mail, videoconferencing and a collaborative work system, these students worked for two weeks on psychology experiments, statistical analysis of their results and writing simple artificial intelligence programs. Via Internet, they 'attended' a lecture by a world expert on human–computer interaction, speaking from the Apple headquarters in California.

Such moves towards the Big Bang raise many questions. Strategic thinking is essential, as is a clear understanding of how to use the technology for teaching at a distance. Is the OU optimistic about the power of the technology to enable education to proceed better than ever and in the OU style? For example, should there be an OU online information base? About what? For whom? Will the information relate only to courses? How will teaching intentions relate to the base? Does anybody know enough yet to use the technology well? Can the rest learn how to do so?

If there is to be general acceptance of the benefits of new technology, academic objectives must be seen to lead rather than follow the technology. Recently, OU course teams have encountered technical difficulties with CD-ROM technology that have placed an extra load on staff already under pressure. Course authors have met increased uncertainty because rights for electronic versions are more difficult (and sometimes impossible) to clear than for print. CD-ROMs can easily carry large libraries of text, but selecting, scanning and processing items is not cheap. Capturing illustrations in electronic form has not proved easy. Use of audio and video has been extremely limited so far – there is no true multimedia teaching on CD-ROMs being distributed to students in 1995. Students using CD-ROMs may not like having to read most of the text on their screens, despite the search facilities. For tutors, problems may arise because such courses permit students a wider choice of materials in answering TMAs. Evaluation will tell the tale.

CONCLUSION

It seems clear that the Big Bang in distance education is likely to happen first in those countries that are the first to have electronic superhighways. Bates (1994) says that Canada's Open Learning Agency has brought its students on thirty-two courses on to computer-mediated communication and Internet. Ehrmann (1994a, b) cites US examples that illustrate a merging of distance and on-campus teaching methods, but Duning (1994) speculates on whether such changes will result in distance education losing its competitive advantage. If she is right, or if the difficulties of using the superhighways for distance education prove insurmountable, the Big Bang could turn out to be a whimper. Meantime, as Duning says, distance educators everywhere had better notice what's happening and decide on their strategy.

REFERENCES

Bates, A. (1993) 'Technology for distance education: a ten-year perspective' in Harry, K. *et al.* (eds).

Bates, A. (1994) Personal electronic communication, 20 July.

BBC (1994) Broadcast on Radio 4, 6 October.

Bell, E. (1994) 'BT stall on superhighway', *The Observer*, 31 July, p. 5.

Bildt, C. (1994) 'Sweden climbs the information technology ladder', *The CTISS File*, No. 17, pp. 50–3.

Duning, B. (1993) 'The coming of the new distance educators in the United States: the telecommunications generation takes off' in Harry, K. *et al.* (eds).

Ehrmann, S. (1994a) 'Looking backwards: US efforts to use technology to transform undergraduate education' in Martin, J. *et al.* (eds).

Ehrmann, S. (1994b) 'US higher education in 1998: how it might use technologies for undergraduate education' in Martin, J. *et al.* (eds).

Eraut, M. (ed.) (1991) *Education and the Information Society*, London, Cassell.

Forrest, J. (1994) 'Digital compression: the most radical revolution since satellites', *Intermedia*, 22(2), pp. 39–43.

Gore, A. (1994) 'Forging a new Athenian age of democracy', *Intermedia*, 22(2), pp. 4–7.

Graves, W. (1994) 'Toward a national learning infrastructure', Keynote address to the Association for Learning Technology Conference '94, 19–21 September, Hull.

Harry, K. *et al.* (eds) (1993) *Distance Education: New Perspectives*, London, Routledge.

Laurillard, D. (1993) *Rethinking University Teaching*, London, Routledge.

Laurillard, D. (1994) 'How can learning technologies improve learning?' in Martin, J. *et al.* (eds).

Mapp, L. (1994) 'Learning from learning technology: a framework of implementation issues', *The CTISS File*, No. 17, pp. 23–6.

Martin, J. (1977) *Future Developments in Telecommunications*, second edition, Englewood Cliffs, New Jersey, Prentice-Hall.

Martin, J. *et al.* (eds) (1994) *Higher Education 1998 Transformed by Learning Technology*, Oxford, Computers in Teaching Initiative.

Mason, R. (1992) 'Computer conferencing for managers', *Interactive Learning International*, Vol. 8, pp. 15–28.

Mason, R. and Kaye, A. R. (eds) (1989) *Mindweave: Communication, Computers and Distance Education*, Oxford, Pergamon.

Scott, B. (1993) 'IBM distance learning developments using video-conferencing' in Harry, K. *et al.* (eds).

Syfret, T. (1994) 'Move over, PPV and VOD: free television will retain the dominant audience share', *Intermedia*, 22(2), pp. 27–9.

Yeomans, K. (1994) 'Towards a blanket licence scheme for the re-use of copyright material in computer courseware development', *The CTISS File*, No. 17, pp. 60–2.

2

A PRACTICAL AGENDA FOR THEORISTS OF DISTANCE EDUCATION

Hilary Perraton

INTRODUCTION

The development of an expanded programme of distance education at the University of the West Indies provides an opportunity for matching practical needs against research questions of wider interest.

The programme needs information both about a set of practical issues and about four practical questions which can be answered within a theoretical framework. First, what guidance can be given to academic staff on the curricular content of their courses? Second, what guidance can be given on the instructional design and presentation of courses? This in turn leads to a search for something more robustly established than the commonly applied heuristics of course development. Third, how can we demonstrate the legitimacy of distance education and design a system that will enhance that legitimacy? Discussion on the quality of distance education may be relevant here. Fourth, how can we justify the use of resources on distance education?

BACKGROUND

The University of the West Indies is constrained by space, time and money – geography, history and economics. It takes more than half a day and US$350 to fly from either of the two campuses in the eastern Caribbean to the third in Jamaica. The University was first set up as a university college in relationship with the University of London, at a time when no British university took distance education seriously. Geography has pressed it towards the use of distance education, initially through the establishment of a teleconference service. The University, funded by governments unhappily dependent on sugar, bananas and tourism, has few resources it can divert from its regular teaching to distance education.

My job is to help the University go beyond what it has done through teleconferencing, and to establish an expanded and effective programme of distance education, making the University's resources more widely and more fairly available to the non-campus countries and to non-campus students.

One starting-point is the Renwick report (Renwick *et al.*, 1992) which sketched plans for the University to become a dual-mode institution. Other guides to policy are knowledge about the needs of the University's host communities, the views of the University staff, and the extensive literature on education in the Caribbean. Many of the planner's questions can and should be answered entirely within the region. But there are others to which answers ought to be available from the research and even the theoretical literature. The opportunity to plan a new distance-education programme can cast a searchlight across the research landscape, illuminating the towers of well-established hypothesis, the unproductive sloughs of ill-conceived enquiry, and the empty heights where our ancestors' neglected footpaths just might lead to new visions of intellectual delight, new mines of understanding.

As the single regional university, the University of the West Indies has a responsibility to meet needs in tertiary education throughout the region. In interpreting that responsibility it needs at the same time to take account of the development of community colleges and other tertiary institutions. The University is therefore faced with general questions about the courses it should offer and the areas of work to be expanded or contracted and specific questions about the distance-education courses it should develop. A subsidiary set of questions is about the way in which these courses should be developed and organised.

Educational theory has little to offer in tackling the first set of problems. Some are political and institutional. How should responsibility for different aspects of distance teaching be distributed between the campuses and the University centres in non-campus countries? What kind of institutional structure will best suit the University? How best should tertiary education be organised in small island states? Many are logistical. Where are print costs lowest? What is the most appropriate way to upgrade the teleconference system? Some are psychological. How does one engender support within the University for changes in working practice? Above all, many are financial. How can we raise the funding for the initial work that has to be paid for, from already hard-pressed budgets, even where there is a long-term economic case for it? Answers to questions of this kind will come from patient empirical study within the region, helped by any synthesis of practice of other institutions.

But there are four research questions, of immediate practical significance, whose answers may be found through educational theory and research. They concern curriculum, methodology, legitimacy and resources.

HOW DO WE DETERMINE WHAT SHOULD BE TAUGHT?

The University has decided that courses taught at a distance should match those taught face-to-face on one or other of the campuses. But that decision, necessary to ensure parity of esteem, does not of itself determine the content of new courses: by convention, syllabuses are described briefly, while course content can vary widely between campuses.

Let me rephrase the question. By posing it I am assuming that classifications of human learning are arbitrary so that we cannot argue for the inclusion or exclusion of any particular subject matter on *a priori* grounds. I assume, too, that a University has a role which is broader than technical training so that one cannot simply ensure that, say, an accountancy course matches the demands of the professional bodies. Given the need to select, we can rephrase it and ask, 'how do we decide what is non-trivial?'

There is little in the distance-education literature to help us, as it has tended to concern itself with means rather than ends. And, if we leave aside the pleas for a new vocationalism, there would appear to be less discussion of curricular issues in the literature on secondary and tertiary education alike than there was a generation ago. Nor can we expect a single and simple criterion; higher education properly serves many purposes. There is, however, one possible line of approach that has a legitimate pedigree and appears to be of wide applicability. Gagné (1966) in his hierarchy of learning suggested the particular value and effectiveness of learning at the higher levels that he identified and laid emphasis on problem-solving. Daniel Bell in the mid-1960s 'proposed a set of courses at the upper-division level that would have two objectives: first to enable students to develop a degree of sophistication about the methodological skills employed by the major disciplines ... and, second, to draw students back into broad contact with the intellectual world when they concentrate on their major specialty' (Martin, 1982, p. 45). More recently Barnett (1992, p. 26) suggests that, 'there is something of value in [an] imagery of ascending levels of understanding'. He justifies this by arguing that higher order concepts, with greater explanatory power, 'are what a genuine higher education is about', that it needs to cultivate critical reflection and that by 'taking on a reflexive attitude we are in effect taking a view of our knowledge from a higher level' (*ibid.*, p. 27).

If we follow this line of attack, then the design of courses that facilitate and encourage higher levels of learning may present particular difficulties for the distance educator: it is easier to design teaching material that teaches the facts and gets examination passes than to encourage reflexivity.

This kind of problem was being addressed by Brian Lewis (1973) at The Open University in a research project that was unfinished when he died. His aim was to set up a theoretical framework that would lead to the solutions of 'hard practical problems of course design'. The framework required elucidation of the notion of critical thinking; it suggested that course design should encourage the development of higher-order problem-solving procedures so that 'the quality student should be able to challenge and extend and even *transform* the knowledge he is given' (*ibid.*, p. 203).

That concern with quality, with higher categories of learning, and with dimensions of quality that are not captured by easy measures of what is conveniently quantifiable, suggests a line of research that would guide us on both curriculum and methodology and, to look ahead, would elucidate the concept of legitimacy. It takes us straight on to questions of methodology.

WHAT GUIDANCE CAN WE GIVE TO COURSE PLANNERS AND WRITERS ON PEDAGOGY?

Here there is no shortage of literature. From Holmberg's admirably brief and simple *On the Methods of Teaching by Correspondence* (1960) to compendiums like *Instructional Message Design* (Fleming and Levie, 1993) or *Teaching Through Self-instruction* (Rowntree, 1990), we have plenty of practical guidance on the development of teaching materials. But the literature has two weaknesses.

First, the advice it gives is not as well grounded as one would like. Hannafin and Hooper (1993, p. 227), at the end of a review of the applicability of learning principles, conclude that they 'identify powerful guidelines and heuristics for which a high degree of consensus exists'. Various reviews have commented on the lack of anything more than rules of thumb to guide the choice of media (for example, Bates, 1982, pp. 320–1; Dodds, 1983, p. 17). Even on one of the staples of distance education – activities in self-instructional text – we have little research data on the effect of activities in learning (Rubin, 1994). So, we have guidance, that probably results in our producing better materials than we did twenty-five years ago, but that still rests on quite shaky theoretical foundations. And we lack pedagogical advice to give to faculty members on some of the most basic questions: given the relative costs of different media, and knowing about their convenience for our students, we cannot say very much about the trade-offs between costs and effects for particular uses and combinations of media. The line of research from, for example, Cantril and Allport (1935) to Chu and Schramm (1968), that compared the effectiveness of different media with repetitive and reassuring findings of no significant difference, seems to have petered out but has not been followed by the development of a well-founded theory to guide the selection of media. We are, in consequence, left sadly short of guides on media choice beyond those simple rules of thumb.

Second, much of the available advice comes out of a narrow intellectual tradition. Again, Lewis identified the problem, noting that although 'considerable efforts were made to make the Behavioural Objectives Approach work – we can now say, quite categorically, that there are severe limitations to what this particular approach can achieve in the field of higher education' (1973, p. 196). Making a similar and general point, Hirst has argued that, 'Most of the central objectives we are interested in are not themselves reducible to observable states, and to imagine that they are, whatever the basis of that claim, is to lose the heart of the business ... States of mind are not analysable into observable states without committing category mistakes of some consequence' (Hirst, 1975, p. 290). Although Bååth (1979) some years ago suggested the need to explore a different starting-point for course development, many writers' training courses around the world still assume the universal validity of an objectives-based approach. I have previously suggested (Perraton, 1992) that one might more usefully begin with Stenhouse's (1975) distinction between training, concerned with skills, instruction, concerned with information, initiation into social norms, and induction, in which students are introduced to thought systems enabling judgement. If this is a useful road to explore it should lead us to decisions about content as well as about methodology.

There may, then, be a much bigger research challenge here than at first sight appears. Perhaps we need a new paradigm of research; at the least we need to generate some more powerful generalisations and explanatory hypotheses than those we have at present.

CAN WE ESTABLISH THE LEGITIMACY OF DISTANCE EDUCATION?

Method and content both have a bearing on legitimacy. I use this term to refer to:

> ... the status and credibility of the organisation as an institutional peer in the higher education system, and to recognition of its academic standards, and quality of its personnel and its educational outcomes. This includes recognition of credentials gained through study at a distance, and the parity of distance education with traditional forms of face to face teaching and learning. Such acceptance is inevitably qualitative and contested.
>
> (Moran, 1991, Ch.1)

We will get some way to establishing legitimacy if we establish 'Exam Success', to use the name of a Nigerian correspondence college. Even here we are short of data: it is only a handful of institutions that publish adequate data on completion rates and examination pass rates. But establishing that distance-education students can pass their examinations is a necessary but not sufficient condition for demonstrating legitimacy: questions about the comparative quality of the process of distance education remain. From his experience as a University Correspondence College tutor a century ago, H.G. Wells made the point in criticising the College which,

> ... procured honours-men already acquainted with the examination ... to divide the proper textbook into thirty equal pieces of reading and further to divide up a sample collection of questions previously set, so as to control the reading done. The pupil after reading each of his thirty lessons

sat down and answered the questions assigned to that lesson in a special copy-book supplied for that purpose and sent it to the tutor, who read, marked, criticised and advised in red ink ...

There is nothing inherently undesirable in the direction and testing of reading by correspondence, and nothing harmful in intelligent examining. But, as it was, we were, with the greatest energy and gravity, just missing the goal. We went beside the mark. The only results we produced were examination results which merely looked like the real thing. In the true spirit of an age of individualistic competition, we were selling wooden nutmegs or umbrellas that wouldn't open, or brass sovereigns or a patent food without any nourishment in it.

(Wells, 1934)

There is a more recent, and perhaps even more disturbing, critique of what we may be doing. Bock and Papagiannis (1983) have suggested that the function of non-formal education is to contain educational demand rather than to meet it. If that is true for distance education, then we will meet our objectives provided we recruit enough students, but will be a long way from establishing legitimacy or offering our students an education of the quality that legitimacy would require.

Again, if we are to do better than produce wooden nutmeg courses, or to contain a troublesome demand for education, we may find help in shaping research from conventional education. In his review of the nature of higher education Barnett found a broad consensus that the:

... cluster of aims, values and general ideas traditionally associated with higher education includes: 1 pursuit of truth and objective knowledge; 2 research; 3 liberal education; 4 institutional autonomy; 5 academic freedom; 6 neutral and open forum for debate; 7 rationality; 8 development of student's critical abilities; 9 development of student's autonomy; 10 student's character formation; 11 providing a critical centre within society; 12 preserving society's intellectual culture.

(Barnett, 1990, pp. 8–9)

If the search for legitimacy in distance education is to get beyond bland assertions, then one productive line of research may be to examine how far distance education can or does achieve any of these purposes.

If, to take one example, we consider our students' capacity to take part in an open forum, to develop their own critical abilities, to participate in dialogue within the conventions of a particular academic discipline and to develop their autonomy, then it would seem a reasonable hypothesis that these qualities are more readily developed in face-to-face dialogue than through study purely at a distance. That suggestion then provokes the severely practical question: what kind of face-to-face study, in what quantities, ought to be provided for our students, for what kind of purpose? The answers to the question will determine the proportion of resources to be devoted to tutorial support and the design of that support. That resource question is, of course, only part of a broader one.

HOW DO WE JUSTIFY COMMITTING RESOURCES TO DISTANCE EDUCATION?

If the research proposed under the previous headings yields results that are encouraging for distance education, and seems to demonstrate its quality and legitimacy, then we have gone a long way towards justifying the use of resources. There remains a strong, old-fashioned case that public resources should be committed to education, not just for instrumentalist reasons but because of the intrinsic value of education, respect for which is a mark of a civilised society. And, if education is to be supported and funded, then there is an arguable case that funds should not be restricted to full-time education of one age-group. Practical questions – of great complexity and importance – then arise about the proportion of costs that ought to be borne by full- and part-time, younger and older students.

But there remain lines of research that might help make the case for committing resources and that have have been comparatively neglected by distance educators. Methodology for costing distance education is now well established (cf. Unesco, 1977; Jamison et al., 1978; Rumble, 1986), but, just as we are short of data on successful completion rates, so we lack figures on costs per student and, more particularly, costs per graduate. Mugridge (1994, p.121), for example, in reviewing studies from a symposium on the funding of open universities, found the data so thin that he concluded: 'If open universities are to advocate a different funding structure or bid for more funds, they will also need to make their case by producing fuller data than have usually been available on completion rates and costs per graduate.'

As well as examining the costs and short-term effects of distance education, we may also wish to look at its longer-term consequences for our students. A wealth of studies – from Psacharopoulos (1973) to Hosain and Psacharopoulos (1994), for example – have examined the rates of return to the full-time education of young people in both industrialised and developing countries. While the conceptual basis of this line of analysis has been criticised (cf. Karabel and Halsey, 1977, pp. 13–14; Eicher, 1980, p. 13), it remains so much part of the armoury of the major world financial institutions that we need at least to know the answers to questions about the rates of return to part-time, mid-career education. Mace (1978) raised questions about the benefits of higher education through the British Open University from this standpoint and we appear still to have few answers to them.

There is at least one further approach to examining the costs and effects of mid-career education which, in contrast to rate-of-return analysis, does not assume that increases in income are a proxy for increases in productivity. Take the case of a mid-career teacher, earning £15,000 ($22,500) per annum, who completes an Open University MA in education at the age of 40. (All figures are hypothetical.) If we assume that the teacher's salary remains the same in real terms over a working life of a further twenty years then, in 1994 currency and assuming 5 per cent interest rates, the current value of the twenty-year salary is £186,933 ($280,400). We can set that figure against the cost of the MA course at, say, £5,000 ($7,500) and see that the cost is less than 3 per cent of the value placed by society on the teacher's remaining years of work. If, then, the teacher's performance in the classroom improves by more than 3 per cent as a result of following the course, then there appears to be a social case for investment in it. (It ought to be possible to establish that better-educated teachers teach better: Beeby (1966) set out the theoretical case; sadly, Lockheed and Verspoor (1991) found the evidence at primary level less reassuring than one would have liked.) The argument at first sight challenges us to find non-trivial measures of performance in various occupations and there is a danger that this approach might lead to unthinking quantification of easy indicators. But, accepting those dangers, if we found across a range of examples that such modest increases in performance were all that was needed to justify investment in mid-career education, then we would have added a potent argument for such investment.

CONCLUSION

That is my shopping-list. It springs from a belief that there is an ideological case to be made for distance education in attacking educational inequality and, in the Caribbean, for attacking geographical as well as other forms of deprivation. But it springs, too, from a concern that arguments about the methods of distance education have been too narrowly based and that arguments about its legitimacy have been too self-serving. The shopping-list is disparate; if it has a common theme it is that the major research needs are, for the most part, shared with the rest of the education service. Research on distance education belongs in the mainstream of educational research.

REFERENCES

Bååth, J. A. (1979) *Correspondence Education in the Light of a Number of Contemporary Teaching Models*, Malmö, Liber Hermods.

Barnett, R. (1990) *The Idea of Higher Education*, Buckingham, Society for Research into Higher Education and Open University Press.

Barnett, R. (1992) *Improving Higher Education*, Buckingham, Society for Research into Higher Education and Open University Press.

Bates, T. (1982) 'Options for delivery media' in Perraton, H. (ed.) *Alternative Routes to Formal Education: Distance Teaching for School Equivalency*, Baltimore, MD, Johns Hopkins University Press.

Beeby, C. E. (1966) *The Quality of Education in Developing Countries*, Cambridge, MA, Harvard University Press.

Bock, J. C. and Papagiannis, G. J. (1983) *Nonformal Education and National Development*, New York, Praeger.

Cantril, A. H. and Allport, G. W. (1935) *The Psychology of Radio*, New York, Harper.

Chu, G. C. and Schramm, W. (1968) *Learning from Television: What the Research Says*, Stanford, CA, ERIC.

Dodds, T. (1983) *Administration of Distance-teaching Institutions: A Manual*, Cambridge, International Extension College.

Eicher, J.-C. (1980) 'Some thoughts on the economic analysis of new educational media' in Unesco, *Economics of New Educational Media*, Vol. 2, Paris, Unesco.

Fleming, M. and Levie, W. H. (eds) (1993) *Instructional Message Design: Principles from the Behavioral and Cognitive Sciences*, Englewood Cliffs, NJ, Educational Technology Publications.

Gagné, R. M. (1966) *The Conditions of Learning*, New York, Holt, Rinehart and Winston.

Hannafin, M. J. and Hooper, S. R. (1993) 'Learning principles' in Fleming, M. and Levie, W. H. (eds).

Hirst, P. H. (1975) 'The nature and structure of curriculum objectives' in Golby, M. *et al., Curriculum Design*, London, Croom Helm.

Holmberg, B. (1960) *On the Methods of Teaching by Correspondence*, Lund, Sweden, Lund universitets årsskrift.

Hosain, S. I. and Psacharopoulos, G. (1994) 'The profitability of school investments in an educationally advanced developing country', *International Journal of Educational Development*, 14(1).

Jamison, D. T., Klees, S. J. and Wells, S. J. (1978) *The Costs of Educational Media*, Beverly Hills, CA, Sage.

Karabel, J. and Halsey, A. H. (1977) *Power and Ideology in Education*, New York, Oxford University Press.

Lewis, B. N. (1973) 'Educational technology at the Open University: an approach to the problem of quality', *British Journal of Educational Technology*, 3(4).

Lockheed, M. E. and Verspoor, A. (1991) *Improving Primary Education in Developing Countries*, Oxford, Oxford University Press.

Mace, J. (1978) 'Mythology in the making: is the Open University really cost-effective?', *Higher Education*, Vol. 7.

Martin, W. B. (1982) 'Alternative approaches to curricular coherence' in Hall, J. W. (ed.) *In Opposition to Core Curriculum*, Westport, CT, Greenwood Press.

Moran, L. (1991) *Legitimation of Distance Education: A Social History of the Open Learning Institute of British Columbia*, (draft) unpublished PhD dissertation, University of British Columbia.

Mugridge, I. (1994) *The Funding of Open Universities*, Vancouver, Commonwealth of Learning.

Perraton, H. (1992) 'Assessment of distance education', University of London MA/Diploma course in distance education.

Psacharopoulos, G. (1973) *Returns to Education: An International Comparison*, Amsterdam, Elsevier.

Renwick, W. *et al.* (1992) *Distance Education at the University of the West Indies*, Vancouver, Commonwealth of Learning.

Rowntree, D. (1990) *Teaching Through Self-instruction: How to Develop Open Learning Materials*, London, Kogan Page.

Rubin, E. D. (1994) 'Review of Lockwood, F., *Activities in Self-instructional Texts*', *Open Learning*, 9(1).

Rumble, G. (1986) *Costing Distance Education*, London, Commonwealth Secretariat.
Stenhouse, L. (1975) *An Introduction to Curriculum Research and Development*, London, Heinemann.
Unesco (1977) *The Economics of New Educational Media*, Vol. 1, Paris, Unesco.
Wells, H. G. (1934) *Experiment in Autobiography*, London, Gollancz and Cresset.

3

TRENDS, DIRECTIONS AND NEEDS

A view from developing countries

Badri N. Koul

INTRODUCTION

If distance education is to serve as a democratising force universally, if the enlightened academic is to serve as a crusader for equity in intellectual terms, if international academic exchanges have to be cleansed of the stigma of 'exploitation', distance education in the developing world needs support in basics. To this end, we need to shift our focus from *research* and *development,* as two disparate activities, to a unified one namely *developmental research.* This is an argument in continuation of an earlier one (Koul, 1993), which presented a case for research and development in distance education (DE) in India. The points made were: (a) there was hardly any such activity going on in developing countries; (b) why it was essential generally and more specifically in developing countries; and (c) how collaborative efforts in research could be usefully effected. To carry the argument further the notion of *developmental research* is expounded briefly in the context of DE followed by: (a) comments on the nature of indigenous research in developing countries; (b) suggestions with regard to the direction current practices should take and what needs to be done to make *developmental research* a possibility; and (c) views on the possibilities such work opens up for the workers in the field. The underlying assumption is that this exposition is generalised enough to represent most of the developing countries and reasonably integrative to emphasise the value of uninhibited participation which the developed world should embark on and practise globally.

DEVELOPMENTAL RESEARCH CHARACTERISED

Developmental research in DE should be a three-axial operation in which growth along each of the axes must be synthesised to achieve tangible results (see Figure 3.1).

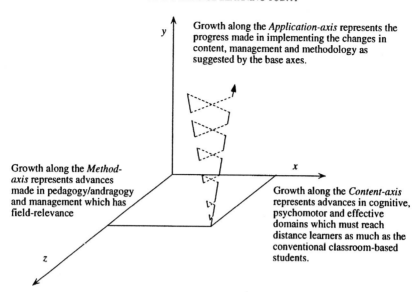

Figure 3.1 Three-dimensional representation of developmental research

The introduction of the *z*-variable into the conventional situation represented by *x* and *y* axes makes the overall operation quite complex. The dominant educational mind-set (which is *x-y*-based) does not easily recognise the *z*-variable; if it does, there are no time-honoured models to accommodate the complexity brought in by this additional variable. Even the basic issue of who works along the *x*-axis, and who along the *z*-axis remains unresolved. Besides, the issue of how to move along the *y*-axis (which is a non-issue in the conventional system) is a still greater complexity which imposes unprecedented demands on institutional governance, operational flexibility and curricular dynamism. Any developments along the *x*-axis, if not used/applied along the *y*-axis, constitute *developmental research* only in terms of the *disciplines* concerned; similarly, any research along the *z*-axis cannot be termed 'developmental' unless it is used for modifying/improving the system. While both may have contributed to the growth of knowledge, skills etc., it is only their application to modify the overall system that characterises them as *developmental research*, otherwise they remain mere research exercises.

RESEARCH IN DISTANCE EDUCATION: THE TRENDS

As in India, research activities in developing countries remain localised mainly to three bases – the university, research institutes or labs and R & D units within industries. At universities research is essentially discipline-based and in the main for the award of research degrees; once obtained, the work quite often gets fossilised as there is no follow-up work on such research. Distance education, a relatively new and developing discipline, is seldom on the research agenda of a university, though some university departments of education have started registering students who wish to work in distance education. The contribution of open universities themselves is no different, as shown by the recent reviews of the Indian DE research scenario (Sahoo, 1992; Panda, 1992). Research institutes/labs for various branches of knowledge were established partly to overcome the consequences of the unproductive research (referred to above) undertaken at universities. With emphasis on fundamental research and creativity these institutions make significant contributions to knowledge, which, however, does not find any easy outlet for dissemination as younger generations of learners are at universities which have hardly any links with these institutes. The achievements of these institutions/labs thus fail to initiate and sustain research activities on a larger scale as an ongoing process of creation and transmission of new knowledge and skills. Distance education is an unknown phenomenon at such institutions, and likely to remain so for quite some time. Industrial R & D activities, too, remain untouched by DE. The picture that emerges is that in developing countries research in DE is neither localised nor coordinated and seldom attracts funds from available sources.

On the other hand, DE as an educational endeavour is developing a momentum of unprecedented dimensions – in India alone there are over fifty distance education institutions (single and dual mode operating from lower to higher levels of instruction), covering most of the university and lower level disciplines, with an enrolment of over 500,000 students in higher education alone. More and more open universities are being established all over the developing world and more and more non-educational agencies, governmental as well as non-governmental, engaged in in-service training/instruction are now turning to DE to meet the overwhelming pressure of numbers, diversity of needs and growing awareness about the importance of professionalism. The overall scene points to what may be called a 'utilisation explosion' of DE courses and DE methodology all over the developing world, involving millions of people in various capacities; and yet the concept of DE remains alien and its methodology primitive and static – alien in the sense that DE in developing countries continues to depend on models developed and tested elsewhere without indigenising them, and static in the sense that innovations are hardly ever attempted, and so the potential of DE in difficult and diverse settings remains unexploited.

The institution of education has entered a phase of 'change' manifest in the progressive expansion and application of DE methodology. This change is a social imperative, and yet we in the developing countries display an inexplicable unpreparedness for meeting the demands being made by this 'change' – we must comprehend it, plan for it, effect it, sustain it and thus build for the future.

RESEARCH IN DISTANCE EDUCATION:
DIRECTION FOR DEVELOPMENTAL PURPOSES

Current trends reveal an expanding use of DE on the one hand and, on the other, no relation between research and associated developmental activities. In the context of research, if we label these trends 'research as an academic exercise', the new direction it must take may be labelled *'developmental research'*, research not to become fossilised but to be used in improving the system and thus opening up new ways of imparting education more effectively and purposefully, at lower costs, and serving not only larger populations but also more diverse clientele groups in adverse situations.

DEVELOPMENTAL RESEARCH IN
DISTANCE EDUCATION: NEEDS

For such *developmental research* to come into existence and then sustain itself, it must fulfil three needs: (a) context specificity, (b) statutory provision and (c) globalisation.

Context specificity

There are now well-established and universally accepted areas of research in DE. For example, Panda (1992) has identified nine broad themes being researched in India, themes which are being researched in the developed and the developing countries. In the latter, however, work on these themes seldom serves the desired purpose, since it is 'borrowings dependent'; it fails to break cultural traps. For example, the theme 'concept and methods of counselling in DE' brings a certain philosophy and certain processes to the mind of a distance educator, but they have yet to find a place in the educational ethos of developing countries. As a consequence, when applied, the philosophy gets misinterpreted and the processes/activities dissolve and fade into culture-specific practices.

The cultural trap in this case is that in operational terms students believe and feel they have been taught only if lectured to. The teacher believes and feels that teaching means delivering a lecture, for that is 'teaching', that is what a teacher is there for. This being so, the teacher is seldom satisfied with the duration of time allowed to cover a subject, and the students feel cheated as not all the portions of the syllabus are covered through lectures. At the philosophical level, too, the notion of counselling in general remains alien to an average student in developing countries, where joint and extended family is still the basic unit of the society. Such a unit has in-built mechanisms to cater to those needs which are usually satisfied by counselling in highly industrialised societies in which the extended family system is not the norm. Children, adolescents, youths and adults, all get their problems, psychological or otherwise, solved by means of interaction within the family;

personal problems are seen as intimate issues which must have intimate people to resolve them; these issues are not for the market-place or an outsider to explore. In fact, in certain cases there is a taboo against divulging such problems to the world outside the family. However, personal problems which affect studies, difficulties which arise in the course of studies and which are seen as the consequence of personal inadequacies, difficulties which are born of unpreparedness in certain cases and aimlessness in others do not find solutions within the intimate circle of the family. Such families, especially in countries with high rates of illiteracy, seldom have the skills and experience to provide hlep and advice. It is not possible for an average family, and certainly not for the families of first-generation learners, to whom DE is specifically directed, to relate one's personal problems with one's studies, much less provide solutions for them. The culture-based counselling mechanism having thus become useless as far as one's studies are concerned, one does not know how to or where to resolve one's difficulties. The expressly appointed educational counsellors are not approached, since they are seen as a teacher; a teacher's task is to teach (read 'lecture') and not to help solve one's personal problems, however intimately they may be related to one's studies. Having come from the same cultural base, neither do the counsellors expect to be, nor are they pre-prepared to see themselves as, looking into personal issues of students. Counselling is thus neither asked for, nor available, so cannot be provided. What research does one conduct in an area that does not exist?

Turning to the actual teaching–learning transaction as it occurs in academic-counselling sessions, one would still be satisfied if, as referred to earlier, lecturing had a purpose beyond what the self-instructional materials are supposed to serve. But, invariably these sessions become (a) note-giving sessions, (b) sessions for the linguistic simplification of the study materials by translating them into the regional language concerned or by linguistically diluted presentation of the content, or (c) sessions for providing clarification on assignments. If this is what 'academic counselling' is meant to be in practice, the options, which will have approval on economic as well as managerial grounds, are to prepare 'made-easy' versions of the materials, and to provide materials in regional/mother tongues as aids to work on assignments. These options may not be considered undesirable in themselves, but they certainly do not constitute 'academic counselling', which has been identified as an area worthy of research.

Thus whether we look at the issue of counselling from a socio-cultural or actual transactional viewpoint, there is nothing to research. There is no basis for it, yet we know how significant this activity is in DE. *Developmental research* in DE in developing countries has to begin from a search for, and an understanding of, the actual contextual basis of each research area. This is the first need.

Statutory provision

For the sake of argument let us assume that we started our research activities from the beginning – that we assessed the nature of the cultural base and environment, and discovered or identified a method of purposeful counselling/tutoring in a given situation. A subsequent issue will be that of using this research, i.e. that of implementing the discovered/identified method, of who will implement the change suggested by research. However, a prior question is – who will conduct this research?

As is the convention, it is academics at the universities/institutions of higher learning who conduct research in their respective disciplines and share it with their colleagues, peers and students through the mechanisms of seminars/conferences and teaching. Such research, however, pertains to their respective disciplines. Few, if any, of them conduct research in the methodology they use in teaching, nor in the system within which they work. *Developmental research* in Distance Education pertains more to the methodology of teaching and the system in which it is operated than to a discipline. The discipline-oriented academics would, and do, prefer to give their time to discipline-based research, as that is what concerns them and provides for their professional recognition and growth. Who is there to conduct research in DE? The issue is old and well-known (Calvert, 1988).

If not the discipline-oriented academics, then a group of people who either by sheer coincidence or in certain cases by choice come to be in units like the Institute of Educational Technology at The Open University, UK. But it is not unusual to come across academics at that university who would pretend not to know what the IET is doing. Of course, some gains will have been derived by the academic units from such work, and the IET will have learnt how to make themselves more acceptable to academic units, and thus some convergence in mutual concerns and utilisation of such research for developmental purposes must have been achieved. However, even the UK OU does not support a mechanism to utilise IET research dynamically for such developmental purposes. It is likely that the time-gap between a finding and its application is too long to have optimal utility, and it is equally likely that it is not utilised at all. Here it is not clear whether we are stretching an anomaly too far to fit into a recognised and time-honoured paradigm or we have accepted that some should exclusively research in distance education, while others use their findings to develop the system.

A different model is the Open Learning Agency (OLA), Canada, where the academic remains discipline-centred at the constituent university or college, while the DE personnel at OLA contribute to systemic development. This model provides for easier application of research findings for developmental purposes, as in the former case every academic is expected to become aware of the findings, learn to apply them and then apply them, but in the latter, an academic may or may not bother about them, while the DE personnel will be up-to-date with the findings and keen to apply them at the earliest.

There is a third case – the universities where a beginning has been made, with the help of consultants, but where there is no provision for *developmental research*, nor any for its application. In many such universities, there is seldom any significant discipline-based research being conducted. Is there a case for the academics of such institutions to get involved in research in DE? If they do, the findings could find ready application and faster propagation. But then that amounts to accepting that an academic in a DE institution is more a facilitator than an *academic*.

Going beyond these illustrative cases, we also need to consider some of the obvious cues from the consumer industry, which displays a deliberately planned approach to *developmental research*. It appears that market trends have to be studied in terms of the obsolescence of educational items available in the market, new educational requirements emerging from the changing character of the labour-force needed and new requirements in relation to technological advances as well as in terms of changes in human aspirations. Such studies must point to new curricula, new combinations of the existing disciplines and subdisciplines and certainly new disciplines, new skills and new attitudes leading to new cultures which are more universal. The implication is that such studies, without interfering with discipline-based research or pretending to be discipline-based themselves, will point to and ask for curricular changes which may not be in line with well-established, though less relevant now, discipline-based curricula. Mechanisms to accommodate such shifts also have to be provided.

The four situations discussed above indicate it in no uncertain terms that we have not squarely met the two questions which came up earlier: (a) who conducts research and (b) who must implement it? It appears that we cannot find answers to them unless the overall system makes legislative and statutory provision for regular developmental changes, besides demanding, as a matter of routine, contributions to purposeful changes from the people involved. In other words, for *developmental research* to come into being, and to serve its purposes, it will always depend on a statutory provision for the 'management of change' through institutional support; without this, *developmental research* is not likely to occur in DE.

Thus the second major need is a shift in the basic paradigm of the governance of open universities and distance education institutions. This is equally relevant to the developed and the developing countries. Incidently, it points to a very fertile but unexplored area of research – dynamic governance of open universities/distance education systems.

Globalisation

Should advanced countries listen to or consider the questions outlined above? Seemingly, they have discovered and identified their basics long ago, taken off in timely fashion and are cruising along satisfactorily in their own skies: why should they even think of situations discussed above, much less get interested in them and work in them! But have they? In the area of research they have made reasonable strides, but can we say the same about *developmental research*? Yet, the developing countries find themselves gaping at what they see (hear or read) about the research activities in the advanced countries. The lag perceived in the relative rates of growth, the visible difference between the individual as well as institutional confidence for chalking out a direction or building a conviction for operationalising research, and the demoralising contrast between the facilities available for effecting plans and projects, undermine a practising distance educator from a developing country. Escalating international prices for services and products of all kinds perpetuate a dependence which increases with every international conference held and every new title placed in the market. Contributions of the developing countries in such conferences remain inconsequential; this situation needs to change.

Nobody knows what a newborn child may achieve when adult. From its birth over a century ago, distance education is maturing. As it advances to the centre-stage, its potential and application in diverse as well as adverse situations have to be the concerns of all researchers – individuals, groups and institutions. In situations where human beings belonging to specific cultures constitute the main raw material for an investigation, there is no alternative but to make that investigation culture- and location-specific. If *developmental research* in DE is aiming for powerful, universally applicable generalisations, such research needs to be conducted wherever the locale is available: this points to the 'democratisation' and 'universalisation' attributes of DE. Should we not go to those locations?

From the viewpoint of fundamental research, the developmental utility of which may be looked into only secondarily, it is worth researching into culture-cum-locale specific learning strategies, mind-sets, perceptions regarding the need for education, characteristics of achievement in educational endeavours, actual educational requirement for improving the quality of life etc. We have moved far away from the position in which 'learning' by rats, pigeons or dogs was seen as a process no different from that by human beings. It is time we took another step away and overcame the fallacy that all human beings, whatever their cultural base and local imperatives, 'learn' the same way, should learn the same things for the same purposes, using the same techniques and the same materials. For example, is there anything to be done for 'first nations', except directing and/or pulling them to the so-called 'mainstream'? Are there other streams? Are we aware of them? Should we find them? This points to the 'vast reach' and the 'mode for the hitherto deprived populations' attributes of DE. Do these areas appeal to researchers from the advanced countries?

Both the points made above appear at best 'idealistic invocations'. But education has already become a commodity for global transactions. It may not take long for territorial restrictions to collapse completely and for the dominant, prestigious and influential suppliers to discover that their supplies glut their own native markets and to seek other markets. A pragmatic approach for the supplier countries/institutions may be to enter the developing world, study the market and then modify their wares according to the local needs with the help of local industry and labour-force on something like royalty bases. Furthermore, if the local industry is found suitable technically, cheaper quality products could be returned home as the labour and raw material in the developing local settings is bound to be cheaper for years to come. This approach promises a long-term symbiotic relationship which should benefit the collaborating countries – the developed and the developing, as both of them will have a stake in its success.

CONCLUSION

Developmental research in DE is certainly a new line of thought and action for developing countries, and the developed world. To make this shift a reality, we need to research into the basics in culture-specific domains and also into the existing paradigms of governance and establish one which makes such research possible, while the developed world should enter the developing one with the objective of improving life globally by enriching others while they enrich themselves.

REFERENCES

Calvert, J. (1988) 'Distance education research: the rocky courtship of scholarship and practice', a Keynote paper presented at the 14th World Conference on Distance Education, ICDE, Oslo.

Koul, B. N. (1993) 'A case for collaborative research and development in distance education', *Media and Technology for Human Resource Development*, 6(1).

Panda, S. K. (1992) 'Distance educational research in India: stock-taking, concerns and prospects', *Distance Education*, 13(2).

Sahoo, P. K. (1992) 'Researches in distance education at university level in India: trends and perspective', *Kakatiya Journal of Distance Education*, 1(1).

4

AMERICAN DISTANCE EDUCATION

A short literature review

Michael G. Moore

INTRODUCTION

In this chapter a selection of articles from *The American Journal of Distance Education* will be used to illustrate some of the main directions of American research. Considerable space has been contributed to the reference list, which it is suggested be studied as a substantive part of this chapter; a good impression of the scope and nature of American research can be gleaned from a careful reading of the titles of the research articles listed.

DELIVERY OF DISTANCE EDUCATION IN THE UNITED STATES

In the United States there is no autonomous integrated multimedia delivery system such as those of the open universities in other countries. There are tens of thousands of instructional programmes for distant learners, provided by universities, colleges, schools, corporate training departments and the armed forces. Most of these are delivered by a single teacher using a particular medium. The vast majority of what claims to be research about distance education consists of descriptions of how one or more or these communications media have been used to link a classroom teacher to one or more distant classes.

The media used are: correspondence, broadcast and recorded video, audio, audio-graphic, video- and computer-conferencing.

Correspondence education

About 250,000 Americans enrol annually in correspondence courses provided by over seventy members of the National University Continuing Education Association (NUCEA). There are some 500 private correspondence schools enrolling around 5 million students in technical and vocational courses. Each branch of the armed forces has its own correspondence school as do many government departments. Research on correspondence education goes back to the beginning of the century, but today there are only a few studies each year, since the method is overshadowed in the popular and academic imagination by distance teaching using electronic communications. Recent studies have focused on teaching (Holstein, 1992), design (Diehl, 1987), certain subject areas (for example, Martin, 1993), students' workload (Malan and Feller, 1992), course completion (Billings, 1988) and students' perspectives regarding effectiveness of instruction (St Pierre and Olsen, 1991) and student support services (Tallman, 1994).

Television courses

College-level television courses, known as telecourses, are produced by universities, public broadcasting stations and, above all, by community colleges, such as Kirkwood, Dallas, Miami-Dade and Coastline Community Colleges. More than 1,000 post-secondary institutions sign on each year for courses broadcast by the Public Broadcasting Service. A model was provided by The Annenberg/CPB Project which, between 1981 and 1990, provided funds, typically in the 2–3 million dollar range per course, for the production of over 170 high quality television-based university courses. Telecourses are bought by colleges and universities and distributed on video tape or by local cable networks. They usually have a printed study guide; tutoring and student support is given on campus, or through correspondence (Brock, 1987; Whittington, 1987; Anderson, 1987). The Annenberg/CPB Project stimulated much evaluation research in the design, use and effectiveness of telecourses.

Teleconferencing

The delivery method that has led to the explosion of interest in distance learning in the United States is the teleconference, provided either by two-way video, one-way video accompanied by two-way audio, by audio, audio-graphics, or computer network. One of the reasons for the growing acceptability of distance education by teleconferencing is that this family of media allows groups of distant learners to be taught in real-time by a classroom teacher. Teachers frequently believe they can thus teach at a distance while making few changes in their assumptions about teaching and learning, or even their teaching techniques. The assumptions about education of this 'candid camera' or 'hairy arm' approach are those of the traditional classroom, as are the techniques used in teaching, i.e. lecture and overhead notes (Gehlauf et al., 1991).

All major universities have satellite up-link hardware, production studios and personnel. Programmes are produced at undergraduate and postgraduate level, with a large proportion being for continuing professional education (Barker and Platten, 1988). Major and Shane (1991) describe satellite programmes for training nurses, Merkley and Hoy (1988) for teacher training, Anderson (1989) for training about use of natural resources. Satellite programming by community colleges is described by Kitchen (1988).

The National University Teleconference Network (NUTN) is a consortium of 260 organisations providing or receiving a range of over 100 college programmes by satellite. Another consortium, The National Technological University, consists of ninety-four engineering colleges; most courses are broadcast directly to workplaces. The Public Broadcasting National Narrowcast Service (NNS) transmits programmes by satellite to twenty-five affiliate stations who then redistribute them locally to schools or workplaces by Instructional Television Fixed Service (ITFS) and cable (Brock, 1987; Whittington, 1987; Anderson, 1987).

Satellite teleconferencing is used by most of America's big companies. Typical of these is IBM's Interactive Satellite Education Network (ISEN). This is a one-way video, two-way audio network, with originating studios in four cities, and receiver sites across the country. Corporations with similar programmes include: Federal Express, Kodak Corporation, Tandem Computers, AETNA Life and Casualty corporation. As well as private systems there are 'turn-key' organisations that produce and sell programmes or sell satellite time and production resources. Examples are American Management Association, Bankers TV Network, and The American Rehabilitation Educational Network. The Department of Defense has several educational satellite systems, such as the Army Logistics Management College's Satellite Education Network and the navy's Video Teletraining System (Maloy and Perry, 1991).

Satellite-delivered instruction in the schools has been stimulated by grants from the Federal Government for demonstration projects known as the Star Schools projects. A large proportion of teachers believe that satellite programming significantly improves their schools and their own professional development (Martin and Rainey, 1993). There is evidence that children's achievement and attitudes are both positively affected in these programmes. Especially important in the success of these programmes is the role of local site facilitators (Moore *et al.*, 1991).

Computer-conference

An example of distance education delivered by computer-conference is the Electronic University Network, in which member universities provide credit courses on floppy disks for home computers, augmented by e-mail and on-line data searching. An idea of the potential of the method is given by the Bangkok Project, which linked educational computer networks worldwide in a professional development activity for members of the distance education community (Anderson and Mason, 1993).

Conventional teaching institutions increasingly use computer-conferencing to extend their classes, and to individualise their instruction. In the view of many, computer-conferencing shifts the emphasis away from the mass production model of distance education to one which is more responsive to the needs of individual learners, and is a medium that supports learner empowerment and autonomy (Davie and Wells, 1991).

Research in the area of computer-conferencing has focused on effectiveness, including cost-effectiveness (Phelps *et al.*, 1991; Cheng *et al.*, 1991), the instructors' role (Boston, 1992), the nature and usefulness of text-based dialogue, and the pedagogical value of the permanent transcript (Davie and Wells, 1991). There is evidence that computer-conferencing permits a higher quality of interaction among students and between students and instructor than conventional instructional environments (Lauzon, 1992).

Audio and audio-graphics

Using the telephone with microphones and amplifiers is technically the simplest teleconference medium, but often highly effective and certainly cost-effective, especially with well-educated students who work in a highly conceptual field (Burge and Howard, 1990).

A number of software packages support low-cost real-time transmission of graphics to accompany an audio-conference. Research so far indicates the practical difficulties that groups have in interacting graphically and point to the need for both training and substantial up-front design time to make the technique successful (Gunawardena, 1992). Wolcott (1993) undertook a qualitative study of the course planning procedures used by eleven instructors teaching by audio-graphic teleconference.

LEARNERS AND LEARNING

There are hundreds of one-shot case studies of the effects or effectiveness of particular communications media in bringing about learning. Since they focus on general effectiveness of learning in a particular programme, they add little to knowledge about the learning process itself. Their aim is to identify the general student variables that appear to interact favourably with instruction delivered by their particular medium with a view to making the programme more effective. In reality the focus is on the independent variable, the programme, rather than the dependent, the learner. Many of these studies focus on students who drop out or withdraw from study (Dille and Mezak, 1991). Perhaps inevitably in an educational culture that regards every student as a fee-paying customer who must above all else be satisfied, there are many studies of student satisfaction with courses and with such course features as organisation, content and instructor (Wilkes and Burnham,1991; Egan *et al.*, 1992; Biner *et al.*, 1994).

One step in sophistication beyond the one-shot case descriptions referred to above, and next most common, is a genre of studies in which attempts are made to compare the results of teaching by two or more media. For an example using relatively good methodology, see Grimes *et al.* (1988), a study that compared the effectiveness of a telecourse with a lecture course. Similar studies include Beare's (1989) work on the comparative effectiveness of videotape, audiotape and telelecture in teacher education, Cheng *et al.*'s (1991) comparison of performance and attitude in traditional and computer-conferencing classes and Souder's (1993) comparison of traditional versus satellite-delivered management of technology courses. Although Dubin and Taveggia should have said the last word on the subject of which medium is more effective, when they wrote, as long ago as 1968, 'The results of this research are clear and unequivocal – no particular method of teaching is measurably to be preferred over another when evaluated by student examination purposes', there remains an apparently insatiable appetite for this kind of comparative study.

Among the few areas of basic research with regard to distance learning is that of Atman (1987, 1988) who has investigated goal accomplishment style and the role of conation (striving) in being a distance learner. Reviews of literature have been provided by Cookson (1989) and Coggins (1988).

THEORETICAL MODELS

There are now twelve American graduate Schools of Education that provide courses in distance education (Dillon, 1992). In spite of this, the vast majority of research is atheoretical, and consequently of limited value. In this land of unbounded free speech, where every opinion is as weighty as any other, there remains a propensity for individuals to engage in ad hoc theorising, to offer fresh, naive descriptions in place of the more demanding work of filling in the theoretical spaces that have, over twenty years become apparent. Of major importance, given the emergence of the new media, is the need to study course structures, dialogic procedures and learner behaviours when teleconferencing is used, with a view to refining or redefining the relationships between these variables that were established before these highly interactive media appeared. One author who has made an important contribution in this regard is Saba, who has expanded the concept of transactional distance and produced a model of the dynamic relationship between dialogue and structure by using integrated system dynamics (Saba, 1988; Saba and Shearer, 1994). Garrison and Baynton (1987) and Baynton (1992) have furthered understanding about learner autonomy, even if indirectly, as they conceptualise and investigate the idea of learner and teacher control. Oxford and Florini (1990) led a discussion about the relationship of distance education to certain other disciplines. One of these discussions, led by Wagner (1990), about the conceptual relationship of distance education and educational technology has generated particular interest.

TEACHING AND TEACHERS

The most common questions about teaching are how to modify normal classroom teaching to be effective in the 'candid classroom'. Clark (1993) provides an excellent study of attitudes of faculty in a sample of fifty-seven higher education institutions. The question of faculty attitudes seems especially important since negative attitudes are seen by many administrators as the main obstacle to change. In reality, it seems that most instructors who have taught by teleconference like it, but they fear that their colleagues and their administrators do not perceive their distance teaching as favourably as they do (Dillon and Walsh, 1992). When asked how they can be helped to become effective distance educators, most faculty ask for more resources, especially of time and for in-service training programmes that deal with how to teach at a distance, not merely how to manipulate new technology.

A rare view of teaching in a total systems approach is that of Beaudoin (1990) who described the roles of a teacher who facilitates learning from prepared study materials rather than transmitting information in person. There is much interest in the theory and practice of interaction. Wagner (1994) has reviewed several models and related them to contexts of instructional delivery, instructional design, instructional theory and learning theory in an attempt to establish conceptual parameters for the function of interaction. Hillman *et al.* (1994) have attempted to add to Moore's (1989) typology of interaction, which they call learner–interface interaction.

POLICY RESEARCH

A growing number of agencies are trying to take advantage of the technological developments that have made it possible to deliver academic programmes to learners off-campuses, across the state, nationally and internationally, and the growth in this activity is causing a welter of problems. Among the most serious are the issues arising from the conflict between delivery across state borders and the traditional, indeed constitutionally protected, rights of individual states to regulate education. A specially difficult problem concerns approval requirements. An institution that wants to operate nationally can face as many state assessments as there are states (Reilly and Gulliver, 1992). Other policy issues include questions regarding the use of state money that might be used for such instruction; how to monitor and control the quality of out-of-state programmes; inter-institutional resource-sharing and programme articulation; integration of alternative instructional delivery systems; programme prioritisation; programme curricular review and approval; academic residency;

establishment of fee structures; and support services (Olcott, 1992; England, 1987).

CONCLUSION

The above review has described some of the main trends in distance education research in the United States. There are two trends that have not emerged in this account that should be noted in concluding this review. One of these trends is the merging of computer and video technologies and the proliferation of highly interactive, low-cost, desktop computer-based communications media. The other trend is the homogenisation and globalisation of the communications environment as a result of satellite-delivered programming. The former of these technologies is leading to greater individual control of learning and the second to the continuance of group-based instruction. The former might be seen as stimulating greater learner autonomy with a concomitant risk of administrative chaos, while the latter gives greater stability to the educational programme with control held by the teaching institution, with an accompanying risk of control by other socially conservative, perhaps reactionary agencies. The former is leading to the breakdown of established institutional and administrative arrangements, and the development of the 'virtual university', while the latter tends to reinforce the influence of traditional agencies. The former might be seen as breaking the social, if not economic, control of poorer countries by the technologically advanced countries, and the latter as perpetuating it. Some needs for research that arise from these trends include the following:

- What teaching arrangements are optimum when learners can access instruction and information from a wide range of sources?
- How can individual learners be assisted so they do not become isolated learners and develop the skills of negotiating the information resources available to them?
- What preparatory support and counselling arrangements are appropriate in an environment marked by such distributed teaching sources?
- What teaching is appropriate in the group arrangements so that homogenisation is avoided and learners obtain maximum benefit according to individual talents?
- What accreditation, certification and quality control mechanisms are appropriate for the 'virtual university'?
- What are the trends and needs for faculty development?
- What policy-making structures and procedures are needed to promote better quality distance education?
- What are the international obligations regarding distance education of the technically advanced countries?

REFERENCES

(All references are to *The American Journal of Distance Education*, with one exception, for which the full citation is given.)

Anderson, J. (1987) 'A historical overview of the application of telecommunications in the health care industry', 1(2), p. 53.

Anderson, S. (1989) 'Natural resources education through videoconferencing', 3(3), p. 58.

Anderson, T. and Mason, R. (1993) 'International computer conferencing for professional development: the Bangkok Project', 7(2), pp. 5–18.

Atman, K. (1987) 'The role of conation (striving) in the distance learning enterprise', 1(1), p. 14.

Atman, K. (1988) 'Psychological type elements and goal accomplishment style: implications for distance education', 2(3), p. 36.

Barker, B. and Platten, M. (1988) 'Student perceptions on the effectiveness of college credit courses taught via satellite', 2(2), p. 44.

Baynton, M. (1992) 'Dimensions of "control" in distance education: a factor analysis', 6(2), pp. 17–31.

Beare, P. (1989) 'The comparative effectiveness of videotape, audiotape and telelecture in delivering continuing teacher education', 3(2), p. 57.

Beaudoin, M. (1990) 'The instructor's changing role in distance education', 4(2), p. 21.

Billings, D. M. (1988) 'A conceptual model of correspondence course completion', 2(2), p. 23.

Biner, P., Dean, R. and Mellinger, A. (1994) 'Factors underlying distance learner satisfaction with televised college level courses', 8(1), pp. 60–71.

Boston, R. (1992) 'Remote delivery of instruction via the pc and modem connections: what have faculty learned?', 6(3), pp. 45–57.

Brock, D. (1987) 'And six to grow on', 1(2), p. 34.

Burge, E. J. and Howard, J. L. (1990) 'Audio-conferencing in graduate education: a case study', 4(2), p. 3.

Cheng, H. C., Lehman, J. and Armstrong, P. (1991) 'Comparison of performance and attitude in traditional and computer conferencing classes', 5(3), pp. 51–64.

Clark, T. (1993) 'Attitudes of higher education faculty toward distance education: a national survey', 7(2), pp. 19–33.

Coggins, C. (1988) 'Preferred learning styles and their impact on completion of external degree programs', 2(1), p. 25.

Cookson, P. (1989) 'Research on learners and learning in distance education: a review', 3(2), p. 22.

Davie, L. and Wells, R. (1991) 'Empowering the learner through computer-mediated communication', 5(1), pp. 15–23.

Diehl, G. (1987) 'Hidden agenda in course construction and revision', 1(1), p. 25.

Dille, B. and Mezak, M. (1991) 'Identifying predictors of high risk among community college telecourse students', 5(1), pp. 24–35.

Dillon, C. (1992) 'The study of distance education in the United States: programs of study and coursework', 6(2), pp. 64–9.

Dillon, C. and Walsh, S. (1992) 'Faculty: the neglected resource in distance education', 6(3), pp. 5–21.

Dubin, R. and Taveggia, T. (1968) *The Teaching–Learning Paradox*, Eugene, University of Oregon Center for the Advanced Study of Educational Administration, p. 33.

Egan, W., Welch, M., Page, B. and Sebastian, J. (1992) 'Learners' perceptions of instructional delivery systems: conventional and television', 6(2), pp. 47–63.

England, R. (1987) 'Engineering education through telecommunications: policy recommendations for the states', 1(3), p. 41.

Garrison, D. R. and Baynton, M. (1987) 'Beyond independence in distance education: the concept of control', 1(3), p. 3.

Gehlauf, D. N. *et al.* (1991) 'Faculty perceptions of interactive television instructional strategies: implications for training', 5(3), p. 20.

Grimes, P. (1988) 'The performance of nonresident students in the "Economics U$A" telecourse', 2(2), p. 36.

Gunawardena, C. (1992) 'Changing faculty roles for audiographics and online teaching', 6(3), pp. 58–71.

Hillman, D. *et al.* (1994) 'Learner–interface interaction: an extension of contemporary models and strategies for practitioners', 8(2), pp. 30–42.

Holstein, J. (1992) 'Making the written word "speak": reflections on the teaching of correspondence courses', 6(3), pp. 22–33.

Kitchen, K. (1988) 'Interactive television at community colleges in Minnesota', 2(1), p. 73.

Lauzon, A. C. (1992) 'Integrating computer-based instruction with computer conferencing: an evaluation of a model for designing online education', 6(2), pp. 32–46.

Major, M. and Shane, D. (1991) 'Use of interactive television for outreach nursing education', 5(1), pp. 57–66.

Malan, R. and Feller, S. (1992) 'Establishing workload equivalence: independent study courses and college residence classes', 6(2), pp. 56–63.

Maloy, W. and Perry, N. (1991) 'A navy video teletraining project: lessons learned', 5(3), pp. 40–50.

Martin, E. and Rainey, L. (1993) 'Student achievement and attitude in a satellite-delivered high school science course', 7(1), pp. 54–61.

Martin, H. (1993) 'Foreign language study by correspondence: who and why?', 3(2), p. 76.

Merkley, D. and Hoy, M. (1988) 'Using satellite uplink in teacher training', 3(2), p. 67.

Moore, D. *et al.* (1991) 'The role of facilitators in Virginia's electronic classroom project', 5(3), p. 29.

Moore, M. (1989) 'Three types of interaction', 3(2), pp. 1–6.

Olcott, Jr., D. (1992) 'Policy issues in statewide delivery of university programs by telecommunications', 6(1), pp. 14–26.

Oxford, R. and Florini, B. (1990) 'What distance education can learn from other disciplines', 4(1), pp. 3–10.

Phelps, R. *et al.* (1991) 'Effectiveness and costs of distance education using computer-mediated communication', 5(3), pp. 7–19.

Reilly, K. and Gulliver, K. (1992) 'Interstate authorization of distance higher education via telecommunications: the developing national consensus in policy and practice', 6(2), pp. 3–16.

Saba, F. (1988) 'Integrated telecommunications systems and instructional transaction', 2(3), p. 17.

Saba, F. and Shearer, R. (1994) 'Verifying key theoretical concepts in a dynamic model of distance education', 8(1), pp. 36–59.

St Pierre, S. and Olsen, L. (1991) 'Student perspectives on the effectiveness of correspondence instruction', 5(3), pp. 65–71.

Souder, W. (1993) 'The effectiveness of traditional versus satellite delivery in three management of technology master's degree programs', 7(1), pp. 37–53.

Tallman, F. (1994) 'Satisfaction and completion in correspondence study: the influence of instructional and student support services', 8(2), pp. 43–57.

Wagner, E. (1990) 'Looking at distance education through an educational technologist's eyes', 4(1), pp. 53–68.

Wagner, E. (1994) 'In support of a functional definition of interaction', 8(2), pp. 6–29.

Wilkes, C. Wynn and Burnham, B. (1991) 'Adult learner motivations and electronic distance education', 5(1), pp. 43–50.

Whittington, N. (1987) 'Is instructional television educationally effective? A research review', 1(1), p. 47.

Wolcott, L. (1993) 'Faculty planning for distance teaching', 7(1), pp. 26–36.

5

CREATING THE FUTURE

Developing vision in open and distance learning

A. W. (Tony) Bates

COPING WITH CHANGE

Imagine you are the Dean of the humanities department in a dual-mode institution, and you are on the university's planning committee. The present, slightly left of centre government has been holding down the university budget to just below the rate of inflation for the last five years, and is at the same time demanding that the university increases the number of students it will serve within its current financial plan. The government, however, is in trouble, and looks like losing heavily in an impending election to a right of centre party that is committed to drastic cuts in public expenditure.

The Vice-Chancellor has set up a programme review committee, to see if resources can be switched out of some programme areas (humanities in particular has been targeted) into others (such as science and technology). You are under pressure from the Division of Continuing Education and some junior members of your faculty to make many more courses available through compressed videoconferencing off-site, although other faculty members have grave concerns about the quality of such teaching, and the university's planning office has warned there is no additional funding available for this purpose. The Centre for Educational Technology is also deeply critical of the cost-effectiveness of the videoconferencing proposal and is pressuring staff in the faculty to use computer-conferencing, even though there is no computer-conferencing system currently available, and most staff do not seem to want to use it.

You, together with all the other Deans, have been asked by the planning committee to present a new programme plan for the next three years. Lastly, your partner complains that you constantly bring work home, and seem to be irritable most of the time.

... I could go on, but I suspect that the picture is not an untypical one, even though the details may vary.

All educational institutions, conventional or dual mode, autonomous distance teaching universities or training organisations, are undergoing tremendous pressure for change, mainly due to external circumstances over which they seem to have little control. Several chapters in this section have made clear the importance of strategic planning for institutions engaged in or about to embark upon distance education. However, while many institutions have a strategic plan, they still continue to be driven by external forces, and forced to deal with unexpected events on an ad hoc basis. What can an institution do to take more control over its fate, and to make the problems faced by our exemplary Dean more manageable?

A STRATEGY FOR CHANGE

What I aim to do in this chapter is to:

- look at some of the major trends and changes impacting on open and distance learning;
- describe a strategy for managing change;
- show how such a strategy can impact on the day-to-day decision-making within one part of an organisation, by using decisions around the use of technology as an example.

CURRENT TRENDS

The first thing is to know what is happening in the outside world that may impact on the institution and its activities. This means conducting an annual environmental scan. This can be divided into several sections.

Political

This analyses what is happening in national and local politics. Much of this analysis will reflect local context, but to give examples of what such an analysis may reveal, I will list four common political agendas at work that have direct impact on open and distance learning:

- *access and equity*: the need to make more places available for post-secondary education (especially school-leavers), and to ensure that minority and equity groups, such as single parents, women, the unemployed, low-paid workers, new immigrants, and other ethnic groups (e.g. black people, aboriginal and low-caste people) are able to access learning opportunities;
- *economic development and workforce training*: increasingly, governments are recognising and promoting the link between continuing, life-long learning in the workplace, and economic development; this may be accompanied by a greater emphasis on national standards, competency training, and vocational training (e.g. apprenticeship regeneration) rather than on academic courses;
- *improving the cost-effectiveness of education and training*: in many contexts, governments are holding education budgets at or just below the

rate of inflation, or are looking to cut public spending substantially; at the same time, governments are demanding higher standards and/or vocational 'relevance', as well as lower average cost per student; in the private sector, companies are looking at ways to reduce travel and accommodation costs in order to get better value for training;

- *improving the accountability of the education system*: not only are governments expecting educational institutions to increase their cost-effectiveness, they are also increasingly expecting institutions to justify to the public what they are doing, in terms of measurable 'outputs' and value for money.

Depending on the political (and economic) mood of the country at any one time, and the party in power, one of these agendas may dominate.

The key issue is not so much the changing political climate, but the fact that the political climate does change, and increasingly quickly. It is critical, then, that for the purposes of survival, open and distance learning institutions need always to be able to demonstrate *both* their ability to widen access and reach equity groups, *and* to meet the education and training needs for economic development. They also need to be able to shift emphasis quickly between these two goals as the political climate changes. They also need continually to search for more cost-effective ways of operating, and now also to provide concrete measures of their impact on society.

Economic development and the labour market

This is a huge area (see Bates (1992a) for a fuller discussion). In brief, though, the trends can be summarised as follows:

- a move away from resource-based and manufacturing industries as job-providers towards an information- or knowledge-based economy, with a consequent shift in the profile and nature of the workforce;
- increasing demands for a better educated workforce, and in particular a workforce that continues to learn throughout life (see Reich, 1991; Government of Canada, 1991; Porter, 1991);
- the emergence of a major new market for education and training – those already in the workforce: for example, in British Columbia, workforce education and training, if provided by traditional means, would require a 50 per cent expansion of the traditional post-secondary education system (Bates, 1992b);
- conventional time- and place-dependent teaching is not usually suitable for the work structure and lifestyle of those in the workforce;
- individuals or employers will often pay the full cost of high-quality education and training delivered flexibly; thus alternative sources of funding for open and distance learning are rapidly expanding;
- governments vary considerably in their understanding of the change in the educational market, and in the priority or support that they give to open and distance learning for workforce development.

In many fields, politicians and even governing boards are unaware of the growing importance of open and distance learning worldwide, and its impact on economic development. Politicians can come and go quite quickly; ministers change (roughly every two years) and new backbenchers and board members are elected or appointed every three or four years. It is critical, then, not only to brief fully and continually all major political parties, but also to ensure that the more permanent civil servants and governing boards are fully aware of and understand the importance of open and distance learning for economic development.

Social trends

This deals with issues such as developments in entertainment and leisure, demographics (including immigration and ethnic issues), community activities and citizenship, health and crime issues, and changes in lifestyles (e.g. home working, 'cocooning'). This is particularly important for the non-formal, non-credit areas of open and distance learning.

As an example of analysis of social trends, we are seeing in Canada an increasing proportion of home-workers and single-parent families, an increasing proportion of women in the workforce, high immigration rates from south-east Asia, an ageing population, increasing awareness of, involvement in and attempts by the general public to take direct control of community issues such as crime and health, and a very strong and growing voluntary sector. These trends are particularly important in defining priority target groups and new programme areas for open and distance learning.

Technology

Any scan for a distance-teaching organisation must cover key developments in computer, telecommunications, television and entertainment technologies and industries. Current trends include:

- increasing power and sophistication of multimedia computer development, thus rapidly increasing its educational potential;
- dramatic decrease in the cost/power ratio, making sophisticated technologies available to the general public at moderate cost;
- convergence of telecommunications, television and computing, both in terms of technology and businesses;
- fast-track developments towards low-cost, on-demand access to digital technologies and services in the home and workplace, but with public access to technology becoming increasingly fragmented and diverse;
- political moves towards developing public learning networks on the information highway, but a lack of policy or strategies by education ministries for the development, application and co-ordination of educational telecommunications.

As well as these more general trends, it is also essential to have intelligence about specific local conditions. The availability of new technology to the general public is critical, and will vary between countries and regions. For instance, we found in 1994 that 79 per cent of our students at the Open Learning Agency (OLA) had access to a suitable computer for study purposes (up from 37 per cent three years earlier); this situation will be very different for distance teaching institutions in the West Indies or even the United Kingdom. While wide-band information highways are already linking main city centres together in North America, it will be many more years before more remote areas or smaller towns are connected. Constant monitoring is essential.

The 'local' education system

This tracks significant developments in the local education scene: establishment of new universities, colleges, or changes in mandate, government education policy, local funding issues for education and training, developments in the private training sector, etc.

Key developments in British Columbia (Bates, 1992a; Black, 1994a, b) are:

*   building more campus-based institutions to increase access (new universities, university-colleges), and getting existing institutions to take more students for the same money;
*   move towards more skills-based education/training, competency testing;
*   a commitment by *all* post-secondary institutions to become more open, flexible and responsive to education and training needs (BCHRDP, 1992);
*   development of local community learning centres, independent of local colleges, focused on training, and networked together;
*   development of a provincial learning network;
*   government 'creaming' or holding back funds from institutions to promote innovation.

An important element in this part of the scan is to identify similar services being delivered by other organisations within your geographical area.

An annual environmental scan is an important element in a strategy for managing change. Despite the broad scope of a scan, and the wealth of possible sources of information, it does not need a great deal of staff time. One person co-ordinates the scan at OLA, but draws heavily on input from heads of departments and other managers. Information is collected and stored throughout the year, and the scan is assembled over a three-week period. What is essential is a clear focus in selecting and analysing information. This comes from having a clear vision for the organisation (see below), and a good understanding of its current strategic directions.

46

DEVELOPING VISION

Even more important than an environmental scan for managing change is the development of a long-term vision.

Several distance teaching organisations already use a North American business approach to strategic planning, based on management by objectives. This means developing a number of strategic objectives, and one-year and three-year plans for achieving these objectives. This has its value, but is often not sufficient for dealing with a fast-changing environment, for several reasons. Firstly, most strategic planning processes require a highly participative approach from staff, so take a great deal of staff time each year. Consequently, many institutions end up each year with a large number of strategic objectives, to ensure that each staff interest group is accommodated. Also, each year a new set of objectives, designed to respond to the changing external environment, is brought in, while staff are still struggling to implement the strategic objectives from previous years. This can lead to criticisms from staff that an institution is 'a mile wide and an inch deep' and 'lacks direction'.

For somewhat similar reasons, the OLA's President, Glen Farrell, decided that the Agency lacked a shared, common vision of what it wanted to accomplish. He decided to develop such a vision. A firm of consultants was hired to train staff throughout the Agency in the process of creating a vision, based on the work of Robert Fritz (1989).

While the method has proved to be a very powerful planning tool, the concept is relatively simple. Organisations collectively decide what they *really* want to achieve, irrespective of current reality, and then develop strategies to move them closer to that goal. This moves an organisation (or individual) from a situation where short-term problem-solving drives decision-making, to one where each problem is addressed in terms of the long-term vision or goal, and how any solution might move the organisation closer to that goal.

In Fritz's method, there are certain requirements to be met in a satisfactory 'vision':

- it must be concrete: it must spell out in some detail what the vision will actually look like when implemented. This is important, because academics tend to define visions conceptually ('open access'), which can mean different things to different people, rather than concretely ('no prior qualifications required for any of our foundation courses'). Concrete, detailed definitions force into the open differences in values and objectives, which then need to be resolved. A vision statement, unlike a mission statement, will be many pages long, and may even contain illustrative scenarios.
- it must reflect what those working in the organisation *really* want to do, irrespective of current reality. This can be very difficult. The tendency of staff is to say 'Get real – we'll never get the money to do that.' While

that may be true in the short term, if key stakeholders buy into the vision, then anything *is* possible.

- a vision – or more likely parts of the vision – can originate from anyone in the organisation, but all those directly associated with the organisation (especially the governing board or council) must be fully involved in the process of developing and agreeing it. This means extensive consultation, both internally and externally, during its development.
- consensus must be achieved without compromising what people really want. Quiescent acceptance without commitment is also unsatisfactory. 'Either/or' positions need to be avoided, by looking for a creative third alternative that satisfies all sides in contention.
- visions are 'nested'. It may be necessary to develop a vision for the education system as a whole before one for the institution can be developed. While it is helpful if a system vision has already been developed (for example, by the government), it is perfectly valid for an organisation to create its own system vision. Once an institution has developed a vision for its own operation within that system vision, then each of the sub-units within the organisation can develop visions for their work, within and consistent with the overall institutional vision. Thus it begins to impact directly on the work of all staff within the organisation.
- it is very important to try to get full understanding of, and commitment to, the institutional vision from key stakeholders. Key stakeholders will include the primary funding ministry, the institution's board or governing council (indeed, vision-building should be their most important task), all regular staff of the organisation (including tutors), partner institutions, key employer groups and current students.

The final version of the Agency's vision statement (OLA, 1994), which is 15 pages long, eventually reflected a major shift in the overall direction and intentions of the Agency, away from being an institution in competition with other institutions for students, to one where it plays a co-ordinating and support role within an overall system, and provides direct instruction only where no other institution is able or willing to do so. The whole process took about a year. However, once agreed, a vision statement should last for at least five years, or until there are major changes that demand it.

A vision statement does not replace strategic planning, but sits on top of it. It is the vision statement that drives the definition and prioritising of strategic objectives or 'end-results'. The three-year strategic objectives/'end-results' are recommended by staff, and agreed and prioritised by the board, as a result of analysing the environmental scan, and current progress towards the vision. Financial and other resource allocations (such as technical facilities), especially for new developments, are made against each strategic objective or set of end-results, by a budget committee, consisting of the heads of the main operational areas, guided by the vision statement and by the priorities set by the board. End-results are stated in measurable terms (e.g. x no. of students in y courses; z no. of hours of TV, audioconferencing, computer-conferencing, etc.).

Each operating area then develops action plans for achieving these objectives, over a one- and three-year period. The action plans for each strategic objective are determined by an analysis of current reality, conducted by each operational area. This includes an analysis of the financial and other resources allocated to each strategic objective.

It is an iterative process, with one- and three-year end-results, and priorities, being modified as events are analysed. However, the vision does not change and the main strategic *directions* do not change a great deal, although the speed at which any given strategic direction is being achieved will vary from year to year. Fritz uses the analogy of a sailing-boat, with a clear 'destination' (vision), but tacking first one way then another as the wind changes, but always moving slowly but surely towards the set destination.

DEPARTMENTAL DECISION-MAKING

Once an institutional vision has been crafted, each operational area should develop its own vision statement 'nested' within the institution-wide vision. Because of the commitment to the use of technology for delivery of courses and services within OLA's institutional vision, it was necessary to develop a vision statement for technology use in the Agency.

To summarise, the technology vision for the Agency is that all services, academic and administrative, will be available on demand and on-line electronically within five years. Also, because different target groups will have differing levels of access to technology, delivery of services will be available in a variety of modes or formats, depending on the needs of the 'client'. This means for instance that course materials, however originally created (video, hard-copy print, etc.) will be converted and stored digitally, and can be made available in any format (downloaded digitally, on CD-ROM, video-cassette or print). Lastly, the teaching model would be based on resource-based learning and group work, moderated and guided by a remote tutor, via electronic networks.

This vision statement has now driven our decision-making regarding hardware and software purchase and internal and external networking. The information technology infrastructure will be based on a networked, multi-media relational database distributed across an open-architecture client-server hardware system. This means that certain applications, such as student registration, will 'sit' on a particular computer, but that computer will be networked with other computers holding other applications, and will be able to share and combine information from other computers.

This year, we are replacing our ten-year-old mainframe computer system, and our equally old, in-house developed student registration system. The decisions on what hardware and software to purchase have been much simplified both by the overall vision and by the information technology vision. Even though all the resources needed may not be available this year, we can move in steps towards the overall plan.

CONCLUSIONS

In the case of the OLA, regular staff surveys have shown substantially greater agreement about there being a shared vision now than three years ago. Our biggest problem has been getting 'true' buy-in from other organisations. The advanced education minister, the senior civil servant and his deputy, and the manager and staff directly responsible for the Agency, have given their full support to the new vision. However, other middle managers in our key ministry still behave as if nothing has changed. We need to do a great deal more to get buy-in for our vision from these staff.

Several colleges have responded well at a senior level, and a number of new collaborative arrangements are being developed, although this also happened before the development of the new vision. There was already in place, before the development of the vision statement, a mechanism for collaboration between the Agency and the universities, for coordinating university distance education programmes at a provincial level. However, in terms of technology, the universities still operate autonomously, developing plans, and usually being funded by the ministry, without consultation or collaboration with the Agency (or each other, for that matter).

It is early days yet to know the extent to which we will be able to offer provincial-wide services used and valued by other institutions. However, from an internal planning point of view, there is a great deal more confidence and cohesion in our decision-making. It would be wrong, then, to suggest that an environmental scan and a detailed vision statement will make all the problems of an organisation disappear. It is a time-consuming process to develop a fully supported vision statement, and many staff will feel that the seemingly endless discussions get in the way of their 'real' work. However, once developed, a good vision statement does simplify the planning process in subsequent years. There will always be some people within an organisation who will not feel comfortable with the institution's (new) vision. With luck, they will drift away to another organisation that is closer to their own vision. Many more will reserve judgement until they see how the vision impacts on their day-to-day work. Once a vision statement is agreed, it needs discipline and consistency in working towards it. Nevertheless, the scan and the vision statement make it easier to know when to say 'no' to new initiatives, and enable resources more easily to be re-allocated internally. These two planning tools do provide more stability for an organisation in fast-changing times, without reducing its flexibility to change and adapt, while maintaining its long-term goals. Lastly, it should reduce the number of times our Dean comes home with a headache.

REFERENCES

Bates, A. (1992a) *A Scan of the British Columbia Environment 1991–94 and the Implications for the Open Learning Agency,* Burnaby, BC, The Open Learning Agency.

Bates, A. (1992b) *Lifelong Learning and Human Resource Development,* Burnaby, BC, The Open Learning Agency.

BCHRDP (1992) *Report of the Steering Committee,* Victoria, BC, British Columbia Human Resource Development Project.

Black, D. (1994a) 'Mixing modes and institutions: university distance education in British Columbia, Canada' in Dodds, A. (1994) *Distance Education: Windows on the Future* (Conference Proceedings) Wellington, New Zealand, The Correspondence School.

Black, D. (1994b) *Environmental Scan, 1995–1998,* Burnaby, BC, The Open Learning Agency.

Fritz, R. (1989) *The Path of Least Resistance,* New York, Fawcett Columbine.

Government of Canada (1991) *Learning Well, Living Well,* Ottawa, Government of Canada.

Open Learning Agency (1994) *Mission and Vision Statement: Internal Working Document,* Burnaby, BC, The Open Learning Agency.

Porter, M. (1991) *Canada at the Crossroads: The Reality of a New Competitive Environment,* Ottawa, Business Council on National Issues/Government of Canada.

Reich, R. (1991) 'The REAL economy', *The Atlantic Monthly,* February.

Part II

THE STUDENT
EXPERIENCE

6

STUDENT LEARNING AND STUDENTS' EXPERIENCES

Research, theory and practice

Alistair R. Morgan

INTRODUCTION

How do students experience their courses in open and distance education? What is it really like to study at a distance (usually part time) in contrast to the more familiar setting of conventional higher education? How do students approach their learning and what is the nature of the corresponding learning outcomes? This chapter aims to address these questions which underlie much of the debate about the quality of learning.

The various methodologies will be explored in terms of research and evaluation of student learning, particularly for how they can contribute to the development of theory and improvement of practice.

The chapter sets out a model of student learning which is grounded in students' realities of study; it also indicates the types of 'interventions' which are available to teachers and course designers to improve the quality of student learning. The chapter also addresses some of the recent criticisms of research in student learning and the policy issues originating from it.

WHY IS 'APPROACH TO LEARNING' IMPORTANT?

One of the fundamental concepts developed in the recent research in student learning is 'aproaches to learning' and the distinction between a 'deep approach' and a 'surface approach' (Marton and Säljö, 1976). Students' approach to learning describes the way they set out to tackle a particular learning task or piece of work. Also it is important to note that approach is context-specific to a particular task in which the learner is engaged. The crucial importance of approach to learning is that it is linked directly to the quality of the learning outcomes. In the original studies of Marton and Säljö (1976), students who tackled their studies in a way which was called a 'deep approach' gained a thorough understanding of the material studied. In contrast, students who tackled their studies in a very different way, labelled a 'surface approach', failed to gain a grasp of the material which had been studied. The importance of a deep approach, then, is that it is linked to the quality of the learning outcomes. The original research has been extended to a wide range of contexts (see, for example, Marton *et al.*, 1984). The same concepts have been identified with students in open and distance education (Morgan *et al.*, 1982; Morgan, 1993). Ramsden (1988) provides a useful summary of how the distinction of a deep/surface approach has been described in a wide range of studies, as follows:

Approaches to Learning

Deep approach:

Intention to understand

Focus on what 'is signified' (e.g. the author's arguments)

Relate and distinguish new ideas and previous knowledge

Relate concepts to everyday experience

Organise and structure content

Internal emphasis: 'A window through which aspects of reality become visible, and more intelligible.'

Surface approach:

Intention to complete learning task requirements

Focus on the 'signs' (e.g. the text itself)

Focus on discrete elements

Memorise information and procedures for assessment

Unreflectively associate concepts and facts

Fail to distinguish principles from evidence, new information from old

Treat learning task as an external imposition

External emphasis: 'Demands of assessment, knowledge cut off from everyday reality.'

(Ramsden, 1988, p. 19)

To gain a thorough understanding of a subject area, and for the students to 'construct' meanings from the learning activities with which they engage, are generally regarded as two of the key aims and outcomes of higher education. The former CNAA described a degree-level programme of study as follows:

... the development of students' intellectual and imaginative powers; their understanding and judgement; their problem-solving skills; their ability to communicate; their ability to see relationships within what they have

56

learned and to perceive their field of study in a broader perspective. The programme of study must stimulate an enquiring, analytical and creative approach, encouraging independent judgement and critical self-awareness.

(quoted in Gibbs, 1992, p. 1)

Although there are contested views about what constitutes quality, and various stakeholders – namely, academic bodies, government and funding agencies, and students – will have different priorities, the CNAA statement would seem likely to have quite wide support. These learning outcomes specified in the CNAA statement are those which are linked directly with a deep approach to learning.

Dave Harris (1994) raises important questions about the research in student learning as follows:

The deep/surface dichotomy might well reflect real cognitive differences, but the question is still why one approach should be positively valued, and this returns us to the analysis of universities and their cultures, both in proximal and distance contexts. After all, mere success in assessment is relatively easy to guarantee, especially in the less public areas of proximal teaching, providing lecturers teach to their own tests ... It is clear that proponents of active learning would be unhappy to endorse these (increasingly common?) coaching or guided practices, of course 'deep approaches' are valued, therefore, for reasons which exceed their technical or cognitive merits. How did they come to be so valued? Who benefits and who loses from these values?

(Harris, 1994, p. 203)

In response to Harris's questions, from a philospohical standpoint, whether the aims of education are seen from a rational-technicist, liberal-humanist or critical-structural perspective view, I would expect some agreement to the view that students should be able to go 'beyond the information presented' to them in their teaching. All the research indicates that a 'surface approach' to learning fails in developing learning outcomes which enable student to do this. Harris (correctly in my view) is critical of the 'teaching' or 'coaching' which is merely focused on assessment requirements. It seems likely that this type of teaching will tend to foster surface approaches – of question spotting, rehearsing model answers and memorisation of information. The power of the assessment system to influence the nature of student learning and to trivialise learning as an 'unintended side-effect', i.e. to induce a surface approach to learning, is well documented in the classic studies of Becker, Geer and Hughes (1968). It is for these reasons that a 'deep approach' is to be valued. The strength of the research is that the deep/surface dichotomy provides a more sophisticated model of learning than a distinction of active/passive learning. In this sense a deep approach is valued on cognitive grounds, although there is also an emotional dimension of feelings of satisfaction, as initial confusion about a new topic is replaced by a feeling of understanding. The new material is understood in a different manner, from a 'new gestalt', or whole picture, and it is not possible to 'unlearn' the material and return to the initial position of confusion.

I think the criticism of Harris (1994), from a structuralist perspective, that dominant groups claim a legitimacy of their own 'readings' of educational process is too pessimistic. He continues his critique as follows:

> The implication is that the 'deep' approach is not a merely cognitive (or metacognitive) technique but an aesthetic, connected to much wider cultural predispositions, a source of pleasure and power, a matter of social distinction, social solidarity and social reproduction.
>
> (Harris, 1994, p. 199)

Whilst I believe that the critique of Harris informed by the work of Bourdieu (1986) is too pessimistic, it does highlight the issue of gaining the 'cultural capital' to participate in post-compulsory education. In terms of helping students to adopt a 'deep approach' to their learning, it points to the importance of raising students' awareness of what learning consists of, that is of helping them to develop their conceptions of learning. This is particularly important as the student population becomes more diverse with increased participation rates in post-compulsory education.

To digress for a moment into the world of fiction, in the play (and associated film) *Educating Rita* by Willy Russell (1986), how do we understand the learner's experience? I think we can see Rita's attempt to tackle the essay question 'Suggest how you would resolve the staging difficulties inherent in the production of Ibsen's *Peer Gynt*' with the brief response 'Do it on the radio' as an indication that she lacks the 'cultural capital' to engage in the type of discourse that was expected. Helping Rita is about enabling her to become familiar with the discourse of the subject area, to develop a more sophisticated notion of what learning consists of and then to change in order to reduce the 'cultural distance' from the education.

Returning to Harris's critique of the phenomenological research in student learning, although his analysis gives valuable insights into some of the origins of students' difficulties, the research in student learning provides a framework for what teachers and course designers need to do to help students improve their learning.

RESEARCH AND PRACTICE

From the above discussion, it should be clear that in order to improve student learning, we need to help students to adopt a deep approach to their learning. Harris (1994) provides a valuable critique; however, the strength of the 'phenomenographic project' for improving learning is that it is grounded in the qualitative differences in learning outcomes, i.e. the quality of learning. Although learning outcomes are primarily a cognitive issue, 'deep learning' also has an important emotional dimension, parallel to Carl Rogers' (1969) notion of personally meaningful, learning. (Deep learning can be seen as a 'short-hand' which encompasses both a deep approach and quality learning outcomes.)

If the research in student learning can be used to inform practice, what sorts of course designs and strategies for helping students with their studies are available? The research suggests that there are two key areas for 'intervention' by teachers and course designers to improve the quality of student learning. First, certain aspects of course design and assessment are more likely to encourage students to adopt a deep appproach, in contrast to a surface approach. Secondly, activities to help students develop and change their conceptions of learning are likely to facilitate students to adopting a deep approach.

The aims of these interventions to improve student learning have been summarised by Biggs (1994, p. 4) under four key areas of: (a) positive motivational context; (b) high degree of learner activity; (c) interaction with others; and (d) a well-structured knowledge base.

Students' motivation is more likely to be intrinsic, when they have some responsiblity for what they learn and how they learn it. Adults learn better when the learning activities are relevant for them in terms of needing to know the material being studied. So, for example, project-based learning – learning related to some work project or problem-based learning – is likely to generate a greater feeling of 'ownership' of the teaching and learning.

Learning should be active; hence the crucial importance in open and distance learning is that learners are encouraged to interact with the various 'texts' in a particular course. However, in the case of written text, this requires more than merely inserting in-text questions, as learners are not that easily manipulated with such devices (Lockwood, 1992). Hence, far more attention needs to be given to the types of activity which will encourage reflection in learning and help learners to construct their own meanings. This leads directly to encouraging 'interaction with others'. This is probably one of the more difficult areas to address. How can interaction and dialogue be set up in open and distance learning? Dialogue can be developed within the text (Evans and Nation, 1989a), but it should reflect a philosophical commitment to a form of discourse which informs all teaching and learning, rather than seeing it as merely a technical issue.

The well-structured knowledge base, usually provided by the printed teaching text, is the crucial starting-point for learners; it introduces them to the key concepts in the field and the nature of the discourse in the subject matter. Although Biggs was not working specifically in the field of open and distance learning, these key issues for improving learning translate directly. Interaction in learning, dialogue in learning, helping students towards more reflexivity in their studies encourage the student to 'construct' meaning.

Is the 'return of the technical fix', as suggested by Dave Harris, a serious threat? Although I believe much of the work of the CVCP's 'Effective Learning and Teaching in Higher Education' initiative is firmly grounded in the research and has drawn out policy issues sensitively, there is definitely a serious risk that study skills packages will attempt to 'teach' skills out of any context, with no consideration of the discourse of particular subject material. Various study skills manuals and packages have a potentially large market with a 'vulnerable' readership, searching for quick remedies and 'handy hints' to help them as they struggle with their studies. (See Gibbs (1981) for discussion of these issues.)

Developing skill in learning is not concerned with prescribed techniques, in the manner set out in some (now dated) study manuals. Skill in learning is concerned with a deep approach to learning, particular conceptions of learning and particular orientations to education (Svensson, 1984) and with developing an awareness of the discourse of the subject area (Northedge, 1990).

So far, I have made relatively little specific mention of open and distance education as contrasted to proximal education. This is intentional. The research in student learning suggests that the detailed processes of how students tackle their studies in both conventional higher education (proximal) and open and distance learning are similar. Also, with the changes in conventional settings, the distinction between the forms are rapidly becoming blurred as self-study material of various forms is being introduced into conventional settings.

The relationship between research and practice in phenomenological research in student learning is very different from that underlying traditional instructional technology. One of the basic tenets of educational technology is the use of feedback data for course improvement. Many writers in this area suggest that change in educational practice and organisational change can be understood in terms of a rational systems approach and engineering models of feedback (see, for example, Rowntree, 1982). Although this rational systems model of understanding change is a useful starting-point, this model provides only a partial explanation of change in practice. There is a lack of congruence between much of the writing on course development in open and distance education and the processes in practice, or, as Schon (1983) says, there is a mismatch between 'espoused-theory' and 'theory-in-use'. He contrasts the 'technical-rationality' with 'reflection-in-action' as a more realistic model of how professionals operate in practice. In the case of educational change and course improvement, student feedback does not necessarily inform and influence change in the manner assumed in rational models of change. Other complex factors concerned with the history, culture and politics of the organisation are crucial for understanding change (Pettigrew, 1985); these factors are likely to be of equal if not greater importance. (The link between research and development and organisational change is discussed further by Terry Evans in Chapter 7 in this volume.)

The 'active learning project' – to use the term sometimes applied to the publications from the Universities' Staff Development and Training Unit, 'Effective Learning and Teaching in Higher Education' (CVCP, 1992) – has been influential because the relationship between research and practice has been informed by the notion of the 'reflective practitioner' (see also Entwistle, 1994). Within the UK, the staff development departments and teaching and learning units that have been successful appear to have adopted Schon's work and ideas from experiential learning to underpin their activities (for example, the Oxford Centre for Staff Development at Oxford Brookes University). More recently, Evans and Nation (1989b) have articulated the work of Habermas and of Giddens (1984) to develop the idea of 'critical reflection' to draw together theory, research and practice in open and distance education.

A MODEL OF LEARNING

Figure 6.1 sets out a model of learning, which is grounded in students' realities of learning. So far in this chapter, we have explored why approach to learning is so important and how it is related to the learning outcomes. We have also seen how helping students to develop their awareness of what learning itself consists of, is crucially important as we work to encourage them to adopt a deep approach to learning. Säljö's (1979) research on students' conceptions of learning identified five qualitatively different conceptions. Säljö's Levels 1, 2 and 3 are concerned with memorisation, reproducing information and using set algorithms to solve problems, in contrast to Levels 4 and 5 which are concerned with constructing meaning. The importance of conception of learning is that it seems to have a limiting influence on students' approaches to learning (van Rossum and Schenk, 1984). At the same time we have discussed briefly how certain assessment demands can so easily induce a surface approach to learning.

Returning to the model, the 'organisational context and learning milieu' is the wider institutional context in which the learner is studying. Besides the details of a specific learning task, what is the overall organisational context of learning? What sorts of traditions exist within the organisation (or within a course) for how the teaching and learning is organised? How are the more implicit messages about the curriculum conveyed to students? Is there freedom for learners to pursue their own interests? Are students encouraged to draw their own experiences and opinions into their work? What is the dominant conception of teaching which informs a particular course or department within an organisation? These factors will have a crucial influence on how students approach their learning.

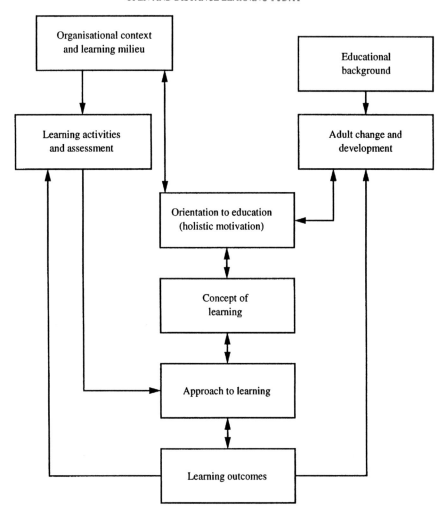

Figure 6.1 A model of student learning

The model aims to provide a holistic model of learning; it is a relational model which draws togther the key elements which influence how students tackle their learning and the quality of the learning outcomes. It is developed as a heuristic model rather than a causal model so as to provide a basis for critical reflection on teaching and learning.

The concept of orientation to education is central to the model. It describes how students come to be engaged in their studies; it describes a holistic motivation for study as they experience it (in contrast to a mechanistic view focusing on push/pull factors.) The key orientations to education which have been identified, with both conventional and open and distance learners, are academic, vocational and personal, and with an extrinsic/intrinsic distinction within each of them (Gibbs *et al.*, 1984). The concept of orientation to education serves to relate the detailed processes of learning to the broader issues of adult change and development.

If we look at the wider issues about the experiences of adult learners, how does learning interact with people's lives? It is generally recognised that adult learners are seeking some sort of change in their lives. Of course, there will be a great diversity in the nature of these changes desired by students. Some students are seeking to change jobs, to gain employment, or to increase their chance of promotion; some feel unfairly judged by the educational system and want to prove to themselves and their peers that they are capable of academic study, others are taking up something new after redundancy or other personal crisis. These aspirations will 'translate' into various orientations to education which describe how a learner engages with a particular course. However, for many students there are other changes which arise from the interactions of studying with their everyday lives, some of which are unanticipated – for example, the limitations of a current job, the shortcomings of a peer group or the constraints of a relationship. Being an adult learner is inextricably connected with *human change*.

For example, Morgan and Holly (1994) described changes with a group of Open University students under the themes of: confidence and self-esteem; an awareness of self in society; a move towards 'empowerment'; and a change in relation to the social and domestice context of learning. Evans (1994) describes numerous cases of the gendered experience of being a learner in open and distance education. At the same time, there is considerable potential for *change* for women students through open and distance education. As Evans explains:

> As with many social problems, gender inequalities are seen as being, at least partly, solved through education. In particular, open and distance education have been nominated in some societies as a key means for providing educational opportunities for women who have previously been disadvantaged.
>
> (Evans, 1994, p. 53)

Again, to quote Evans (1994) on the relationship between studying and the broader issues of adult change and development, 'A question for prospective or new students could well be "Do they realise the potentially far-reaching implications of studying?"'

So, if we return to the model (Figure 6.1), the aim is to provide a framework for a holistic understanding of the learners' experiences. It draws together the key issues which influence the quality of the learning outcomes, both change at the conceptual level, as well as broader issues of adult change and development.

METHODOLOGICAL COMMENTARY

It should be clear by now that the majority of the research on student learning referred to has been carried out using qualitative methodologies. However, the aim is not to polarise qualitative and quantitative methods; on the contrary, there is a need for a complementarity of methods so there is a cumulative development of theory. In fact this mixing of methods is an important feature of the research in student learning.

The research of Ference Marton and the Gothenburg Group, using qualitative methodologies, has provided a major foundation in the research in student learning, and the research approach has subsequently been labelled 'phenomenography' (Marton, 1981). Other researchers (Entwistle and Ramsden, 1983) have adopted both interviews and inventory questionnaires for investigating students' approaches to study. This work also identified a 'strategic approach' where students focus on the demands of the assessment tasks and possible ways to gain cues about the assessment and gradings with the overall aim of gaining the highest grades. The research labelled 'illuminative evaluation' (Parlett and Hamilton, 1977) provides another important strand for looking at research in open and distance education; again this research has adopted both qualitative and quantitative methodologies to describe what is 'really going on' in education programmes. Of course, there are major methodological difficulties in researching learning and teaching, as Dave Harris points out clearly in Chapter 8 in this volume, 'Still seeking the audience?'. However, the challenge is to adopt a range of methodologies, which are most appropriate for the research or evaluation questions or, in the words of Martyn Hammersley (1992), to 'deconstruct the qualitative–quantitative divide'.

Earlier in this chapter, I outlined how the current research in student learning set out to draw research, theory and practice into a closer relationship. The model of student learning presented in Figure 6.1 is an attempt to develop a theoretical framework grounded in learners' experience, which serves to inform practice. Reflection in action (Schon, 1983) and critical reflection (Evans and Nation, 1989b) provide insights into the research–theory–practice relationship which are very different to the prescriptive approaches of traditional educational technology. Every new teaching and learning situation will be different; however, research and theory grounded in the learners' experiences provide a basis from which to draw links and parallels and so inform practice in the new settings.

CONCLUSION

In this chapter I have attempted to outline some of the key concepts for understanding learning from the learner's perspective in open and distance education. Approach to learning is discussed as one of the central concepts for understanding student learning. The model of student learning provides a basis for theorising teaching and learning. Of course, there are many unanswered questions – for example, the concerns of Dave Harris about how to develop the 'cultural capital' required to participate in open and distance education. How can open and distance education contribute to lifelong learning and the development of the idea of a learning society and the sorts of teaching and provisions are most likely to facilitate these changes? How can research be drawn closer to the development of policy and practice in open and distance education?

REFERENCES

Becker, H., Geer, B. and Hughes, E. C. (1968) *Making the Grade: The Academic Side of College Life*, New York, Wiley.

Biggs, J. (1994) 'Student learning research and theory: where do we stand?' in Gibbs, G. (ed.) *Improving Student Learning: Theory and Practice*, Oxford, Oxford Centre for Staff Development.

Bourdieu, P. (1986) *Distinction: A Social Critique of the Judgement of Taste*, London, Routledge.

Brannen, J. (ed.) (1992) *Mixing Methods: Qualitative and Quantitative Research*, Aldershot, Avebury.

Committee of Vice-Chancellors and Principals (1992) *Effective Learning in Higher Education*, Sheffield, CVCP Universities' Staff Development and Training Unit.

Entwistle, N. (1994) *Teaching and the Quality of Learning*, London, Committee of Vice-Chancellors and Principals of the Universities of the UK.

Entwistle, N. and Ramsden, P. (1983) *Understanding Student Learning*, Beckenham, Kent, Croom Helm.

Evans, T. (1994) *Understanding Learners in Open and Distance Education*, London, Kogan Page.

Evans, T. and Nation, D. (1989a) 'Dialogue in the theory, practice and research of distance education', *Open Learning*, 4(2), pp. 37–46.

Evans, T. and Nation, D. (eds) (1989b) *Critical Reflections on Distance Education*, Lewes, Falmer Press.

Gibbs, G. (1981) *Teaching Students to Learn*, Milton Keynes, Open University Press.

Gibbs, G. (1992) *Improving the Quality of Student Learning*, Bristol, Technical and Educational Services Ltd.

Gibbs, G., Morgan, A. and Taylor, E. (1984) 'The world of the learner' in Marton, F., Hounsell, D. and Entwistle, N. (eds).

Giddens, A. (1984) *The Constitution of Society*, Cambridge, Polity Press.

Hammersley, M. (1992) 'Deconstructing the qualitative–quantitative divide' in Brannen, J. (ed.).

Harris, D. (1994) '"Effective teaching" and "study skills": the return of the technical fix?' in Evans, T. and Murphy, D. (eds) *Research in Distance Education 3*, Geelong, Deakin University Press.

Lockwood, F. (1992) *Activities in Self-instructional Texts*, London, Kogan Page.

Marton, F. (1981) 'Phenomenography – describing conceptions of the world around us', *Instructional Science*, 10(2), pp. 177–200.

Marton, F., Hounsell, D. and Entwistle, N. (eds) (1984) *The Experience of Learning*, Edinburgh, Scottish Academic Press.

Marton, F. and Säljö, R. (1976) 'On qualitative differences, outcomes and process I and II', *British Journal of Educational Psychology*, 46, pp. 4–11, 115–27.

Morgan, A. (1993) *Improving your Students' Learning: Reflections on the Experience of Study,* London, Kogan Page.

Morgan, A. and Holly, L. (1994) 'Adult change and development: the interactions of learning with people's lives' in Gibbs, G. (ed.) *Improving Student Learning: Theory and Practice,* Oxford, Oxford Centre for Staff Development.

Morgan, A., Taylor, E. and Gibbs, G. (1982) 'Variation in students' approaches to studying', *British Journal of Educational Technology,* 13(2), pp. 107–13.

Northedge, A. (1990) *The Good Study Guide,* Milton Keynes, The Open University.

Parlett, M. and Hamilton, D. (1977) 'Evaluation as illumination' in Hamilton, D., Jenkins, D., King, C., MacDonald, B. and Parlett, M. (eds) *Beyond the Numbers Game,* Basingstoke, Macmillan.

Pettigrew, A. W. (1985) *The Awakening Giant: Continuity and Change in Imperial Chemical Industries,* Oxford, Blackwell.

Ramsden, P. (ed.) (1988) *Improving Learning: New Perspectives,* London, Kogan Page.

Rogers, C. (1969) *Freedom to Learn,* Columbus, Ohio, Merrill.

Rowntree, D. (1982) *Curriculum Development and Educational Technology,* 2nd edn, London, Harper and Row.

Russell, W. (1986) *Educating Rita,* London, Methuen.

Säljö, R. (1979) 'Learning about learning', *Higher Education,* 8, pp. 443–51.

Schon, D. (1983) *The Reflective Practitioner: How Professionals Think in Action,* London, Temple Smith.

Svensson, L. (1984) 'Skill in learning' in Marton, F., Hounsell, D. and Entwistle, N. (eds).

van Rossum, E. J. and Schenk, S. M. (1984) 'The relationship between learning conception, study strategy and learning outcome', *British Journal of Educational Psychology,* 54, pp. 73–83.

7

THE POTENTIAL OF RESEARCH WITH STUDENTS TO INFORM DEVELOPMENT

Terry Evans

INTRODUCTION

The relationship between research and development is often taken for granted in academic and scientific communities. Research is assumed to be a 'good thing' and development is assumed to occur through the trickle-down effects of publication and conference presentation. Some companies engage researchers to work specifically on research projects which have a prospect of leading to a profitable development. In such circumstances the development stages and outcomes are the 'real' measures of research productivity, whereas in the former circumstances, research productivity is measured by competitive grants won and publications accepted. In most cases, research in distance education has been more like the former, although often tinged with the constraints of funding bodies requiring research into particular areas. In Australia, one way in which research into open and distance education has been promoted is through the tendering processes of the Australian Government's Department of Employment, Education and Training. Such research is focused on government priorities, for example, in the areas of new communications technologies, and is often constrained by very tight deadlines for both the submission of tenders and final reports.

Notwithstanding the advantages of these research funds, there are questions about the effectiveness of such approaches for encouraging and supporting research leading to worthwhile and sustainable developments in the field. There is a dilemma here. The fact that the Government has identified an area as important gives it a very good start in the potential development stakes. However, the tight prescription of the research topic and the even tighter schedules mean that many active researchers are too busy to meet the schedules and, if they did, they may wish to shape the topics into more useful ones. This is development-led research of a rather restricted kind; however, 'unrestricted' research does not necessarily lead to worthwhile developments either.

The relationship between research and development is complex in any context and the field of open and distance education is no exception.

Achieving development in open and distance education requires bringing about informed change or reform to educational practices which are deemed to be improvements ('developments'). An important part of this process is having powerful support for the changes from, for example, government, policy-makers and institutions' managers. However, generally speaking, these are only significant in the development or implementation phases. The quality of a development, it seems, is absolutely dependent on its usefulness for the students concerned. Therefore, there is an imperative that potential developments to educational practice are based on and informed by research with students.

DEVELOPMENTS FOR WHOM?

The educational process requires that there is an interdependent relationship, however attenuated it may be within forms of open and distance education, between the teachers and learners. Clearly this dependence extends beyond those who might formally be seen as teachers to include everyone whose work involves sustaining an educational institution's endeavours. But the initiatives for developments within an educational organisation often come from interests which are somewhat removed from the immediate relationship between teachers and students. This does not mean that the developments are not in the students' interests, at least partly, or that they are even counterproductive, although this may occasionally be the case. However, it does mean that often the prime motives behind the developments in education are located outside of the teacher–student relationship, but nevertheless have an important effect thereon.

Some common examples may help here. Over the past decade in both developed and developing nations there has been an economic rationalist imperative that institutions need to adopt a more 'user-pays' approach to their activities. This led to the development of various educational practices and services more closely geared to their cost–income relationship, rather than, for example, to student needs and interests. Institutions' activities have shifted to those which can be 'sold' on a full-cost, plus margin, basis. Economic rationalism suggests that, if learners are prepared to pay, then in terms of market processes, they must be satisfied 'customers' and, therefore, the educational endeavour has been worthwhile, *educationally*. This logic can be dissected in different ways; however, the point here is to illustrate that educational developments have taken place with an imperative which is not, of itself, based on an understanding of students' educational needs and interests.

Other examples include developments in the areas of new communications and computer technologies. The cry is heard frequently that many such developments are more in the interests of hardware and software manufacturers or service-providers, than in the interests of educational institutions or their students. This is probably an over-simplification, because often the equipment, services and software have lured the educator with the promise of some improvement, increased efficiency or enhancement to their own practices or services. But it does raise the question of whose interests are being served by the major developments taking place in open and distance education. Often the answer to such a question is very difficult to ascertain. Most major developments have political and ideological foundations, and are constructed with a variety of institutional interests. Therefore, the answer depends largely on one's own ideological and private concerns; however, it can be argued that students' interests are not paramount. This is not to argue for a 'warm and cuddly' ideology of student-centredness, rather it is to make the point that, if any effective educational developments are to occur, they must directly accommodate student contexts, interests and needs; one of the best ways to understand, analyse and represent these interests is through useful *research.*

WHAT STUDENT RESEARCH CAN SHOW

One of the features of distance education is its relatively long preparation and course production phases. For new educational ventures the prospective students are almost invariably unknown to those preparing the courses and, logically, the prospective students themselves are unlikely to know that they are, indeed, 'prospective students'. This means that 'student research' itself has to be interpreted fairly widely to include prospective students, existing students and past students within research activities. The implication of this is that some 'student' research activities need to be conducted with people who are not students, but who are or may be *prospective* students. Arguably, this is akin to some forms of market research which deal with the development of new products.

Good student research needs to adopt approaches, methods and methodologies which can record and analyse the diversity which any broad array of people will embody (Evans, 1994, pp. 122–33). Often students in general are reduced to one or a few archetypes which are used to focus the attention of those developing new educational practices. Whilst it is useful occasionally to have a typical student (or students) in mind, the hard reality of the sorts of mass education in which distance educators are involved is that diversity needs to be recognised or else developments will only be partially successful at best. In particular they are likely to exclude people who are often routinely excluded from other mainstream activities and concerns, for example, those with disabilities, older people or other specific minority groups.

Failure to recognise the diversity of people in student research can lead to courses and procedures which may not fulfil the needs or meet the requirements or circumstances of particular students who have enrolled in good faith. Such people may find themselves unable to meet course requirements or deadlines, or find other aspects of their educational experience do not fit with their expectations, needs or circumstances. These students are susceptible to withdrawing from their courses which may have profound negative consequences for their self-esteem and futures, and also for the educational organisations concerned. Here one of the most researched aspects of distance education comes to the fore: 'drop-out'.

Retention or 'drop-out' rates have been of concern to distance education institutions internationally for decades. A good deal of institutional research has been deployed, and also several studies with a theoretical basis have sought to explain the 'drop-out' phenomenon (for example, Kember, 1989; Roberts *et al.*, 1991). Much can be learned from 'drop-out' research to inform future developments, but it is analogous to aeroplane crash investigations – the benefits come to others from the tragedies of those who have gone before. In this sense, 'drop-out' research is research into the failures of educational institutions' previous developments; hence, it is research *after* development. ('Drop-outs' do, of course, often occur for reasons beyond the control of the institution (Evans, 1991).)

The research and development process is not a simple one from the former to the latter. Indeed, the (ideal) research and development process is cyclic, with one informing the other sequentially. Therefore, 'drop-out' research or evaluations of courses and educational services, are important aspects of the cycle, but they follow at least the first offering of a course or service, which means the first cohort of students has encountered its strengths and weaknesses. Evaluations, in a sense, are more positively focused than 'drop-out' studies because they reflect all the students' experiences and not (just) those who have withdrawn. Course evaluation has been routinely more prevalent in distance education than in most other forms of education. With the advent of the 'quality' movement, evaluation has flourished as another element of 'instructional industrialism' (Evans and Nation, 1989) in the sense that the production, distribution and analysis of evaluation 'instruments' have become virtually an automated process of 'mindless' data collection (Morgan, 1990). Much course evaluation can thus be seen as among student research of the worst kind. The use of 'closed' survey questionnaire items on limited aspects of a course or service which are then coded, analysed and reported to satisfy the quality 'inspectors' does not constitute good research of any kind and is a dangerous impediment to the sorts of thoroughgoing and well-grounded research which Morgan advocates (Morgan, 1990; Morgan, 1992). It is dangerous for at least three reasons: it masks the findings of good evaluations; it diverts resources from worthwhile evaluation and other student research; and it exhausts the students from participating in further evaluations and research.

One form of research which generally does focus its activities in a thoroughgoing review of the elements of a course or educational service is developmental research. In this category one may place 'developmental testing' or 'formative evaluation', for example. In some instances, not only is this form of research useful in itself for producing findings for the development of subsequent courses or services, but it can also yield direct benefits for the participating students. Their efforts on courses, for example, may be counted towards assessment, and in the case of both courses and services, the weaknesses participants identify may be promptly remedied or compensated to their direct benefit. The beauty of developmental research is that it closely links the needs and contexts of the students to the development of the course or service in question, but it is reactive to an existing development which may not necessarily be based on a sound understanding of students' needs, requirements and contexts.

There is a significant body of research into students' contexts, experiences and orientation to study in distance education which has contributed to literature in the field. Some of the contributors to this volume have played their own parts (for example, Evans, 1994; Evans and Grace, 1994; Gibbs *et al.*, 1984; Lockwood, 1992; Morgan, 1993) as have other researchers (for example, Farnes, 1992; Holt *et al.*, 1990; Holt, 1993). Such research is sometimes closely related to the development process in that, for example, it relates to the researchers' work with course teams in the development of courses. In other instances, the research relies on the usual research publication processes to filter gradually into the practical developmental work of others or, perhaps, into the policy decisions of government or institutions. It is here that we can begin to see the weakness emerging in the research and development relationship. Sometimes the most substantial and potentially useful research with students has insufficient relationship to the development of educational courses and services. Principally this occurs because the links between research, publication and the development of practice are tenuous. This is something which both Calvert (1989) and Nation (1990) have lamented.

LINKING RESEARCH AND DEVELOPMENT

If, after so many decades, the link between student research and educational development is rather weak, then there is good reason to believe that the countervailing forces are quite strong. As was argued previously, the powerful forces of government and ideology, for example, are such that educational developments proceed for other than principally student-centred reasons. Thus, a pragmatic approach suggests that student research can only improve its relative position. In addition, its chances of so doing are prosecuted best by demonstrating that a stronger student research and development link will actually improve the chances of education being effective more generally, to national economic interests, for instance. The politics of such a position are not without their difficulties, especially where, for example, improved education leads to a greater critical awareness amongst people who then are moved to challenge injustice. Powerful interests in open democracies prefer to avoid such challenge; in lesser democracies or autocracies they insist on avoiding or crushing it.

From adopting a pragmatic approach we can assume that improving the links between student research and the development of open and distance education is a matter of both improving the effectiveness of the ways in which current research is implemented, and also encouraging forms of research which directly link with practice in their methodology. What follows are some suggestions which are indicative of the forms of research that may prove useful.

Clearly, some forms of research discussed previously, such as good quality evaluation and developmental research are grounded in practice. They span activities which explore a course in action, or immediately after its completion. Depending on the subsequent analysis and implementation, these forms of research are ones which should have an important place in connecting student research to student-oriented educational developments. These forms of work (and they can encompass a range of different quantitative and qualitative approaches) have the advantage of scrutinising an existing course or educational service; the students involved are thus dealing with something which actually affects them directly. However, it does not prevent the development of courses which are seen to reflect the interests of teachers more than students, or some 'new technology'-based services which reflect an institution's or manufacturer's interests.

However, there are also strengths and weaknesses to using student research in the development phases of new courses or services. Clearly, the people who are generally best able to suggest new ideas for both curriculum and pedagogy are the teachers; it is what they are paid to do. So, being too dependent on students for such ideas would be a significant weakness; however, if the 'draft' ideas for new courses were prepared by the teachers with a 'critical eye' on, for example, their institutions' routinely collated data on matters such as geographical distribution, sex and disability, then the initial planning of the course would have an important reference point. If this planning was also done with an understanding of student research more generally, such as on matters of student (dis)abilities, characteristics and orientations to study (Gibbs *et al.*, 1984; Newell and Walker, 1991; Taylor *et al.*, 1981; Walker, 1994), the ways in which students use course materials (Lockwood, 1992; Marland *et al.*, 1990, 1992), gender concerns (Grace, 1994; Prümmer, 1994), students' career and life paths (Farnes, 1992; Morgan, 1992), then the course would be even more firmly grounded in student experiences and contexts.

An intriguing area of student research which is neglected concerns students' lives and careers beyond the completion of their courses. It is quite understandable that this is under-researched because it presents several difficulties, such as establishing and maintaining contact with people who are no longer enrolled, and a potentially wide geographical dispersal. However, such research should be able to produce very useful information for course planners and developers concerning what aspects of their studies students found to be valuable for their lives and what things they believe could be better. Potentially there are also the great publicity stories for institutions which can emerge, as Woodley (1988) noted in one of the few examples of this research.

Using past, present and potential students in forms of 'focus group' research could produce some valuable information and ideas for institutions seeking to develop their courses and services. This is an approach used in 'applied' forms of social research, such as opinion polling or marketing analyses, but seems to be a rarity in open and distance education. As with most forms of research with students at a distance, undertaking group research can be particularly difficult. It is possible to mediate such research using telephone or computer means, with the participants focusing on the identified themes or topics which the researchers have presented. These themes or topics can be relatively tightly prescribed or very open, depending on what the institution seeks to achieve. In the case of using different student groups, rather than a diversity within each group, there is the opportunity of comparing and contrasting any views or ideas related to their quite different positions to the course or service in question. A strength of these forms of research is their grounding in the development process because the express purpose and 'focus' of the research spring from the desire or need to develop a course or service.

Action and participatory forms of research are by their very nature interlinked with development. Typically, these forms of research in educational contexts are a good means of encouraging collaboration between a group or team of staff working towards reflecting on and developing their practice. There are examples of these being used in distance education with students and staff with a view to understanding students and enhancing their. courses or services (Altrichter *et al.*, 1991a; Guy, 1994). However, again the problems involved in obtaining genuine participation with students at a distance militate against such forms of research, although the prospects of configuring research which is mediated in some ways by telephone and computer could be explored further. A key feature of participatory research is the attempt to ensure 'symmetrical communications' between those involved. This is something which is difficult to achieve in circumstances, such as distance education, where the power relations are asymmetrical (Evans, 1989; Kemmis, 1984). Clearly, the power relationships between students and staff need to be understood and managed equitably in participatory or action research. Predominantly the actions taken, and the responsibilities for them, rest with the staff; however, the research process itself can ensure that, through the cycle of reflection, theorising, ideas for action and action

(Altrichter *et al.*, 1991a, p. 15), the students have a valued and substantial role.

CONCLUDING COMMENT

The purpose of this chapter has been to argue a case for the importance of recognising the special contribution that student research can make to the research and development process in open and distance education. Existing research provides a very substantial basis upon which to build; however, like most forms of research it is often relatively poorly linked to development. Some ideas have been suggested for adopting forms of research which are more vigorously linked to development. In these ways student needs and requirements can be better reflected in the practices of open and distance education. This brief chapter can only be suggestive of the potential of student research to inform development and it complements others' arguments in this regard about research and practice. It is now necessary to explore these ideas further by seeing them in action and evaluating the consequential developments.

REFERENCES

Altrichter, H., Evans, T. D. and Morgan, A. R. (1991a) 'Introduction: distance education, evaluation and action research' in Altrichter, H., Evans, T. D. and Morgan, A. R. (eds).

Altrichter, H., Evans, T. D. and Morgan, A. R. (eds) (1991b) *Windows: Research and Evaluation on a Distance Education Course*, Geelong, Deakin University.

Calvert, J. (1989) 'Distance education research: the rocky courtship between scholarship and practice', *International Council of Distance Education Bulletin*, 19, pp. 37–47.

Evans, T. D. (1989) 'Fiddling while the tome turns: reflections of a distance education development consultant' in Parer, M. (ed.) *Development, Design and Distance Education*, Churchill, Monash University, Centre for Distance Learning, pp. 117–26.

Evans, T. D. (ed.)(1990) *Research in Distance Education 1*, Geelong, Deakin University Press.

Evans, T. D. (1991) 'An evaluation of *Classroom Processes*' in Altrichter, H., Evans, T. D. and Morgan, A. R. (eds), pp. 139–73.

Evans, T. D. (1994) *Understanding Learners in Open and Distance Education*, London, Kogan Page.

Evans, T. D. and Grace, M. (1994) 'Distance education and the gendered privatisation of learning', *Journal of Curriculum Studies*.

Evans, T. D. and Juler, P. A. (eds)(1992) *Research in Distance Education 2*, Geelong, Deakin University Press.

Evans, T. D. and Nation, D. E. (1989) 'Critical reflections in distance education' in Evans, T. D. and Nation, D. E. (eds) *Critical Reflections on Distance Education*, London, Falmer Press, pp. 237–52.

Farnes, N. (1992) 'Life course analysis and research in distance education' in Evans, T. D. and Juler, P. A. (eds), pp. 89–104.

Gibbs, G., Morgan, A. R. and Taylor, E. (1984) 'The world of the learner' in Marton, F., Entwistle, N. and Hounsell, D. (eds) *The Experience of Learning*, Edinburgh, Scottish Academic Press, pp. 165–88.

Grace, M. (1994) 'Meanings and motivations: women's experiences of studying at a distance', *Open Learning*, 9(1), pp. 13–21.

Guy, R. (1994) *A Postpositivist Understanding of Distance Education in Papua New Guinea*, PhD thesis, Geelong, Deakin University.

Holt, D. M., Petzall, S. and Viljoen, J. (1990) 'Before ... and after: MBA participants' first-year experiences of distance learning' in Evans, T. D. (ed.), pp. 157–79.

Holt, D. M. (1993) 'Changing conceptions and practices of management: professional learning from an MBA experience by distance education', *Distance Education*, 14(2), pp. 232–59.

Kember, D. (1989) 'An illustration, with case studies, of a linear-process model of drop-out from distance education', *Distance Education*, 10(2), pp. 196–211.

Kemmis, S. (1984) 'The use of video for developing symmetrical communication' in Zuber-Skerritt, O. (ed.) *Video in Higher Education*, London, Kogan Page, pp. 136–41.

Lockwood, F. (1992) *Activities in Self-instructional Texts*, London, Kogan Page.

Marland, P., Patching, W. and Putt, I. (1990) 'Distance learners' interactions with text while studying', *Distance Education*, 11(1), pp. 71–91.

Marland, P., Patching, W. and Putt, I. (1992) 'Thinking while studying: a process tracing study of distance learners', *Distance Education*, 13(2), pp. 193–217.

Morgan, A. R. (1990) 'Whatever happened to the silent scientific revolution? Research, theory and practice in distance education' in Evans, T. D. (ed.), pp. 9–20.

Morgan, A. R. (1992) 'Theorising adult change and development through research in distance education' in Evans, T. D. and Juler, P. A. (eds), pp. 81–8.

Morgan, A. R. (1993) *Improving Your Students' Learning*, London, Kogan Page.

Nation, D. E. (1990) 'Reporting research in distance education' in Evans, T. D. (ed.), pp. 83–107.

Newell, C. J. and Walker, J. (1991) 'Disability and distance education in Australia' in Evans, T. D. and King, B. (eds) *Beyond the Text: Contemporary Writing on Distance Education*, Geelong, Deakin University Press, pp. 27–55.

Prümmer, C. von (1994) 'Women-friendly approaches to distance learning', *Open Learning*, 9(1), pp. 3–12.

Roberts, D., Boyton, B., Buete, S. and Dawson, D. (1991) 'Applying Kember's linear-process model to distance education at Charles Sturt University', *Distance Education*, 12(1), pp. 54–84.

Taylor, E., Morgan, A. R. and Gibbs, G. (1981) 'The orientation of Open University students to their studies', *Teaching at a Distance*, no. 20, pp. 3–12.

Walker, J. (1994) 'Open learning: the answer to the government's equity problems: a report on a study of the potential impact of the Open Learning Initiative on people with disabilities', *Distance Education*, 15(1), pp. 94–111.

Woodley, A. (1988) 'Graduation and beyond', *Open Learning*, 3(1), pp. 13–17.

8

STILL SEEKING THE AUDIENCE?

David Harris

INTRODUCTION

Central to social theory at the moment is the serious attack launched by 'post-modernism' on the 'foundational' claims in social sciences, and on the 'emancipatory narratives' which they deploy rhetorically to claim legitimacy. Some aspects of this debate have entered discussions on the organisation of education generally (such as Green, 1994), and of distance education specifically (see, for example, Campion, 1989; Gillard, 1993; Edwards, 1991).

The broader issues are well-known too, of course. Lyotard (1986) is particularly aware that the university as an institution is seriously threatened by a general 'scepticism towards metanarratives', and Bauman (1987) is one of several writers who have connected this scepticism with a general decline in the role and influence of intellectuals.

There are implications for research methodology too, though, including the methodologies used to investigate audience reactions in various mass media contexts. I think the work of Baudrillard (1983) is particularly appropriate to a discussion of these specific problems: Baudrillard takes further than most the implications of the old observation that (teaching) media structure the audiences that they address. Research strategies also do the same sort of structuring, however. Briefly, Baudrillard argues that the gap, or distance, between the message (educational argument or research question) and the response by the audience has vanished or 'imploded'. Audience responses to research are so determined by the style and mode of research, that it is impossible to say any longer whether any independent data exists for researchers to discover: the relay between question and answer has been 'short-circuited'. These problems have long been acknowledged, of course, in methodological debates about how to do research which avoids 'observer effects' or 'leading questions', but Baudrillard connects the problems to much wider social and cultural trends, and is thus much more pessimistic about a technical solution, or one which dismisses these effects as merely minor distortions.

This implosion is part of the general dominating effect of media representations on reality that Baudrillard refers to as 'simulation' and it also seems to arise from a form of audience resistance to a saturation of messages and enquiries, a coping strategy of deliberate passivity, produced, 'fatally', by the very explosion of such messages and enquiries in the first place.

Finally, Baudrillard suggests that this development is effaced by the continuing activities of researchers (in public opinion polling in his specific case) whose role is to proceed as if there still were an independent 'reality' out there to be researched (instead of a 'hyper-real' fusion of realities and mediated representations); in practice, the apparently collective and genuine responses of audiences are, in a very strong sense, methodological artefacts.

Baudrillard writes at a high level of abstraction, with excess, and with a clear disregard for any attempts to provide rigorous supporting evidence, of course. Commentators have also found him excessively pessimistic, even 'thanatoid', and this has probably been transmitted to this piece, as Morgan suggests (see Chapter 6 in this volume). It can be a useful pessimism, though, to take to extremes a number of existing insights for the purposes of argument, and the threads of his critique can be seen winding through a number of more specific debates about audience research, both in distance education and in another parallel field – the film and television audience. The rest of this chapter traces some of these debates.

AUDIENCE RESEARCH: A PARTIAL HISTORY

Gathering feedback

Official research on the student audience at the UK Open University (UK OU) began inside the Institute of Educational Technology (IET) as part of a general interest in gathering 'feedback' from students in order to undertake a particular kind of evaluation. The story has been told elsewhere (Thomas, 1977), but it is convenient to abstract out of the variety of techniques two main kinds: questionnaire-based techniques such as the original Course Unit Report Form (CURF) or the more recent Annual Survey of New Courses, and more subjective or qualitative devices such as 'developmental testing'.

Debates about each of these techniques offer familiar dilemmas: simple 'objective' data are convenient to manage but hard to interpret, while the more open-ended comments derived from developmental testing, say, are variable (sometimes more informative), and likely to be of unknown reliability. Certainly, neither technique seemed able to provide the sort of conclusive data required to test the effectiveness of the system as in the 'rational curriculum planning' model in use, officially, at the time. There was an irreducible element of subjective interpretation, even of political or tactical usages of evaluation data. When this becomes apparent to all the participants, it is no longer possible to claim neutrality, objectivity or naturalness for the findings as a justification for political activity.

Data gathered primarily to inform course design in a specific (then rather didactic) teaching system must operate with only a limited model of the audience, of course. The audience is there to provide feedback on issues decided by the course designers, and any excessive responses could be interpreted as either irritating 'noise' or as a bonus, a kind of gift of a good idea. This kind of approach operates within certain macro constraints, much as do similar operations in commercial media or opinion polling: as long as general levels of satisfaction are maintained (reasonable drop-out rates, viewing figures, support for policies), there is no need to pursue investigations of detailed responses.

It is possible to suggest that the early work on broadcasting specifically entered new levels of investigation because the macro constraints were unusually severe. To generalise again, levels of 'use' of television and radio programmes in particular proved disappointing, yet these items were among the most expensive ones to provide. Bates (see, for example, Bates, 1984) was led to pursue the issues in more detail, and in rather specific ways.

The debate spread beyond the official interest in 'uses and gratifications', to include a classic concern in Media Studies more generally – how the audience for TV was able to resist the 'educational' mode of address of OU TV programmes and impose their own 'readings'. Thompson's contribution (1979) argued that OU students came to 'case-study' programmes, for example, with certain competencies and expectations already, and tended to read those programmes as if they were the sort of documentaries they would have seen routinely as part of normal television viewing. Ironically, something about the structure of the programme, as opposed to its manifest content, encouraged these conventional readings.

A debate then ensued about how to discourage them, so to speak, or to signal to students that specifically 'educational' readings were required. Policy implications were obvious – television programmes had to be structured to close off these subjective readings, using parallels to those devices used to structure written texts (advance organisers, in-text questions and assignments based on programme contents). Another popular option was to attempt to prestructure audience perceptions using 'Broadcast Notes' to be read before viewing or listening.

The research and its policy links demonstrate a clear strategic intent, in other words, to establish audience responses in order to validate, or assess in a broad sense, pedagogic policy which was to be largely determined at the centre. Audience research was the feedback cycle of course design, at best plebiscitary, to borrow a term. As with all kinds of strategic communication, though, information was being ignored or lost in this process.

Apparently, very high CURF returns for 'difficulty' led to one OU unit being withdrawn (but only where the course team was already suspicious of it), and one study of developmental testing (Henderson *et al.*, 1977) claims it had a considerable impact on course design. But the usual kinds of responses in the usual ranges led to very unclear implications for policy: if 50 per cent of a sample found some material 'difficult', it is not immediately clear whether this is a desirable or undesirable form of difficulty or whether the material should be modified and, if so, how exactly.

The same kind of problems can arise for the data gathered from developmental testing or from student assessment scores as a measure of teaching effectiveness (for further discussion, see Harris, 1987). The best use of such data, possibly, is an (important) political one – OU spokespersons then (and those who use similar instruments to measure 'student satisfaction' now) can use results from those exercises to claim some generalised assent to course design policies and thus to demonstrate that various publics can have confidence in them. These issues are particularly relevant in the 1990s with the teaching quality assessments of the Higher Education Funding Councils. The tensions between a need for research into student diversity, and the political constraints, which often lean in a different direction, are explored far more fully in Evans' contribution in Chapter 7 of this volume.

Entering the world of the learner

A different kind of research began to gather momentum at the UK OU in the mid-1970s, with some laboratory research on learning styles undertaken by Pask and his associates (e.g. Pask, 1976). This work initially identified two major approaches to learning – 'serialism' and 'holism'. The work of Marton and Säljö (e.g. 1976a, b) also became known, and the 'deep/surface' dimension became incorporated into a major part of the work of the influential Study Methods Group (SMG) at the UK OU (see, for example, Morgan, 1993; Beaty and Morgan, 1992; see also Chapter 6 in this volume). An astonishing work of synthesis of these approaches and others can be found in Entwistle and Ramsden (1983), and in subsequent works, including major UK staff training intiatives and a recent and widely published package on 'active learning' in conventional higher education compiled by the British CVCP (e.g. Eastcott and Farmer, 1992).

I have discussed these initiatives elsewhere (Harris, 1994). This research did much to gain much fuller knowledge of the conditions in which students actually receive, study and manage learning materials. Various research instruments were used, especially in Entwistle and Ramsden (1983), including ethnographic techniques, while the OU SMG employed an effective qualitative approach involving longitudinal phenomenographic 'action research'. The policy implications are well known too: briefly, students must be encouraged to develop suitable learning styles (usually some variant of the 'deep' approach, sometimes combined with 'syllabus independence'), and these can be fostered by a variety of programmes providing 'study skills' There are course design implications too, such as the CVCP initiative on designing 'active learning' sequences.

Yet, despite the admirable results achieved, this sort of work still has limits to its desire to explore the subjective worlds of the learners. For example, the important student behaviour associated with 'instrumentalism' or a 'strategic orientation' has been underemphasised and glossed. There still seems to me to be some kind of commitment to 'deep learning' as 'proper learning', closely connected to the professional ideologies of pedagogues, which maintains a longstanding reluctance to acknowledge coping strategies (including 'selective neglect', sophisticated plagiarism and collective authorship by students, tutor sponsorship or 'over-supervision' of 'independent study', and other semi-deviant activities).

A strategic orientation appears clearly in Entwistle and Ramsden as a successful stance, and many studies recognise the bad effects of excessive assessment in encouraging a 'surface' approach, but the discussion tends to be limited. We tend to hear far more of the 'good side' of the orientation via the discussion of 'syllabus independence' in work like Beaty's and Morgan's.

Of course, this could be because students are simply not instrumental in a 'bad' sense. Given the semi-deviant nature of the activity, though, it is possible that students decline to exhibit it in the company of researchers (although I uncovered some in my own very limited research: see Harris, 1987).

It is also possible, though, that the more psychometric research designs privileged certain kinds of data. The focus on the rather abstract notion of 'learning style', for example, might impose a rather tight frame on explorations of the world of the learner and lead to research on that actual moment of cognitive encounter with specific texts. It is apparent that Morgan's work offers a different interest, however, seeing the 'concept of "orientation to study" as ... [enabling] one to relate theoretical ideas at the detailed level of the learner engaged in a particular task, to the broader structural issues concerned with interactions of study with people's lives' (Morgan, 1991, p. 83). The same interest in context or holism, of course, lies behind the use of student journals in evaluation (see, for example, Guy, 1991). However, the close connections with policy implications can provide other sorts of frames around explorations.

Morgan illustrates this 'holist' approach very effectively in a number of places, as Evans' piece reminds us. One particularly telling example concerns his discussion of the impact of 'the prevailing convention and social structures ... [on women who] are required to fulfil the "traditional" domestic demands of providing meals etc., instead of studying'. For such women, 'studying is done almost in secret' (*ibid.*, p. 86). It is pleasant, insightful and encouraging for all committed pedagogues to note instances where education has empowered such individuals, and it is a triumph for the 'deep' approach, but in this consciousness-raising mode it is easy to overlook those individuals who have hardly been affected by the stirring materials they read and who respond to these and other pressures by rather desperately attempting to find 'short cuts' to good grades.

There are other problems, too. Social class as well as gender might structure the context of learning in higher education, for example, as in the work of Bourdieu (see Harris, 1994). The collective and largely unconscious 'predispositions' arising from the different amounts and types of 'cultural capital' acquired by course designers and students might explain rather well the 'deep' and 'surface' behaviours described by phenomenographers, and their links with professional ideologies suggested above. In the context of a conventional university system saturated with these unconscious predispositions which structure the whole debate about (proper) learning styles, it becomes difficult to acknowledge alternative approaches as anything other than 'deviant', and thus as able to be ignored.

If the audience in higher education is structured by social class in ways which reveal few differences in orientation, gender, of course, is another matter. Here differences are plentifully distributed, and personal experiences of gender politics are likely to be at the forefront of consciousness, and thus to appear in students' subjective accounts. (Ethnic differences are another area which requires research, perhaps – as in Guy's (1991) work and his subsequent thesis, focused on cultural differences and distance education in Papua New Guinea.) But it is unlikely that 'proletarian' or 'popular' predispositions are equally widespread, at least in the UK higher education system, so it is hardly surprising to find little immediate evidence of their effects even in the phenomenographic studies.

In popular culture more generally, though, there is more research. De Certeau charts the 'proletarian' strategies used to cope with and resist the dominance of those with cultural capital – 'poaching, tricking, speaking, reading, strolling, shopping, desiring' (Frow, 1991). These have attracted much attention in cultural studies, and in 'activist' accounts of the popular television audience such as that of Fiske (1989). The popular audience in cultural studies, apparently, is capable of ironic and intertextual readings, and it responds well to films and television programmes that are relatively unstructured, unfinished, or 'producerly' in Fiske's (originally Barthes') terms. Less optimistic and 'committed' writers (e.g. McGuigan, 1992) have replied to Fiske's work by pointing to the fleeting and rather vulnerable nature of this sort of behaviour as 'resistance', and there is a possibility that much of it is itself an effect of playful commercial media productions, rather than something occurring 'beyond the text'.

However, we might expect increasingly to find such responses as our (UK) student body becomes less 'conventional' perhaps, although again these aspects will have to be actively sought in research, against the tradition that includes conventional academics and which sees popular culture as worthless and its participants as passive. It is possible that some sort of interaction with more 'producerly' educational texts might effect these responses, although whether educational media can ever be playful is debatable. To return to the general point, though, even the best phenomenographic research cannot uncover a variety of 'readings' as responses unless that diversity is permitted by a class system (or a cultural pluralism in terms of ethnicity).

Further, the role of the researchers themselves in constructing and limiting a context can not be ignored, even for the most 'holistic' and 'qualitative' approaches. Some indication of the interplay of research strategies and policy interests has been given above. More generally, ethnography has recently attracted attention, along with all the other approaches, from 'post-modern' sceptics (like Clifford, 1988, or Clough, 1992).

Two arguments seem especially relevant for the phenomenographic approaches. First, ethnography classically used participants' utterances as 'data' to construct an account of a lifeworld which still privileges the categories and interests of the researchers: this contributes to the tendency to routinise or 'exoticise' its subjects, despite emancipatory intentions. Secondly, the sense of insight, discovery, even 'surprise', generated by the best ethnographic accounts is produced to an extent by the writing itself, often using the same classic narrative devices of story-telling found in novels, sensationalist newspaper reporting, realist films or even soap operas. The sort of research carried out by ethnographers or phenomenographers would need to be far more explicit about its use of data and its argumentational strategies to avoid this sort of criticism in the future. Journals written by subjects themselves might overcome some problems, but the same sort of general point remains – journals too would derive their effect from writing strategies and could no longer be seen simply as transparent or naive accounts of 'real' experience.

Finally, there is another obvious 'methodological' point in this sort of criticism. Researchers seem aware that their own long-term participation in close research with students might have had an effect in actually teaching those students how to pursue effective study strategies – and in 'action research' of this kind, this is quite desirable, of course. In a slightly more uncomfortable discussion, however, Buckingham (1991) notes that even young children are aware that there is something special about a research context, something that requires special answers. The children interpreted Buckingham's invitation to discuss television programmes as a pretext to display certain 'attitudes' or 'opinions' which they deemed appropriate, and which seemed to be shaped not by the programmes themselves so much as the desire to engage in the discussion of them. Pedagogues have long 'taken positions' in seminars in order to 'provoke discussion': here, it seems, the students were doing something pretty similar. Sophistry may be more widespread than we think.

CONCLUDING THOUGHTS

Far from being a rather dull area with some well-worked options based on various permutations of questionnaires and ethnographic techniques, audience research seems to be an area where much remains to be done. Indeed, there could be some major new challenges to solve. The diversity offered by gender differences is probably still to be pursued, of course, and the debate about whether a specific feminist methodology is required to tap specifically female orientations is still a lively one (see, for example, Hammersley, 1994). If audiences become more diverse along the dimensions of social class and ethnic origins, then further explorations of the cognitive or aesthetic world of the learner seem essential, and approaches must be open to far more possibilities than those provided by even a holistic version of permutations of the variables in current research on learning styles.

Then there is Baudrillard's metaphor for the current audience – a mass of rather cynical individuals, a 'black hole' into which research initiatives pour questions with little in the way of meaningful reply. There is still an important assumption in much audience research that 'the audience' exists as some kind of genuine entity, that some real social bond unites the students on an OU course, or some collective interest (including 'political' interests for activists). There is still often a lingering humanism, celebrating individuals and their 'rebellious subjectivity' as units comprising an audience: this view is again deeply rooted in the pedagogic world-view, of course.

We might begin to suspect these assumptions, however, given all the recent work on the more general impact of social change on hitherto stable identities (seen best, perhaps, in doubts about 'the family' as a metaphor for the TV audience), and the longstanding scepticism about 'the individual subject' as an author of his or her works. Can the mere participation of people in a course of study act any longer to bind them together somehow, to overcome their other diverse or nomadic identities and the play on them of other texts or of other participations? What actually is an audience? In this light, the most intractable 'practical' problem may well be that audience research cannot construct its audience well enough to produce anything more than meaningless statistical aggregates.

REFERENCES

Bates, A. (1984) *Broadcasting in Education: An Evaluation*, London, Constable.
Baudrillard, J. (1983) *Simulations*, London, Semiotext(e).
Bauman, Z. (1987) *Legislators and Interpreters*, Cambridge, Polity Press.
Beaty, E. and Morgan, A. (1992) 'Developing skill in learning', *Open Learning*, 2(3), pp. 3–11.
Buckingham, D. (1991) 'What are words worth? Interpreting children's talk about television', *Cultural Studies*, 5(2), pp. 228–44.
Campion, M. (1989) 'Post-Fordism and research in distance education' in Evans, T. (ed.) *Research in Distance Education 1*, Geelong, Deakin University Press.

Clifford, J. (1988) *The Predicament of Culture: Twentieth Century Ethnography, Literature and Art*, London, Harvard University Press.
Clough, P. (1992) *The End(s) of Ethnography*, London, Sage.
Eastcott, D. and Farmer, R. (1992) *Planning Teaching for Active Learning*, Module 3 of the Effective Teaching and Learning Project, Sheffield, CVCP Universities Staff Development and Training Unit.
Edwards, R. (1991) 'The inevitable future? Post-Fordism and open learning', *Open Learning*, 6(2).
Entwistle, N. and Ramsden, P. (1983) *Understanding Student Learning*, London, Croom Helm.
Evans, T. and Juler, P. (eds)(1991) *Research in Distance Education 2*, Geelong, Deakin University Press
Fiske, J. (1989) *Reading the Popular*, London, Unwin Hyman.
Frow, M. (1991) 'M. de Certeau and the practice of representation', *Cultural Studies*, 5(1), pp. 52–60.
Gillard, G. (1993) 'Deconstructing contiguity' in Evans, T. and Nation, D. (eds) *Reforming Open and Distance Education*, London, Kogan Page.
Green, A. (1994) 'Postmodernism and state education', *Journal of Educational Policy*, 9(1), pp. 67–83.
Guy, R. (1991) 'Privileging others and otherness in research in distance education' in Evans, T. and Juler, P. (eds).
Hammersley, M. (1994) 'On feminist methodology: a response', *Sociology*, 28(1), pp. 293–300.
Harris, D. (1987) *Openness and Closure in Distance Education*, London, The Falmer Press.
Harris, D. (1994) '"Effective teaching" and "study skills": the return of the technical fix?' in Evans, T. and Murphy, D. (eds) *Research in Distance Education 3*, Geelong, Deakin University Press.
Henderson, E., Hodgson, B. and Nathenson, M. (1977) 'Developmental testing: the proof of the pudding', *Teaching at a Distance*, 10, pp. 77–82.
Lyotard, J.-F. (1986) *The Post-Modern Condition: a Report on Knowledge*, Manchester, Manchester University Press.
Marton, F. and Säljö, R. (1976a) 'On qualitative differences in learning, I: outcome and process', *British Journal of Educational Psychology*, 46, pp. 4–11.
Marton, F. and Säljö, R. (1976b) 'On qualitative differences in learning II: outcome as a function of the learner's conception of the task', *British Journal of Educational Psychology*, 46, pp. 115–27.
McGuigan, J. (1992) *Cultural Populism*, London, Routledge.
Morgan, A. (1991) 'Theorising adult change and development through research in distance education' in Evans, T. and Juler, P. (eds).
Morgan, A. (1993) *Improving Your Students' Learning: Reflections on the Experience of Study*, London, Kogan Page.
Pask, G. (1976) 'Styles and strategies of learning', *British Journal of Educational Psychology*, 46, pp. 128–48.
Thomas, A. (1977) 'Problems of evaluation, with special reference to the evaluation of Open University counselling', unpublished doctoral thesis, Milton Keynes, The Open University.
Thompson, G. (1979) 'Television as text: Open University "case study" programmes' in Barrett, M., Corrigan, P., Kuhn, A. and Wolff, J. (eds) *Ideology and Cultural Production*, London, Croom Helm.

Part III

INFORMATION TECHNOLOGY

9

INFORMATION TECHNOLOGY AND DISABLED STUDENTS

Overcoming barriers to learning

Tom Vincent

Developments in information technology are often referred to as 'solutions looking for a problem'. This is not surprising when a technology-led approach is adopted and the needs of the individual who might use the technology are an afterthought. A major concern is that such an approach, which is common, can undermine the potential of using information technology.

In relation to the application of information technology to the needs of disabled learners, there is considerable evidence of success (Hawkridge and Vincent, 1992). A key reason for this has been the importance attached to assessing individual needs. This process identifies barriers to learning, and how information technology could contribute to overcoming these barriers.

This chapter provides some examples of the exploitation of the potential of information technology for disabled learners. It draws on the outcomes of projects which seek to overcome barriers to learning in distance education. This includes the transformation of print-based teaching materials into alternative media, and access to computers.

BARRIERS TO LEARNING

Distance education has provided an alternative way of learning for many people; this includes those who have a disability. Evidence for this comes from the UK Open University where there are over 5,000 disabled undergraduates (approximately 5 per cent of all students), and this number continues to increase at 10 per cent per year, a rate which exceeds the general increase in student numbers.

Why should distance education be an attractive option for disabled people?

There are some obvious advantages, such as being home-based and thereby eliminating travel to a conventional institution which can be difficult for some students with a physical or sensory disability. However, such factors are likely to be less influential than the provision of support services that meet individual needs. For example, a severely physically disabled student may find it advantageous to study at home but if the principal teaching medium is print and the student is unable to turn the pages of a book independently then a barrier to learning exists. The provision of services such as audio transcription may depend on the number of students who require the service. Providing fifty students per year with an audio recording of the same course does have an advantage in scale compared to a situation where there is only one student on a course. This factor has been critical at the UK Open University in terms of the scale and scope of the provision for disabled students.

Barriers to learning relate to both the method of teaching and a student's disability. For example, if videotapes are used for teaching then there are potential barriers for those students with a visual or hearing impairment. By contrast, it may be a good medium for students with a physical disability. It would be unwise, however, to generalise in this way as all students have individual needs which need to be identified. Experience shows that categorising students by medical condition is far less satisfactory than categorising them by learning needs. At The Open University, there are over 700 students who are unable to use, or have difficulties with, print-based teaching materials and prefer to receive these materials on audiocassette. The reasons for this requirement are many and diverse and, in terms of providing this service, have less significance than the identification of the need. This popular service does, however, have limitations. A course may require in excess of 100 C90 cassettes (150 hours of audio) for the course units alone. The linear access to the audio results in a relatively passive learning environment. There are also difficulties with managing this amount of audio and finding particular pieces of information.

Numerous barriers to learning exist including:

• Written communication – essays, correspondence, examinations
• Reading – finding information, text, diagrams, pictures
• Non-print-based media – audio, video
• Computing courses and computer-assisted learning
• Laboratory work – experimental kits.

There already exist ways of overcoming many of these barriers to learning. For example, videotapes can be subtitled for hearing-impaired students, and computers can have a synthetic speech output to enable blind students to write with the aid of a wordprocessor.

The use of information technology to overcome barriers to learning has continued for more than a decade. Of particular significance has been the use of desktop computers which became available in the 1970s and, through the adaptation of software and the provision of alternatives to the keyboard and visual display (enabling technologies), have made a significant contribution to meeting individual learning needs. Research in this area continues and there are many examples of the important part played by information technology in overcoming barriers to learning (Hawkridge and Vincent, 1992).

The following examples of using information technology to meet the needs of disabled students are drawn from experience at the UK Open University.

ALTERNATIVES TO PRINT

In an educational context, access to books is essential for learners if a broad-based curriculum is to be pursued. For some students, books may not be an appropriate medium because of physical or sensory disabilities or specific learning difficulties such as dyslexia. These students, referred to as print-disabled students, may prefer to use print that has been transformed into other media such as braille or audio. The Alternatives to Print project has exploited developments in electronic publishing and compact disc technologies to give further choice of media for students in distance education. The project set out to:

- identify how existing services for print-disabled students could be enhanced and extended through the transformation of existing print-based course materials into alternative media
- develop a computer-based workstation that gives access to course materials on CD-ROM that could be integrated with commercially available enabling technologies
- identify how large print could be produced within an existing electronic publishing system.

Electronic text

Desktop or portable computers, with CD-ROM drives and appropriate enabling technologies, have been used by students to access modified versions of electronically published print materials. This modification involves the replacement of mark-up commands used for publishing through print. Alternative mark-up commands provide an appropriate layout of text for the CD-ROM delivery medium as well as taking into account that the text will be used with screenreaders (synthetic speech) or other enabling technologies. A retrieval program, ReadOut (Taylor, 1994) has been developed that is compatible with enabling technologies, and allows for a more structured presentation of the course material and a higher level of interactivity. The transformation of print course material into alternative electronic versions has involved close collaboration between The Open University's publishing department and academic staff. It is essential that the pedagogic features introduced into print are not lost during the transformation process. This may not be possible with every feature but techniques such as supplementary notes attempt to provide equivalence.

Digital audio

More recent research at The Open University has identified ways of providing effective access to digital audio versions of course material. As with digital text, the delivery medium is CD-ROM. The digital audio is indexed so that an interface can be added to provide non-sequential access so that an active medium can be created (cf. the passive medium of audiotape). The ReadOut program provides links between the text and audio, and allows for a change of medium as appropriate to study needs. Pictures and diagrams have text and audio descriptions. Other facilities include word and phrase searching, bookmarks and extracting selected text.

An integrated workstation

An important outcome of research at The Open University into the use of computers by blind people has been the design of an integrated workstation that is optimised for each individual user. Integration is achieved by assessing individual needs in terms of software applications, and providing additional software that enables links to be made between applications where appropriate. One example is the 'menu' approach. The interface for the user is a menu of options which are selected by single digits (reducing number of key actions). The menu is accessible with the enabling technology (such as screenreading with speech output) and, on selection, the particular application becomes available with individual preferences set and the enabling technology optimised for that application (for example, the rate of speech may vary depending on the activity).

This approach has been used as a basis for a workstation for print-disabled students (Figure 9.1) (Vincent, 1994). The design allows for choice of medium for particular study needs. It is an example of a delivery environment discussed by Valcke and Vuist (Chapter 18 in this volume). For example, a blind student might search – with the aid of a screenreader – for key words or phrases, then use the digital audio to listen to associated passages of text. The auto-tracking retains pointers to equivalent positions in each medium to allow rapid changes between the media. Another important feature is that the digital audio can be listened to at variable rates – many blind learners use high rates of audio for study purposes to facilitate reading.

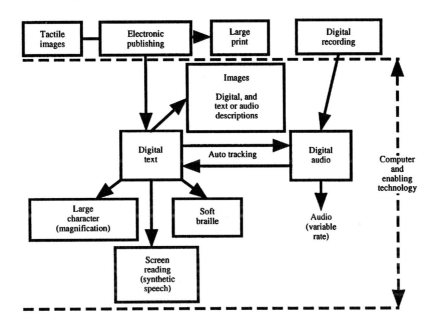

Figure 9.1 An integrated computer-based learning environment

Courses involved in the project

Over seventy students have been involved in the Alternatives to Print project. In each case the most appropriate medium has been provided which includes a choice from large print, and digital text and/or digital audio on CD-ROM.

The Social Sciences Foundation Course is a popular course for disabled students including many who cannot use conventional print. This is the first course to be completely transformed to large print with a supplementary portfolio of pictures and diagrams included in the course units. The course has also been made available on CD-ROM (text and audio). Parts of five other courses have been transformed in a similar way to extend the evaluation of the learning environment that has been created.

Large print

The approach taken to produce large print was to seek a way of integrating this requirement into existing publishing facilities rather than create an independent facility. This 'piggy-back' approach was seen as providing the maximum opportunity for large print production to become embedded within existing publishing services. The method adopted was based on an 'on-demand' (Docutech) workstation that had been introduced for low volume printing (it is understood that other universities have installed, or are considering, similar 'on-demand' print services). One of the benefits of this approach is that the cost per publication is only marginally influenced by the number of copies produced (conventional printing costs per publication are dependent on quantity). This is a key consideration for large print production in an educational institution where the number of copies is likely to be small.

Outcomes

An assignment question from the Social Sciences Foundation Course illustrates the problems faced by students unable to use conventional print:

> 'Behind even the simplest of objects lie complex social stories.' Illustrate this statement using the example of sugar in Unit 1.

The advice to students includes:

> ... the story of sugar features in several sections of the unit, including passages in Sections 1, 2.2, 2.3 and 3.1, 3.2 and 3.3 ...

The first problem the students faces after receiving this advice is finding the information that is referred to and which appears in various sections of the unit. It is typical of what is expected on many similar occasions. Feedback from students who completed this assignment showed that by having access to the text in digital media, it provided an independent means of finding, reading and extracting notes associated with this task.

There is no doubt from all student feedback that having access to conventional print-based course materials through alternative media is beneficial. For students who are blind, access to course materials using a combination of electronic text and enabling technologies gives an increased degree of independence. A key factor in this is the facility to rapidly search and retrieve from large amounts of text which cannot be achieved independently by other means – essential in a learning situation.

THE IMPLICATIONS OF A 'HOME COMPUTING POLICY' FOR STUDENTS WITH DISABILITIES

In 1987 the UK Open University adopted a policy whereby the use of a microcomputer would be a major and compulsory component of selected courses. Prior to 1988 some courses had contained a practical computing element. Generally, this was not a major part of the course and students usually did not have to use a computer at home. For most of these courses students accessed university mainframe computers through terminals in local study centres or at residential schools. Where students had access to the appropriate equipment (a suitable terminal and a modem), they were allowed to use them to dial into the university's computers instead of using study centres.

The Home Computing Policy (now known as the Personal Computing Policy) was adopted 'because it is no longer practical to support the requirements of computer science and some other courses through study centre based facilities'. In its early days the policy was to apply only to courses to which computers have a direct relevance. However, one implication of the adoption of the policy was that the use of computers would spread to more courses, which previously would not have had a computing component. This has proved to be the case.

Adoption of the policy had a number of other implications and raised several fundamental questions, many of which had particular relevance to disabled students. The Open University is committed to openness in being accessible to potential students as far as possible, regardless of factors such as their level of physical and sensory ability, their educational background and their financial means. The adoption of the Home Computing Policy was likely to affect that openness. If the student was to be expected to fund the acquisition of the computer, some might find it an intolerable additional financial burden. Some students have disabilities which make use of a computer difficult, and they might thus be excluded from courses included within the Home Computing Policy. One question was: who was going to pay for the computers? Another was: which computer (or family of computers) should be adopted? As well as the hardware, choices had to be made about the software which would be used. These are all difficult questions, which could only be resolved by consultation between several interested parties.

Some students with visual or physical disabilities might be disadvantaged because they have difficulty in using a microcomputer. A survey was conducted in an attempt to assess whether disabled students would be deterred from taking courses with a home computing element and to identify potential problems (Edwards, 1988).

On the whole, the results of the survey were positive. It was concluded that, assuming that suitable finance is available, the Home Computing Policy would

93

not disadvantage the majority of students who are disabled. For many it may indeed represent an improvement in their educational and work opportunities. It was recognised that there would be a number of students who would be seriously handicapped because they have disabilities which make access to computers difficult. In some cases they may be totally excluded from home computing courses. The university has accepted its responsibility to support and aid these students as much as possible. This implies providing equipment and adaptations as required, and supporting research and development of new adaptations where they are not currently available.

The Open University/NFAC scheme

The scheme was established in October 1987 with the National Federation of Access Centres (NFAC) and its associated members (mainly further education colleges) and had the following general aims:

1   To provide a national assessment resource, and information base from which a service could be developed for Open University students with disabilities, especially those with complex, sensory and motor difficulties.
2   To recognise the need for a formal rather than informal level of service which would provide students with individual assessments, advice, hardware support and training.
3   To act as consultants to regional and advisory staff.

When the scheme was established, a key consideration was the level and extent of service which would be offered to students. It was felt that the service should provide:

(a) Assessment facilities for all students referred by The Open University.
(b) The organisation and adaptation of equipment and software to meet individual user needs.
(c) Training in the use of microelectronic-based study aids.
(d) Allocation, installation, reclaim and redistribution of equipment.
(e) On-going support including evaluation of equipment and repair advice.
(f) Routine/regular professional exchange between staff working with students with disabilities, staff concerned with the implementation of the Home Computing Programme, and staff of the National Federation of Access Centres.
(g) Research and development activities in conjunction with a network of centres and organisations already involved in work in this area and in collaboration with research activities in progress at The Open University.

Outcomes

Since 1987 nearly 400 students have received assessment training and support in relation to the provision of equipment that has allowed them to participate in courses where the access to a computer is essential. Although priority has been given to students taking courses in the Home Computing Policy, the Scheme is open to potential Home Computing students and also to students for whom access to microelectronic-based study aids is essential to their independent communication.

The assessment scheme provides an opportunity for students to discuss study issues and difficulties and to investigate possible solutions. In the majority of cases, a further day is spent installing equipment at the student's home and further initial instruction is also given on the operation of the equipment and software.

The emphasis is on assessing the study situation, rather than the students, and considering the range of options which might be appropriate. Students on the Scheme usually attend the nearest college-based ACCESS Centre for the day, unless this presents mobility problems. Because of the difficulty of predicting in advance the full range of hardware and software that might be required, home-based assessments remain the exception.

The short training period available to all students in the Scheme inevitably means that only a limited amount can be achieved during the training sessions. Students' confidence, motivation and the time they have available therefore became key factors in determining the extent to which the potential of the equipment is maximised. Encouragement is given to identifying a local 'facilitator' who can assist with minor technical problems and queries. Also, considerable benefits have been seen by students setting up small user groups where similar enabling technologies are used. Feedback from students suggests that some have progressed swiftly to the point where the computer directly serves their needs. For others, however, problems have been encountered and additional training provision has been essential.

DEVELOPMENTS IN COMPUTER TECHNOLOGY

One of the most significant recent developments in desktop computing has been the introduction of the Graphical User Interface (GUI) for IBM-compatible computers. For some disabled students this has created difficulties, for others it has provided new opportunities. Of particular significance is the use of computers by blind students. The enabling technologies (such as screenreaders) that have been developed in the past decade are incompatible with the Microsoft Windows GUI. Unfortunately this development cannot be ignored because many computer applications are now being produced for this GUI. Research continues (Gill, 1993) in providing blind people with access to these applications but progress is slow because of the nature of the problem. The difficulties with access to GUIs are compounded by many computer applications incorporating images and video (multimedia). One effect is the reduction in the use of text. Even if the text could be made accessible to a blind person, it would have limited meaning without a full description of the associated image.

By contrast, multimedia techniques have created new opportunities for other disabled students. One example is the simulation of a laboratory exercise which involves the identification of minerals from thin sections of rock samples under a polarising microscope. The Virtual Microscope (Vincent and Whalley, 1994) has provided access for physically disabled students to this laboratory exercise which was previously denied. This application of multimedia is also an example of a new method of teaching being introduced for disabled students which has also benefited all students – the Virtual Microscope is now used at Residential Schools for *all* students.

Meeting individual needs

With the current widespread use of new technology in society, the range and diversity of technological devices that may be used or adapted to meet the needs of disabled people continues to increase. The crucial question for individual disabled people is whether, and how, this technology should be applied to their specific needs. The need for the assessment of individuals in relation to the most appropriate new technology has been increasingly recognised over the past few years. It has also been recognised that the assessment process requires professional expertise, and that it will often require this expertise to be drawn from more than one discipline. On-going assessment is equally crucial because of factors that include: technological changes, and personal factors such as intellectual development, physical changes and different environments. Assessment is a continuous process.

The training requirements for individuals has to be directly associated with the assessment process. Clearly, there is a need for a general training in the use of any new technological device; however, it is the training in relation to individual needs that determines the overall effectiveness and efficiency in meeting individual needs.

The assessment, provision, training and support for the use of new information technology represent a significant investment of time and resources. Not least, this is true for an individual disabled person who may have to invest a considerable amount of time and effort before seeing any return on that investment. In this context, the objectives for using new technology need to be clearly established for each individual.

In a distance education environment, such as the home, the lack of immediate advice and support places even greater demands on providing appropriate, accessible and effective technology. For this reason, hardware and software projects at the UK Open University have actively engaged students with disabilities within the research team. In turn, this has led to the identification of important factors that need to be taken into account when matching new information technology to individual needs.

REFERENCES

Edwards, A. D. N. (1988) 'Use of computers in the education of Open University students with disabilities', Proceedings of the Fifth International Conference on Technology and Education, Vol. I, Edinburgh.

Gill, J. (1993) *Access to Graphical User Interfaces by Blind People*, London, RNIB.

Hawkridge, D. and Vincent, T. (1992) *Learning Difficulties and Computers: Access to the Curriculum*, London, Jessica Kingsley.

Taylor, M. E. (1994) *ReadOut*, The Open University, Internal Report.

Vincent, T. (1994) 'Transformation of course material into digital media for print disabled students', *The CTISS File*, No. 17 (July).

Vincent, T. and Whalley, P. (1994) *The Virtual Microscope*, Internal Report, The Open University.

10

SEE WHAT I MEAN?

Where compressed digital videoconferencing works

Colin Latchem

INTRODUCTION

The two-way video and audio-compressed digital videoconferencing Tanami Network is owned and operated by Aboriginal communities in Australia's 'red heart' (Mitchell *et al.*, 1994b). This six-site network links four remote communities by satellite with sites in Alice Springs and Darwin and via Integrated Services Digital Network (ISDN) with facilities throughout Australia and overseas. The communities' primary requirement of the Network was for access and privacy in conducting community, ceremonial and family business; it has become an important means of maintaining traditional law, knowledge and social frameworks. The Tanami Network has also proved to be a cost-effective and culturally appropriate means of providing education and telemedicine, links with distant students, patients and prisoners, evidence at hearings and enterprises within the communities. It has also been used to auction the community artists' distinctive 'dot paintings' at Sotheby's in London, assess the suitability of an overseas academic wishing to undertake research into these paintings, discuss Aboriginal culture with an audience in London's Festival Hall and establish links with interstate Aboriginal communities. By allowing them to speak as a group from the places where they live, the technology has enhanced the confidence of these communities (Granites and Toyne, 1994).

The Network has also been used for cultural exchanges with other indigenous communities with videoconferencing systems – Alaska Natives above the Arctic Circle and Native Canadians in northern Alberta. These exchanges have covered ceremonial matters, education and land rights and have included traditional painting, drumming and dance.

The Alaskan videoconferencing network is used primarily to achieve educational equity and optimum learning opportunities for all K-12 students within the North Slope Borough School District, the largest school district in the US. Studies indicate that distant students learning through this medium score higher than students in the same classroom as the instructor (Renaud and Pennino, 1992). The network is also used by teachers and students discussing problems outside the formal instructional setting and for enhancing communication between younger and older elements of the communities.

The Little Red River Cree Nation in Alberta use their three-site system for educational, medical and social services applications. Their network embodies the 'Cree way' of exploring and shaping ideas by allowing the expertise of Cree people (particularly the elders), resident instructors and university-accredited instructors to be shared and developed in a two-way process (Williams, 1994).

While distance educators wrestle with decisions about new technologies, it is interesting how readily these traditional communities have used videoconferencing to gain local ownership and control of educational and social services, overcome geographical and social disadvantage, leverage limited resources and develop mutually beneficial partnerships. They have used this technology in contexts where interactive and synchronous communication apply. They have shown that the medium is sufficiently transparent for users to organise events for themselves and that telecommunications technologies may allow new, sometimes surprising agencies to take the initiative and bypass traditional providers of distance and equity programmes.

With some notable exceptions, educators and trainers have been relatively slow to adopt videoconferencing. Even the corporate sector has been slow to respond. *Broadcast Engineering News* (1993) cited a survey of 200 US businesses employing over 3,000 staff which concluded that 'videoconferencing is failing to ignite the passions of the corporate or government user to the extent predicted when the technology was introduced in the eighties'. Over two-thirds of the organisations had no plans to use videoconferencing and half of those using the technology reported a lack of employee interest. Lange (1993) suggests that such user reluctance may be due to ignorance of the technology and its benefits, fear of trying out new ideas, or lack of incentive to do things differently. It may also be the case that users' needs can be met through other technologies. For example, the above survey reported a general corporate opinion that fax, e-mail and LANs were adequate to their business communication needs and that the benefits of 'head shots' were insufficient to justify the additional costs of videoconferencing.

Compressed digital videoconferencing is a relatively new technology. Digital codecs are barely ten years old and compression techniques only became capable of delivering motion video at 384 and 128 kbit/s in the late 1980s. There are ISDN networks in Western Europe, the Middle East, North and South America, Australia, New Zealand and some Asia/Pacific countries, all connected to world ISDN, but these networks are neither all-pervasive nor standardised. Capital and transmission costs are reducing, performance is improving, and inter-operating conventions are eliminating incompatibility. The relatively slow picture-refresh rates imposed by the restricted bandwidth of Basic Rate ISDN and current compression techniques will give way to something more akin to broadcast-quality video when videoconferencing can operate over such systems as Broadband ISDN. Videoconferencing is also moving to the desktop level. It remains to be seen whether this technology will fulfil its potential but this chapter summarises recent applications of this technology and the key issues that these raise.

INTER-CAMPUS AND REGIONAL APPLICATIONS

Videoconferencing is capable of supporting multi-campus institutions and regionalised teaching where it is difficult to provide specialist teachers or assure reasonable class sizes. Australia has rapidly embraced videoconferencing within its tertiary education system, largely as a consequence of federal government initiatives. About two-thirds of Australia's 37 public universities (many multi-site institutions) and many Technical and Further Education (TAFE) colleges now have videoconferencing facilities, most of which are the Basic Rate ISDN 128 kbit/s two-way video, two-way audio systems (Latchem et al., 1994).

A nationwide survey of videoconferencing in Australian higher education confirmed that it is generally regarded as an important addition to the institutions' delivery systems. Most users perceive the educational and managerial benefits, cost savings and productivity gains as outweighing any inherent limitations in the technology such as picture resolution or motion effects (Mitchell et al., 1994a).

Australian universities use videoconferencing for meetings, interviewing overseas candidates and interstate or international 'guest lectures', but find it less easy to encourage staff to teach via this technology. Appropriate staff development programmes are essential but, even so, from induction to successful use to frequent use is often a slow process (Youngblood et al., 1991).

Findings of no significant difference in learning outcomes are common in comparisons of videoconferenced and classroom teaching. The effectiveness of videoconferenced teaching appears to depend more upon instructional design and presentational and contextual variables than any inherent characteristics of the medium. Most successful applications combine videoconferencing with distance education packages and/or local tutorials. Students at remote or rural sites who have previously had no access to particular courses or to real-time interaction are generally more favourably disposed towards videoconferencing than their metropolitan counterparts (Arger *et al.*, 1989; Hansford and Baker, 1990; Schiller and Mitchell, 1992; Waldrip *et al.*, 1993).

South Australian TAFE's eleven-site network makes heavy use of point-to-point and multi-point videoconferencing combined with distance education materials and face-to-face tutorials to deliver programmes from metropolitan campuses to aggregated classes at regional sites. New programmes in tourism, customer service and sales techniques, rural property planning, French for wine-makers and wine appreciation have been made possible by this medium (Mitchell, 1991). The capacity of the technology to sustain the distant learners' motivation is demonstrated by the fact that within two years of introducing videoconferencing into certain programmes between the Light College of TAFE in Adelaide and the regional sites, completion rates had increased fivefold (Donaghy, 1993).

Dallat *et al.* (1992), reporting on videoconferencing at the multi-campus University of Ulster, conclude that the capacity to offer psycho-social support to distant learners is one of the most important attributes of the medium. Harris and Hague (1991), describing trials of videoconferenced English language tutorials for adult migrants in Western Australia, also acknowledge the medium's potential to build learner–teacher relationships, motivate and support learners and maintain learner progress. The tutors also valued the feedback provided by distant learners' non-verbal behaviour and the ability to review their delivery and interactions through video-recordings.

A number of institutions report on using videoconferencing to provide cost-effective advanced level programmes by combining lecturers' expertise at various sites and aggregating classes. In 1992, the fibre optic UNINET videoconferencing network linking Sydney University, University of Technology Sydney, Macquarie University and University of New South Wales was used for a jointly offered postgraduate course on medical imaging. The participating students felt that lecturer–student interaction had been inhibited by the use of the technology but that the course had been enriched by the cross-campus, cross-faculty collaboration (Braun *et al.*, 1993). Sydney University's Faculty of Veterinary Science and counterparts at Murdoch University in Western Australia, the Universities of Melbourne and Queensland and Massey University in New Zealand have formed a videoconferencing alliance to share teaching and research. The University of London's fibre optic LIVE-NET has been used extensively for inter-collegiate undergraduate and postgraduate programme delivery. LIVE-NET covers a small geographic area but its cost-effectiveness comes through time-tabling efficiency, enhanced course options and savings in staff and student travel time. Beckwith (1994) reports that cross-site videoconferenced delivery has been useful in the humanities where the ability to take a wide variety of options is attractive to students and in science and medicine where more students can observe close-ups of live experiments and operations than normally obtains. He also observes that lecturers using videoconferencing make greater and better use of visual material and pay more attention to student feedback than typically applies in conventional teaching.

INTER-SECTORAL COOPERATION AND CONSORTIA

As knowledge and skill life-cycles grow ever shorter, working and learning become indivisible processes and just-in-time learning becomes essential in the workplace. In such an environment, educational and training providers have the opportunity to combine their strengths and resources in strategic alliances and consortia and use technology for delivery into the workplace and classroom. Duning (1990) observes that one of the most striking effects of videoconferencing in the US has been a greater receptivity to consortia and partnerships among otherwise non-cooperating, disparate parties. Borbely (1994) suggests that the technology and the costs have now reached the point where individual faculties and middle-level managers feel empowered to join in developing distance education programmes.

A number of inter-sectoral partnerships are developing within Australia. The Catholic Education Office in Inner West Sydney has installed videoconferencing in three of its schools, partly to reduce the need for specialist staff to brave the heavy traffic between sites and partly to link these schools to universities and TAFE colleges for the purposes of teaching and staff development. The universities of New South Wales, New England and Western Australia, partners with the Commonwealth Scientific and Industrial Research Organisation in the national Co-operative Research Centre for Premium Quality Wool, use video-conferencing to share their staff resources for undergraduate programmes in wool science. The University of Queensland's Mining and Metallurgical Engineering Department is engaged in a joint initiative with the national Co-operative Research Centre for Mining Technology and Equipment to use videoconferencing for the delivery of a Master's and other advanced level programmes to students at mine sites around Australia. The Queensland Government Videoconferencing Network (QGVN) delivers educational and state government services across a twenty-two-site network including fourteen TAFE sites. QGVN saves depart-ments and agencies many thousands of dollars, but its main benefits are claimed to be convenience and flexibility of delivery, responsiveness to special needs at short notice, and a capacity to do things that are otherwise impossible (*Connecting Queensland*, 1993).

In Norway, education, industry and Norwegian Telecom have collaborated in using videoconferencing to provide lectures to remote nursing students, teaching and in-service training for remote schools, adult education programmes and opportunities for deaf children and adults to communicate through sign language (Klingsheim and Kristiansen, 1993). Norwegian Telecom has also experimented with videoconferencing for telemedicine and continuing education for remote area practitioners. The participating specialists and practitioners regarded these trials as achieving better educational outcomes than the more traditional hospital-based training and saw the technology as having the potential to increase the recruitment, stability and competence of medical personnel and ensure sound and safe medical services in remote areas (Akselen and Lillehaug, 1993).

In the US, Stanford University School of Engineering, which has a long tradition of using one-way video, two-way audio to deliver advanced level engineering and science courses to corporate sites, introduced two-way videoconferencing into its delivery in 1991. Lecturers and students are positive towards this medium and the students appreciate the real-time feedback, feel less isolated from the campus class and believe that the quality of interaction is better than with one-way video, two-way audio. Other findings are that the technology needs to be used in ways that minimise interference with lecturers' autonomy and teaching styles, that the videoconferencing room needs to be as similar as possible to the normal classroom, that the best classes are small and less lecture-based, and that students at remote sites should have the same electronic access to campus resources and support as the on-campus students (DiPaolo, 1993).

Stanford is a founding member of the Collaboration for Interactive Visual Distance Learning group which aims to use two-way videoconferencing to strengthen educational/industrial links and comprises the engineering schools of Boston University, Columbia University, Massachusetts Institute of Technology, Pennsylvania State University, Rensselaer Polytechnic Institute, Stanford University and five major corporations – AT&T, IBM, PictureTel, 3M and United Technologies Corporation. Boston University also collaborates with United Technologies Corporation in providing a postgraduate engineering programme and Columbia University delivers postgraduate programmes in engineering and materials and computer science and to such clients as Intel Corporation (Lange, 1994).

Such consortia deliver significant programmes through 'talking-heads' presentations. Some critics may refer disparagingly to such methods but Bates (1991) suggests that this approach can be effective where students are highly motivated, have highly developed learning skills and have already mastered the key concepts. He further suggests that the most successful applications of this model in the US have been in postgraduate and professional education.

INTERNATIONAL APPLICATIONS

ISDN facilitates worldwide videoconferencing at relatively low cost – typically that of two peak-rate telephone calls. There are some disparities within international connections: for example, there is not yet complete harmony within the EC while North America and some Asian countries use a transmission speed of 56 kbit/s rather than 64 kbit/s, but these have not prevented some exciting international applications.

The University of New England in Australia has used the technology for trialling English language teaching between Armidale and Tokyo (Arger and Wakamatsu, 1992). International delegates at the 1993 Conference of Economists at Curtin University in Western Australia were able to engage in a two-hour discussion with Nobel Laureate Professor of Economics Lawrence Klein, located at the University of Pennsylvania, Pittsburgh (Latchem and Puls, 1994). The 1993 international colloquium, Videoconferencing and Audiographic Groupware in Distance Education and Training, was presented by The Open University at Milton Keynes and University College London sharing videoconference delivery via ISDN and by PictureTel and Columbia University demonstrating applications of the technology from the US. The entire event was videoconferenced to delegates in Aberdeen and one hour was shared with European viewers via the Eurostep satellite educational channel (Mason, 1994).

The University of Sundsvall-Härnösand in Sweden has used intensive videoconferenced language exchanges as a strategy for implementing a two-term, part-time French course in collaboration with the University of Orléans, France. The videoconferenced sessions were found to allow for adult language learning and the teachers and students did not feel that videoconferencing dehumanised the teaching. They found that talking to someone on a screen changes the relationship, but not necessarily in a negative way. The frame of the screen focuses interest on the person and this was found to influence the participants who tried to be brief, clever and to the point (Enkvist, 1993).

International collaboration may be of value to students in institutions where resources are limited, departments are small and the main expertise of the staff is not within the areas of specialisation needed by the students. For example, in 1992, the University of Technology in Trondheim (Norway) and Chalmers University of Technology in Gothenburg (Sweden) used ISDN videoconferencing to share resources and courses and enable doctoral students to receive advice from experts at both universities (Kristiansen, 1994).

CONCLUSION

Videoconferencing has been shown to work in a wide range of 'mixed-mode', multi-campus, regional, collaborative and international applications. It lends itself to applications requiring real-time interaction and visual communication. It can achieve economies of scale, serve the needs of access and equity, maximise teaching expertise and bring value-added benefits in linking institutions, staff and students. It avoids the domination and control of broadcast communication links and allows for strong local control structures. Sessions can be conducted without the complexities of traditional television production and set up at short notice.

Some of videoconferencing's potential strengths and weaknesses derive from its being a technology which draws upon more traditional forms of communication, including the classroom. Its main limitations lie in the currently high installation costs which inevitably impose limits on sites and access, and the need for distance students to attend at pre-determined dates, times and venues while many of them value flexible timing over interaction.

Videoconferencing offers teachers, trainers and service-providers with new ways of communicating across geographical boundaries. For a second, wider phase of videoconferencing to take place, a mind set is needed which values equity, is shaped by a vision of the regional, national and international potential and can conceive technology as integral to collaborative enterprise and outreach provision.

REFERENCES

Akselen, S. and Lillehaug, S. I. (1993) 'Teaching and learning aspects of remote medical consultations' in Davies, G. and Samways, B. (eds), pp. 89–98.

Arger, G., Jones, G., Smith, R. and Hansford, B. (1989) UNE/Telecom trial of interactive video using data compression techniques between UNE Armidale and UNE Coffs Harbour, 3–13 October, Armidale, NSW, University of New England.

Arger, G. and Wakamatsu, S. (1992) 'Experimental international language teaching between Japan and Australia using 64/128 kbps compressed video via ISDN', paper presented at the Pacific Telecommunications Conference, Honolulu, Hawaii.

Bates, A. W. (1991) 'Third generation distance education: the challenge of the new technology', *Research in Distance Education*, 3(2), pp. 10–15.

Beckwith, R. (1994) 'The integration of ISDN into a multi-functional visual communications network' in Mason, R. and Bacsich, P. (eds), pp. 219–34.

Borbely, E. (1994) 'Challenges and opportunities in extending the classroom and the campus via digital compressed video' in Mason, R. and Bacsich, P. (eds), pp. 65–82.

Braun, M., Town, G., Hudson, M. and Holley, L. (1993) 'Multi-university postgraduate course run over UNINET in Sydney' in Nunan, T. (ed.) *Distance Education Futures*, University of South Australia, Underdale, SA, pp. 73–80.

Broadcast Engineering News (1993) 'Videoconferencing fails to line up to hype', *Broadcast Engineering News*, October, p. 6.

Connecting Queensland (1993) 'Bridging the gap', 2(4), October.

Dallat, J., Fraser, G., Livingston, R. and Robinson, A. (1992) 'Teaching and learning by videoconferencing at the University of Ulster', *Open Learning,* 7(2), pp. 14–22.

Davies, G. and Samways, B. (eds) (1993) *Teleteaching,* Proceedings of the IFIP Third Teleteaching Conference, TeleTeaching '93, Trondheim, Norway.

DiPaolo, A. (1993) 'Stanford University: experiences in distance education' in Davies, G. and Samways, B. (eds), pp. 23–6.

Donaghy, B. (1993) 'Videoconferencing retains TAFE students', *Campus Review,* vol. 3, no. 35, September 16–22, p. 6.

Duning, B. (1990) 'The coming of the new distance educators in the United States: the telecommunications generation takes off', *Distance Education,* 11(1), pp. 24–9.

Enkvist, I. (1993) 'Videoconferencing technology in foreign language teaching' in Scriven, B., Lundin, R. and Ryan, Y. (eds) *Distance Education for the Twenty-first Century,* selected papers from the 16th World Conference of the International Council for Distance Education, Thailand, 1992, pp. 270–3.

Granites, R. J. and Toyne, P. (1994) 'The Tanami Network: alleviating isolation through regional, national and global networking', presentation to The Multimedia Communications Community of Interest Conference, Tanami Network, Yuendumu, NT.

Hansford, B. C. and Baker, R. A. (1990) 'Evaluation of a cross-campus interactive teaching trial', *Distance Education,* 11(2), pp. 287–307.

Harris, C. and Hague, M. (1991) 'Meeting at a distance: how videoconference tutorials enhance teacher–learner relationships' in Atkinson, R., McBeath, C. and Meacham, D. (eds) *Quality in Distance Education,* Proceedings of the Australian and South Pacific External Studies Association Forum 1991, Charles Sturt University, Bathurst, NSW, pp. 193–8.

Klingsheim, K. and Kristiansen, T. (1993) 'The importance of user participation in telecommunication development' in Davies, G. and Samways, B. (eds), pp. 27–35.

Kristiansen, T. (1994) 'ISDN telephony in Norway' in Mason, R. and Bacsich, P. (eds), pp. 115–26.

Lange, J. (1994) 'ISDN videoconferencing for education and training' in Mason, R. and Bacsich, P. (eds), pp. 127–43.

Latchem, C., Mitchell, J. and Atkinson, R. (1994) 'ISDN-based videoconferencing in Australian tertiary education' in Mason, R. and Bacsich, P. (eds), pp. 99–113.

Latchem, C. and Puls, M. (1994) 'Videoconferencing in education', *Curtin Gazette,* 7(2), pp. 14–17, Curtin University, Perth, WA.

Mason, R. (1994) 'The educational value of ISDN' in Mason, R. and Bacsich, P. (eds), pp. 219–34.

Mason, R. and Bacsich, P. (eds) (1994) *ISDN Applications in Education and Training,* London, The Institution of Electrical Engineers.

Mitchell, J. (1991) 'Videoconferencing in the SA DETAFE: using state-of-the-art technology to enhance teaching and learning' in *National Technology in Education and Training Conference Proceedings,* Technology in Education and Training Committee, Redfern, NSW.

Mitchell, J., Atkinson, R., Bates, T., Kenworthy, B., King, B., Knight, T., Krzemionka, Z., Latchem, C. and Schiller, J. (1994a) *Videoconferencing in Higher Education in Australia: An Evaluation of the Use and Potential of Videoconferencing Facilities in the Higher Education Sector in Australia,* Higher Education Division, DEET

Occasional Papers Series, Canberra, ACT, AGPS.

Mitchell, J., Latchem, C. and Schiller, J. (1994b) *Tanami Network – Flourishing but Fragile: The Canvassing of the Potential for Improved Provision of Commonwealth Services to Remote Areas through Use of the Tanami Network,* Adelaide, SA, Open Learning Technology Corporation.

Renaud, B. and Pennino, L. (1992) *United States' Largest School District Uses Videoconferencing to Bridge Gaps in Distance and Education for Students in Remote Alaskan Villages,* Edelman Public Relations Worldwide press release, 26 October, VideoTelecom, Austin, Texas.

Schiller, J. and Mitchell, J. (1992) 'Interacting at a distance: staff and student perceptions of teaching and learning via videoconferencing' in *Educational Research: Discipline and Diversity,* proceedings of the AARE/NZARE 1992 Joint Conference, Geelong, VIC, Deakin University, pp. 22–6.

Waldrip, B., Horley, J., Treagust, D. and Milne, C. (1993) *Evaluation of ISDN Videoconferencing involving Two Campuses and Two Different Courses,* Science and Mathematics Centre, Curtin University of Technology, Perth, WA.

Williams, B. (1994) Personal communication from KAYAS Cultural College, Fox Lake, Alberta.

Youngblood, P., Mahoney, M. and Tonkins, S. (1991) 'Issues in the implementation of a trans-campus videoconferencing network' in Atkinson, R., McBeath, C. and Meacham, D. (eds) *Quality in Distance Education,* Bathurst, NSW, Australian and South Pacific External Studies Association Forum, pp. 512–19.

11

TEACHING AND LEARNING BY SATELLITE IN A EUROPEAN VIRTUAL CLASSROOM

Desmond Keegan

TEACHING FACE-TO-FACE AT A DISTANCE

The recent literature of distance education contains a number of attempts (Garrison, 1985) to divide technologies used in distance education into generations. Although this type of classification has its values, it needs further development to show how first generation technologies can be both more popular and more successful than final generation. A more fruitful approach may be to analyse educational provision, as seen by the distance educator, into face-to-face provision, teaching at a distance, and teaching face-to-face at a distance, and then to show how each complements the others and enriches the provision of education and training.

Historians of western education (Boyd and King, 1969) trace the origins of conventional face-to-face education back through the centuries, showing how it evolved through the dialogue, lecture, seminar, tutorial, laboratory practical and library resource centre to the provision in schools, colleges and universities today. This is characterised by (a) face-to-face provision, (b) between teacher and learner in the learning group, (c) based on interpersonal communication.

Teaching at a distance is more recent, going back only 150 years to the developments of technology associated with the Industrial Revolution, especially in transport and communications. It is characterised by the separation of the teacher from learner and of the learner from the learning group, with the interpersonal communication of conventional education being replaced by a mode of communication mediated by technology. Correspondence schools, open universities and other structures today provide this complement and enrichment of conventional provision.

Rapid advances in information technology associated with what may be called an electronics revolution of the 1980s made it possible for the first time in history to teach face-to-face at a distance. By electronically linking students and teacher at various locations by cable, microwave or satellite it becomes possible to create a virtual classroom.

A VIRTUAL CLASSROOM

A virtual classroom comprises an electronic classroom from which the class is taught, a network of specially equipped electronic classrooms at which the students are present, and the satellite, microwave or cable linkages between them. For teaching purposes, virtual classrooms can be either two-way video with two-way audio (often called 'videoconferencing' or, more accurately, 'videoteaching' and the subject of Chapter 10 by Colin Latchem) or one-way video with two-way audio.

This chapter deals with a one-way video, two-way audio satellite system used for the University College Dublin (UCD) Certificate in Safety and Health at Work in the 1993–4 academic year. It gives a detailed account of a specific application rather than a broad-ranging survey of satellites in education. It seeks to raise questions that are generalisable to other users: what is the difference between an information technology project and a distance education course? If this is the first university-accredited virtual classroom course by satellite in Europe, why is it the first? Does electronic teaching face-to-face at a distance, as analysed in this and related chapters on information technology, justify the abandonment of Wedemeyer's 'a distance education course should be available any time, anywhere there are students or only one student' which has become a guideline for distance education for at least the last two decades?

THE PROBLEM

The university wished to respond to the urgent need of small and medium-sized enterprises (SMEs) for professional training in a current issue – that of workplace safety and health legislation. It also wanted to meet in part the reasons cited by Azevedo for the low take-up of open and distance learning by small and medium-sized enterprises: 'providers are said to do too little to discover the needs of small and medium-sized enterprises, to be disinclined to target economic sectors or training needs, to be unresponsive to feedback, to provide materials that are not tailored to particular requirements' (Azevedo, 1993, p. 10).

The challenge is to provide the course from the university to students at or near their workplace in such a way that these students would be absent from work for only about two hours per week and in such a way that academic excellence would be achieved.

The problems addressed by virtual classroom courses are:

- many small and medium-sized enterprises need and want to have staff trained in up-to-date technologies and in legislation that affects them;
- even in a small country it is difficult for staff to travel to the university at regular intervals to attend the course;
- live, interactive didactic strategies and technologies are needed by the nature of the course and the expectations of business students;
- it is difficult for lecturers in a multidisciplinary course, most of them based in the capital, to travel at regular intervals to sites thoughout the country.

THE SOLUTION

The solution was for the lecturers to lecture in a broadcast-standard educational television studio at the university, with sound and vision output sent by a permanently installed microwave link to the national television transmission centre. From here it is retransmitted by a permanently installed European Broadcasting Union uplink to the Eutelstat II, flight 4 satellite at 7° East and is then downlinked to the satellite dishes at colleges and centres and other receiver sites throughout Europe. The satellite footprint is from Morocco to Moscow and from Iceland to Israel.

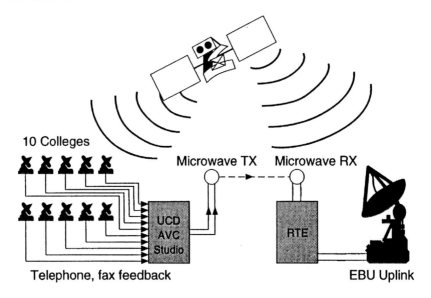

Figure 11.1 Technical structure of the European virtual classroom

The enrolment fee was set at £545 and 218 students enrolled. Electronic classrooms were set up at ten Regional Technical Colleges (RTCs) or similar centres throughout the country and the students were allocated to the nearest centre. Centres were asked to provide a suitably located classroom, tiered if possible, adequate for thirty adult students. Each electronic classroom was equipped with £5,000 worth of equipment:

- 1 x 1.2m satellite dish and receiver
- 1 x screen (approximately 1.5m x 1.5m)
- 1 x Liquid Crystal Video Projector
- 1 audioconferencing unit (to eliminate howl-around during talkback)
- 1 telephone
- 1 fax.

DIDACTIC STRUCTURE

Great attention was paid to didactic structure as it was felt that the success or failure of a distance education system lies in the structure whereby learning materials are linked to actual learning by students (Keegan, 1990, p. 110). The quality of student learning and the status and costs of the learning were issues throughout.

The didactic structure had to meet these goals:

- to provide a course designed for SMEs and their staff
- to provide training at or near the workplace of each student
- to use live and interactive technologies
- to bring university lecturers and their expertise to local areas
- to contribute to the development of local college provision
- to enrol students in a fully accredited university course
- to provide an academically rigorous university course.

To respond to all these exigencies a comprehensive delivery system was needed. The system comprised five interlocking didactic strategies:

- printed distance education materials
- 26 x 40-minute satellite lectures
- 26 x 20-minute live, interactive discussion sessions
- 26 x 1 hour face-to-face tutorials
- assessment activities.

The result is a one-year, part-time study programme of about 150 hours. The university's mature age entry regulations apply. Orientation lectures are given in each of the colleges or centres in September when the students receive their materials. Lectures and tutorials are held each Friday morning for twenty-six weeks from October to May. The university examinations are held at all centres in May 1994 and the graduation ceremony is held at the university in July.

The following procedures were followed for the 1993–4 academic year. Each student received two volumes of printed distance education materials. They were written by leading authorities on safety and health at work, chosen from universities, business and semi-government sectors, who were already experienced in lecturing on this subject at diploma level. The same lecturers gave the live satellite lectures.

At 9.00 am (10.00 am European time) on each of the twenty-six Fridays, the lecturer began lecturing from a desk in the studio to the two cameras, with the third camera over his/her head. At the lecturer's side sat the Course Director who did the introductions, provided continuity and managed the discussion/questions sessions. A self-controlled teaching space was designed for the lecturer, with full dual control either by the lecturer or production crew. Nearly all the lecturers chose to control the technology themselves, depressing buttons as they lectured to show either themselves or sophisticated computer graphics specially prepared for the course on the overhead camera.

At 9.40 am each Friday morning, the lecture finished and the Course Director opened the discussion session by asking the lecturer to deal with faxes which had been sent in during the lecture and then taking live questions and clarifications from students throughout the system on STD lines direct to the studio. It proved possible to handle ten calls per week as each question and reply averaged two minutes.

At 10.00 am each morning, the satellite was switched off and the tutorials began, given by expert local tutors who had been present throughout. At 11.00 am the students left their electronic classrooms to return to their companies.

Twenty-four self-assessment questions which were analysed during the tutorials provided formative assessment, two university projects provided both formative and summative assessment and the final examination was held in May 1994. Each project is worth 15 per cent of the final grading with the examination counting for 70 per cent.

COSTS AND HIDDEN COSTS

The costs of Year 1 amounted to £300,000. A grant of £191,000 was received from the EU as seeding funding for the European Virtual Classroom for Vocational Training project, of which this is the first stage. The enrolment for Year 2 (1994–5) is 300 students at £660 each at fifteen centres on a commercial basis with no subvention.

It would be unrealistic to propose this system as a model for other institutions without detailing the expertise, plant and personnel that the university provided and underlining the costs of replicating these.

The university's Audio Visual Centre regularly produces educational television programmes for transmissions on national television. It had transmitted an engineering course by satellite to Jordan in 1988 and provided satellite transmissions for the EU Delta Multimedia Teleschool.

Plant included a professional educational broadcasting studio with three Sony MT cameras and a switching system for inputs from cameras, computer and overheads. There is a studio production suite with vector scope and wave form monitor to control quality of outgoing video signal to EBU standards; a CAR (Central Apparatus Room) with Quantafont graphics generator for graphics and titles; Robert Leacroft telephone unit to receive and hold telephone calls; master sync generator and finish video microwave fed by cable to an antenna on the roof of the university to a similar facility at RTE.

Each lecture used a producer, cameraperson, graphics supervisor, director, vision mixer, production coordinator/sound controller, production assistant/telephone operator and satellite engineer.

EFFECTIVENESS

The technology and the system design worked superbly, in spite of the fact that the satellite lectures occurred only once per week in non-dedicated rooms in busy colleges. On one occasion, due to human error beyond the control of the university, the whole system failed and, on another, one centre failed to receive transmission and the pre-recorded videotape – sent in advance to each centre – had to be used.

The satellite delivery model was evaluated from five aspects:

- *Academic excellence*: could academic excellence be achieved? Was it possible to produce a rigorous university-level teaching and learning system by satellite?
- *Access*: did students enrol who would otherwise have been unable to do the course?
- *Quality of learning*: would students be hampered in their learning by the absence of lectures from a physically present lecturer?
- *Results*: would students be confident of passing? Would they drop out in large numbers? Would their assignment and final examination results be as good as a student who travelled regularly to the university?
- *Status*: after the experience of a satellite university course would they enrol again in satellite-delivered courses?

The effectiveness of the delivery system was evaluated by a questionnaire completed by all students ($N = 218$) in December 1993, soon after they became familiar with the system.

1 It is possible to achieve academic excellence in a satellite-delivered course.
Strongly agree 23% *Agree 63%* *Uncertain 14%*
Disagree 0% *Strongly disagree 0%*

2 My enrolment was dependent on the course being offered by satellite at a centre near to me.
Strongly agree 41% *Agree 33%* *Uncertain 7%*
Disagree 15% *Strongly disagree 3%*

3 My learning from the course was hampered because I did not attend face-to-face lectures.
Strongly agree 1% *Agree 5%* *Uncertain 11%*
Disagree 66% *Strongly disagree 16%*

4 My examination results will be just as good as if I had studied with face-to-face lectures at Belfield.
Strongly agree 16% *Agree 56%* *Uncertain 23%*
Disagree 5% *Strongly disagree 1%*

5 I would enrol again in a satellite-delivered course.
Strongly agree 40% *Agree 54%* *Uncertain 6%*
Disagree 0% *Strongly disagree 1%*

No fewer than 94% of the students enrolled in Europe's first satellite-delivered university accredited course stated they would enrol again in a similar course.

It was important to repeat the questionnaire at the end of the course in May 1994 to see whether exposure to the treatment (studying by satellite lectures) had confirmed or altered their evaluation. Again the results are reported as percentages on a Likert scale:

1 It is possible to achieve academic excellence in a satellite-delivered course.
Strongly agree 23% *Agree 63%* *Uncertain 13%*
Disagree 1% *Strongly disagree 0%*

2 My enrolment was dependent on the course being offered by satellite at a centre near to me.
Strongly agree 41% *Agree 42%* *Uncertain 5%*
Disagree 10% *Strongly disagree 2%*

3 My learning from the course was hampered because I did not attend face-to-face lectures.
Strongly agree 2% *Agree 11%* *Uncertain 21%*
Disagree 55% *Strongly disagree 11%*

4 My examination results will be just as good as if I had studied with face-to-face lectures at Belfield.

Strongly agree 9%   *Agree 49%*   *Uncertain 37%*
Disagree 5%   *Strongly disagree 0%*

5 I would enrol again in a satellite-delivered course.

Strongly agree 28%   *Agree 62%*   *Uncertain 9%*
Disagree 1%   *Strongly disagree 0%*

Not only has a significant innovation in the use of information technology in university education been evaluated, a surprisingly warm reception has been given by students employed in Irish SMEs, many of whom had extensive previous experience of conventional university education.

It was important to establish whether the students' replies to both questionnaires could have been anticipated or not. To ascertain this, a randomly selected control group ($N = 90$) was set up and the same questionnaire administered to them. To evaluate whether the observed distribution of sample answers equals the expected distribution if the two groups did not differ, the chi-square test was used. Ten different chi-square tests were conducted comparing the answers of the control group to those of the enrolled students.

The effectiveness of the system can be further evaluated by the results of the projects. Project 1 had to be submitted to the tutors by 14 January 1994 and 213 of the 218 enrolled presented it. One hundred per cent reached the pass mark and there was a very large number of outstanding scores. Project 2 had to be submitted by 15 April 1994 and pushed the students into original work beyond the content of the distance education printed materials and the satellite lectures. All 208 of the students presenting Project 2 passed and many of the results were outstanding.

The university examination was held at ten centres on Friday 27 May 1994. At this time 209 students sat the examination and 207 passed. The external examiners were from the University of Surrey at Guildford, Queens University Belfast and The Safety and Health Authority, Dublin. The two failing students are permitted by the university to resit the examination in the Summer of 1995. They do not have to attend the satellite lectures a second time and, as both had passed both projects, these results stand.

Over 80 per cent of the students were paid for by their company and the low drop-out rate may reflect the possibility that students do not drop out from distance education courses when paid for by their company or when they do the course in company time.

EDUCATIONAL USES OF SATELLITES

If, then, satellites have such potential as an educational delivery system, why are they not more widely used in Europe?

First, one needs an uplink. There are two in this country: the one used for this course and a commercially-owned mobile one. They cost £180,000 and few universities have funds of this size available for purchase. Secondly, there are regulatory issues, with PTTs in control in many countries. Finally, costs are high at about 1,500 ecus per hour, excluding production costs, and Telecoms are usually only interested in selling block hours.

Outside Europe there are numerous examples of the use of satellites in education, notably from China, the USA, India and Latin America. Satellite transmission is the kernel of China's distance university system, linking the central Chinese Radio and Television University in Beijing to the network of forty-three other open universities throughout the country (Wei and Tong, 1994). The best-known US example is the National Technological University system headquartered at Fort Collins, Colorado. It is claimed that by using digital compression and splitting the transponder into ten channels and transmitting for twenty-four hours a day, it is possible to get the cost of transponder time down to $60 per hour and a break-even point of nine students per course. This is achieved by having four cameras in a conventional lecture room in which a lecturer is lecturing to fee-paying students, and eliminating production costs by transmitting the class.

There is extensive literature on the uses of satellites in education in Europe, for instance Van den Brande (1993). This focuses mainly on the Olympus satellite, Channel e, Europace and Eurostep, but these are best characterised as educational technology projects rather than accredited distance education courses. Olympus had a chequered career before burning out last year. Europace was disbanded in late 1993 and reconstituted as Europace 2000. Present plans are for Eurostep to merge with Europace 2000 on 1 January 1995.

The course described differed from the other European satellite initiatives in the literature in some or all of the following:

• It was a distance education course, rather than an information technology project or experiment. The students of the first intake have graduated and two have failed. The concept of university failure is absent from the other initiatives.
• In this course the satellite lectures are the content of the course; the satellite provides background, motivation, administrative details in some of the other uses.
• The course described was approved by the Faculty of Science, by the

Academic Council and by the Governing Body of the university in early 1993 so that satellite students could become students of the university like other enrolled students. The course is included in the Euopean Credit Transfer Scheme (ECTS) schedule and is believed to be the first satellite course so accredited.

- Regulations were put in place for students from all over Europe to enrol, to be tutored by the university tutors, be examined and receive certification in their own countries.

CONCLUSION

Future uses of satellites in education in Europe will depend on resolution of the regulatory issues and reduction of costs, especially by digital compression, splitting of transponders and the use of new hot-bird, high-powered, wide-beam satellites.

The present course, and courses similar to it, raise questions on university affiliation, transnational certification and transnational teaching at a distance.

Some graduates remarked at the graduation ceremony in July 1994 that the first time that the students had come to the university was for their graduation ceremony. This was clearly true of a course directed to safety officers in SMEs in remote parts of the country, 6 per cent of whom were admitted on mature age entry and 15 per cent of whom had no previous higher-level study.

Transnational certification was set up for this course though, in the event, no students from outside Ireland enrolled. Two initial questions arise: (a) why would any EU citizen want Irish certification and, conversely, would an Irish citizen enrol in a French or Italian qualification if it was available by satellite?; and (b) what is the language and content of instruction, as besides the EU legislation there is in addition complex national legislation?

Transnational teaching face-to-face at a distance is now a reality and successful systems have been reported in the literature. There is, for instance, cable from Dublin to Stockholm, so it is entirely feasible to set up a two-way video, two-way audio virtual classroom between the two cities. For the first time in history, a student fidgeting in Stockholm could disturb the teacher and the rest of the class in Dublin or a student in Dublin could interact with the teacher in Stockholm. Eutelsat II F4 has a footprint that covers the whole of Europe and viewers from the Netherlands, France and Italy participated live by telephone in the 1993–4 academic year course. Students can now participate in an international classroom in which students from all over Europe are classmates.

REFERENCES

Azevedo, R (1993) 'Creating a new European dynamism through open learning activities', *Epistolodidaktika*, 1, pp. 6–24.

Boyd, W. and King, E. (1969) *The History of Western Education*, London, Black.

Garrison, D. (1985) 'Three generations of technological innovation in distance education', *Distance Education*, 6(2), pp. 235–41.

Keegan, D. (1990) *Foundations of Distance Education*, London, Routledge.

Van den Brande, L. (1993) *Flexible and Distance Learning*, Chichester, Wiley.

Wei, R. and Tong, Y. (1994) *Radio and TV Universities: The Mainstream of China's Adult and Distance Higher Education*, Nanjing, Yilin Press.

12

A DIMENSION OF IMAGE TYPES IN EDUCATIONAL MULTIMEDIA MATERIALS

Peter Whalley

OVERVIEW

Developments in multimedia technology have meant that more complex forms of image can now be used in educational multimedia materials. The purpose of this chapter is to examine the pedagogic and organisational significance of these developments. It is seen as being important to question the largely technology-driven impetus towards the use of video in educational multimedia, and in particular the use of 'full-screen' video.

The most appropriate educational use of the more complex image types is likely to follow from their being made available to course authors in ways that are technically simple to manipulate and thus experiment with. A brief review is made of some aspects of the multimedia authoring platforms that can serve as 'thinking tools' for authors without requiring them to invest a lot of time acquiring technical skills that become redundant almost as soon as they are learnt.

A DIMENSION OF IMAGE TYPES

It is possible to conceive of a dimension of image types ranging from the *still* through to *film* in terms of the extent to which they can be seen as being 'time-based' (Figure 12.1). Conventionally authors of distance teaching materials will have only been concerned with the types of image at the each end of this dimension. The recent technical progress made with interactive multimedia systems can be viewed in terms of the proposed dimension as permitting the greater ease of manipulation of dynamic images: see Figure 12.1.

Moving along the dimension from *still* to *film* could be thought of simply as an increase in complexity. However, it is interesting to note that the possible interactivity – or degree of learner control – peaks between *animation* and *video*.

In terms of the educational use of multimedia it therefore seems likely that the most interesting developments will be in this area.

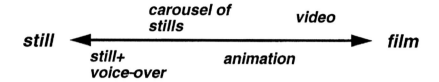

Figure 12.1 A continuum of image types

EXAMPLES

The best way to consider the relevance of a dimension of image types to the creation of educational materials is to apply it to a series of images taken from a practical multimedia system. The following examples have all been taken from a single multimedia database designed to illustrate the variety of electric wheelchairs available in the UK, while also providing higher-level advice about their purchase and use. (The *Adviser* system was developed by colleagues of the author in the Institute of Educational Technology at The Open University, UK, with a grant from the Department of Health.)

Still

The initial core of the information system was made up of the text descriptions and still images provided in the manufacturers' catalogues: see Figure 12.2. The arrangement adopted was that images would be embedded within a context of other images and text, but that when 'clicked' they would expand to fill the screen. Another click would reduce them again.

Figure 12.2 Still

120

Still and voice-over

Early versions of the information system had followed the 'video with everything' pattern. However, the designers realised that in many instances simply giving the user interactive control of a commentary with an associated still image made the features being detailed much easier to understand (Figure 12.3).

Figure 12.3 Still + voice-over

Carousel of stills

Because the *Adviser* system was designed for an audience who would be totally new to the problems of disability, the basic structure of the information system was formed of 'carousels' of examples. The user can simply browse through the sets of examples and gain an appreciation of the diversity of types available, without having to know anything of the features that are conventionally used to categorise them: see Figure 12.4.

Figure 12.4 Carousel of stills

Animation

The key aspect of animations is that they are made up of a series of discrete steps, and it is the choice of image at each step and the way that simple temporal

121

continuity is replaced by voice-over or graphic cueing that can make them so powerful. The course author's prior analysis of a continuous process into conceptually discrete 'stages' can make it much easier for the learner to understand the importance of particular parts of the process. An example is portrayed in Figure 12.5.

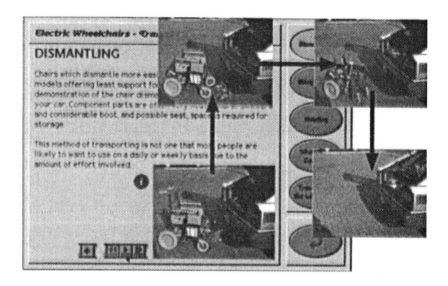

Figure 12.5 Animation

Animation/video

Animation/video is in many ways the most interesting part of the dimension, and might itself merit being considered as a dimension of new image types. At the border with video are the various 'morphing' techniques available that effectively turn discontinuous images into continuous video. The author's Virtual Microscope (discussed by Tom Vincent in Chapter 9 of this volume) would be another example: in this case discontinuous images have been processed so that they can be used to emulate the continuous rotation of a slide. The example shown in Figure12.6 from the *Adviser* system is intriguing in a different way, because here continuous video is made to appear as a 'staged' animation by the use of overlayed graphic annotation and a discontinuous voice-over.

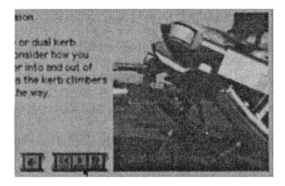

Figure 12.6 Animation/video

Video

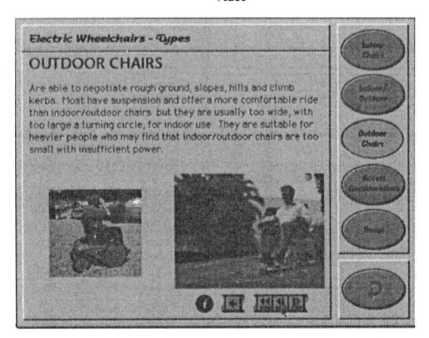

Figure 12.7 Video

Short fragments of video formed an important part of the final information system. Some were made especially for this project but many were derived from promotional film materials made by the manufacturers of the various wheelchairs. No use of 'full-screen' video was made in this project as it was always important to embed the video fragments within a context of still image and text description: see Figure 12.7.

Fragments of video

In other versions of multimedia databases we have experimented with having video fragments that 'blow up' to full screen if they are clicked – as with the *still* image type in this database. It is also possible to provide interfaces where the same fragment of video is shown in different linear combinations, with the linking voice-overs that provide continuity changing as the learner accesses the same video fragments at different conceptual depths. The author's *Topic Accessed Video* interface is an example of these new more powerful forms of access to video that can be provided for the student: see Figure 12.8.

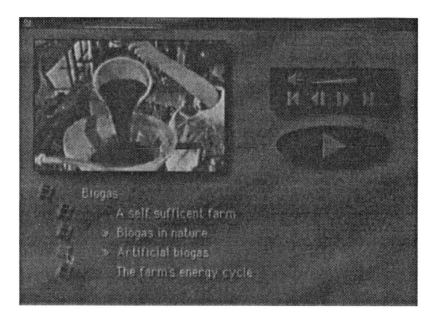

Figure 12.8 The Topic Accessed Video interface

As powerful microcomputers and video compression technology become cheaper and more readily available, the temptation on the part of developers to use full-screen video becomes greater. However, it must always be at the expense of some loss of interactivity, and most important of all, contextual information for the learner. Once full-screen video from microcomputers becomes commonplace as a delivery system for film, the temptation to overuse it in educational multimedia materials may lessen.

AUTHORING SYSTEMS

The key to the successful and sensitive use of the whole range of image types is the form of authoring system made available to the course author. In the development of educational multimedia materials it is important that the authors have available to them systems that allow them to easily manipulate image, sound and video fragments in order to obtain the best combination for their particular teaching purpose. Design should not be relegated to the role of superficial embellishment, but must be taken into consideration from the outset.

 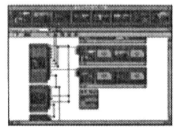

Figure 12.9 Macromedia's *Director* and Kodak's *Arrange IT* authoring systems

Professional authoring systems such as Macromedia's *Director* can appear rather daunting at first sight. However, it is quite possible to set up 'template' subsystems that allow the author to concentrate upon the teaching components without having to concern themselves with all the intricacies of 'inking effects', screen 'transitions', etc. (see Figure 12.9). Getting these right is crucial to the successful *look and feel* of the final multimedia system, but it is important that they do not dominate in the early prototyping stages. Recent commercial developments aimed at the home market such as Kodak's *Arrange IT* multimedia system have a much simpler 'direct manipulation' interface. Systems such as these are ideal for the rapid prototyping of ideas, which may then be passed over to designers and programmers to be further enhanced.

CONCLUSIONS

It is becoming accepted that good multimedia courses are likely to be the product of team work and to require a greater cooperative overlap of skills than other media. To take this beyond the level of rhetoric it is necessary for the course authors to be properly supported in the early 'envisioning' stages, where they can experiment with and test their ideas in this new medium. The significance of thinking of images in a 'time-based' dimension, as suggested by this chapter, lies in the extent to which it cuts across the traditional domains of professional expertise in the creation of distance teaching materials. This is likely to be viewed by organisations as either a problem, or as a fruitful source for innovative collaboration.

It is easy for educators to develop an artistic inferiority complex when first confronted with the design decisions required by the programs used in multimedia work. However, no film director or graphic designer is any more likely to possess the complete range of skills required to successfully manipulate the time-based media in an educational context. The advent of desk-top publishing did not turn everyone into typographers and designers overnight. However, our early amateurish efforts have given way to a more considered use of the technology and, perhaps more importantly, an appreciation of other professional skills.

Part IV

LEARNER USE
OF MEDIA

13

OVER THE THRESHOLD

Media technologies for home learning

Adrian Kirkwood

INTRODUCTION

In developing educational materials for open and distance learning, much effort is usually expended on the form and structure of the teaching. Written materials, still the most widely used means of teaching distance learners, are prepared and scrutinised with the aim of maximising accessibility and clarity, while minimising errors, omissions and unintended ambiguity. Attention is paid not only to what is being taught, but also to how it is being taught. However, when materials are designed to be studied at home by means of the media, it is not sufficient to concentrate just on the form and content of the teaching: it is also necessary to take account of the context within which learning will take place and the ways in which equipment and media materials will be used.

LEARNING AT HOME

Most people who enrol for distance education courses undertake much, if not all, of their studying in locations outside of an educational institution. In the higher education sector, distance learning is offered not only by single mode institutions but is increasingly being offered by universities and colleges that have previously relied almost entirely upon traditional face-to-face instruction. In an attempt to increase numbers and, possibly, to recruit a wider range of students, many institutions throughout the world have recently started to explore the educational use of media and information technologies (IT) to provide a distance learning alternative to their classroom-based teaching or to share expertise across a number of geographically dispersed sites. In the early 1990s the economic and political pressures to increase student numbers while reducing direct contact time and unit costs has coincided with a phase of rapid technological development in the field of information and communications technologies.

Swinburne University of Technology in Melbourne, Australia is an example of an institution seeking to diversify its profile of students through the use of new technologies. A short video entitled *Education for the People* has been produced to promote its use of distance teaching methods. The video argues that higher education need no longer be confined to the minority who can study in close proximity to their teachers and focuses on the potential of home-based learning when facilitated by the use of media technologies. The commentary on the video includes this statement:

> Each student will have a personal computer with a CD-ROM, modem, VGA graphics monitor and access to domestic TV, radio, telephone and VCR. Link these everyday items and they can access and communicate with staff and other students at Swinburne and around the world.
>
> (Swinburne University of Technology, undated)

There is no suggestion that the university will provide some or all of the equipment mentioned to home-based learners. Within the video *Education for the People* this level of access to technologies is presented not as a desirable goal to be achieved for home-based learners at some unspecified time in the future, but as the current position!

Technology-led assertions of this kind are not unusual in the distance education world of the 1990s. They include these unwarranted assumptions that will be challenged in this chapter:

(a) that home-based learners already have access to, or are willing to acquire, a wide range of high specification information and communications technologies;

(b) that the information and communications technologies to which home-based learners do have access can be used (singly or in combination) at times and in circumstances that are convenient for learners and optimal for effective studying; and

(c) that learners studying by themselves have sufficient familiarity with or experience of using media (singly or in combination) for effective learning to take place.

In essence, people who make such assumptions appear to be largely unaware of the domestic circumstances and the social and physical environment of home-based learners. A recognition of the diverse contexts within which much distance learning takes place is essential, not only for those directly involved in the development of distance learning materials, but also for the policy-makers responsible for the introduction and maintenance of the teaching system. When it comes to the use of IT and media, teachers and administrators have been used to having the main variables of the context of learning under their control, whether that be in a classroom or laboratory of a conventional institution or in a study centre or residential school utilised by a distance teaching institution. With home-based learning those variables are much more difficult to control, but policy and teaching decisions often seem to ignore or seriously underestimate that fundamental difference.

Research aimed at developing an understanding of the context within which distance learning takes place is scarce, but should be an essential element in the design process:

> Most open and distant student learning occurs independently of the teachers' presence, but dependently on the course materials they have prepared. Open and distance teachers have to make complex educational decisions, if not exactly in the dark, certainly in the gloom of speculation, interpretation, extrapolation and guesswork! Then, if these decisions are in error in some way, this often can only be discovered when it is too late (at least for the first students) as assignments come in or evaluation sheets are returned.
>
> (Evans, 1994, pp. 15–16)

Evans makes the case that research with students is necessary to reveal the significance of the diversity of learners' experiences and contexts and that 'open and distance educators can use this knowledge to frame their planning and course development phases' (*ibid.*, p. 127).

It is usual for distance learners to undertake much of their studying at home. While text-based materials offer considerable flexibility in terms of the location of studying, media-based materials constrain learners to a greater extent by their need for suitable equipment. Whether intended for the purpose of 'instruction' or for promoting 'dialogue' or 'conversation', the design of media-based distance teaching materials or systems needs to take particular account of research into access to media technologies in the home and their patterns of use.

Some media are more flexible than others: for example, audiocassettes can be played in fixed domestic entertainment systems, in battery-operated portable sets, or in many car radio/cassette players. A VCR or computer tends to be used in a fixed location, whether for entertainment or for study purposes. Distance learners usually have to schedule their studying to suit their other commitments and responsibilities (paid employment, child care, domestic activities, etc.). Ideally they would like the ability to study in a location and at a time that is most convenient for their own requirements, but the use of media technologies can bring learners into competition (or conflict) with other members of the household. They also need to be able to use whatever media technologies they have access to in ways that are conducive for effective learning to take place.

The following sections will discuss in more depth the issues of home access to equipment, the domestic context of learning and students' familiarity with information and communications technologies and their experience of using them for educational purposes.

TECHNOLOGIES IN THE HOME

Distance educators involved in the development and dissemination of media-based materials for home study need to be aware, at the very least, of the extent to which their students are likely to have access to suitable equipment at home that could be used for studying. Research on domestic access to information and communications technologies is often undertaken on a national basis by a variety of agencies. In the UK, for example, the government's Office of Population Censuses and Surveys (OPCS) undertakes its General Household Survey on an annual basis and this usually includes questions about leisure activities, domestic appliances and other equipment in the home. Regular surveys of access to television, video and other entertainment media are also undertaken by broadcasting and trade organisations, for example the Independent Television Commission in the UK. For more detailed and targeted information, distance teaching institutions need to survey their own students, who are unlikely to be a representative sample of the general population.

The public surveys indicate that in 1993 almost all UK households (99 per cent) contained at least one television set and that video recorders were located in about four-fifths of homes, although access to cable and satellite TV is relatively low (Gunter *et al.*, 1994). Computers in the home, like television and videos, are very often used for leisure and entertainment. During the 1980s computer manufacturers promoted their wares as multi-purpose devices that no home could afford to be without. Educational uses almost always featured prominently in the marketing output and home computers were usually promoted as being particularly suitable for children. By the early 1990s just over one-fifth of households in Britain contained a home computer of some kind (OPCS, 1994).

A decade ago predictions were being made that there would soon be a computer in most households, that prices would fall dramatically and that growth in ownership would follow the pattern of the video recorder. Figure 13.1 shows that in the UK ownership of home computers has increased little since 1987 (18 per cent to just 23 per cent in 1992). Over the same period there has been a steady growth in the number of households with a video recorder and, more recently, with a CD player (from 15 per cent in 1989 to 33 per cent in 1992).

The definition of 'home computer' used in the General Household Survey is very imprecise and can be applied to a wide range of machines. Unlike domestic video technology, for which there is now a high degree of standardisation, computers operate on a range of differing systems and compatibility between machines remains a problem for users.

The forecasts of cheap computers becoming as ubiquitous as VCRs in the home have clearly not been realised. This is due, at least in part, to the pricing policy of manufacturers that increases the technical specification of machines rather than reduces the base price. The development of ever-higher

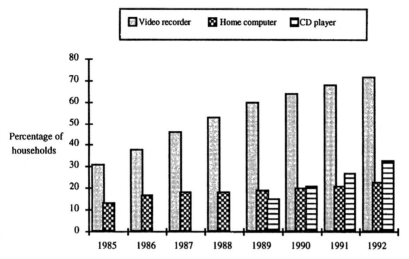

Figure 13.1 Households in Great Britain with video, home computer
and CD player, 1985–92
(*Source*: General Household Surveys, 1987 and 1992,
Office of Population Censuses and Surveys)

specification machines continues apace. Digitised audio and video material
can now be stored and processed on multimedia computers, but such
equipment costs a great deal more than a basic home computer and
significantly more than existing domestic technologies. It is only possible to
speculate how many (or few) of these machines have found their way over
the threshold into a domestic setting. Perhaps the multi-purpose, multimedia
home computer is not the route to *mass* marketing. It may be that leisure
activities mediated by IT will enter the majority of homes by other, cheaper
means: user-friendly equipment that is operated by familiar, minimal controls
may prove to be more readily accepted, providing a multi-function 'gateway'
to a range of services and leisure activities.

The direction taken by developments in IT and the media for domestic
purposes is of considerable importance for distance teaching organisations
that seek to utilise equipment already in the homes of learners. There is a
need to monitor trends in the population at large and among students. On a
regular basis, The Open University, UK, monitors the extent of students'
access to new technologies. In 1991, 90 per cent of OU students had a VCR
at home – greater than the national figure (Taylor, 1992). Although an
increasing amount of OU television material is distributed to students on
videocassette, the majority is transmitted by the BBC (see Kirkwood, 1990).
Because transmission times are often inconvenient for many students,
extensive use is made of 'time-shift' recordings. The 1991 survey found that
38 per cent of students with a VCR recorded OU programmes to watch later,
while a further 28 per cent watched and concurrently recorded their

programmes (Taylor, 1992). However, recording off-air is not always achieved without problems. In 1993 the OU used open transmission as a means of distributing video material to students on several courses (rather than sending out cassettes by mail). Many difficulties were encountered, due mainly to problems with video equipment and with the information provided by the university about transmission times (Kirkwood, 1994).

Home access to a computer is also monitored regularly at the OU. The situation is complicated by the fact that a limited number of courses (17 in 1995) *require* students to arrange good access to a PC in order to undertake practical activities. Any surveys of the general population of students need to take account of this special sub-set. Taylor's 1991 survey of a random sample of undergraduate students revealed that 24 per cent had access to a computer at home, with a further 17 per cent having access both at home and at their place of work (Taylor, 1992). A survey in 1993 (Kirkwood *et al.*, 1994) monitored access among students beginning their undergraduate study with the university.

Thus, research can provide information about the extent to which media technologies that could be used for studying are to be found in the homes of students or potential students. If there is no suitable domestic equipment already, it is also important to know if is it feasible to arrange for equipment to be acquired (from the distance teaching institution or elsewhere). However, knowing that learners have suitable equipment at home is insufficient: there is also a need to recognise the environment within which it is likely to be used.

THE SOCIAL AND PHYSICAL CONTEXT OF LEARNING AT HOME

Research on the location and patterns of use of media technologies may also be available from media organisations. For example, although a large proportion of households in the UK has more than one television set – 67 per cent in 1993 – a much smaller proportion (15 per cent) has more than one VCR (Gunter *et al.*, 1994). In most homes, the video is located in the main living-room, connected to the sole or main TV set and for use by all members of the household. This is certainly the situation for OU students with a VCR at home; the 1991 survey found that in almost all cases the video equipment was located in the main living-room (Taylor, 1992).

Home-based students cannot just use the television and VCR whenever their study schedule suggests; they often have to negotiate a convenient time with other members of the household or wait until everyone else is out or asleep. Institutions teaching with television need to be aware of domestic patterns. The OU survey in 1991 found that in terms of the *quality* of access to the household VCR, one in seven students (14 per cent) experienced difficulties gaining access to the equipment when they needed to record a

134

programme or play it back, and one-third of students (33 per cent) reported inconvenience to other members of the household resulting from their use of the VCR for study purposes (Taylor, 1992).

The location and use of computing equipment are less clearly defined. Successive OU surveys have found that a large proportion of those students with home access to a computer have the machine located in a quiet, 'private' area like a study or spare bedroom. However, a significant minority have to undertake computing activities using equipment set up in a 'public' part of the household; some have no permanent location, but have to set up their machine as and when needed. Another important feature of using a computer at home for study purposes is the inconvenience caused to other members of the household. Using the computer, especially when printing, can cause noise that may disturb others. The equipment may monopolise space or facilities that others may want to use, particularly if the computer is not set up in a 'private' location. It is also possible for other household members to cause noise or to inconvenience the student when he or she is trying to work. The general access survey undertaken in 1991 (Taylor, 1992) indicated that about 30 per cent of students were aware of inconvenience caused to others when using the computer for their studies. Women tend to be more likely than men to report the inconvenience to others: it often seems that female students consider the computer they use to be a family resource, while male students use equipment that is theirs.

Studies of students learning with media technologies at home should inform decisions about the design of materials. Because learners may face competition for use of a VCR or computer, video sequences or computing exercises should not be too long, and the study schedule should allow sufficient flexibility to enable media-based materials to be studied when learners find it most convenient.

AN APPROPRIATE APPROACH TO THE MEDIA

Students may have the necessary information and communications media at home and they may have arranged to make use of them at a convenient time and/or location – but are they themselves suitably prepared to use the media effectively for study purposes? What guidance and support needs to be provided within or alongside the learning opportunities?

If students have acquired equipment in order to take a particular course, they face the double challenge of learning the practicalities of how to use that equipment effectively, as well as the intellectual demands of studying their chosen subject. For example, learning how to use a computer can be extremely frustrating and time-consuming, particularly when in the privacy of one's home. It is often a matter of developing confidence as much as acquiring competence. When The Open University introduced its Home Computing Policy, from 1988, a large proportion of students were 'novices':

the course being studied provided many learners with their first experience of using a computer (see Jones *et al.*, 1992). A variety of support mechanisms were established to provide assistance, including specially prepared guidance notes and a Help Desk that students could telephone for advice on how to overcome problems they encountered with their computing activities. Even students who were not computing 'novices' needed to make use of the OU's support systems, as many experienced problems with particular software packages, had difficulties with items of equipment or were unfamiliar with the type of computer system used for OU home computing courses.

Media technologies such as audiocassette players, televisions and videos may be familiar to students and potential students, but their use is primarily recreational. When people use technologies normally associated with leisure for study purposes, they may adopt an inappropriate approach to the learning situation. For example, if an educational television programme adopts a documentary format to present 'real-life' material to be analysed or evaluated using theoretical models or approaches taught in a course, students may be too passive in their approach to the programme – perhaps just sitting back and 'going with the flow' – as a result of their normal viewing expectations:

> Students do *not* automatically know *how* to use instructional television to the best advantage. The further a programme moves away from overtly didactic teaching, the more help students need to develop the necessary skills to benefit from such programmes.
>
> (Bates, 1983, p. 67)

Programmes may need to deploy explicit teaching strategies to alert students to the need for an active approach to the material presented. In addition, distance education courses rarely use media-based materials in complete isolation; it is far more likely that they will constitute one or more components of the total course materials. Very often text materials will be used to make explicit links between various course components, for example focusing attention on particular evidence or issues, providing reference to the explanation of appropriate theories or principles, and so on. This helps students to develop skills for actively engaging with media-based materials.

But there is more to using one medium in conjunction with another than just providing support (however important that may be). Very often media are used in combination for particular learning purposes. The integration of materials using different media can optimise educational opportunities; for example, a spoken commentary and sounds from an audiocassette can complement the visual examination and manual manipulation of a model or piece of apparatus. But it is easy for course designers to underestimate the problems for learners of handling and attending to a variety of materials. Crooks (1993) has reported the experiences of students working with multiple media for integrated exercises in the developmental testing of an OU course teaching French:

Integration of media was very pronounced in [the sequence] *Le Service National* which combines video and print with a third medium, audio, in a follow-up exercise. Several students commented that using all three media was very inconvenient. Individual comments were that too much switching between media disturbed concentration and that it was difficult to pay attention to the spoken words and keep an eye on the text at the same time.

> 'I sometimes felt I needed the skills of a concert pianist, having to control so many buttons, switches, etc. as well as taking notes, concentrating and reading.'
>
> (Crooks, 1993, pp. 16–17)

CONCLUSIONS

Information and communication technologies undoubtedly have great potential for distance education, but the domestic environment within which students work often seems to be overlooked or its constraints underestimated by those advocating the wider use of such technologies. This chapter has argued the need for all institutions to undertake research on both the *quantity* and the *quality* of students' access to media technologies and has provided some illustrations from UK studies. Course designers and policy-makers need to shed some light on those processes by finding out more about how students actually learn with and from information and communication technologies in the home.

REFERENCES

Bates, A. (1983) 'Adult learning from educational television: the Open University experience' in Howe, M. J. A. (ed.) *Learning from Television: Psychological and Educational Research*, London, Academic Press.

Crooks, B. (1993) 'Combining video, audio and print: the formative evaluation of the audiovisual media policy of L220, French One', Paper No. 32, Programme on Learner Use of Media, Institute of Educational Technology, Milton Keynes, The Open University.

Evans, T. (1994) *Understanding Learners in Open and Distance Education*, London, Kogan Page.

Gunter, B., Sancho-Aldridge, J. and Winstone, P. (1994) *Television: The Public's View 1993*, an Independent Television Commission Research Monograph, London, John Libbey.

Jones, A., Kirkup, G. and Kirkwood, A. (1992) *Personal Computers for Distance Education*, London, Paul Chapman.

Kirkwood, A. (1990) 'Into the video age: Open University television in the 1990s', *Journal of Educational Television*, 16(2), pp. 77–85.

Kirkwood, A. (1994) 'The video cassette downloading scheme: report of a survey in 1993', Paper No. 43, Programme on Learner Use of Media, Institute of Educational Technology, The Open University.

Kirkwood, A., Jones, A. and Singer, R. (1994) 'Computing access survey 199: Foundation course students', Report No. 191, Centre for Information Technolog in Education, Institute of Educational Technology, Milton Keynes, The Ope University.

Office of Population Censuses and Surveys (1989) *General Household Survey 198* London, HMSO.

Office of Population Censuses and Surveys (1994) *General Household Survey 199* London, HMSO.

Swinburne University of Technology (undated) *Education for the People* (video Melbourne.

Taylor, J. (1992) 'Access to new technologies survey 1991: Access to televisual an video-recording equipment for study purposes', Paper No. 19, Programme o Learner Use of Media, Institute of Educational Technology, Milton Keynes, Th Open University.

14

THE EMPATHY TEMPLATES

A way to support collaborative learning

Bob Zimmer

Collaborative learning is natural, but much in ordinary life prevents it. The openness, warmth and empathy on which it depends are often blocked by hard words. The result is competitive opposition or withdrawal: fight-or-flight.

In computer-supported collaborative learning-at-a-distance, the problem is worse. Usually missing are the voice-tone, facial expression and body language which can soften the impact of hard words – which often are inadvertent. Interactions frequently break down in 'flames'.

If open, warm empathy can be reinstated through clear words, then the problem of hard words can be solved. The Empathy Templates are three short statement-pairs which are designed to do this. They have been tested successfully in computer-supported collaborative learning-at-a-distance. This account shows how they work.

SITUATIONS YOU MIGHT RECOGNISE

Situation 1

You're meeting with someone. You say something that really matters to you. And instead of evidence of empathic comprehension, you get back only dismissal or contradiction: hard words of invalidation. So you can't listen properly in return. What do you do?

How can you invite the empathic comprehension that you need? If you say, 'Did you understand me?', or 'I'm not sure you heard me', or 'Was that clear?', you're leaving the other person to decide whether *you* have been understood. You're giving up your authority on the one subject on which you are the only authority there is: your own thoughts, feelings and needs. On the other hand, if you say something coercive like, 'C'mon, gimme some understanding!' – you won't get any. It can only be given freely. What can you do?

Situation 2

You hear someone telling you what to think and what to do – instead of openly disclosing his or her own thoughts, feelings and needs and perhaps asking your help. You're receiving hard words of dogmatism. So if you respond as apparently expected, you can't give empathic comprehension; you can only knuckle under. What do you do?

How can you invite the open disclosure that you need? If you ask questions, you're likely to be seen as probing, and the other person will harden up still more – or else dry up completely. On the other hand, if you try to set an example by sharing your own views and feelings, you're likely to be seen as interrupting – as changing the subject from the other person's concerns to your own. What can you do?

Situation 3

Worse, you hear someone laying on to you a load of fantasies about your species, your ancestry or your motives – instead of warmly affirming you as a fellow human being. You're receiving hard words of disparagement. There is no way in which you can respond with open disclosure of your own thoughts, feelings and needs, without getting back a response that almost certainly will degrade them. What do you do?

How can you invite the warm affirmation that you need? If you oppose, you will be attacked. If you placate, you will be seen as weak, and the disparagement will escalate until you do oppose – or flee. What can you do?

Worse still

You encounter such situations, with the added complication that you are using computer-mediated communication. With current technology, the non-verbal channels – the voice-tone, facial expression and body language – which can soften the impact of hard words are largely missing. The competitive opposition which all too often results is known internationally on e-mail networks as 'flaming' (Bitar, 1987; Slade, 1987; Coate, 1992; Kiesler and Sproull, 1992; Shea, 1994). It can seriously harm collaborative learning.

WHAT'S WRONG

If you have noticed that collaborative learning quite often breaks down into competitive opposition or withdrawal – fight-or-flight – you're not alone. The continuous diet of reported conflict served up by news media and self-help media, for example, provides ample public evidence.

Jean Liedloff's analysis of the problem may prove reassuring (Liedloff, 1975; 1989). Her view, on comparing different cultures, is that much of this conflict springs from a singularly unfortunate, socially institutionalised tradition in our own culture – the belief that human beings are anti-social by nature and have to be beaten by authority into pretending to be good.

Specifically, the older generation uses children's natural sociality to get listened to and to convince them of this belief, and of course the children have to agree with their elders in order to survive. But they survive only at the cost of internalising this belief and passing it on to the next generation. The fear-based behaviours which inevitably result inhibit natural cooperation – and render self-fulfilling the dismal belief on which they are founded.

That's the bad news. The good news is that in having an identifiable source, this fear-based pattern can be changed.

WHAT'S NEEDED

If open, warm empathy can be offered and invited in the face of competitive opposition, then the fear-based pattern can be broken, and in principle the problem can be solved. Moreover, if this can be done through clear words alone – without reliance on non-verbal communication – then the problem can be solved even in computer-mediated communication.

Open disclosure, warm affirmation and empathic comprehension – as discussed in the three situations above – are the three factors which Carl Rogers (1962) identified as the core behaviours behind successful communication: communication which results, for all participants, in a sense of togetherness in shared understanding.

These three factors are shown in bold print in the inner ring in Figure 14.1. Each of them is followed (counter-clockwise) by an invitation which it implicitly makes, for the other person to give another of the same three factors in return.

Through these implicit invitations, the three factors combine to form a continuous cycle of collaborative learning. The way in which this cycle works can be visualised metaphorically as a two-person circle dance, with the inner ring drawn on the floor beneath them. The two people remain always on opposite sides of the circle, and they can begin anywhere along it. For example, if one of them moves into warm affirmation inviting open disclosure, then the other in response moves into open disclosure inviting empathic comprehension. If the first then moves into empathic comprehension inviting warm affirmation, then they are halfway around the circle already, and so it goes. This sequence of actions is traced by the arrows at the centre of the circle, where each cross-over at the centre represents the changeover from one person's actions to the other's.

So what's needed is a way for people to lead one another around this collaborative circle, when some may have forgotten it, or may not know how it goes, or may not even know that it exists.

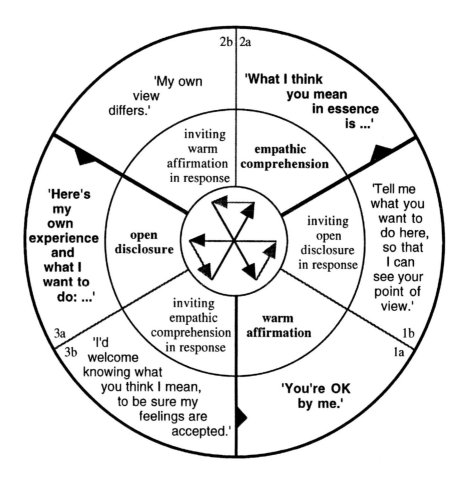

Figure 14.1 The collaborative-learning cycle and the Empathy Templates

A SOLUTION OFFERED: THE EMPATHY TEMPLATES

The Empathy Templates offer a way in which people can lead one another through this collaborative-learning cycle explicitly, so long as all participants remain free to leave – i.e. no one has to fight just to get out. This chapter explains how the templates work, reports on their tested effectiveness and draws implications for further development.

What they do

The Empathy Templates do three things. Firstly, they directly model and support the collaborative-learning cycle.

Secondly, in so doing, they indirectly dissolve competitive opposition, by displacing it and demonstrating an alternative in which the views, feelings and needs of one person and those of another are kept together, side by side.

Thirdly, they directly dissolve competitive opposition, by inviting open disclosure, warm affirmation and empathic comprehension in direct response to perceived dogmatism, disparagement and invalidation. They presume that such perceptions in the receiver are the result of inadvertence (Hussey, 1980) or distress patterns (Jackins, 1978) or fear structures (FIP, 1975) in the sender or receiver, and never reflect the sender's deepest and real intentions – since they can act only to prevent the sender from receiving warm affirmation, empathic comprehension and open disclosure in return.

How they do it

The Empathy Templates do these three things by sending the minimum amount of information which is needed, for someone who knows the collaborative-learning cycle to keep it going with someone who does not know it.

What's in them

First, to model the collaborative-learning cycle, the Empathy Templates use six particular messages: three offers which express the Rogerian factors of open disclosure, warm affirmation and empathic comprehension, plus three invitations which make the implicit invitations in these three factors absolutely explicit. The offer and explicit invitation which make up each template are numbered in Figure 14.1 in the outer ring of the diagram.

Secondly, to distinguish between the views, feelings and needs of one person and those of another, the templates keep these all literally on different sides of the circle, side by side. The right-hand side deals entirely, for each participant, with other people's concerns. The left-hand side deals entirely with the participant's own concerns.

In doing this, the templates embody the principle that differing views, feelings and needs are themselves *never* in conflict (Gordon, 1974; Jackins, 1975): views of the same thing inevitably look different from different points of view; this doesn't put them into conflict. The same goes for individual feelings and needs: difference doesn't mean conflict. Conflict arises *only* from solutions – actual courses of action – which are inadequate for meeting people's differing needs; in principle, better solutions always are possible through sufficiently creative negotiation.

Thirdly, to provide a direct response to perceived dogmatism, disparagement and invalidation, the templates explicitly invite opposites of these using Invitations 1b, 2b, and 3b.

The wordings of these explicit invitations are very carefully chosen. The theory behind them is dense (Zimmer, 1993a) and especially involves experiential learning (Houston, 1984; Kolb, 1984), transactional analysis (Berne, 1964) and driver theory (Kahler, 1979; Hay, 1983; Stewart and Lee, 1986). So the wordings have to fulfil a large number of conditions simultaneously. Nonetheless, the wordings are not set in concrete: they are subject to continuous refinement towards better fulfilment of the conditions. For example, a current contender for Invitation 2b, instead of 'My own view differs', is the more direct 'I'd like you to hear my own view'. And one for Invitation 3b, instead of 'I'd welcome knowing what you think I mean', is the simpler 'I'd like your sense of what I mean'.

Their degree of necessity

The templates explicitly model three support elements: affirmation inviting disclosure (A-ID), comprehension inviting affirmation (C-IA) and disclosure inviting comprehension (D-IC). What matters in a real conversation is how thickly and evenly these support elements are spread around. Collaborative learning progresses with each message sent, on average, so long as the density and distribution of these support elements satisfy three minimum conditions:

- each message contains, on average, at least one support element
- each support element appears, roughly, at least once every three messages
- any opposing, anti-supportive elements are immediately neutralised.

Use of such explicit models becomes necessary when the spontaneous density and distribution of these support elements drops below these thresholds, whereupon degradation into competitive opposition can be rapid.

TESTING: THE APPROACH TAKEN

The Empathy Templates have been tested successfully in computer-supported collaborative learning, in a situation wherein all participants knew about them and had easy access to them.

From October 1993 to January 1994, an eight-week experimental Open University course called XT001: *Renewable Energy Technology* (Alexander, 1993) was presented entirely through computer-mediated communication. This course was designed and advertised as a resource-based course for collaborative learning-at-a-distance through computer-conferencing. Twenty-four volunteer students from all over Europe took part. Thirteen staff also took part, making thirty-seven participants in all.

The course was run on the FirstClass™ conferencing system, and it embodied the Interactive Learning Support Environment (ILSE) developed by Alexander (Alexander, 1993) and Matheson (Matheson, 1993). It took place through five linked collaborative-learning conferences.

In a section (Zimmer, 1993b) of the user-guide for the course, the common problem of 'flaming' in computer-mediated communication was explained, and the Empathy Templates were offered for dealing with it. (Version: 'You're OK by me' was rendered as 'Hi, <Person's name>'.)

The purpose of each Empathy Template also was explained in a brief on-screen user-guide which was placed prominently in the main XT001 conference area as a reminder (Zimmer, 1993c).

Model wordings for the templates were placed in a special on-screen ILSE-panel menu for ready reference (Zimmer, 1993c). (As a technical feature, each of these menu items was designed to key its model wording automatically into the message being composed by the user – but many users reported this inoperative due to memory limitations in their machines.)

OBSERVATIONS AND CONCLUSIONS

Observation 1   The collaboration was remarkably polite and peaceful overall, and it produced substantial documents of high quality in each of the three topic areas of the course.

Conclusion 1   The collaboration was a success.

Observation 2   There were 363 messages in the five collaboration conferences taken together, containing 1,108 identifiable supportive and anti-supportive elements in all. The three kinds of support element (A-ID, C-IA and D-IC) were distributed quite evenly throughout the messages – together with the instances of their opposites, which participants neutralised quickly.

When the number of anti-A-ID elements was subtracted from the number of A-ID elements, and the same was done for the C-IA and D-IC elements, it was found that each of the 363 messages contained a net average of 1.2 of the first support element, 0.3 of the second, and 1.2 of the third – a support density of 2.7 net – as shown in Figure 14.2. Further information is available.

These support densities were four times the density needed for the first and third elements, and just adequate for the second (C-IA).

Inspection of the profile suggests that in this case, the collaborative-learning cycle ran essentially like a three-cylinder engine with one cylinder just adequate but the other two supercharged. Its greatest potential problem was unrecognised misunderstanding, but its warm enthusiasm got it there.

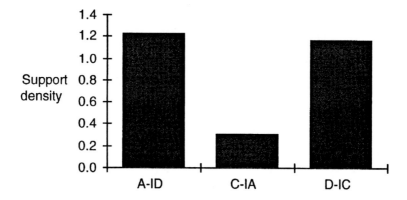

Figure 14.2 All participants, all conferences, 1,108 elements from 363 messages, total support density 2.7 net

Conclusion 2 The thirty-seven participants as a group were strongly committed to collaborative learning, as shown by the high density of support elements in their conference messages overall.

Observation 3 The average profile of support densities remained much the same in shape from individual conference to conference. The shape in each case was much the same as in Figure 14.2. (The five profiles for the individual conferences are omitted here because of space limitations; these are available from the author.) This basic profile shape – i.e. spectrum of behaviours – was a stable characteristic of this group of people working in this environment.

Conclusion 3 The method for analysis of conference messages into support elements was consistent and reliable.

Eighteen students completed this collaborative course, out of the twenty-four volunteers who started. At the end of the course, as part of a larger questionnaire about all aspects of the course, these eighteen were asked the following three questions about their experiences of the templates:

1 Whether you actually used the Empathy Templates or not, how helpful did you find their presence and the explanations of their purpose?
2 Did you knowingly use any of the Empathy Templates in spirit or principle, if not word-for-word?
3 Did you ever soften what you said to someone to try to avoid getting an Empathy Template back?

Observation 4 Fourteen students responded.
   Two of these had 'flamed' other people throughout the course. They were regarded as insufficiently committed to collaborative learning to be relied on

as judges of the helpfulness of the Empathy Templates for collaborative learning. Accordingly, they were removed from the sample.

The twelve remaining, demonstrably committed students had sent 127 messages to the five conferences, with a total of 364 support elements in all and no anti-supportive elements. Each message contained, on average, 1.4 of the first element, 0.2 of the second, and 1.3 of the third – a total support density of 2.9 – as shown in Figure 14.3.

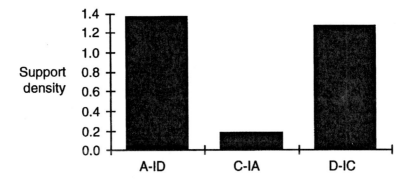

Figure 14. 3   Demonstrably committed respondents, all conferences, 364 elements from 127 messages, total support density 2.9 net

This profile is very similar to the profile (cf. Figure 14.2) for all 363 messages which were sent to the course conferences by all thirty-seven people who participated in it at any time – staff and students together. The only significant differences are a 7 per cent increase in total support density (2.9 instead of 2.7), and a decrease in the already small density of the comprehension-inviting-affirmation (C-IA) support element.

Conclusion 4   As a group, the twelve students responding to the questionnaire who were demonstrably committed to collaborative learning were reliably representative of all thirty-seven participants as a group, both in the overall spectrum of their behaviours and in their commitment to collaborative learning.

In contrast, Figure 14.4 shows the behaviour profile of the two students who engaged in 'flaming'. It does not include their behaviour in role-plays, where, of course, anything was 'fair game'. Most of their anti-supportive behaviour opposed the A-ID support element (affirmation–inviting–disclosure), and seriously diminished the density of this element in their messages.

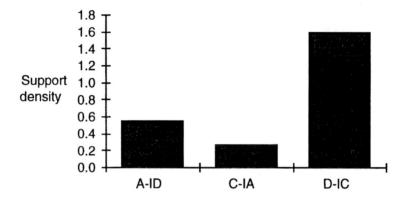

Figure 14.4 Respondents who 'flamed', all conferences, 255 elements from
76 messages, total support density 2.5 net

Credibility of the twelve demonstrably committed students needed further analysis.

People can only judge the helpfulness of a tool to the extent that they are trying to use it for that purpose. So responses from the twelve were weighted by their individually demonstrated commitments to collaborative learning. This was measured by the number of support elements which each of them individually put into the conferences: 364 support elements in all.

In effect, they were each given voice in direct proportion to their demonstrated commitment.

The outcome was as follows.

Observation 5 Weighted responses from the twelve as a group:

• With 51 per cent of their weighted response, they said that they took care at least once not to bring out an Empathy Template from others.
• With 73 per cent of their weighted response, they said that they consciously used an Empathy Template themselves at least once – presumably to cope with those who 'flamed'.
• With 86 per cent of their weighted response, they said that they rated the very presence of the Empathy Templates as helpful or very helpful.

Conclusion 5 With the weight of their 364 contributed support elements, these twelve committed students judged the Empathy Templates to be effective aids for collaborative learning.

Observation 6 Conclusion 4 (representativeness of the respondents) and Conclusion 5 (evaluation by the respondents) together imply the following:

Conclusion 6 The thirty-seven course participants as a group regarded the Empathy Templates as effective aids for collaborative learning.

Observation 7 Conclusion 1 (success of the collaboration) and Conclusion 6 (rated helpfulness of the templates for collaborators) together imply the following:

Conclusion 7 The Empathy Templates were effective aids for collaborative learning.

SUMMARY AND IMPLICATIONS

The Empathy Templates model a basic collaborative-learning dialogue cycle – and invite it.

In principle, they can be used to replace competitive opposition with collaborative learning, in any situation wherein all participants remain free to leave. The very existence of the templates shows that the self-perpetuating cycle of competitive opposition is not inevitable.

In practice, the templates have been tested in the demanding conditions of computer-mediated communication, and there they have proved themselves to be effective aids for collaborative learning.

In the test situation, all participants were fully aware of the existence and availability of the templates. Use of the templates by an individual in situations where others don't know about them remains to be formally tested. Speaking informally as an individual, the author has found them very helpful at critical moments.

The relative scarcity of empathic comprehension inviting warm affirmation (C-IA) in all of the support-element profiles may reflect a widespread cultural deficiency. People simply are not aware of the 75 per cent chance that their clear understanding of what someone has said actually is wrong (Nolan, 1987). Widening awareness of models like the Empathy Templates may encourage people to check their understanding.

Wording of the Empathy Templates is subject to continual development. Suggestions for alternative forms are welcome.

REFERENCES

Alexander, G. R. (1993) 'XT001: Guide to ILSE (Interactive Learning Support Environment)', Centre for Electronic Education, September, Milton Keynes, The Open University.

Berne, E. (1964) *Games People Play: The Psychology of Human Relationships,* New York, Grove Press.

Bitar, P. (1987) 'Inquiry concerning misunderstandings arising from computer mail', posted on Computers and Society Digest, February. Available also from R. Slade: roberts@mukluk.decus.ca.

Coate, J. (1992) 'Cyberspace innkeeping: building online community', published in numerous electronic conferences, 1992–3, available from John Coate, tex@well.sf.ca.us.

Foundation for Inner Peace (1975) *A Course in Miracles,* London, Arkana (entire volume).

Gordon, T. (1974) *T.E.T.: Teacher Effectiveness Training,* New York, Wyden, pp. 272ff.

Hay, J. (1983) 'Effective communication', One-day workshop, Harrow, Action Development.

Houston, G. (1984) *The Red Book of Groups: And How to Lead Them Better,* London, Gaie Houston.

Hussey, M. (1980) 'Reflections on convergent communication', Buckingham, personal communication.

Jackins, H. (1975) *Quotes from Harvey Jackins,* Seattle, Rational Island Publishers, pp. 3, 16.

Jackins, H.(1978) *The Human Side of Human Beings: The Theory of Re-evaluation Counseling,* Seattle, Rational Island Publishers, pp. 63ff.

Kahler, T. (1979) 'Process Communication Model™ (in brief): an interactive approach for successful communication', Little Rock, AR, Taibi Kahler Associates.

Kiesler, S. and Sproull, L. (1992) 'Group decision making and communication technology', *Organizational Behavior and Human Decision Processes,* Vol. 52, pp. 96–123.

Kolb, D. A. (1984) *Experiential Learning: Experience as the Source of Learning and Development,* Englewood Cliffs, NJ, Prentice-Hall.

Liedloff, J. (1975) *The Continuum Concept,* London, Duckworth, pp. 76–9.

Liedloff, J. (1989) 'The easy way', talk given at the 1989 Dartington Conference, 'Imagination, Discipline and Education', Totnes.

Matheson, S. (1993) 'ILSE Design – Version 3', Centre for Electronic Education Report No. 48, Milton Keynes, The Open University.

Nolan, V. (1987) *Communication,* London, Sphere Books, pp. 7ff.

Rogers, C. R. (1962) 'The interpersonal relationship: the core of guidance' in Stewart, J. (ed.) *Bridges Not Walls: A Book About Interpersonal Communication,* London, Addison-Wesley (1977), pp. 240–8 (reprinted from *Harvard Educational Review,* Vol. 32, Fall 1962, pp. 416–29).

Shea, V. (1994) *Netiquette,* San Francisco, Albion Books.

Slade, R. M. (1987) 'Misunderstandings in messaging systems', posted on Computers and Society Digest, February. Available also from R. Slade: roberts@mukluk.decus.ca.

Stewart, I. and Lee, A. (1986) 'The Kahler "Process Communication Model"', Two-day Transactional-Analysis workshop, Nottingham, 25–26 January.

Zimmer, R. S. (1993a) 'The Empathy Templates: to invite collaborative learning', Teaching and Consultancy Centre Report No. 79, Institute of Educational Technology, Milton Keynes, The Open University.

Zimmer, R. S. (1993b) 'The Empathy Templates – user guide: for maintaining creative communication', appendix in Alexander, G. R. (1993).

Zimmer, R. S. (1993c) 'The Rogerian Interface: mediating openness, warmth and empathy for collaborative learning-at-a-distance', paper presented at the 1993 Teaching and Learning Exchange, 'Quality, Creativity and Renewal', conference organised by the Institute for Teaching and Learning, California State University, held at San José, California, October.

15

ELECTRONIC HIGHWAY OR WEAVING LOOM?

Thinking about conferencing technologies for learning

Liz Burge

Information highways are high-speed data networks used to transport information and link people who want to be connected with others. E-mail, bulletin boards and computer-conferencing are common activities on the Internet and other electronic networks. The metaphor of a highway is used to reflect qualities of speed, volume, power and efficiency (Menzies, 1994a, p. 7). Any decontextualised look at a real highway shows how we may travel efficiently without too many interruptions and delays. However, any contextualised look at highways, as they operate in the natural environment, suggests some limits in the usefulness of the metaphor for learning contexts. The highway is a rigid metal and asphalt ribbon imposed on the countryside and it enables large quantities of fast-moving traffic to travel as single, unrelated units using laws to regulate traffic flow.

In the early stages of electronic data networks the highway metaphor attracted much attention, but now, as 'pot-holes' and 'road-kill' become evident, users react more cautiously.

> Is the information highway the road to a common future or just another trip to the mall?
>
> (Menzies, 1994b, p. 3)

> Internet is more than a highway; it's a virtual community where multiple things happen.
>
> (de Boer, 1994)

> Computer conferencing is like riding the rapids, you've got to get in a boat and you've gotta keep going – you have to keep that boat moving along the river of information, because if you ever stop you're going to go down.
>
> (Burge, 1994, p. 32)

When such reactions illustrate the limitations of high-speed, high-volume 'traffic', what do we do with the highway metaphor? One solution is to jettison it altogether and develop others. One metaphor raises very different associations: one of lower speeds and volumes of activities, and creative activity:

> ... computer-mediated communication is like a loom. The threads of experience each participant brings to the loom form the warp and weft of the fabric of learning. The weaver first threads the warp threads on the loom, determining the overall pattern of the cloth. The course planner threads the education loom with warp threads of course outline and plan. With warp threads in place, weft threads are added. Qualities of the threads used affect the design decisions and the pattern of final woven fabric. The weft threads of the educational loom are spun by the life experiences of all participants, each with a different texture. Every weft thread added to the cloth causes it to change and grow. As each learner contributes a thread of discussion to the learning experience, the cloth of learning is formed.
>
> (von Weiler, 1994)

This metaphor helps my understanding of interactive learning. But what am I to do with these very different metaphors of highway and loom? Do I choose between them, or change my perspectives (Menzies, 1994a)? How flexible and creative is my thinking for that task? Barker's prophecy may apply here (note how it relates to the highway metaphor):

> I believe the next few years are going to be filled with people coming around blind curves and yelling things at you. If you have paradigm *flexibility,* then what they are yelling will be opportunities. If you have paradigm *paralysis,* then what they will be yelling at you will be threatening. The choice will be up to you.
>
> (Kemp, 1991, p. 18)

Will my behaviour show paradigm paralysis, flexibility or compromise? What kind of paradigm is needed anyway (Farnham-Diggory, 1994; Jonassen, 1991)?

Distance educators confront much fast-paced activity and hype in the use of conferencing technologies (CTs). We continuously have to make choices, using the lens of informed critique. Postman sees this process as negotiation:

> ... every culture must negotiate with technology, whether it does so intelligently or not. A bargain is struck in which technology giveth and technology taketh away. The wise know this well, and are rarely impressed by dramatic technological changes ...
>
> (Postman, 1992, p. 5)

Which knowledge and values inform our negotiation? How do we understand technology in its natural contexts of use? Before we decide how to respond to the latest billboards on the highway, or change the weaving threads, we have to examine a variety of paradigms (Hlynka, 1991), including our own. The rest of this chapter, therefore, reflects my selection of paradigm components that are key for metaphorical and analytical thinking about CTs. The exploration will cover a variegated landscape: a forest of concepts, some sunlight of new knowledge about CTs, and trails to guide our travel. The technologies are audio, audio-graphic, video- and computer-conferencing – formats that enable synchronous and asynchronous group communications, and which I have used personally. The exploration will avoid extensive reviews of practice because the literature on CTs is still emerging (see, for example, Burge, 1994; Burge and Roberts, 1993; George, 1990; Harasim, 1990; Hiltz, 1994; Kaye, 1992; Laurillard, 1993; Macdonald, 1994; Mason, 1994; Wells, 1992). Consequent development of practice will be informed by references to concepts and strategies developed by colleagues in other fields. The forest of ideas has four key areas – media research, constructivist learning theory, adult learning and gender issues.

Media researchers continue to debate the usefulness of research that depends on objectivity, causality principles and the analysis of selected components of the learning context (for example, Ullmer, 1994). Hooper and Hanafin (1991) explain their findings carefully:

> ... unique causal relationships between technology and learning have not been established conclusively ... the effectiveness of IT [instructional technology] is more likely contingent upon the informed application of time-tested learning strategies than the technological capabilities of a medium.
>
> (Hooper and Hanafin, 1991, pp. 69–70)

Clark and Kozma continue to exchange opinions about research into the effect of media attributes. Clark argues that media do not in themselves cause learning; they act only as delivery vehicles. Media attributes may affect the 'cost or speed of learning but only the use of adequate instructional methods will influence learning' (Clark, 1994, p. 27). Kozma supports the new systemic paradigm in educational research, i.e. seeing how every component in a dynamic system operates and influences each another in naturally complex and unpredictable settings. He argues therefore for media research that looks at situation-specific strategic use of learning media:

> In what ways can we use the capabilities of media to influence learning for particular students, tasks, and situations?
>
> (Kozma, 1994, p. 18)

Jonassen, Campbell and Davidson (1994) respond to Clark and Kozma by emphasising the unpredictable complexity in learning contexts and the futility of analysing only selected components in a system:

> We delude ourselves when we manipulate attributes of the medium and expect these manipulations to have a predictable effect on a process as complex as learning. We certainly cannot know which affordances (to use Clark's terms) are 'necessary' let alone 'sufficient' causes for learning.
>
> (Jonassen *et al.*, 1994, p. 25)

What are we to make of these expert debates? How do we negotiate our own trails through the thickets of conflicting opinions? We do know that the features of a medium bias the way in which information is represented. Representation often reduces the amount of information available for cognition, reflects the producer's own mindset about knowledge processing, and creates media-induced forms of thinking (Johnson and Johnson, 1993). The medium acts as both message and massage (Menzies, 1994a, p. 8). Norton adds another explanation:

> To represent ideas with speech is to give primacy to memory, rhythm, personalistic and vivid imagery ... To represent ideas with print is to give primacy to the analytical, the sequential, the propositional, the hierarchical, and the rational ... To represent ideas visually through photograph, television, or film is to give primacy to the presentational, the emotive, the non-rational, and the subjective ...
>
> (Norton, 1992, p. 38)

Given these effects, how might we visualise and differentiate the functions of CTs? CTs may be experienced, for example, as tools that 'give'. They are synomorphic when they fit into natural human behaviour, as, for example, a glove is synomorphic to a hand, but not to a foot (Knuth and Cunningham, 1993). Draper defines the kinds of tools needed for learning:

> In asking what computers can do to support education, we must not look to large machines or even tools in the traditional sense, but to devices like gloves that fit human ability much more intimately by complementing it. Their essential advantage however is analogous to that of tools: to extend the range that can be brought within the scope of personal interaction – of action but especially of perception.
>
> (Draper, 1992, p. 170)

One example is the fax machine when it enables fast and reliable transmission of handwritten material produced by learning groups. Another example is e-mail, where time, location, flexibility and speed of transmission make message-sending convenient (the highway enables traffic to flow smoothly).

CTs may be experienced also as tools that 'taketh away'. For example, as well as biasing the presentation of information, they can amplify the impact of unhelpful interpersonal behaviours, as in an audio-conferenced student discussion where certain vocal interaction patterns can reinforce dominance and plays for 'air power', or vocal qualities such as monotones, nasality or tension can diminish vocal attractiveness and vocal maturity, and hence reduce attention to the listener (Pittam, 1994). One problem with learners' use of CTs is what I term the 'mitten effect' – reduction of flexibility in use. Learners may not feel or think that the technology helps them to learn in their preferred styles. One classic example of this restriction effect is the audio-conferenced class in which the teacher lectures for 80 per cent of the time, or acts as an all-controlling 'traffic cop' of discussions. What should happen is more natural behaviour: learners talking across the teacher to each other and the teacher consciously timing her/his contributions so that they help as and when necessary. Such a dialogue model, however, depends on the learners coming to class having worked already with the information delivered; then valuable class-time is spent working at higher cognitive and affective levels.

The second forest area is the renewed interest in the learning theory of constructivism (Brown *et al.*, 1988; Collins, 1991; Duffy and Jonassen, 1992; Duffy *et al.*, 1993; Jonassen, 1991; Jonassen *et al.*, 1993; Lebow, 1993; Merrill, 1991; Shuell, 1988; Winn, 1990). Constructivism links with the weaving-loom metaphor rather than with the highway metaphor because of its focus on creativity, multiplicity and growth:

> Constructivism, like objectivism, holds that there is a real world that we experience. However, [constructivists argue] that meaning is imposed on the world by us, rather than existing in the world independently of us. There are many ways to structure the world, and there are many meanings or perspectives for any event or concept.
>
> (Duffy and Jonassen, 1992, p. 3)

Constructivist learning is about the elaboration of concepts, but as they operate in real contexts. Learners elaborate via questioning, critique, application, reflection-on-action (Reigeluth, 1983). Thinking is done interactively and iteratively, as in cross-country skiing across the intellectual landscape. Discussions about constructive learning and teaching are sprinkled with terms that reflect the work in learning, such as cognitive apprenticeship (Collins *et al.*, 1989), cognitive load (Chandler and Zweller, 1991), cognitive ergonomics (Zuchermaglio, 1993) and cognitive flexibility (Spiro *et al.*, 1988).

To learn constructively is to actively process new information, use structured experiential activity and analyses of life experiences, solve problems, examine critically one's existing mental frameworks, accept ambiguities in knowledge, explore belief systems and assess one's learning. The learner's existing mental framework and learning needs are the key agents in interpretation and construction of knowledge. She/he knows that there is no single 'truth' in interpretative contexts.

To teach constructively is to provide opportunities for complex information processing related to a learner's needs and knowledge of the world, design relevant and real world (authentic) tasks, help to identify conflicting ideas and attitudes, provide complex and controversial stimuli, challenge the learner's existing knowledge structures and values, acknowledge vague structures in knowledge, help learners revisit material in greater depths, confirm the learning identified by learners, and guide learners to generate correct solutions. Teaching constructively also means skilful attention to learning strategies, not just the content. It means, for example, managing structured tasks for groups, helping learners to acquire and use learning skills, not 'rescuing' learners as they experiment with sharing responsibility for class process, and ensuring emotional safety for expressions of need, trust and uncertainty. Avoided at all costs is the reinforcement of passive dependency in learners and also signs of both cognitive oversimplification and lack of transfer of knowledge from one context to another.

Applying constructivist thinking to how learners' use CTs means asking first the 'why and when and for what?' questions before asking the 'how?' questions. The 'when?' question is especially important for CT use: it relates to controlling the timing of our interventions in learning processes and our mixing of the contextual elements that affect those processes. The 'what?' and 'why?' questions are linked – learning outcomes and learning strategies have to be integrated, but not in ways that deny choices for the learner. Balancing the amount of freedom available within a sense of structure is a key challenge. Another – and one which is the biggest challenge for many teachers using CTs – is to move out of the lecture mode and into facilitative models.

The third forest area contains issues of adulthood. Deserving of more space than is available here, adult characteristics – as they help and hinder learning – need some new angles of analysis, especially away from medical models and towards client-centred models. We could further examine our assumptions behind such terms as student support, autonomous learners and self-discipline. Adults do not want to realise they are guinea-pigs for clumsy experimental usage of CTs, nor do they want to feel as if asking for help (a deficit model) is the only reason to 'talk' in CT mode. But their learning group may need help in working through the inevitable stages of development (Tuckman and Jensen, 1977).

The fourth forest area is heavily populated – by women distance students. A growing literature (for example, May, 1994; Kirkup and von Prümmer, 1990) recognises many women's existing learning skills and preferences, especially collaborative and expressive ones, which are brought to any learning contexts. Women do not need to be told about cooperation and respectful climates; their gender socialisation has been strong and they need the freedom to use those skills with confidence. Research into technology equity and use indicates cultural issues (Bush, 1983) and many women bringing expectations of easy efficiency and little patience with unfriendly software (Kantrowitz, 1994; Tannen, 1994).

Where is the sunlight in our landscape? What do we know so far about learner use of CTs? A recent analysis of articles (Murphy, 1994) suggests relatively fragmented, linear descriptions, with little evidence of interdisciplinary theoretical links to actual practice. Examples could include linking research in audioconferenced learning groups to theories on voice perception and its relationship to social identity (Pittam, 1994), applying constructivist learning strategies to computer-conferenced learning contexts, or the deliberate design of controversy into CT use (Davie and Inskip, 1993; Davidson and Worsham, 1992).

We appear to be using the technologies to produce amplificatory impacts, that is, carrying out much the same kind of activity that we have in walled classrooms, but with more efficiency (Kiesler, 1992). This means that both the lecture models and dialogical models of teaching are being tried.

We know some principles for promoting relational ways of learning. The principles suggest that CTs have to mediate people, not distance. CTs can help to reduce interpersonal conditions that impede productive talk. In CT use we can help learners to share responsibility for class process and also to act as cognitive screens or sieves that sort out and clarify the thinking of their peers.

Effective CT use recognises that a learner's idea of the effort required to learn from a particular medium will influence her/his cognitive work in processing the information delivered by that medium (Cennamo, 1993). Time is needed for learners to adjust their neurological processing of information to adapt to the particular skills demanded by the medium (Simpson, 1994). The two-way talk of CTs has to be designed for receiving, processing and sending messages in ways that facilitate active learning (for example, talking in order to think or to arrive at a tentative conclusion). To use CTs as a vehicle for one-way transmission of pre-digested information, or perfunctory summaries of student work, or for students asking only for help, is a waste of the technologies, especially given the costs. Evidence of cognitive synchronicity (my term for everyone being 'connected' to the topic at hand) and social energy for learning are key criteria for effective use. A third criterion is enabling learners to exercise creativity in thought and peer interaction (Post, 1994).

We know that careful attention has to be paid to the affective elements of the environment, such as vocal presence, eye gaze, acoustic courtesies, tactful phrasing of written text, visual presence and a comfortable, energised climate. In my experience of audioconferenced events since 1982 (as teacher, chairperson and participant), for example, I've learned that novices have to be helped to understand the benefits and duties of collaborative learning, and many have to learn expression skills in order to think aloud effectively. I've learned, too, that many people have little or no self-awareness of their vocal presence, and how to use it effectively for group-based talk. I know also that some participants need time and listening space before they speak.

How do we identify effective use of each CT? Audioconferenced classes (AC) can show evidence of learners referring to each other by name, and doing so across the tutors without fear that their dialogue will be interrupted, working in small groups or tasks before reporting back to the whole, hearing critically constructive feedback from a designated respondent group, venting their frustrations, getting substantive but appropriately timed input from their tutors or teacher, and paying respectful attention to the practical knowledge of their peers. We know that learners' use of AC is enhanced when the teacher uses 6 'Cs' – *connect* learners to resources, *create* the climate, *confirm* new learnings, *challenge* to greater understanding, *correct* misunderstandings and *change* the agenda as necessary (Burge and Roberts, 1993, p. 13). The absence of visual cues means that students at local sites can feel 'liberated' to engage in dysfunctional group behaviour – all without the teacher ever knowing, unless she/he knows to ask directly, or to have the learners complete assessments of their group process.

Use of text-based computer-conferencing (CC), with its lack of vocal cues and strength in text format and relative ease of sending messages to peers, depends on relationship building and focused contributions. Focused messaging is essential, not only to help maintain cognitive synchronicity, but also to avoid information overload and the effect of fragmented thinking. As people contribute at their convenience, the threads of discussion may appear split at the ends and disentangled because the topic of one contribution can appear on the screen after a contribution thirty seconds earlier that referred to quite another thread in the same discussion. Contributing into a twenty-four-hour-a-day, seven-days-a-week classroom has its demands:

> ... it's asynchronous, but it's not atemporal; you can't be out of step with [class discussion] ... it doesn't mean that time is not important. There is a time factor, a window within which you have to be involved.
>
> (Burge, 1994, p. 31)

Grint's (1992) perspective on the challenge of contribution quality is relevant: we have to create the conditions for creative 'volatility of conversation' without producing prattle, or what one Open University (UK) student called 'chewing-gum for the eyes'. CC enables much contributive energy (my term) for people to talk as often as they like, when they like, but one person's freedom to write is another's deluge of information (trying to drink a glass of water from a fire hydrant). Learners' use of this medium is enhanced when the teacher enables adequate time for preparation of learners, and provides efficient trouble-shooting for technical problems. In other words, render the medium as transparent as possible so that the learner feels efficient and not loaded with perceptions that she/he has to make a huge effort. The paradox of elegance applies here: expert performance appears effortless. Preparation for CC includes showing learners how to direct contributions to relevant conferences so that jumbled and fragmented messaging is reduced. In addition to using strategies listed already for AC, the CC teacher has to keep a keen eye on cognitive synchronicity and contributive energy.

Videoconferencing (VC) poses a particular challenge because its visual element tends to encourage recidivism into lecturing modes. Educators are finding ways to use the somewhat limited visual channel to enhance the cues necessary for communicating ideas and understanding the feelings behind the expression. Text and pictures can be transmitted relatively easily using cameras but their function has to support the talk and their legibility maximised. Creating social presence means that learners have to be taught to look directly at the camera in order to be present metaphorically with their peers in another site. Any impersonal styles reduce psychological connection. Participants need also to acquire visual composition skills to avoid the screen being filled with empty table-tops, cluttered backgrounds and distant faces.

Audio-graphics (AG) also pose challenges in visual composition for the expression of ideas. AG enables real-time talking by AC and the use of pre-prepared and on-line, ad hoc information, so the teacher is integrating two channels of information. The temptation is to use the computer screen as a blackboard that transmits everything, even information that could be more efficiently delivered in paper format. Adult learners will not easily tolerate uninformed use of CTs by people seduced by the medium. Because of the voice and visual links, attention has to be paid to the correspondence of information presented, i.e. visuals and spoken words have to work together without undue redundancy.

Having seen the forest and felt the sunlight, how am I guided to travel on new CT trails? One strategy is to explore the links between the structural elements of learning (the loom) and the process elements (the threads and the weaver). For example, in audioconferencing, three structural elements are participants, synchronous vocal communication, and no visual cues. Learning tasks such as being attentive, generating ideas, elaborating concepts and getting feedback are enhanced when the teacher talks less and listens to/responds more than she/he may do using a lecture mode. The challenge therefore is to change teaching functions without reducing academic rigour and the teacher's sense of importance. Adult learning facilitators already have those insights. With each CT, collaborative styles of learning will be designed quite deliberately; it does not happen just because people have been collected together. This connection issue relates to the synergy of learning: '... creating a shared experience of learning is qualitatively different from helping individuals share their prior experience' (Johnson and Johnson, 1993, p. 146).

Another trail strategy is to think functionally – about gloves and tools, not mittens and weapons. To redefine my ideas about control and empowerment that swirl around the CTs: from meaning access to fire-hydrant quantities of information and unlimited opportunities for one-to-many opinion-giving, to meaning the selection of glassfuls of information and the creation of community contexts for critically examining that information. To provide opportunities for learners to talk in order to help their thinking, rather than always the reverse process. To connect a functioning group; don't just collect an aggregate of bodies. This last goal means thinking about holistic learning. To consider Heather Menzies' warning to avoid education being 'increasingly transformed into educational packages ... and [being] less and less a holistic experience in real life, grounded in real communities' (Menzies, 1994b, p. 12). To examine each emerging CT first for how it helps learning, and how its use can be sustained. Identify our own metaphor for the CTs, for in such descriptions do we display our professional paradigm and avoid paradigm paralysis. Finally, to ask about our key goals for CT use: are they technological mastery – functional skills, or conceptual mastery – asking the why and the when questions before the how questions? When integrated into the whole learning context, as one component among many, conferencing technologies offer learners and educators flexible ways to connect with one another, not surpass one another.

I acknowledge the research help given by Judith Murphy, Janet von Weiler and Daniel Yakimchuk for background in parts of this chapter.

REFERENCES

Brown, J. S., Collins, A. and Duguid, P. (1988) 'Situated cognition and the culture of learning', *Educational Researcher,* 18(1), pp. 32–42.

Burge, E. J. (1994) 'Learning in computer-conferenced contexts: the learner's perspective', *Journal of Distance Education,* 9(1), pp. 19–43.

Burge, E. J. and Roberts, J. M. (1993) *Classrooms with a Difference: A Practical Guide to the Use of Conferencing Technologies,* Toronto, The Ontario Institute for Studies in Education.

Bush, C. G. (1983) 'Women and the assessment of technology: to Think, to Be; to Unthink, to Free [sic]' in Rothschild, J. (ed.) *Machina ex Dea: Feminist Perspectives on Technology,* New York, Pergamon Press, pp. 151–70.

Cennamo, K. S. (1993) 'Learning from video: factors influencing learners' preconceptions and invested mental effort', *Educational Technology Research and Development,* 41(3), pp. 33–5.

Chandler, P. and Zweller, J. (1991) 'Cognitive load theory and the format of instruction', *Cognition and Instruction,* 8(4), pp. 293–332.

Clark, R. (1994) 'Media will never influence learning', *Educational Technology Research and Development,* 42(2), pp. 21–9.

Collins, A. (1991) 'Cognitive apprenticeship and instructional technology' in Idol, L. and Jones, B. F. (eds), *Educational Value and Cognitive Instruction: Implications for Reform,* Hillsdale, NJ, Lawrence Erlbaum, pp. 12–37.

Collins, A., Brown, J. S. and Newman, S. E. (1989) 'Cognitive apprenticeship: teaching the craft of reading, writing and mathematics' in Resnick, L. (ed.), *Learning, Knowing and Instruction: Essays in Honor of Robert Glaser*, Hillsdale, NJ, Lawrence Erlbaum, pp. 453–94.

Davidson, N. and Worsham, T. (eds) (1992) *Enhancing Thinking through Cooperative Learning*, New York, Teachers College Press.

Davie, L. E. and Inskip, R. (1993) 'Fantasy and structure in computer-mediated communication', *Journal of Distance Education*, 7(2), pp. 31–50.

de Boer, A. (1994) Personal communication with author.

Draper, S. W. (1992) 'Gloves for the mind' in Kummers, P. A. M., Jonassen, D. H. and Mayes, T. (eds) *Cognitive Tools for Learning*, Berlin, Springer-Verlag, pp. 169–81.

Duffy, T. M. and Jonassen, D. H. (eds) (1992) *Constructivism and the Technology of Instruction: A Conversation*, Hillsdale, NJ, Lawrence Erlbaum.

Duffy, T. M., Lowyck, J. and Jonassen, D. H. (eds.) (1993) *Designing Environments for Constructive Learning*, Berlin, Springer-Verlag.

Duffy, T. M., Lowyck, J. and Jonassen, D. H. E. (eds) (1993) *Designing Environments for Constructive Learning*, Berlin, Springer-Verlag.

Farnham-Diggory, S. (1994) 'Paradigms of knowledge and instructions', *Review of Educational Research*, 64(3), pp. 463–97.

George, J. (1990) 'Audio conferencing: just another small group activity', *Educational and Training Technology International*, 27(3), pp. 244–8.

Grint, K. (1992) 'Sniffers, lurkers, actor networkers: computer-mediated communications as a technical fix' in Beynon, J. and Mackay, H. (eds), *Technological Literacy and the Curriculum*, London, Falmer Press, pp. 148–70.

Harasim, L.M. (ed.) (1990) *On-line Education: Perspectives on a New Environment*, New York, Praeger.

Hiltz, S.R. (1994) *Virtual Classroom*, Norwood, NJ, Ablex.

Hlynka, D. (1991) 'Postmodern excursions into educational technology', *Technological Literacy and the Curriculum*, London, Falmer Press, pp. 148–70.

Hooper, S. and Hanafin, M. J. (1991) 'Psychological perspectives on emerging instructional technologies: a critical analysis', *Educational Psychologist*, 26(1), pp. 69–95.

Johnson, D. and Johnson, R. (1993) 'Cooperative learning and feedback in technology-based instruction' in Dempsey, J. and Sales, G. (eds), *Interactive Instruction and Feedback*, Englewood Cliffs, NJ, Educational Technology Publications, pp. 133–59.

Jonassen, D. H. (1991) 'Objectivism versus constructivism: do we need a new philosophical paradigm?', *Educational Technology Research and Development*, 39(3), pp. 5–14.

Jonassen, D., Mayes, T. and McAleese, R. (1993) 'A manifesto for a constructivist approach to uses of technology in higher education' in Duffy, T. M., Lowyck, J. and Jonassen, D. H. (eds), pp. 231–47.

Jonassen, D. H., Campbell, J. P. and Davidson, M. E. (1994) 'Learning with media: restructuring the debate', *Educational Technology Research and Development*, 42(2), pp. 31–9.

Kantrowitz, B. (1994) 'Men, women and computers', *Newsweek*, 123(20), pp. 48–55.

Kaye, A. R. (ed.) (1992) *Collaborative Learning through Computer Conferencing: The Najaden Paper*, Berlin, Springer-Verlag.

Kemp, J. E. (1991) 'A perspective on the changing role of the educational technologist', *Educational Technology*, 31(6), pp. 13–18.

Kiesler, S. (1992) 'Talking, teaching and learning in network groups' in Kaye, A. R. (ed.), pp. 105–16.

Kirkup, G. and von Prümmer, C. (1990) 'Support and connectedness: the needs of women distance education students', *Journal of Distance Education*, 5(2), pp. 9–31.

Knuth, R. A. and Cunningham, D. (1993) 'Tools for constructivism' in Duffy, T. M., Lowyck, J. and Jonassen, D. H. (eds), pp. 163–88.

Kozma, R. B. (1994) 'Will media influence learning? Reframing the debate', *Educational Technology Research and Development*, 42(2), pp. 7–19.

Laurillard, D. (1993) *Rethinking University Teaching*, London, Routledge.

Lebow, D. (1993) 'Constructive value for instructional systems design: five principles toward a new mindset', *Educational Technology Research and Development*, 41(3), pp. 4–16.

Macdonald, D. (1994) 'Connecting the voices', *Learning*, 6(4), p. 16.

Mason, R. (1994) *Using Communications Media in Open and Distance Learning*, London, Kogan Page.

May, S. (1994) 'Women's experience as distance learners: access and technology', *Journal of Distance Education*, 9(1), pp. 81–98.

Menzies, H. (1994a) 'Learning communities and the information highway', *Journal of Distance Education*, 9(1), pp. 1–16.

Menzies, H. (1994b) 'Hyping the highway: is the information highway the road to a common future or just another trip to the mall?', *Canadian Forum*, 73(830), pp. 3–8.

Merrill, M.D. (1991) 'Constructivism and instructional design', *Educational Technology*, 31(5), pp. 45–53.

Murphy, J. (1994) Unpublished paper.

Norton, P. (1992) 'When technology meets the subject matter, disciplines in education. Part 2: Understanding the computer as discourse', *Educational Technology*, 32, pp. 36–46.

Pittam, J. (1994) *Voice in Social Action*, Thousand Oaks, CA, Sage.

Post, P. (1994) Personal communication with author.

Postman, N. (1992) *Technopoly: The Surrender of Culture to Technology*, New York, Vintage.

Reigeluth, C. M. (1983) 'The elaboration theory of instruction' in Reigeluth, C. M. (ed.), *Instructional Design: Theories and Models*, Hillsdale, NJ, Erlbaum, pp. 335–82.

Shuell, T. J. (1988) 'The role of the student in learning from instruction', *Contemporary Educational Psychology*, 13, pp. 276–95.

Simpson, M. S. (1994) 'Neurophysiological considerations related to interactive multimedia', *Educational Technology Research and Development*, 42(1), pp. 75–81.

Spiro, R. J., Coulson, R. L., Feltovich, P. J. and Anderson, D. K. (1988) *Cognitive Flexibility Theory: Advanced Knowledge Acquisition in Ill-structured Domains*, Technical report no. 441, Champaign, IL, University of Illinois, Centre for the Study of Reading.

Tannen, D. (1994) 'Gender gap in cyberspace', *Newsweek*, 123(20), pp. 52–3.

Tuckman, B. and Jensen, M. (1977) 'Stages of small group development revisited', *Group and Organizational Studies*, 2, pp. 419–27.

Ullmer, E. J. (1994) 'Media and learning: are there two kinds of truth?', *Educational Technology Research and Development*, 42(1), pp. 21–32.

von Weiler, J. (1994) Unpublished paper and personal communication.

Wells, R. (1992) *Computer-mediated Communication for Distance Education: An International Review of Design, Teaching and Institutional Issues*, State College, PA, Pennsylvania State University, The American Centre for the Study of Distance Education.

Winn, W. (1990) 'Some implications of cognitive theory for instructional design', *Instructional Science*, 19, pp. 53–69.
Zucchermaglio, C. (1993) 'Toward a cognitive ergonomics of educational technology' in Duffy, T., Lowyck, J. and Jonassen, D. (eds).

16

USE OF HYPERMEDIA AND TELECOMMUNICATIONS FOR CASE-STUDY DISCUSSIONS IN DISTANCE EDUCATION

Alexander J. Romiszowski

INTRODUCTION

The particular focus of this chapter is on the effective implementation of group discussion, or 'conversational', methodologies on electronic telecommunications networks. This focus is particularly important, as we know much less about how to converse effectively on electronic networks, than we do about electronic self-instruction. There is a long history and fairly developed technology of the design, development and delivery of self-study materials in different (including electronic) media. There is much less known about the running of effective group-discussion sessions at a distance. Such teaching methods as seminars (where a group critiques and comments on a prepared paper or presentation) or case-studies (where groups exchange ideas on how to explain or deal with a problem situation) are traditionally implemented in small or medium-sized groups, led by skilled and experienced 'facilitators'. Much of the success of these teaching methods is ascribed to the facilitators and the skill with which they focus discussion, guide the approaches adopted by the participants, use the natural group dynamics to stimulate interest, participation and deep involvement, pull together what has been learned in the final debriefing discussion, and so on. Can such participatory discussion methods be effectively orchestrated at a distance? How might this be done? The answers to such questions are vital if we are to learn just how we can utilise the new electronic communication media for education and training.

TWO PARADIGMS COMPARED

To begin, let us review a little theory and also some of the research that is already available on this topic. To start with the theory, it may help to compare and contrast two alternative paradigms for teaching: the 'instructional' and the 'conversational' paradigms. These are summarised in tabular form in Table 16.1.

Table 16.1 Instruction vs conversation

Paradigm:	'Instruction'	'Conversation'
OBJECTIVES: (OUTPUT) (why?)	specific pre-defined products standard	general negotiable processes variable
MESSAGES: (INPUT) (what?) (when?) (who?) (whom?)	designed pre-prepared instructor one-to-many	created on-line participants many-to-many
INTERACTION: **(PROCESS)** (focus) (analysis) (feedback) (complexity)	behaviours criterion-ref corrective one-layer thick	ideas contents/structure constructive interwoven layers
DISTANCE EDUCATION: example	Correspondence courses	Teleconferencing Videoconferencing
	Computer-mediated Communication (CMC)	

The instructional paradigm is the one that has driven much (though by no means all) of the research and development of the past thirty years that has been performed under the label of educational (or instructional) technology. The conversational paradigm may be seen as the basis of much of the work done on small group work, group dynamics, experiential learning and so on.

In relation to distance teaching specifically, one may notice at the bottom of Table 16.1 that the conventional correspondence course model may serve as a good example of the instructional paradigm. Teleconferencing, both audio- and video-based, is on the other hand a good example of the conversational paradigm in action. So is computer-conferencing, as it is most commonly practised. Computer-mediated communication (CMC) is, however, able to support both conversational and instructional procedures. This 'versatility' of CMC is a potential advantage which is an addition to others mentioned in the literature, such as: asynchronous communication, ability to attract more and richer comments and contributions from students, a permanent record of study, including student comments and annotations, non-linear study, random access and so on.

PROBLEMS OF STRUCTURE AND CONTROL IN CMC

In order to give some background to the work reported here, it is necessary to mention, very briefly, some earlier work which attempted to use a simple, unstructured, electronic communication system for seminars at a distance. Two specific problems were observed. These were labelled the problems of *structure* and *control* (Romiszowski and Jost, 1989; Romiszowski and DeHaas, 1989).

The problem of structure is that participants who take part over a long time-period by occasionally logging on to an ongoing discussion on electronic mail have difficulty in maintaining an overall view of the content and structure of the previous discussion. The messages are received in chronological order and seldom is it clear to which previous messages they relate.

The problem of control refers to the ease or difficulty with which the seminar organiser can keep the participants on task. What tends to happen in this form of discussion over time is that most participants respond to messages as they read them, thus extending the discussion on some hot issue that someone else has just mentioned. If this issue happens to deviate from the originally intended discussion topic, the chances are that discussion will, from that point onwards, ignore the formally assigned task and wander ever further into other topics. Our observation in the electronic seminar was that it became more difficult to bring discussion back on track than would normally be the case in a conventional meeting.

Several similar electronic seminars were run, confirming that the problems of structure and control were inherent to the methodology. A review of the literature concerning educational computer-conferencing revealed that others had experienced similar problems. One way to diminish them that had been tried was to develop special software for computer-conferencing. It was for these reasons that we turned to hypercard, to experiment with ways of storing an electronic discussion in a structured manner.

A STRUCTURED CASE-STUDY DISCUSSION ENVIRONMENT

A methodology that depends heavily on relatively open-ended and rather 'deep' conversation between participants and course leaders is the case-study. The object of the case-study methodology is to engage the participants in analysis and evaluation of a given case, in order to develop their skills in handling a range of similar real-life situations later on, or, alternatively, to create a better and deeper understanding of the general principles that are illustrated by the facts of the case presented. Learning must go beyond the specific case itself in order to be useful. The key to the effectiveness of a case-study exercise is the quality of the case *discussion*, and this depends in turn on the quality of the case-discussion leader. One unfortunate result of this is that effective learning from case-study exercises is not always achieved. Also it is always instructor-intensive and, therefore, relatively expensive. This factor unduly limits the use of the case-study method. An approach to overcoming the frequent unavailability of a competent case-discussion leader, as well as increasing the efficiency of the available leaders, was implemented by means of a networked case-study discussion environment (Romiszowski, 1990). This is a 'hybrid' system that combines some of the best aspects of computer-based learning for presentation and initial discussion of the case materials, with some of the best aspects of computer-conferencing, to provide opportunities for reflective discussion of the deeper implications of the case, between various participants and a discussion leader who may be separated by both distance and time.

The computer-based learning element is constructed according to the principles of the 'Structural Communication' methodology of 'conversational self-instruction' (Hodgson, 1974; Egan, 1972; Romiszowski, 1986; Pusch and Slee, 1990). The structural communication methodology was an attempt to develop self-instruction techniques that would be valid and powerful enough to use on higher order learning objectives.

In order to promote such objectives, it is postulated that one must present stimulating initial learning materials, followed by a dialogue which will provide challenges to the learner to solve new and multi-faceted problems. This dialogue must be two-way (obviously) and highly personalised and interactive.

Such dialogue can be simulated in printed texts which, after presenting a basic reading assignment, pose a number of open-ended discussion problems (somewhat like essay questions). However, in order to respond, the reader, rather than structuring and writing the essay, would construct a sort of essay outline, by selecting the factors that make up the 'best case' or 'solution' from a long list (usually between twenty and thirty) of candidate statements.

Given a list of twenty or more items from which to make a selection of any number of items, the combinations run into many millions. The structural communication methodology handles the dialogue by means of a diagnostic tool called a *discussion guide* (like a small expert system) which directs the student to various feedback comments stored as a form of hypertext.

One early application of Structural Communication (SC) was a series of correspondence course units for top-level management decision-making, published in the *Harvard Business Review* and responded to voluntarily by a large body of the readership (Hodgson and Dill, 1970a, b; 1971). However, the technique did not get widely accepted. One contributory factor may have been the somewhat unwieldy search procedures that learners have to engage in when using the discussion guide and moving from comment to comment in a printed text. Of course, these difficulties pale into insignificance in the context of computer-based dialogue in a hypertext environment.

RESEARCH ON STRUCTURAL COMMUNICATION

Romiszowski *et al.* (1988a) examined the use of structural communication to increase the processing of information in a business simulation. They designed a structural communication unit for the purpose of 'debriefing' students in order to increase their processing of information. Students who participated in the structural communication debriefing exercise did, in fact, significantly improve their scores. This suggests that the structural communication debriefing helped learners to analyse the case information more effectively and thereby acted as an aid to deeper processing. A computer-based version of the debriefing exercise was developed (Romiszowski *et al.*,1988b).

In another study using mainframe technology to present a Structural Communication case-study in management information systems, Slee examined 'interactivity' and increasing learner interaction (Pusch and Slee, 1990). All learners were given the opportunity to make a comment after each question investigated. Finally, upon completion of the case-study, all learners commented to the instructor regarding the computer-based training experience via electronic mail. A significant number of students continued an 'academic dialogue' when they were given the opportunity to make a comment, arguing in response to the discussion comments received.

More recently, a structural communication shell has been developed in Hypercard which enables the selection of a variety of study units that may be presented automatically to the student. The shell also tracks exactly how the learner utilised the unit. A characteristic of this shell is that it allows for student-generated comments and insights to be added to the already prepared materials and to be shared between students and tutors as a form of an in-depth, student-generated seminar. This fusion of pre-designed study exercises with collaborative group discussion by e-mail has been further applied to the computer delivery of case-study methodology (Romiszowski and Chang, 1992).

The case-discussion network

The following section describes the use of a case-discussion environment, developed by Chang and now installed on the Syracuse University campus computer network. The system is fully reported elsewhere (Chang, in press).

When a student logs on to the network and selects the Activity 'Case Study', the business case is displayed in a scrollable field (Figure 16.1). By clicking the 'Next' button, the next phase called *investigation* presents a series of open-ended problems.

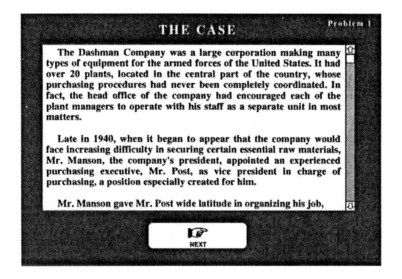

Figure 16.1 The Harvard business case in a scrollable field

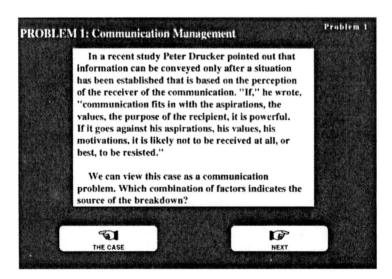

Figure 16.2 The problem

After each problem has been presented (Figure 16.2), students are introduced to the next and essential phase of SC methodology, the *response matrix* phase. The response matrix is a randomised array of items which summarise concepts or principles applicable to the case. The student composes a response by selecting any combination of these items as a 'best' response to the given problem (Figure 16.3).

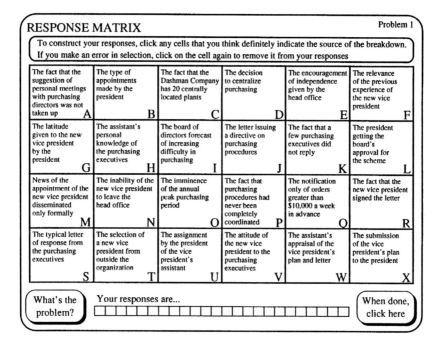

Figure 16.3 Response matrix

On clicking on a cell, the letter of the cell shows up in the designated place located at the bottom of the screen. When the student indicates completion by clicking the 'When done ...' button, a 'Discussion Guide' is presented. Based on student selections, the system recommends the reading of certain feedback comments located in a browsable hypertext environment.

The comments are constructive statements which discuss in depth the rationale for including or excluding certain items. After reading the comment, the student can return to the Discussion Guide card to read another comment. The reading of the comments completes the first activity.

The second activity is a group discussion of the finer points of the case. After reading any one of the set of expert's comments, students can type their own comments or reactions in another field. Since it is a scrollable field, students can type as much as they wish. When the student moves on, the system transfers anything typed in the student comment field to a field named 'DISCUSSION LOG'. As discussion among group members continues, the 'DISCUSSION LOG' field accumulates more information. But there is a separate discussion log for each separate aspect of the original case and its proposed solution. This enables students to maintain a sense of the structure of the overall discussion, while engaging in any one of the issues. In addition to keeping the DISCUSSION LOG files, the program also records data on students' performance.

CONCLUSION

The case-discussion environment described above is now regularly used to extend access to Harvard business cases to School of Management students at Syracuse University. In reality, as the case materials and the SC software are on the campus server and are accessible from any of the computers linked to the campus network, the materials are accessible to a much wider audience. The system is so configured as to automatically form separate small discussion groups of about six to ten participants, so as to maintain the characteristics of in-depth small-group work. Future developments involve the incorporation of multimedia in the presentation of the basic case information and the extension of access to the system via Internet. The system is seen as a prototype for future public-access case-discussion environments.

REFERENCES

Chang, E. (in press) 'Investigation of constructivist principles applied to collaborative study of business cases in computer-mediated communication', Doctoral dissertation, Syracuse University.

Egan, K. (1972) *Structural Communication*, Belmont, CA, Fearon Publishers.

Hodgson, A. M. (1974) 'Structural communication in practice' in Romiszowski, A. J. (ed.), *APLET Yearbook of Educational and Instructional Technology*, London, Kogan Page.

Hodgson, A. M. and Dill, W. R. (1970a) 'Programmed case: the misfired missive', *Harvard Business Review*, Sept/Oct, pp. 140–6.

Hodgson, A. M. and Dill, W. R. (1970b) 'Programmed case: sequel to the misfired missive', *Harvard Business Review*, Nov/Dec, pp. 105–10.

Hodgson, A. M. and Dill, W. R. (1971) 'Programmed case: reprise of the misfired missive', *Harvard Business Review*, Jan/Feb, pp. 140–5.

Pusch, W. S. and Slee, E. J. (1990) 'Structural communication: a forgotten application of cognitive theory to instruction', *Instructional Developments*, 1(2), Syracuse, NY, Syracuse University School of Education.

Romiszowski, A. J. (1986) *Developing Auto-instructional Materials*, London, Kogan Page.

Romiszowski, A. J. (1990) 'The case study methodology: interactive media and instructional design' in Klein, H. E. (ed.), *Problem Solving with Cases and Simulations*, Proceedings of the Seventh International Conference on Case Method Research and Case Method Application. Produced and distributed by the World Association for Case Method Research and Application (WACRA), Waltham, MA, Bentley College Press.

Romiszowski, A. J. and Chang, E. (1992) 'Hypertext's contribution to computer-mediated communication: in search of an instructional model' in Giardina, M. (ed.) *Interactive Multimedia Environments*, pp. 111–30, Heidelberg, Springer-Verlag.

Romiszowski, A. J. and DeHaas, J. (1989) 'Computer mediated communication or instruction: using e-mail as a seminar', *Educational Technology*, October.

Romiszowski, A. J., Grabowski, B. L. and Damadaran, B. (1988a) 'Structural communications, expert systems, and interactive video: a powerful combination for a nontraditional CAI approach', paper presented at the Meeting of the Association for the Development of Computer-Based Instructional Systems, Washington, DC.

Romiszowski, A. J., Grabowski, B. L. and Pusch, W. S. (1988b) 'Structural communication: a neglected CAI methodology and its potential for interactive video simulations', paper presented at the Meeting of the Association for the Development of Computer-Based Instructional Systems, Washington, DC.

Romiszowski, A. J. and Jost, K. (1989) 'Computer conferencing and the distance learner: problems of structure and control', paper presented at the 1989 Conference on Distance Education, University of Wisconsin.

Part V

COURSE DESIGN AND ASSESSMENT

17

THE CHALLENGE FACING COURSE DESIGN

Mary Thorpe

THE THEORETICAL CHALLENGE

The limitations of behaviourism, especially for conceptual learning and the development of critical understanding, are well rehearsed (Case and Bereiter, 1984; Winn, 1990). Course designers have, for two decades and more, been using a cognitive approach to learning and searching for ways in which learners can mobilise their existing knowledge and create new frameworks which integrate old and new learning in new forms of understanding. Advance organisers, in-text activities, tutor-marked assignments and project-based assessment are some of the approaches which assume a cognitive model of learning.

However, cognitive learning theory is itself under challenge from evidence that learning involves more than the construction and manipulation of mental models. Social constructivism has reconstructed the theoretical status of the social milieu of the learner and its role in learning. It has been recognised that social context, roles and relationships are central to what is learned and how learning occurs, rather than merely a source of distorting effects on the learner–stimulus event (Carugati and Gilly, 1993).

Winn (1990) also draws upon extensive research which demonstrates that the way in which people solve problems is very context-dependent and that human reasoning does not conform to the models of logic embedded in mathematical or philosophical analysis. He draws on Collins' idea of 'plausible reasoning' as a more appropriate interpretation of how people think in everyday situations, and points to the importance of non-logical processes such as intuition and perception (Collins, 1978; Streibel, 1989). When we add to this the evidence that learners can and do make their own decisions about the nature of a learning task and the most appropriate strategy for them to use on a task (Laurillard, 1978), we are faced with a conceptualisation of learning as dynamic and, in many ways, unpredictable. The idea that courses can be designed in advance so as to work *equally* effectively with successive cohorts of learners, is undermined by this.

The purpose of course design

Course designers are therefore faced not only with the challenge of finding new ways of teaching, but with a reconsideration of what their purpose is, or ought to be. We have also seen the rise during the 1980s of the concept of facilitating learning which has attained such popularity that teaching and its role threatens to be displaced by the idea of the management of learning. The goal of facilitating learning has been to support the development of independent learning which, though conceptualised variously, includes a core aim that learners in effect become able to teach themselves. This is a desirable and an appropriate goal for higher education, but it also has some dangers associated with it. Some of these arise from the tendency for one prescriptive model to be replaced by another. In place of a transmission model of teaching we now have the facilitation of learning, which may in practice take on a variety of less than satisfactory forms. It is all too possible, for example, to hand back to the learner all the responsibility for what and how to learn, while retaining all the power to judge whether or not such learning has been successful.

The other source of danger in shifting attention wholly away from teaching and on to learning, is that we know as yet too little about the process of how confident independence is achieved, and about the proper role of teaching in that process. There may be a danger that the learner is effectively abandoned at a stage when they lack the grasp of large-scale structures of knowledge and of advanced study skills, both of which are necessary prerequisites for complete independence at the higher education level (Lisewski, 1994).

We need to develop procedures and approaches which generate learning and develop self-aware learners and which also avoid either giving learners all the responsibility and no power, or leaving them to sink or swim. It will not be enough merely to provide the extensive multimedia resources which are being introduced in many institutions of higher education. Laurillard has argued, for example, that the rich resources of a CD-ROM or an interactive videodisc are only as good as the enquiry frameworks that the learner brings to them (Laurillard, 1993). She proposes a model of learning which requires both interaction and reflection by the learner and the provision of feedback from a teacher who is able to frame and reframe the content of teaching to take into account both subject matter and student response.

Laurillard situates her model of the academic learning process firmly in the category of mediated learning, and different in kind from experiential learning. Here I would sound a note of caution against the dualism this suggests, of two categorically distinct modes of learning. Even in the context of higher education, learning is about more than the development of ever more sophisticated mental frameworks, difficult and subtle a process as this is. Higher learning also involves the person, the experience that the person brings to the higher learning context, and the experience that that person has during the learning process, whatever form it takes. If course design is going to reframe its purpose to include that of facilitating learning, it cannot ignore the issue of learner identity, the social context in which learning takes place, and the quality of awareness learners bring to their own learning.

Self-evidently this is a considerable challenge for distance education practice which is predicated on the finalisation of teaching material in advance of its use. Winn (1990) argues that the unpredictability of learning requires that courses be delivered by human tutors, tutors moreover who have the skills of the instructional designer to respond to learner reactions and to generate modifications to the original design of materials. Winn's conclusion is that to continue with attempts to perfect instruction in advance, on the assumption that what has been shown to work effectively with one group will continue to work as effectively with others, is inescapably flawed as a strategy. His recommendations, as an alternative way forward, include emphasising evaluation and the development of instructional materials throughout their use, and working directly out of a base in learning theories rather than from a 'principles of instructional design' approach. Any attempt to 'read off' from theory, principles which can be applied confidently, whatever the context, is likely to lead to less effective provision than a continual return to theory to create the best 'fit' for a particular programme with particular students. Winn effectively rejects the principles approach as a reductionist strategy for instructional design:

> A complete theory, having predictive power, allows new rules to be invented when they are needed. Schon (1983) has called this invention process 'reflection in action' and characterises it as a kind of spontaneous research ... To succeed then, instructional designs need to be made while instruction is under way and need to be based on complete theories that allow the generation of prescriptions rather than on predetermined sets of prescriptions chosen ahead of time by a designer.
>
> (Winn, 1990)

THE PRACTICAL IMPLICATIONS

Reconstructing the role of course delivery

The implications for distance education materials are not difficult to derive from this critique. Although Winn does not reject task analysis and pre-specified instruction wholesale, he does advocate the extension of instructional design to the stage when students are using course materials. This would significantly modify the current assumption that instructional design is more effectively concentrated in the production stage of materials development. This means both that 'teachers' (i.e. those in direct contact with students as they use course materials) need to monitor student progress and intervene to modify the prescribed instructional strategies, when students

177

meet unforeseen difficulties. It also means that after implementation instructional designers themselves need to monitor the use of the systems they design (Winn, 1990, pp. 64–5). Winn's view is that 'instructional decisions need to be made while instruction is under way' and therefore that 'human teachers or trainers will deliver instruction'.

Winn's account reads almost like a rationale for the UK Open University's system of local tuition – almost, but not quite. His tutor or teacher role resembles more the on-site engineer, able to step in and adjust the pedagogical machinery of the course, the better to meet user needs. However, The Open University tutor has a direct *teaching relationship* with his or her students, or as it was put in 1979:

> The tutor stands in the key and difficult position of one who perceives the interest and requirements of both course team and students. It is the tutor who must articulate these different requirements and establish a dialogue between them; ... understanding ... requires interpretation and ... the tutor's role as interpreter is a powerful and significant one for students.
>
> (Thorpe, 1979)

It is the course team during course presentation or use which comes closest to the on-site engineer role, and which ought, following Winn's prescription, to receive sufficient resource – and recognition – for its role in developing the course beyond production, and jointly with the students who enrol on it.

Applying progressive theory to course design

Winn rightly argues against 'design by numbers' and advocates a continual return to theory as the creative source of new approaches to instruction. The question is, what theory? One starting-point is the phenomenographic approach, which proposes that how learners conceptualise a learning task constitutes a phenomenon which influences their learning and which ought therefore to be taken into account in the content and process of teaching. The study of learners' conceptions and misconceptions about an area of study, has produced important insights about their learning which have led to significant revisions by course designers of their assumptions about what learners know and how they react to the tasks set for them in course materials (see, for example, McCracken and Laurillard, 1994). Such insights may operate in an inspirational fashion for the teacher/designer, who, having seen deeply into the thinking and imagination of a small number of students is sensitised to the *potential* for misconstruction and misunderstanding among the hundreds (perhaps thousands) of students who will use the finished material in future. This sensitivity is vital, and may ensure that a course is produced which works well generally, as far as we can see, using the evidence of student feedback and examination success.

Discourse theory is also being used to inform approaches to course design in the arts and social sciences. It has been used to illuminate the process whereby learners move from a starting-point in everyday language, to a point where they are using the language of a discipline with confidence. Northedge suggests that distance education materials have successfully provided simplified versions of an academic discourse and thus created frameworks within which students can develop confident and independent use of the language of the discipline (Northedge, 1994).

These are important theoretical foundations out of which new approaches can be developed to the role of teaching through course design, oriented towards more effective development of understanding and conceptual change. However, neither discourse theory nor phenomenography address issues noted earlier, around learner identity and the quality of the learning process experienced during study.

Course design oriented to the learning process

The reconstruction of course design so that it embodies a more sophisticated conception of teaching, is a considerable advance and one which will surely be elaborated further as multimedia configurations are developed for distance teaching. However, this is still not enough. If it is indeed impossible to foresee and to forestall all the misunderstandings and problems that learners will experience, course designers need to respond strategically to the implications of this for effective learning. They need to address the existence of a process of learning running in parallel with their teaching process, and a person who is learning and managing that process alongside the many other events and narratives of everyday life.

One type of strategic response is to argue, as Winn has done, that instruction should always involve a person at the point of delivery or presentation. Such a conviction was part of the educational strategy of the UK OU from the start (Perry, 1976, pp. 115–18), and led to the establishment of an extensive programme of person-to-person tutorial support, at a distance and (to a modest extent) face-to-face. I would argue, however, that, even where such tutorial interaction exists, course designers should also have a strategy for *recognising and supporting the student's process of learning* and the quality of their experience of learning as the teaching and instructional programme proceeds. The need for such a strategy follows directly from the conclusion that course design and instruction can achieve at best a good enough but not a perfect fit for successive cohorts of students, and thus that students themselves need to be pro-active in recognising their own learning difficulties and taking appropriate action to keep their own learning process alive and effective.

Social relationships and learning

I believe that neither discourse theory nor phenomenography adequately recognises what is involved for the learner in doing this, in fulfilling their side of the bargain on the road to achieving independence in learning and deep learning outcomes. Learning requires not only conceptual development and skill in learning, but an ability to manage the self as learner and the social relationships through which learning occurs. There is a categorical difference between, for example, 'interaction' and 'relationship'. The one need not involve any knowledge of us as a person – one can interact with a software program designed for that purpose, for example. A relationship, however slight, involves knowledge of another and resonances with our existing experiences of relationships, especially those of teacher and learner with all their emotional baggage of being judged and experiencing success and failure.

Although interpersonal relationships are not what I want to focus on here, the issue of teacher–learner relationship is still relevant even where course instruction is limited to text. Rowntree and others have written tellingly of the influence of written style in recreating a 'virtual relationship' via the tutorial in print. Personality and an atmosphere of open-minded friendly guidance *can* be mediated, and thus create the conditions for open-minded involvement by the learner (Rowntree, 1986; Holmberg, 1989; Thorpe, 1993a).

Study skills

Course designers, however, have not often progressed beyond this. Learner identity and self-management have either gone unrecognised or been left to the realm of local tuition and support, if such exists. The exception to this has been study skills where student difficulties have often been recognised but the responsibility for positive action located elsewhere – either with the student who is recommended preparatory study, or with specialist study skills courses. One notable and honourable exception to this has been the OU Technology Foundation Course, which embeds study skills teaching and awareness-raising 'inside' the course teaching itself. Guidance on the processes required to study the course materials successfully – and reflection on their use – is the focus of a strand of commentary and activities which are presented alongside the content-specific course texts themselves, identifiable by the use of different coloured ink and given equal status in the teaching. The development of study skills is also made an explicit aim of the course itself.

The embedding of study skills (rather than separate teaching in 'add-on' courses) is a progressive strategy in relation to students' perception of what the skills are and their importance. Study skills, however, remains an area where increases in ability are not easily achieved and convincing evidence that improvements are the result of study skills teaching is difficult to provide. Study skills are to some extent an expression of more general approaches, which reflect differences of personality as well as prior experience or its lack. Such differences are not likely to be changed by short-term bursts of practice which address isolated techniques. Morgan and Beaty (1992) have reported on the ways in which students hold general orientations to study which appear to be linked to actual practices, whether deep, surface or more strategic. These general orientations can change and become both more sophisticated and more integrated with personal change throughout extended study.

Learner identity and self-management

An orientation to study may change for a variety of reasons, some of which may be open to influence from course design. In addition, the process of studying involves for most adults various changes in behaviour, involving the breaking of existing habits of spending time, to fit in the new course-related activities. Students are involved in self- and environment management in order to achieve this, with numerous decisions, many of them taken with little or no structured thought. Taken together, the existence of general prior orientations to study, with (more or less) semi-conscious attempts to manage the self during study, mean that many students feel a degree of powerlessness when it comes to their own learning. One strategy which course designers can adopt in this context, is to encourage students to develop heightened awareness of the self as learner, acknowledging also that what must be managed for effective study includes not only a different use of personal time and space, but strong feelings, both positive and negative, with accompanying changes in self-esteem.

This may feel like a much more risky strategy than that of integrating study skills. Much less of substance is on offer; no techniques or detailed step-by-step approaches. The contribution comes from a process of *legitimation for the student of how it feels to learn*, and strategies for *increasing awareness of one's own learning process, the better to shape it.* Candy *et al.* (1985) have put forward the idea of a learning conversation, in which the tutor initiates discussion about the learner's perception of their own learning experiences. With practice, such conversations should be internalised so that learners can develop their learning practices for themselves, through internal dialogue. These insights have also been applied to the distance education context.

A number of OU courses, for example, have drawn on Schon's work on reflective practice and used the concept of reflection as a focal point for student activities and review of learning goals and progress (Thorpe, 1993b). Several have encouraged students to use writing to capture thoughts and feelings about course-related learning, building up a personal portfolio or learning file alongside study of course materials. This approach is currently being used in a suite of new and innovative courses for mathematics foundation level study.

Evaluation of two courses which have implemented such a learning process orientation (Thorpe, 1993b) provides evidence of the potential of distance study in this respect, building on the centrality of assessment for student learning and motivation which has been well established in numerous prior studies (Marton *et al.*, 1984). The commitment to learning development as well as understanding new subject-based knowledge needs to be an *explicit course aim*, embedded in the teaching as a whole. It should also be localised in explanations and discussions which communicate the reasons for and the arguments in favour of an emphasis on the *process of* students' own learning as well as on course content.

As important as the generation of such material is that the course team or instructional designer creates space for students to reflect on their own learning in ways which encourage them to 'think out' to their own histories and current circumstances. This resembles the creation of a 'window' for reflection which has elements both of time and space. Thus students will not reflect on the outcomes and the processes of their own learning if they are overwhelmed by course material which they perceive must take priority. Study time must be calculated to include time for reflection; space must also be created in the sense of creating areas of the course where reflection is required and is discussed and legitimated. In the courses which were evaluated, these areas are built around two elements in the main: first, there are course materials which set activities stimulating students' reflection on their own learning processes; second, reflection is built in to the tasks and marking criteria specified in the assignment (Thorpe, 1994).

CONCLUSION

The evidence of evaluation of this strategy of active reflection on and support for the students' own learning process suggests that, as we would expect, some students are more profoundly affected than others by the emphasis on reflection (Thorpe, 1994). The majority, however, have expressed personal outcomes in the area of new awareness and approaches to their own learning. There is also considerable, unprompted evidence of the transfer of this learning to other contexts of study, work and personal life, as this interview extract makes clear:

'... I think the other thing that has been interesting is that I have also passed on some of the work I did through my teaching in that I am getting the adults that I work with to reflect on their learning ... Well I think particularly the whole thing about experiential learning and learning cycles and that kind of work goes down very well because it can be easily grasped by people, and for adults I think there is a sort of enthusiasm to understand about their own learning. It puts them more in control so, certainly the two groups that I have done some work on this with were very responsive to it.'

(an associate student, already a graduate but new to the OU; quoted in Thorpe, 1994)

We do not advocate a formula approach for a 'new direction' in course design, based on reflection. Each course team or instructional designer has to face anew the creative task of working out how an explicit emphasis on the students' own learning processes can be expressed through the course in hand. That goal, however, is a new point of departure, since ability to learn, ability to develop as a learner, has always been assumed to happen automatically, as a by-product of effective study of a discourse of texts or of laboratory and seminar experience.

The approaches discussed here also suggest that course designers should work *with the grain* of the known pressures on students, of time and of the wish to succeed in the assignment process. It also suggests that learners will need to be convinced that reflection on learning is both legitimated by the course as a whole, and leads to rewarding outcomes related both to course content and to learning abilities of general personal value. These are ambitious goals, but it has been demonstrated that such goals are not beyond the capacities of teachers and instructional designers in distance education.

REFERENCES

Boud, D., Cohen, R. and Walker, D. (eds) (1993a) *Using Experience for Learning*, Buckingham, Open University Press.

Boud, D., Cohen, R. and Walker, D. (1993b) 'Experiential learning at a distance' in Boud, D., Cohen, R. and Walker, D. (eds).

Candy, P., Harri-Augstein, S. and Thomas, L. (1985) 'Reflection and the self organised learner: a model of learning conversations' in Boud, D., Keogh, R. and Walker, D. (eds) *Reflection: Turning Experience into Learning*, London, Kogan Page.

Carugati, F. and Gilly, M. (1993) 'The multiple sides of the same tool: cognitive development as a matter of social constructions and meanings', *European Journal of Psychology of Education*, (8)4.

Case, R. and Bereiter, C. (1984) 'From behaviourism to cognitive behaviourism to cognitive development: steps in the evolution of instructional design', *Instructional Science*, 13, pp. 141–58.

Collins, A. (1978) *Studies in Plausible Reasoning: Final Report*, October 1976 to February 1978, Vol. 1: *Human Plausible Reasoning*, BBN Report No. 3810, Cambridge, MA, Bolt, Beranek and Newman.

Holmberg, B. (1989) *The Theory and Practice of Distance Education*, London, Routledge.

Laurillard, D. (1978) *A Study of the Relationship Between Some of the Cognitive and Contextual Factors in Student Learning*, PhD thesis, University of Surrey.

Laurillard, D. (1993) *Rethinking University Teaching*, London, Routledge.

Lisewski B. (1994) 'The Open Learning Pilot Project at the Liverpool Business School', *Open Learning*, 9(2).

McCracken, J. and Laurillard, D. (1994) *A Study of Conceptions in Visual Representation: A Phenomenographic Investigation of Learning about Geological Maps*, OU/CITE Report 196.

Marton, F., Hounsell, D. and Entwistle, N. (eds) (1984) *The Experience of Learning*, Edinburgh, Scottish Academic Press.

Morgan, A. and Beaty, E. (1992) 'Developing skill in learning', *Open Learning*, 7(3).

Northedge, A. (1994) 'Making open learning work at access level' in Thorpe, M. and Grugeon, D. (eds) *Open Learning in the Mainstream*, Harlow, Longman.

Perry, W. (1976) *The Open University*, Milton Keynes, Open University Press.

Rowntree, D. (1986) *Teaching Through Self-Instructions: A Practical Handbook for Course Developers*, London, Kogan Page.

Schon, D. (1983) *The Reflective Practitioner*, London, Temple Smith.

Streibel, M. J. (1989) 'Instructional plan and situated learning: the challenge of Suchman's theory of situated action for instructional designers and instructional systems', paper presented at the annual meeting of the Association for Educational Communication and Technology, Dallas, Texas.

Thorpe, M. (1979) 'When is a course not a course?', *Teaching at a Distance*, Winter, pp. 13–18.

Thorpe, M. (1993a) 'Experiential learning at a distance' in Boud, D., Cohen, R. and Walker, D. (eds) (1993a).

Thorpe, M. (1993b) 'Reflective learning at a distance' in *Research in Relation to New Developments in Distance Education Materials*, Heerlen, The Netherlands, Open universiteit.

Thorpe, M. (1994) *The Evaluation of EH266 Learning Through Life: Education and Training Beyond School: First Year of Presentation*, TCC Report No. 78, Institute of Educational Technology, Milton Keynes, The Open University.

Winn, W. D. (1990) 'Some implications of cognitive theory for instructional design', *Instructional Science*, 19, pp. 53–69.

18

A MODEL-BASED DESIGN APPROACH FOR THE FLEXIBILISATION OF COURSES

Martin M. A. Valcke and Guillaume P. W. Vuist

CONTEXT: DISTANCE EDUCATION, OPENNESS AND LEARNING MATERIALS

The Open universiteit (Ou) of the Netherlands develops and provides higher distance education for adults. Apart from the age level of 18, no constraints are put forward as entry requirements. This results in a student population with a very heterogeneous profile: differences in aptitudes, study intentions, prior knowledge levels, prior educational levels, motivation and so on. Students are free to set their own pace and study completely independently; there is little contact between the student and the institution.

Considering this distinctive approach to distance education, the quality of the educational products and processes is of prime importance. In this perspective the Ou learning materials play the key role in fulfilling the learning objectives of students. The learning materials produced by the Dutch Open university are mainly text-based. They consist of printed study books in which the basic content is enriched with embedded support devices (ESD), such as advance organisers, pre- and post-questions, tasks, content pages, indexes, margin texts, examples, schemes, etc. These support devices are designed to motivate and activate the student to access the study content, to process the content and to test their own mastery of the course objectives. Embedded support devices comprise up to 40–45 per cent of the content of the printed learning materials.

THE NEED FOR FLEXIBILITY: PROBLEM STATEMENT

The learning materials are designed to cover a broad set of learning objectives so that they can be used for a large group of potential students. The learning materials are evaluated for their quality and relevance to the individual learning processes of students. However, the traditional approach to designing learning material is not compatible with the idea of providing flexible, demand-driven education (Kirschner and Valcke, 1994) and tailor-made learning materials. As indicated above, due to the openness of our educational system the student population is very heterogeneous, thus making demand-driven education and tailor-made learning materials even more important.

Another problem associated with the production and exploitation of learning materials is economic. The efficiency of these processes, in terms of production time, the ease of revising existing materials, the opportunities to re-use materials for different purposes (e.g. commercial exploitation) is questioned.

Developing learning materials that meet the requirement of flexibility, necessitates that a course development team pay explicit attention to their 'design'. In this chapter we focus on the design features that require course developers to adapt a 'model-based' design approach for learning materials. This results in a collection of learning materials that can be used in a much more flexible way than the current Ou learning materials allow. The design approach we propose is embedded in a computerised environment that we are currently developing. This system is used for the whole life-cycle of learning materials (i.e. design, maintenance and delivery). We have termed this system an *Interactive Learning and Course-development Environment* (ILCE). Since the learning materials are stored digitally, their multimedia characteristics can be enhanced. Moreover, their electronic availability serves as a starting-point to realise a computational interactive learning environment.

REPRESENTING LEARNING MATERIAL IN ILCE

In an ILCE, learning material is stored as a large collection of isolated small units of learning material and a tailor-made course is defined as a selection of a number of units out of this collection with a particular student in mind. Besides the units of learning material, there is an explicit *course model* that encompasses the necessary knowledge about making valid selections. A *repository* is a course model and the associated learning materials; it consists of a *domain model*, a *didactical model* and an *attribute model*.

The domain model

A domain model is a semantic network of the content of the subject domain covered by the learning material. A semantic network consists of nodes and directed links between nodes, representing the relationships (Sowa, 1991).

In a domain model a node represents a particular topic within the subject domain. It serves as an abstract representation of the actual units of learning material, where a unit is a structural entity comprising basic content and a number of embedded support devices. A unit provides the learning material which covers the topic represented by that node. Since a unit of learning material can basically cover more than just a single topic, the question arises as to how a unit should be linked to the domain model. We make a distinction between leaf nodes (i.e. nodes at the bottom of the hierarchy) and intermediate nodes. An intermediate node can be regarded as an organising node, linking a number of subnodes. It points to a unit that discusses the relationship between subtopics (e.g. by introducing common terms, listing differences between subtopics etc.). A unit elaborating one of these subtopics is linked to a subnode in the hierarchy, which can be either an organising node or a leaf node. A unit which points to a leaf node deals with a single topic in the domain. Figure 18.1 shows a domain model in the domain of statistics.

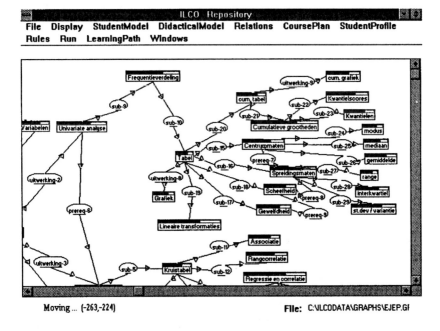

Figure 18.1 A part of a domain model for statistics

Typical relations that appear in a domain model are, for instance, *consists of, subtheme, follows, is a precondition for*. Besides relating units of learning materials, the relations are used to impose a learning path on a selected set of nodes. In production rules associated to the domain model, knowledge about a learning path is formalised.

The didactical model

A didactical model defines what kind of embedded support devices (e.g. a question, a scheme, an illustration, an exercise) can appear in a unit. To each node a didactical model can be linked, but for efficiency reasons a default didactical model is defined for the complete domain model.

The attribute model

The relevant student characteristics are described in terms of attributes such as profession, prior knowledge, content domains and diploma line. These attributes are not a fixed set but can differ for different domain models; the attribute model lists these attributes and their possible values. In an ILCE an attribute acts as a variable with a particular value for a student as well as for a node in the domain model. By matching student variables to node variables, a topic (i.e. a node) can be linked to a particular student.

SYSTEM ARCHITECTURE OF AN ILCE

From a user's point of view, the architecture of an ILCE can be described in terms of three environments that interact with a repository: a *building environment*, a *selection environment* and a *delivery environment*.

The building environment

In the building environment a course team creates a new repository or revises an already existing one; it adopts a model-based design approach. (Later we elaborate on the design tasks of a course team.)

The selection environment

A student interacts in *the selection environment* with the ILCE-system. This process is a negotiation in which the student is prompted to enter her/his personal study needs and requirements. This information is stored in a *student profile*. During the negotiation process the attribute, domain and didactical models are dynamically retrieved from the repository. On the basis of the student profile, a student receives advice on the most suitable set of available learning materials in the repository. These are subsequently retrieved from the repository.

At this stage, an 'individualised course' is generated for that particular student.

The delivery environment

The *delivery environment* is the environment where the student will work (study) with the selected set of learning materials (the individualised course). Two main types of delivery are supported: printed delivery and/or interactive delivery; the two modes can be combined.

Printed delivery, i.e. printing-on-demand, is a first level in tailoring courses to the needs of students. At the Dutch Open university this kind of delivery is particularly interesting for commercial exploitation of repositories by combining subparts into new multidisciplinary courses for specific clients (saving banks, industrial companies, etc.).

In the interactive delivery a student makes use of a computational environment to study the learning materials. The interaction with the system tailors the learning material to the needs of students. These needs can vary according to a specific stage in one's study process: at the start of the process, students need to be able to browse and to travel through the materials. At a later stage they may want to approach the materials from an evaluation point of view. These examples reveal that the interaction with the embedded support devices is vital in this environment. A student can, for example, construct study modes (browse mode, test mode, rehearsal mode, etc.) to work through the materials. Also it is possible to link the ILCE-system to other computer applications (e.g. electronic mail or simulation programs).

FOCUSING ON THE MODEL-BASED DESIGN APPROACH: THE BUILDING ENVIRONMENT

A course builder has basically two tasks to perform in the building environment: (a) defining the course model, and (b) developing the concrete learning materials. Since the course model serves as an index to the actual learning material, it should be obvious that the design of the repository should start with the first task. But once a partly constructed domain model is available, the course builder can start developing learning materials for already defined nodes. The system supports iterative refinement of the attribute and didactical models.

In order to give a detailed account of the design process we present a scenario in terms of a sequence of subtasks. This scenario should be considered for exposition purposes only; once a course team has gained experience with working in the building environment, they will carry out their design tasks in a much more iterative and dynamic fashion than the scenario suggests.

A scenario of working with the building environment

Step 1 Defining the course content

Initially the course team develops a domain model. The system supports this task by providing a graphics editor to construct a network on the screen. The result of this task is a domain model such as the one depicted in Figure 18.1, which lays down the topics that will be covered in the learning materials.

Step 2 Defining the attribute model

In this task the relevant student characteristics that generate a tailor-made course are defined in terms of a number of attributes. The following example shows the attributes linked to the domain 'Statistics':

attribute	values
diploma line	economic, technical and social sciences
prior knowledge of mathematics	high or low prior knowledge

These attributes are in the selection environment used as selection criteria. When a particular student enters the selection environment, s/he can enter values for the specific selection criteria 'diploma line' and 'prior knowledge of mathematics'.

Step 3 Defining the didactical model

A set of embedded support devices (ESD) (for example, a question, a scheme, an illustration, an exercise) is defined as a default to be used in relation to each node. This default set appears in the template for elaborating learning materials for a node (see Step 5).

Step 4 Relating domain, attribute and didactical model

We can indicate that, at the level of the course model, different examples, tasks or cases will be elaborated for three different diploma lines. A typical case is statistics where different 'examples and exercises' are available for economics, social science and technical science students. If, at a later stage, students study these materials and indicate their specific diploma line, they only get ESD that follow their specific diploma line, mathematics prior knowledge, and so on.

As suggested earlier, production rules can also be elaborated. These rules can, for instance, link attributes to specific types of relations between nodes. Due to the complex nature of this type of activity, we will not elaborate this further in this context.

Step 5 Developing learning materials

This task consists of elaborating the concrete learning materials. The model-based decisions associated with a node are automatically translated into a template for a unit of learning material. If, for instance, alternative examples and questions are foreseen for three different diploma lines, the system will indicate this in a template. The system can monitor the input from the course developers in terms of, for example, consistency and completeness. There is also a facility to import data from external sources and to revise already developed learning materials. Figure 18.2 depicts an early version of such a template-driven environment.

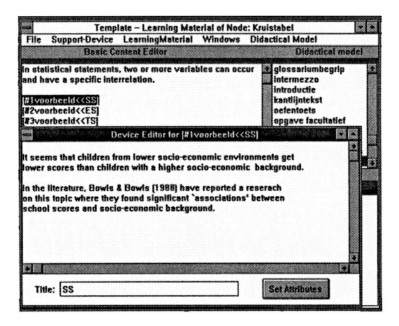

Figure 18.2 Template for elaborating learning materials

191

Step 6 Testing the repository on a particular student profile

In an ILCE, course-builders can test the extent to which the model they have developed works. They can, for instance, define a particular student and ask the system to show what nodes in the domain will be selected.

RELATED RESEARCH

The model-based design approach, outlined above, is in line with recent theoretical and empirical developments in a variety of research contexts. To orient the reader, we summarise some of the typical work in these contexts. Between brackets we indicate where parallels with our work can be found; our aim is to be illustrative not exhaustive within the literature available.

Interactive learning environments

An immediate ILCE-related research context is the area of *interactive learning environments*. Mispelkamp and Sarti (1994) discuss, for instance, the design tool DISCourse where the design focuses on:

- learner modelling where relevant learner attributes and their values are stated (attribute model);
- instructional strategies that focus on the selection of relevant instructional libraries such as examples, tasks, questions, feedback, maps, diagrams (didactical model);
- domain authoring which introduces a domain analysis, learning goal analysis and content analysis (content model).

Merrill, Li and Jones (1990) stress the importance of both a knowledge representation model and knowledge about the learner. The first is inspired by work in the field of semantic data modelling (domain model). The second is realised by adding information about the student's aptitudes, goals and/or previous instruction which will help to filter the most relevant learning materials in a delivery environment (attribute model).

Authoring environments

The activities undertaken in the building environment complement work supported in *authoring environments*.

Ulloa (1994) describes a procedural technique that is in line with the ILCE approach. Of importance is her subdivision between building a 'representation' and elaborating the concrete learning materials. As to the first cluster of activities, she refers to 'Content Definition' (domain model), 'Learner Model Definition' (attribute model) and 'Instructional Strategy

192

Definition', 'Learning Objectives Definition' and 'User Interface Definition' which to a certain extent are to be related to our didactical model.

Lee (1994) introduces a comparable representation model for authoring systems. He distinguishes between a macro and a micro structure. The macro structure is a threaded acyclic directed graph comparable to our semantic network approach. Nodes in the graph correspond to topics in a course and can refer to subtopic pointers ('children nodes'). Each node is also a content pointer which introduces the micro-structure. This is again a network of nodes connected by links. This network can be compared to our didactical model since the nodes are objects with specific didactical functions: presentation objects (basic content) versus elaboration objects, problem anchors, and so on.

Hypercourseware

Thirdly, there is a strong relationship between the ILCE approach and *Hypercourseware* where the focus is, on the one hand, on learner control and, on the other, on the availability of a large knowledge base (cf. Mayes *et al.*, 1990; Thompson *et al.*, 1992). The term 'Hypercourseware' is used to envelop software products which provide some combination of hypertext capabilities. This concept is used in literature to refer to examples such as HyperCard™, SuperCard™, LinkWay™, Guide™, Toolbook™ and Plus™.

Reed (1994) elaborates the latter and explicitly mentions 'semantic networks, concept maps, frames/scripting and schema theories' as theoretical frameworks for Hypercourseware. The 'Concept Mapping Tool' of Reader and Hammond (1994) and the 'Concept Map Metaphor' of McAleese (1990) repeat the opinion of this author when connecting the structure of the domain to the way in which students gain insight into the structure of their knowledge. O'Donnell (1994) set up an experiment that supports the relevance of such knowledge maps.

Adaptive instruction environments

The work of Arshad and Kelleher (1993) introduces the link between model-based design in the ILCE approach and *adaptive instruction environments*. Based on a review of the literature they put forward three selection processes that are basic to these systems:

1 Identification and sequencing of the curriculum.
2 Choosing appropriate goals, policies, materials that will aid learning.
3 Matching to characteristics of the student.

When designing a system, these authors explicitly introduce a 'domain representation' (content model) and a student model (attribute model), next to navigation provisions and the database of teaching materials.

Intelligent tutoring environments

A final, related research context is the field of *Intelligent Tutoring Systems* (ITS) which relates to topic flexibility. Larkin and Chabay (1992) mention, for instance, the possibility of adapting 'instruction to individual student knowledge'.

Grandbastien and Gavignet (1994) criticise the fact that in relation to ITS no authoring environments are widely accepted and even available. They mention reasons for this fact and present a solution to deal with the problem. In their work they concentrate on a formal model for the description of materials and a knowledge-based system using this model (semantic-network approach).

An interesting parallel is between an ILCE and ITS is presented by McCalla (1992) where she links the possibilities to adapt, to realise flexibility and individualisation to the design approach of the curriculum. In her overview the semantic network metaphor is predominantly present in most systems and approaches discussed: for example, 'Genetic Graph', 'And/Or Course Graph', 'Knowledge model' of 'TAPS', the 'Content Knowledge Base' in 'PEPE', and so on. But she also states that the curriculum representation cannot be isolated from other system components. She stresses in particular the importance of the student model (attribute model). Together with Greer, the same author elaborates the concept of student modelling in relation to intelligent tutoring environments as a key to individualised knowledge-based instruction (Greer and McCalla, 1994). This ITS-approach can be considered as the prevailing one as described in the literature (Yazdani, 1987). But, the concept of 'student model' is in the ITS-perspective more dynamic than in the ILCE-approach. Holt, Dubs, Jones and Greer (1994) indicate clearly that a student model in the ITS-viewpoint successively changes and affects continuously the delivery of learning materials.

Our approach as reflected in the design of the building environment of the ILCE seems to incorporate and integrate basic features of a wide variety of instructional technology applications. As stated earlier, the model-based design approach is a starting-point to realise the desired flexibility.

USER EXPERIENCES, FUTURE PERSPECTIVES AND CONCLUSIONS

Several prototypes of subparts of an ILCE-system have been elaborated. In 1993–4 research has focused on testing the functionalities of the environments described above. The results can be summarised as follows:

- *Building environment and repository environment.* Course models for courses from four different content domains have been defined with the system – cultural, social, technical and law sciences. These experiences showed that the approach is thus general and that specific course models could be defined and represented.
- *Selection environment.* Based on an inventory of relevant attributes (student variables) for the four content domains, a prototype showed that it was possible to exploit the course models, resulting in a satisfactory selection profile.
- *Delivery environment.* A prototype to support interactive delivery has been developed and tested in a variety of university settings, exploiting a repository of learning materials in the statistics domain. Research work at the University of Utrecht (Holland) and the University of Gent (Belgium) provided empirical data which indicate the effectiveness and efficiency of interactive learning environments. The possibility of interacting with the embedded support devices was a focus of these studies. The positive impact on learning outcomes was related to specific student characteristics. These outcomes support the need to strengthen the interaction possibilities and to set and integrate attributes to enhance the flexibility of the materials.

At this moment a comprehensive ILCE system is available. In parallel, an iterative test procedure is being used to validate and consolidate the design of the environment and the interface composition. During these test stages, future users of the system (course designers, authors, educational technologists, tutors, counsellors, students, marketing people, etc.) will check the system. This will result in – as well as a consolidated prototype – experimental sets of learning materials in three content domains, outlines for organisational changes when using the system in the Ou, descriptions of procedures for using the ILCE-system and approach.

REFERENCES

Arshad, F.N. and Kelleher, G. (1993) 'SOLA: Students On-Line Advisor', *International Journal of Man-Machine Studies*, 38, pp. 281–312.
de Jong, T. and Sarti, L. (eds)(1994) *Design and Production of Multimedia and Simulation Based Learning Material*, Dordrecht, Kluwer Academic Publishers
Grandbastien, M. and Gavignet, E. (1994) 'ECSA: an environment to design and instantiate learning material' in de Jong, T. and Sarti, L. (eds), pp. 31–44.

Greer, J. E. and McCalla, G. I. (eds) (1994) *Student Modelling: The Key to Individualized Knowledge-based Instruction*, Berlin, Springer-Verlag.

Holt, P., Dubs, S., Jones, M. and Greer, J. E. (1994) 'The state of student modelling' in Greer, J. E. and McCalla, G. I. (eds), pp. 3–38.

Jonassen, D. H. and Mandl, H. (eds) (1990) *Designing Hypermedia for Learning*, Berlin, Springer-Verlag.

Kirschner, P. and Valcke, M. (1994) 'From supply driven to demand driven education: new conceptions and the role of information technology therein', *Computers in Human Services*, 10(4), pp. 31–53.

Larkin, J. H. and Chabay, R. W. (1992) *Computer-assisted Instruction and Intelligent Tutoring Systems: Shared Goals and Complementary Approaches*, Hillsdale, NJ, Lawrence Erlbaum.

Lee, M.-C. (1994) 'A pragmatic course representation model for authoring systems' in Thomas, M., Sechrest, T. and Estes, N. (eds), Vol. 2, pp. 1094–7.

McAleese, R. (1990) 'Concepts as Hypertext nodes: the ability to learn while navigating through Hypertext nets', in Jonassen, D. H. and Mandl, H. (eds), pp. 97–116.

McCalla, G. I. (1992) 'The search for adaptability, flexibility and individualization: approaches to curriculum in Intelligent Tutoring Systems' in Jones, N. and Winne, P. H. (eds.) *Adaptive Learning Environments: Foundations and Frontiers*, Berlin, Springer Verlag, pp. 91–122.

Mayes, T., Kibby, M. and Anderson, T. (1990) 'Learning about learning from Hypertext' in Jonassen, D. H. and Mandl, H. (eds), pp. 227–50.

Merrill, M., Li, Z. and Jones, M. K. (1990) 'The second generation instructional design research program', *Educational Technology*, March, pp. 26–31.

Mispelkamp, H. and Sarti, L. (1994) 'DISCourse: tools for the design of learning material' in de Jong, T. and Sarti, L. (eds), pp. 45–60.

O'Donnell, A.M. (1994) 'Learning from knowledge maps: the effects of map orientation', *Contemporary Educational Psychology*, 19, pp. 33–44.

Reader, W. and Hammond, N. (1994) 'Computer-based tools to support learning from hypertext: concept mapping and beyond', *Computers Education*, 22(1/2), pp. 99–106.

Reed, W. M. (1994) 'The theoretical frameworks for Hypermedia environments' in Thomas, M., Sechrest, T. and Estes, N. (eds), Vol. 1, pp. 533–5.

Sowa, J. F. (1991) *Principles of Semantic Networks: Exploration in the Representation of Knowledge*, San Mateo, CA, Morgan Kaufmann.

Thomas, M., Sechrest, T. and Estes, N. (eds) (1994) *Deciding Our Future: Technological Imperatives for Education*, 2 vols, Texas, University of Texas.

Thompson, A. D., Simonson, M. R. and Hargrave, C. P. (1992) *Educational Technology: A Review of the Research*, Washington, AECT.

Ulloa, A. (1994) 'Open system for collaborative authoring and re-use' in de Jong, T. and Sarti, L. (eds), pp. 83–98.

Yazdani, M. (1987) 'Intelligent tutoring systems: an overview' in Lawler, R. W. and Yazdani, M. (eds) *Artificial Intelligence and Education*, Vol. 1, Norwood, Ablex, pp. 183–202.

19

STUDENTS' PERCEPTION OF, AND RESPONSE TO, FORMATIVE AND SUMMATIVE ASSESSMENT MATERIAL

Fred Lockwood

INTRODUCTION

Student assessment is typically separated into its formative and summative components. Formative components take the form of Self-Assessment Questions or Activities; they are not graded. Summative components may be Tutor Marked Assignments (TMAs), work-place assessment or examinations; they are graded. The balance between these two components and their various forms are many; however, in general, Activities tend to dominate ongoing study of a course whilst TMAs constitute the ongoing grading. These two elements were adopted as representative of the formative and summative elements in typical open and distance learning courses. In a qualitative study data were collected by interview, questionnaire and self-recorded audio-tape (Lockwood, 1991); these elements were explored, with the findings providing insights into students' perception and response to assessment material (Lockwood, 1992).

INFLUENTIAL STUDIES ASSOCIATED WITH STUDENT ASSESSMENT

Of the numerous studies into aspects of student assessment, three were identified as significant. The first involved a group of researchers who became participant observers, followed university courses and involved themselves in university academic and social life (Becker *et al.*, 1968). A major finding was that the academic life of students was dominated by the demands of assessment. Students' study was geared to achieving those grades that would allow them to progress through the university; study was not the stimulating and enlightening experience they had envisaged but rather one of adopting ploys and strategies to survive in the system. These findings were mirrored in a study of the 'hidden curriculum' (Snyder, 1971) where students were interviewed during and after their undergraduate study. Snyder reported the disparity between what students said they were told their study would require – 'creativity', 'imagination', 'originality' – and the rapid realisation that they would be graded on their competence in recall and comprehension on only part of the large body of information presented. The negotiation and prioritisation of the formal curriculum into a hidden curriculum was essential within the competitive environment if the maintenance of high grades and students' self-esteem were to be achieved. These issues were explored further during an exploration of undergraduate learning (Miller and Parlett, 1974). Miller and Parlett combined observation with semi-structured interviews and questionnaires to identify and describe the concept of Cue Consciousness – the extent to which students recognised or actively sought cues from staff to assist them in assignments and in the final examination. Although the theoretical framework that Miller and Parlett describe cannot be applied directly to a distance teaching context, the idea underlying it could be applicable to students studying at a distance and interacting with material associated with continuous assessment. This idea was explored and a concept similar to Cue Consciousness, but applicable in open and distance teaching contexts, was formulated and termed TMA Consciousness.

THE CONCEPT OF TMA CONSCIOUSNESS

Miller and Parlett identified three major strategies; TMA Consciousness eventually identified only two: students were described as either TMA Dominated or TMA Aware.

Cue-Seeking students believed that there were ways of identifying assignment and examination questions, preferences among those likely to mark such scripts and that careful questioning and attentiveness could reveal preferred arguments and likely question areas; they actively sought ways to aid their performance on assignments. In a distance learning context the strategy, described and illustrated below as TMA Dominated, has similar characteristics. Those students described as Cue Conscious were aware that various strategies or methods may be employed, and were being used by fellow students, but were reluctant to commit themselves to them. They preferred to study all aspects of the course, assembled what they believed were appropriate assignments and prepared to answer all possible examination questions. The equivalent student was described in the present research as TMA Aware. Students described as Cue Deaf appeared oblivious of the 'cue-seeking' behaviour of others and of even the possibility of identifying likely examination questions or markers' preferences. They committed themselves to studying all aspects of the course in an attempt to prepare themselves for subsequent assessment. It was speculated that a similar category may exist among students studying at a distance – perhaps regarding each TMA as a mini examination in which they attempted to answer an assignment without consulting the materials they had previously studied. However, the evidence collected failed to suggest a third category within the framework.

The description of Cue Consciousness provides a series of characteristics that could describe students as Cue Seeking and Cue Conscious. Careful analysis succeeded in identifying similar characteristics that differentiated between distance learning students in a similar way. For example, a characteristic that distinguishes those students described as Cue Seeking from Cue Conscious was the selective study of materials: Cue Seekers study selectively whilst Cue Conscious students tried to study all aspects of the course. Among students studying at a distance it was possible to distinguish between those who skipped or ignored materials considered irrelevant to an immediate TMA and others who studied the majority of it irrespective of its immediate relevance. Six characteristics were identified that succeeded in differentiating between students that could be described as TMA Dominated and TMA Aware; they are listed in Table 19.1 and illustrated below.

Table 19.1   Characteristics to distinguish between
TMA Dominated and TMA Aware students

1	Selection of the TMA question
2	Method of TMA assembly
3	Relative worth of course materials/elements
4	Assessment of strategy adopted
5	Importance of TMA grade
6	Allocation of study time

TMA Dominated students

Students described as TMA Dominated geared their whole study to answering a particular TMA question and obtaining a satisfactory grade.

1 Students typically selected the TMA question they intended to answer either before study of the material or after a quick scan through it.

'I always look at the TMA and I have got that in mind ... as I go through the text ... through the unit.'

2 Students systematically assembled material for their TMA as they studied the unit or block.

'I always have a pad and pencil beside me and as I am reading through ... anything that I feel to be particularly pertinent to the TMA, I make a note of.'

3 Material that is considered irrelevant to the TMA question in hand is either skipped or given cursory attention.

'I only read Part 2 ... I don't even know what's in Part 1. I read Part 2 because it's what I was going to do my TMA on ...'

4 Many students regarded their study strategy as restrictive but persisted with it; the content of sections given cursory treatment were identified as potentially important and worthy of study.

'... it's all important and I'd like to study it all but I've got to get the TMA done and so I've got to cut out what's not relevant to the one I'm going to do.'

5 A good TMA grade is regarded as a successful outcome from study. Furthermore, a series of good grades acts as a cushion at the time of final assessment.

'... I do like to get quite a good mark in my assignments to help me with my exams. If I can't do the exam very well, if you've got a reasonable course mark you've got a bit more chance of getting through.'

Many students could not conceive of a situation in which they would follow their interests at the expense of a TMA grade. The award of a good grade were central and of paramount importance.

6 A disproportionate amount of time is typically allocated to assembling the TMA.

'... it says something like 10 hours for an assignment ... I always go way beyond that ... I usually spend about three weeks going through a TMA and really going into it.'

TMA Aware students

Students described as TMA Aware did not gear their study solely to answering the assignment(s) even though they were aware of the TMA questions from which they would need to select, nor was the grade of paramount importance.

1 The TMA questions were often inspected but the actual question not selected until later in their study or at the end of that particular teaching material.

'I do generally have a look at the TMA but I don't really take it in ... [T]hey give you guidelines – what's going to be emphasised and I get a general feeling of it and then I just work through.'

2 Systematic assembly of material for a TMA is typically undertaken after study of the teaching material rather than during study.

'... when I'm studying a unit I'm reading for interest ... I don't have the TMA tucked into the unit as I go through – that would perhaps spoil some of the enjoyment of reading ... if every time I was looking for some reference to a TMA.'

3 Course materials are studied for reasons other than their contribution to a TMA. For example, depending upon the TMA selected it would be possible to omit parts of the teaching material:

'... but [the unit] has things in it that are vital for my education, what I want out of this course ... there's more to this course to me than just writing a few essays and getting a few marks.'

4 The restrictive nature of merely studying material to answer TMAs is often noted.

'... I know we are supplied with the information beforehand, but personally, I think it would be a total waste of time to go through the course units with just the question in mind because it would be so narrow as to be ridiculous.'

5 A successful outcome from study is not equated with good TMA grades but rather with what individuals get out of the course – even though students want to pass rather than fail the course. TMA grades:

'were not really that important ... you've put a lot of work in, it would be nice to get of row of As ... at the end of the year but there's more to studying the course than a list of grades, it's what I get out of it that's important.'

Students could envisage a situation in which they would follow their interests at the expense of the TMA and resultant grade.

6 The limited time available for study is not devoted solely to assembling a TMA but to general study of the course materials and subsequently to answering the TMA.

'I don't stick to the time allocations but I do try to study all of the units and readings before starting on the TMA ... I usually end up rushing to get it together 'cause it takes longer to answer the TMA than I think.'

RESEARCH RELATING TO ACTIVITIES IN SELF-INSTRUCTIONAL TEXTS

A characteristic of self-instructional material is the integration of questions within the teaching material, the opportunity for learners to respond and the provision of a corresponding answer or discussion. A characteristic of the research literature associated with Activities, and their influence upon learning, reveals that it is dominated by experimental studies. The conclusions drawn from literally hundreds of separate studies is not in doubt. However, there has been growing concern over the ecological validity of such research and generalisability of such findings (Anderson and Biddle, 1975; Rickards and Denner, 1978; Duchastel, 1979). Furthermore, recent studies suggest that when the experimental controls are relaxed, or more real-life material and conditions are allowed, the previously identified findings are undermined. For example, many of the experimental studies allowed the learner unlimited time to study material prior to a criterion test. When the time allowed is restricted, which is typical in real learning situations, previously noted effects disappear. Several studies have identified available study time as an important constraint upon learners which directly influences research findings (Carver, 1972; Hamaker, 1986; Wong, 1985). The second part of this chapter describes the benefits and costs associated with Activities in self-instructional material and their link to student assessment.

PERCEIVED BENEFITS PROVIDED BY ACTIVITIES

During an analysis of interview transcripts, questionnaire responses and self-recorded audio-tapes, three common features were identified that students regarded as benefits to their study; they were termed Course-Focused, Self-Focused and Assignment-Focused Benefits.

Course-Focused Benefits

Course-Focused Benefits were those that related to students' learning from the course – the concepts, ideas, arguments under discussion. The Activities were perceived as contributing to their understanding of the course material; the following comment is typical:

'If it looks like it is going to tie in and it is going to increase my understanding later in the course unit, then I will work through it very, very methodically.'

Self-Focused Benefits

Self-Focused Benefits were those that related to a student's learning and development as a person; the opportunities they provided for ideas and arguments to be explored or reconsidered, previous assumptions challenged and personal interest awakened, developed or extended. The central feature is one of thinking critically, or questioning the materials:

'The Activities are just trying to make you take a wider stance and ... think more openly about it and to question your own thinking and to probe your thinking and to probe your own viewpoint.'

Assignment-Focused Benefits

Assignment-Focused Benefits were those that contributed directly to answering an assignment, that provided an opportunity to either think about the issues to be discussed in an assignment or which provided materials to be used in it. The following comment is typical:

> '… it depends on how much it would relate to the assignment … and if I think that this is going to get me thinking more clearly about the issues at stake in the assignment then I might attempt it.'

COST ASSOCIATED WITH ACTIVITIES

The benefits provided by Activities were balanced by a major cost – the study time that Activities consumed; it pervaded virtually all student comments. However, during analysis four constructs emerged that contribute to our understanding of students' perception and use of Activities; these constructs were termed Study time savers–Study time spenders, Degradation–Completion, Deference–Confidence and Inadequacy–Efficiency.

Study time savers–Study time spenders

Some students, in realising the benefits offered by Activities, were no more concerned about the study time that Activities consumed than other elements in the course. They spent as long on the Activity as they felt necessary to satisfy the requirements of it and their own needs. These students, identified as Study time spenders, may be regarded as at one end of a continuum with Study time savers at the other. The following comment is typical of Study time spenders:

> 'I don't have all the time in the world but I do try and spread my time over all the bits in the course – including the Activities. I spend as long as I need to make sure I understand what it's all about.'

For many students, the study time that Activities consumed outweighed the benefits they might offer; students felt they didn't have the time to respond to them. These students were identified as Study time savers. The following comment is typical:

> 'I don't do them because I just don't have the time … if I did I probably wouldn't have time to do the readings and [assignments].'

Degradation–Completion

One of the expectation of authors was that Activities would encourage students to think about the course materials by responding to the various intellectual demands embodied in them. Some students did respond to Activities in this way. Indeed, completion of Activities along the lines suggested by the author may be regarded as one end of a continuum with degradation of Activities at the other. The following comment is typical of a student who completes Activities:

> 'It's possible to skip the Activities, but if you do you're missing a great opportunity to think through your ideas and sort them out ... to analyse things, offer your interpretation.'

Other students reduced the intellectual demands or degraded the activities in two ways. They reduced the intellectual demands thus making it simpler than intended and less time-consuming than expected. Students also collapsed the question(s) and associated follow-up comments into a continuation of the text, focusing on the product of the Activity rather than the process. The following illustrates degradation:

> 'I just read the question and then the comment ... because you know, it's one way again of just cutting down the time and it's all written in the comment anyway so I can't really see the point of slogging through it.'

Deference–Confidence

A student's desire to comprehend the material being presented, to understand the ideas or arguments offered by the author, is a fundamental part of study. It is not unreasonable to assume that students will credit an author with experience and academic competence superior to their own and, in the absence of other authorities, will accept authors' interpretations, analyses and conclusions.

However, many authors maintain that they are not merely providing academic content and opportunities for students to check their understanding but opportunities to challenge previous conceptions, to engage with the material and, above all, to think for themselves. Many students grasped these opportunities and had confidence in their own response. This confidence may be regarded as one end of a continuum with deference at the other. The following comment is typical of confidence:

> 'It's not a case of right or wrong but the balance of the arguments one wants to take and the emphasis you want to give. Quite often I disagree with the way the author has argued his case – stressing some points and omitting others ... so I am just not prepared to accept what he says unless I can see the strength of his argument against the alternative.'

Some students displayed undue deference to authors' comments at the expense of their own. They were judged to incur a cost to their learning when they attempted an Activity and, upon discovering that their response to it differed from the author's, abandoned their own response and adopted the author's. For example, such students explained:

> 'If (my answer) differed I usually choose the author's and changed mine to suit ... I usually end up taking the author's answers in place of my own ... when it comes to revision I would not remember what was right and what was wrong.'

Inadequacy–Efficiency

For some students the decision to ignore Activities, skim them or to complete them less thoroughly than was suggested, was regarded as a legitimate strategy if they were to perform as effective and efficient learners. They believed that they were expected to study selectively since the course materials were a resource for them to draw upon. Students' perception of themselves as efficient learners, as a result of their selective study of course materials, may be regarded as one end of a continuum with feelings of guilt and inadequacy at the other.

The following comment is typical of those who believed they were studying with efficiency.

> 'There's so much in the course that one has to be selective ... I am sure they don't expect you to read every word and do every Activity ... part of being an undergraduate is deciding what areas to follow up, what Activities can be skipped and those you need to do – using your time to best effect.'

Some students acquired feelings of inadequacy as a result of adopting a selective strategy towards their study in general and Activities in particular. Such students were aware of the potential role of Activities in their study but made remarks like:

> 'Oh, [the Activity] aids your understanding, it certainly does ... and I'm a fool to myself for not doing them ... I thought they were all worthwhile, it's a great shame that I just haven't got the time to give to them.'

When students were asked what their reactions would be if Activities were omitted from the course, many said they would feel relieved (a word often repeated); it would remove the feeling of guilt or inadequacy they experienced when skimming over or ignoring them.

CONFLICT, ACCEPTANCE AND BALANCE: A COST–BENEFIT ANALYSIS MODEL

Learners perceive both the benefits to their study that Activities offer and recognise the potential cost of responding to them. When learners reconcile the benefits offered by Activities with the costs they are likely to incur in responding to them, they operate a cost–benefit analysis. Analysis revealed that the majority of learners operated a balance, responding to some Activities and not others as study time pressures and the perceived value of benefits varied.

An intellectual benefit of completing Activities is that learners avail themselves of the Course-Focused, Self-Focused and Assignment-Focused Benefits. A major intellectual cost of not responding to the Activities is that learners miss the opportunity to explore, refine, challenge or apply the particular ideas, concepts or arguments under discussion.

A second intellectual benefit of completing Activities is that learners gain confidence in the arguments they marshal and in views that differ from those of the writer; learners are 'thinking for themselves'. An intellectual cost of not responding to Activities, giving them limited attention and not assembling their own arguments to questions posed, is to lack confidence in their own responses.

The emotional cost that many learners incur during their study, as a result of their decision to save study time by not responding to Activities, is to acquire feelings of guilt and inadequacy. The emotional benefit of spending time on selected Activities, and having confidence in their own arguments, is to acquire feelings of being an effective and efficient learner.

CONCLUDING COMMENTS

Research studies often raise more questions than answers; the above study was no exception. It did succeed in describing two models in which students perceive and respond to both formative and summative assessment material – the Cost–Benefit Analysis and the TMA Consciousness Models respectively. It also revealed, from the limited data available, that the Cost–Benefit Analysis Model was a dynamic process. Students balanced the benefits they perceived from the Activities against the cost, in terms of study time, that they incurred. The importance of the consumed study time, that pervaded students' comments, supports previous studies in the area. In contrast students' perception of summative assessment material appeared to be more rigid, a perception or practice that had been formed at some time in the past and which continued.

REFERENCES

Anderson, R. C. and Biddle, B. W. (1975) 'On asking people questions about what they are reading' in Bower, C. H. (ed.) *The Psychology of Learning and Motivation,* New York, Academic Press.
Becker, H., Greer, B. and Hughes, E. (1968) *Making the Grade: The Academic Side of College Life,* New York, Wiley.

Carver, R. P. (1972) 'A critical review of mathemagenic behaviors and the effect of questions upon the retention of prose materials', *Journal of Reading Behavior*, 4, pp. 93–119.

Duchastel, P. S. (1979) *Adjunct Questions Effect and Experimental Constraints*, Department of Research and Evaluation, Occasional Paper 1, Bryn Mawr, PA, The American College.

Hamaker, C. (1986) 'The effects of adjunct questions on prose learning', *Review of Educational Research*, 56(2), pp. 212–42.

Lockwood, F. G. (1991) *Data Collection in Distance Education*, Geelong, Deakin University and the University of South Australia.

Lockwood, F. G. (1992) *Activities in Self-Instructional Texts*, London, Kogan Page.

Miller, C. and Parlett, M. (1974) *Up to the Mark: A Study of the Examination Game*, Society for Research in Higher Education, Monograph No. 2.

Rickards, J. P. and Denner, P. R. (1978) 'Inserted questions as aids to reading text', *Instructional Science*, 7, pp. 313–46.

Snyder, B. (1971) *The Hidden Curriculum*, New York, Knopf.

Wong, B. Y. L. (1985) 'Self-questioning instructional research: a review', *Review of Educational Research*, 55(2), pp. 227–68.

20

USING ELECTRONIC NETWORKING FOR ASSESSMENT

Robin Mason

INTRODUCTION

A growing number of open and flexible learning programmes are based around telecommunications. Students study in their own time and place, but are connected to their tutor and other students via a computer network based either on the telephone system or a local or wide area network. The primary role of telecommunications in these programmes is the opportunity for discussion and exchange of ideas and queries amongst students and tutors. However, once the problems inherent in providing electronic access have been overcome (for example, equipment, line charges, support costs), it is only sensible to explore the new communications facility to see what other benefits it might bring.

One of the secondary uses of networked connections with students is the opportunity to provide administrative facilities electronically: online registration, payment, queries, and information on courses and even student records. Some campus-based institutions already provide a number of these facilities which their students can access from terminals on the campus. A few distance teaching institutions are also beginning to offer these facilities for their students who access them using a computer and modem over the telephone system from home.

Another growing use of electronic networks is the provision of resources to support teaching and course material. The most obvious example is access to library services, bibliographies and increasingly, electronic inter-library loan requests. However, the whole world of the Internet is also available to the networked student: this includes an overwhelming, unstructured and – as yet – largely untapped resource of educational material, databases and online conversations.

A third area of educational activity which networks support is that of examinations and assignments. Of these three secondary uses, electronic assessment is perhaps the least exploited in current practice. This chapter outlines a range of different uses of networks for assessment and describes a number of applications in detail. The following questions are fundamental to the analysis:

- Does online assessment enhance the practice of assessment in any way?
- Does it make assessment less effective or more superficial?
- What problems are inherent in using electronic media for this purpose?

ELECTRONIC ASSESSMENT AND DISTANCE EDUCATION

The long turn-round time between the student's submission of an assignment, its marking by the tutor, its handling by the administration and its eventual return to the student, has been a continuing source of concern to distance learners. Students feel frustrated when they must submit another assignment before the last one has been returned. Educational researchers have commented on the detrimental effects of delayed feedback to the learning process (Rekkedal, 1983).

Electronic submission and processing of assignments seems to be an obvious way of speeding up the normal postal system which is used by most distance teaching organisations. This consists of the student submitting an assignment via electronic mail (e-mail) to the tutor, who marks the work and makes comments just as usual. In some cases these comments are word-processed onto an electronic form similar to the paper counterpart; in other cases, the tutor simply uses the tools of the word processor to intersperse comments into the assignment, just as is customary with paper and a red pen. The assignment and the accompanying tutor input is then sent electronically to the administrative arm of the organisation for processing in the normal way, before being returned by e-mail to the student. The reduction in turn-round time is derived exclusively from the removal of three postal journeys: this amounts to something between 7 and 14 days.

The content of the assignment is not affected by this process at all, although in principle there are limitations imposed by the nature of word-processing and drawing packages. (Scanners extend these limits, but are not exactly 'domestic equipment'.) Of course, in computer-based subjects where assignments consist of computer programs, electronic assessment allows tutors to evaluate the students' work by running the program themselves. In all subject areas, the primary benefit, however, is the faster turn-round time, which allows students the possibility of receiving feedback on their work while it is still current.

The primary barrier to its adoption on courses where students already have the necessary equipment, is usually organisational. A postal system, whatever its deficiencies, provides a single service for all courses, whereas an electronic handling system inevitably has to run in parallel as an additional service either for some courses, or for some students on a range of courses.

Despite the promise of faster feedback, there are students who are reluctant to choose the electronic route: they may find word-processing their assignments too demanding of their typing skills, for example. In certain disciplines, facility with a drawing package might also be necessary. Faxing assignments to tutors avoids the need for typing or computing skills, but does not allow the tutor to forward the document on to the administrative system. In some institutions where assessments are handled entirely by the lecturer, and particularly where professional updating courses involve students with access to fax machines, this practice works successfully. As far as tutors are concerned, the expectation of very fast feedback which electronic exchange raises in students' minds, may increase the pressure on tutors to mark assignments immediately upon their arrival, rather than at convenient times or even all together after the last one is submitted.

However, these barriers to implementing electronic submission of assignments are not as powerful as the obvious benefits and at least two large distance teaching universities have recently begun offering this service. Of course, educational institutions which provide off-campus courses on a smaller scale without large administrative systems, have had these arrangements in place between the teacher and students for much longer.

Verification of student identities is said to be a possible problem with electronically submitted assignments, although the arguments seem very weak. It could be argued that on courses which involve electronic discussions, the tutor is better able to validate a student's assessed work than on courses in which there is little interaction between student and tutor, whether these courses are delivered by traditional lectures or by print at a distance. The security of the mail system is clearly relevant, however, as the potential for a student to access and change or copy another student's work does exist. In fact, plagiarism is a more significant danger, but the electronic submission of the assignment plays a very small part in the overall problem. Access to a vast range of electronically available resource material via the Internet – much more than any tutor could maintain familiarity with – means that students have greater opportunities to 'cut and paste' material from other sources into their own work. The extent to which this is really a problem of a different order of magnitude from the familiar situation of unattributed ideas, ghost writers and chunks of material lifted from books and articles, is something which the academic community will have to monitor independently of the way in which the final piece of work is submitted. Perhaps the ease of access to information, ideas and interpersonal exchange through electronic networking will eventually lead to a different kind of assessment system, one aimed more usefully at learning to learn, rather than learning others' learning.

Applications of the electronic submission of assignments are currently taking place at two distance teaching universities: Monash University in Victoria, Australia, and The Open University in the United Kingdom.

Electronic assignments at Monash University

Monash University has an extensive system of electronic assignment submission for its distance students in Australia as well as those in other countries, such as Hong Kong and Singapore. On its distance-taught computer studies courses, electronic submission is mandatory, whereas it is offered alongside the traditional postal system in non-computer studies subjects. Using an assignments submission 'area' on its network interface, students submit their assignment directly to their lecturer, who immediately confirms receipt. When marking the assignment, the lecturer intersperses comments between the lines of the student's writing, and keeps a record of student marks on a database set up for the purpose. In some of the larger courses the lecturer may use local tutors for marking, but at the moment the system is handled entirely without intermediaries in the administration.

One of the added benefits of the Monash system is that students can make electronic requests for past examination papers. Furthermore, new staff being trained to mark student assignments, who are themselves remote from each other, use electronic exchanges to practise marking the same assignment and then standardise their marking schemes.

Electronic submission at the UK Open University

From 1995 the UK Open University is planning to offer electronic submission of assignments on several of its courses, one of which will have up to 1,500 students. In the meantime, the University's assignment handling office – which normally processes 3,000 assignments per day through postal submission – is trialling electronic submission on a small LISP programming course of forty students. In fact, this small trial is merely replicating the paper-based process, in that the data received by the assignment-handling staff have to be re-keyed rather than being automatically transferred to the student's records. Tutors complete an electronic copy of the usual feedback form (Figure 20.1) which they submit along with the e-mail copy of the student's assignment to the records office. There it is checked and a random sample sent for monitoring, before being returned to the student. Scaling up this process to a service for thousands of students, automating the re-keying procedure, while at the same time carrying on the usual postal system, is clearly a more significant undertaking.

An additional security feature of the current implementation at the OU, is that copies of the original assignment, the tutor's marked version and assignment handling's returned version are kept in an electronic folder to which the participants can send but not access information. If there were any question of tampering or loss in transit, the original could be accessed as a back-up.

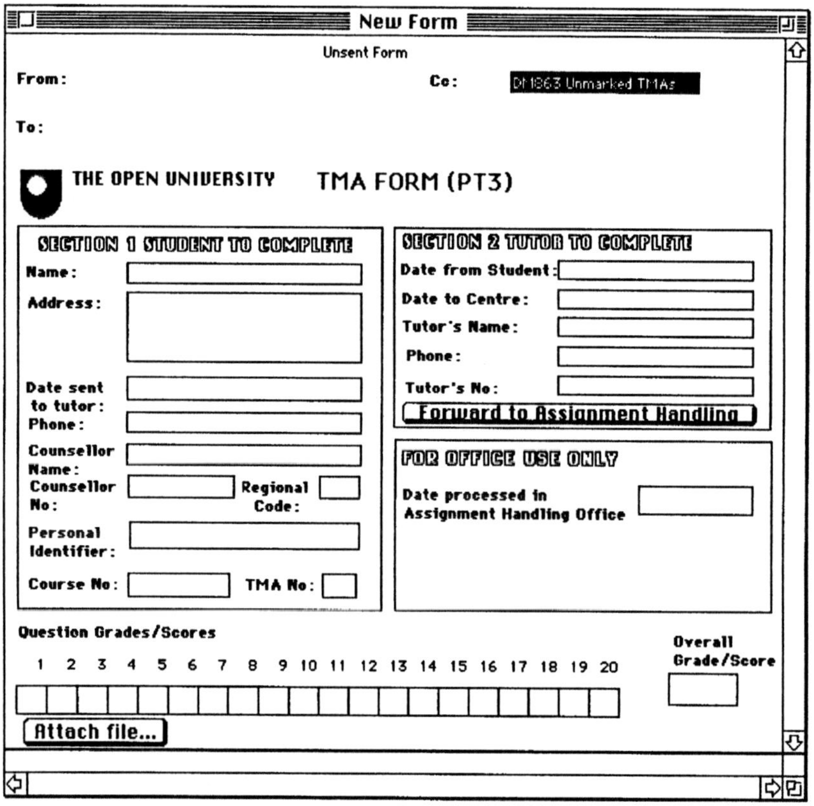

Figure 20.1 Electronic PT3 Form designed by Ches Lincoln and Tony Hasemer, The Open University

At the moment, electronic submission in the University is merely replicating the old system and bringing some advantages (faster feedback) along with some disadvantages (start-up costs, security issues, computer skills). This is the usual route which innovations follow. Not until they begin to change the old ways and to enable altogether new approaches, are the real benefits of the innovation felt.

NEW APPROACHES TO ASSESSMENT

The facility which electronic networking supports, whereby students and tutors can discuss course ideas and issues, exchange documents, and access a range of multimedia materials, has led to a number of innovative approaches in assessment procedures. Just as student use of electronic networking is widespread both in campus-based institutions and in distance learning and other forms of flexible education and training, so these new approaches to assessment are also arising in a range of courses and educational situations.

Staged assignments

One of these is the use of successive drafts of assignments, such that the student can receive feedback on emerging ideas before having to finalise a piece of work. This approach to the process of assessment is not dependent on electronic communication, but it is greatly facilitated by the ease and speed of electronic submission and commenting. In fact, the most extensive use of this technique is at campus-based universities, particularly in the area of creative writing. The approach becomes truly wedded to the electronic network when it moves from being a private interchange between student and tutor to be thrown open to peer commenting as well (see, for example, Barrett and Paradis, 1988).

Online assignments

Another approach to assessment is based on group discussion using a computer-conferencing system: the online assignment. Computer-conferencing allows a discussion to be stored 'centrally', so that students and tutors can read and add comments at any time of the day or night. Ideas and approaches to issues can be refined, clarified and developed through successive messages, thereby offering a rich and powerful forum for learning. The aim of an online assignment is to build on these unique features of computer-conferencing for interactive, written discussion built up over time.

The UK Open University has used online assignments very successfully on a number of its courses in which students are required to have access to its computer-conferencing system. Variations of the basic model have been made, depending on the particular discipline, but the essence of the assignment is that students are marked on the quality of their inputs to the question set. An area on the system is allocated to groups of between ten and twenty students, and discussion of the assignment question lasts for anything up to three or four weeks. Students then select some of their messages to submit for assessment and the criteria for marking includes such items as the following:

- the extent to which the student has used the issues raised in the course material to develop their arguments
- the way in which the student's messages build on and critique the ideas and inputs of other contributors to carry the discussion forward
- the succinctness with which the student's arguments are conveyed.

In one particular application of this approach, a second part was added to the assignment, namely, that students had to write a brief summary of the whole conference discussion, indicating the most important aspects of the debate and any significant issues of the question which were not discussed.

The University's policy is that assignments must be the work of the individual student. Consequently this solution of individual work within the context of group messaging, met University requirements at the same time as it exploited the power of conferencing to support interactive group discussion. Part Two of the assignment, the summary, was included to placate frowning policy committees, but turned out in the end to play a very significant part in the educational value of the work.

(Mason, 1993, p. 571)

Results from these kinds of assignments so far reveal a typical range in the standard of work. Some students complete the work with little intellectual effort: they may give stock views on the assigned question, or ramble on about their personal experience, or avoid addressing the central issues. Those who simply upload pre-prepared messages which do not refer in any way to previous discussions can clearly be penalised on the basis of the marking criteria. In the best examples, however, students really engage in the discussion, taking points further, arguing the other side of an issue, pulling together the previous comments and making thoughtful remarks about the question.

Part two of the exercise, summarising the whole discussion, proved more demanding than it first appeared – much more difficult than summarising an article, lecture or book where arguments are presented in a coherent and structured way. Computer-conferencing discussions are invariably unstructured, rambling and inconclusive. Learning to summarise and evaluate arguments is a fundamental educational skill, which this kind of assignment highlights.

Collaborative assignments

There are many innovative ways in which computer-conferencing is facilitating collaborative approaches to assessment. At the simplest level, tutors can ask students with the highest marks on their assignments to post them in the conferencing system so that others can see and learn from the best work. Tutors, after marking all the assignments, can also make general comments which everyone can access, thus allowing students to assess how they stood relative to other students.

On postgraduate, professional and other non-competitive courses, students can be invited to submit all of their assessed work to a conference where their peers can read and/or comment on it. This work acts as an archive of material for all participants, particularly after the course has finished. Over successive presentations of a course, a database of student assignments can be built up, perhaps consisting of some of the best answers. This can even become part of the content of the course, with students being asked to evaluate previous answers, indicate omissions and comment on arguments (see, for example, Boston, 1992).

More ground-breaking than these rather tentative examples of collaboration is the growing use of assessment through group projects. Again, this form of assessment is hardly unique to electronic networking, but for students studying at a distance it has certainly provided a new opportunity. Just as with their non-electronic counterparts, group projects can involve a number of students each working on relatively separate parts of the assignment, or it can demand an integrated whole produced by the discussions, refinements and reworkings of all the participants jointly. Many models between these two extremes are possible.

Aspects of collaborative work which have proved difficult using electronic media are decision-making and management of the tasks (Harasim, 1986). Unless a leader emerges or is assigned, coordinating the work, allocating tasks and reaching closure on discussions, can be very frustrating and attenuated. However, one of the advantages of modern systems and networks is the ability to exchange multimedia documents, access resources and revise successive versions of the joint work (Alexander and Mason, 1994).

Joint project work can even become the primary learning vehicle of a course, such that resources can be available either electronically or in print form, but the 'content' of the course is the preparation of the group assignment.

ONLINE EXAMINATIONS

There are a few examples of electronic systems being used for examinations. At the simplest level, the Open universiteit in the Netherlands has an electronic bank of exam questions which students access from their local study centre. These computer-based examinations consist of multiple-choice questions, and are felt to be appropriate for some, but by no means all, areas of the curriculum. The questions are prepared by academics in Heerlen and the computer generates questions for each student when they decide to take the examination. The answers are fed in by the student using a local study centre machine and a provisional mark is given immediately on finishing. The final result is confirmed later by Heerlen. This system provides great flexibility for students to study at their own pace, as well as immediate feedback of results.

In the United States where multiple-choice examinations are perhaps more common than in Europe, these have been accessed, filled in and submitted electronically by students studying from home (Eisley, 1991). The growth of 'international' distance education, where courses are offered in countries half-way around the world or to students in widely separated countries, has inevitably led to greater use of electronic examination, usually of the multiple choice kind. Security of the network and the students' IDs are obviously essential. Some academics feel that multiple-choice examinations lead to surface-level rote-learning by students, although the practice continues in many disciplines at traditional campus-based institutions, even at postgraduate level. Ease of marking is an obvious benefit for tutors. In fact, it is the pressure of student numbers without increased faculty which is driving this practice; electronic networking simply extends the possibility to distance students.

In principle, there is no reason why essay examinations could not also be carried out electronically. When multimedia desktop conferencing systems are readily available, verification of student identities could be made through the video camera! Typing skills could be an issue, and the examination would have to be 'open book', but, more significantly, educational institutions would have to be more flexible in their attitude to examinations. From an organisational perspective, the primary advantage is that examination halls and monitors do not need to be provided, and for students it means that they can complete their studies entirely from home and at a distance from the providing institution. As computer ownership increases and telecommunications technologies develop, it seems inevitable that electronic assessment and examination will follow.

CONCLUSIONS

Is technology simply determining the path towards more and more aspects of teaching and learning being carried out electronically? Or are there real educational benefits to be had from the kind of innovations described so far?

The benefits of collaborative work have been analysed by many researchers (Bouton and Garth, 1983); the addition of online access simply extends these benefits to students at a distance. The growth of the open and flexible learning movement has also been expounded at length (Rowntree, 1992; Thorpe and Grugeon, 1987). Electronic access to previous assignments, examinations and databases of 'best answers' is, again, simply an extension of the same princples. Finally, electronic submission of assignments has a very clear benefit, which is hard to refute.

Most of the innovations described, therefore, seem to move assessment (and perhaps, one day, examination) in the direction of increasing flexibility, student benefit and educational value.

REFERENCES

Alexander, G. and Mason, R. (1994) *Innovating at the OU: Resource-Based Collaborative Learning Online*, CITE Report 195, The Institute of Educational Technology, Milton Keynes, The Open University.
Barrett, E. and Paradis, J. (1988) 'Teaching writing in an on-line classroom', *Harvard Educational Review*, 58(2), pp. 154–71.

Boston, R. (1992) 'Remote delivery of instruction via the PC and modem: what have we learned?', *American Journal of Distance Education*, 6(3).

Bouton, C. and Garth, R. (eds) (1983) *Learning in Groups,* San Francisco, Jossey-Bass.

Eisley, M. (1991) *Guidelines for Conducting Instructional Discussions on a Computer Conference,* Proceedings from an International Symposium on Computer Conferencing, Columbus, OH, Ohio State University.

Harasim, L. (1986) 'Computer learning networks: educational applications of computer conferencing', *Journal of Distance Education*, 1(1), pp. 59–70.

Mason, R. (1993) 'Designing collaborative work for online courses' in Davies, G. and Samways, B. (eds) *Teleteaching*, Amsterdam, North-Holland.

Rekkedal, T. (1983) 'The written assignments in correspondence education: effects of reducing turnaround time', *Distance Education*, 4(2), pp. 231–52.

Rowntree, D. (1992) *Exploring Open and Distance Learning*, London, Kogan Page.

Thorpe, M. and Grugeon, D. (eds) (1987) *Open Learning for Adults*, Harlow, Longman Open Learning.

Part VI

LEARNER SUPPORT
AND
MANAGEMENT

21

RESEARCH AND PRAGMATISM IN LEARNER SUPPORT

Bernadette Robinson

INTRODUCTION

In the literature on learner support in open and distance education, description and prescription outweigh empirical enquiry or research. Publications on learner support are often in the form of 'how to do it' guidance or reports of experience. These can have practical value but may be atheoretical, unsubstantiated or lack validity when transferred to other contexts. While many accounts express the conviction that learner support services make a difference to outcomes, demonstrations of the relationships are less easy to find. Learner support has so far received less research attention than other aspects of open and distance learning. Why should this be? There are four possible reasons: learner support may be perceived as a less glamorous activity than some others in open and distance education (support staff often have less power, status and pay); it is often regarded as peripheral to the 'real business' of developing materials; it is an element particularly vulnerable to financial cuts; or it may largely be a pragmatic activity rooted in the lessons of experience.

The last of these possibilities is the focus of this chapter which seeks to examine two questions:

- Is there an established body of research findings on learner support?
- Can decision-making about learner support be based on research findings, or is it essentially a pragmatic activity, contingent on each individual system and context?

WHAT CAN THE RESEARCH TELL US?

Research evidence on learner support in open and distance education comes from several sources:

- investigations of individual elements of a support system, for example, tutoring by the media (audio-tape, audio-graphics, computer-conferencing, telephone and audioconferencing), correspondence tutoring, counselling, turn-round times for course work;

- in the wake of research on drop-out or persistence, in terms of the kinds of interventions that institutions and staff can make;
- analyses of roles and characteristics of 'successful' support staff;
- description and analysis of institutional or individual practice;
- studies of learner satisfaction with support services (such as Rashid *et al.*, 1994), now growing in number along with attempts to measure and assure quality.

In the literature on learner support there are few reviews of research. Of these, some take a wider focus than learner support alone and not all distinguish between empirical research and other kinds of writing. Cookson (1989) identifies empirical work on learning at a distance (but not specifically learner support). Wright (1991) focuses on learner support, but does not distinguish between research reports and other kinds. Sweet (1993) reviews the literature (not the research) on student support and some more general aspects of learning. Faced with the disparate array of research and theory on learners and learning at a distance (a broader focus than learner support alone), Gibson (1990) attempted 'to add order where none ... appeared to exist' by using Lewin's (1936) field psychology of learning to provide a theoretical framework for exploring it. A critical review of the research carried out so far on learner support is still needed.

So what *can* we conclude from the research? The following is an attempt to list broad findings:

- learner–institution contact, such as regular contact with support staff, appears to have a positive effect on learner performance and persistence rates;
- factors which correlate positively with course completion rates include the use of course assignments, early submission of the first one, short turn-round times for giving learners feedback, pacing of progress, supplementary audio-tapes or telephone tutorials, favourable working conditions in the learner's context, the quality of learning materials and reminders from tutors to complete work;
- multiple interacting factors (personal, environmental and course variables) are at work in determining learner success; some institutional interventions can assist if appropriately targeted;
- learners value contact with support staff and other learners, though do not always use the services provided; learners most often report a preference for face-to-face tutoring compared to other media, though where face-to-face meetings are not possible, other forms of contact are rated as acceptable or valuable;
- what happens in the early stages of recruitment and enrolment affects later success or failure;
- personal circumstances and lack of time are the most common reasons given for withdrawal from study.

However, stating these broad conclusions in this way may give some of them more substance than they warrant. Some are based on studies which have produced marginal or equivocal findings. Replication studies are few and frequently produce conflicting findings or fail to confirm the earlier ones. For example, Taylor *et al.*'s (1993) study on student persistence and turn-round times in five institutions in four countries failed to produce generalisable results; it drew attention to the very considerable differences between institutions and their practices, and the difficulties these created for achieving generalisations. Often too narrow a range of research methods are used yet different research approaches can elicit different answers: for example, Garland's (1993) use of an ethnographic approach revealed different reasons for drop-out to those elicited by questionnaires.

SOME ISSUES

There is enormous variation in learner support systems in open and distance learning. Commonalities may lie in similar goals (such as 'providing interactivity and dialogue', 'personalising a mass system', 'mediating between the materials, the institution and the learners', 'institutional responsiveness to individuals', 'differentiation of support services according to different group and individual needs'), but with diverse ways of achieving them.

Concept definition

Definitions of learner support vary. To take just three: one describes it as the elements of an open learning system capable of responding to a particular individual learner (Thorpe, 1988, p. 54); another as the support incorporated within the self-learning materials, the learning system and assignment marking (Hui, 1989, p. 131); and a third as 'the requisite student services essential to insure the successful delivery of learning experiences at a distance' (Wright, 1991, p. 59). Some authors include learner support as an integral part of a course, others place it as a supplement. Some include administration and delivery operations in their definitions, others do not. The range of services included in models of learner support also varies; some include pre-entry services, others do not (see Reid, Chapter 25 in this volume). In some cases support services are provided in partnership with other agencies (such as mentor support for teachers in school-based training, or for in-company learners), adding yet another dimension of variation.

Learner support can be viewed as having three components: the *elements* that make up the system, their *configuration,* and the *interaction* between them and the learners, which creates its dynamic. The elements are:

- personal contact between learners and support agents (people acting in a variety of support roles and with a range of titles), individual or group, face-to-face or via other means;
- peer contact;
- the activity of giving feedback to individuals on their learning;
- additional materials such as handbooks, advice notes or guides;
- study groups and centres, actual or 'virtual' (electronic);
- access to libraries, laboratories, equipment, and communication networks.

Configuration of these elements varies, depending on the requirements of course design, infrastructure of a country, distribution of learners, available resources, and the values and philosophy of the open and distance education provider. Interactivity between the provider and learners differs in level, intensity and function.

The choice and use of these components are based on practicalities as much as on research findings (if not more). For example, though feedback on learning has been identified in at least one empirical study as having beneficial effects on learner progress and course quality (Boondao and Rowley, 1991), some institutions cannot afford to provide it, or see it as a low priority in the face of competing demands, or cannot find enough appropriate people to carry out the tasks, or find the logistics of doing it too difficult given the infrastructure of the country. Reports of practice illustrate that learner support is heavily contingent on local circumstances. Comparisons can be misleading, sometimes based on false assumptions. How far, then, do findings from one context apply elsewhere?

Diversity and generalisation

Some of the problems in generalising are illustrated by differences in the roles of support staff. In some cases different titles refer to essentially the same kinds of roles; in others the same title encompasses quite different tasks. In some systems, 'tutors' do no marking or commenting on learners' course-work; in others, 'tutors' spend 80–85 per cent of their time allocating grades and designing tests for learners, or yet again, use commenting on assignments as the main means of dialogue with learners. The amount of learner support differs as does the proportion of resources allocated to it. The ratio of learners to tutor varies widely: within my own experience it has ranged from 3:1 to 300:1, a difference of scale which has predictable implications for the tutor's role (see Aalto and Jalava, Chapter 24 in this volume). In some cases learner-support staff are selected by qualification, experience and interview, in others they are elected by the group of learners (Warr, 1992). Usually support staff are paid by the open and distance education provider, but sometimes they are paid by the learners, or do the work unpaid. Do these differences matter? I think they do, in two ways: firstly, they make generalisations unsafe for the unwary and, secondly, they have consequences for the motivations of support staff, the meanings they attribute to their roles and work, and for the match between the role as specified by the organisation and as enacted by staff (aspects little researched but of concern to managers).

A similar caution about generalising arises from the myth of 'the learner'. The term has a generic ring about it, but in fact refers to a very wide variety of people with different backgrounds and concerns even within one institution (Evans, 1994). Not all open and distance learners are adults, highly motivated or self-managing. Some are primary school-age children (Forbes and Wood, 1994) or disadvantaged young adults with negative and politicised attitudes to learning (Nonyongo and Ngengebule, 1993), or post-graduate doctors or engineers. Contexts of learning vary from yurt-based, non-formal education for women in the Gobi desert to multinational in-company training by computer networks in Europe.

The research on learner support in open and distance education does not reflect this diversity. Its base is relatively narrow: most published research studies are on formal education, institutionally based, and usually higher education in the more developed countries. Yet cultural contexts have considerable implications for the generalisability of the research findings. Models of 'good practice' developed in western institutions are not always appropriate for other countries and cultures, for example:

> ... given the fact that the socio-religious tradition is one of seeing the younger generation as necessarily in a position when they should take orders, listen to elders, their individuality or independent thinking or decision-making is not nurtured. Often these traditions and customs run contrary to the basic expectations required of open learners.
>
> (Priyadarshini, 1994, p. 458)

and

> while education means spreading awareness and lifting taboos, it does not mean violation of people's customs and traditions. This must be kept in mind while planning a support system.
>
> (*ibid.*, p. 462)

The diversity described points to the situated nature of learner support in three respects: its place in curriculum and course design, the characteristics and milieu of the learners, and the culture and social structures in which it operates (see Koul, Chapter 3 in this volume). What role, then, can research play if concerns are so specific? What are the implications for constructing research agendas?

Practical concerns and research agendas

Some of the difficulties in reconciling practical concerns with broader research agendas are illustrated in a report from a group representing several Asian Open Universities (Sweet, 1993). Practical concerns about learner support were specific, described as 'unique to a particular institution and reflected local conditions, customs and practices' (*ibid.*, p. 97), yet the common research agenda created by them listed broad topics not specifically focused on learner support, for example:

> Explore the feasibility of engaging in various entrepreneurial activities. Develop models of institutional collaboration.
>
> (Sweet, 1993, p. 99)

This contrasts with the research questions from a single institution, following from an empirical study of science students' needs at the Open Learning Institute (OLI), Hong Kong, for example:

> What should be the quantity of provision of tutorials in distance education? Should the attendance of these activities be made compulsory?
>
> (Chan Shui Kin, 1994, p. 53)

As the researcher says, the answers to some of these questions are not simple, needing not just administrative answers but also some which critically examine academic perspectives and educational values. However, answers do need to be sought in the context of the particular institution. For more theory-focused research, some of the questions would need to be re-framed, for example, to become 'in what circumstances should tutorials be compulsory?'

The contrast between these two agendas raises some questions: do research agendas on learner support only become focused when embedded in the context of a particular institution or system? Is applied research only relevant to the institution where conducted?

RESEARCH, PRAGMATISM AND DEVELOPMENT

While both research and pragmatism have influenced the development of understanding and practice in supporting learners, research so far seems to have played a weaker role. What does it add up to?

Is there a theory of learner support?

Theory is essentially an account of how ideas are related, a complex system for organising the ideas through which we conceptualise some aspect of experience. However, 'a few loosely related propositions about causal interconnections do not constitute a theory ... though they may contain elements of one' (Dey, 1993, p. 52). Does this describe the current status of research on learner support? Do the research studies on learner support build convincing models or add up to one or more theories? Not so far, for several reasons. Some of the studies are not linked to any theory. There has been relatively little testing out of propositions, theory or findings from one context to another (Taylor *et al.*'s (1993) study is unusual in this respect). A large number of topics seem to be researched in isolation from previous related work, and do not build on earlier efforts to formulate theoretical explanations. Some studies are single-variable studies resulting in simple explanations for what are clearly complex problems. Sometimes the interpretation of results is over-optimistic. Many studies are descriptive – a necessary part of the research process – but also lack analysis. Some guiding concepts (like 'learner independence' or 'interaction' or 'mediation') are meaningful at one level but not well understood nor well operationalised. 'Learner support' is weakly conceptualised. So, looking at the research on learner support, we cannot claim to have a theory or theories, or even be close to it. But is this too pessimistic a conclusion? What kinds of research are we talking about?

What counts as research?

A distinction is often drawn between 'pure' and applied research. 'Pure' research is primarily concerned with advancing knowledge within a particular field rather than finding solutions to practical problems. It asks broader questions at a higher level of generality than applied research, for example 'how do tutors affect students' approaches to learning?' These kinds of broad questions apply across different contexts and countries. Applied research asks more specific questions, about practical problems focusing on particular programmes and groups ('how did those tutors on that course with that kind of role affect those students' approaches to learning?').

Much of the research in open and distance education generally is applied research (including evaluation) – a problem-solving activity of a practical kind. This reflects the need for managers and course developers to get answers to pressing practical questions. Sometimes it is possible to combine such applied research with more theoretical explorations, but not always. Often institutions or project groups are too small to contain the right kind of expertise within their staff or lack the resources or time. However, research of an applied kind is essential for the effective functioning of open and distance education systems – for getting feedback on the learners, the courses and the systems.

Institutions vary widely in the amount of institutional research they do. Some institutions do little and neglect to compile the necessary baseline data about learners, support staff and their activities. The following situation at the University of Papua New Guinea is, unfortunately, not unique:

> ... records are so bereft of information that students who have already matriculated cannot be easily identified, let alone separated, from those who are still in the process ... the problems caused by this lack of information make the other problems which impact on student performance pale in comparison.
>
> (Geissinger and Kaman, 1994, p. 87)

A starting-point for many applied research endeavours on learner support by an institution must be a set of baseline student statistics (Calder, 1994). This can also assist in the monitoring and review of the development process over time and is helpful for testing out organisational myths about what actually happens. Another source of institutional research is that done by practitioners.

Practitioner research

There is a broad spectrum of what can count as research in learner support. It includes more than the studies that appear in journals. The results of systematic enquiry also appear in the form of internal reports, discussion papers, learner guides and supplementary materials, and feed into training materials, staff development workshops and the development of institutional policy and practice. Dissemination of this kind of research tends to remain at the local or institutional level where it can contribute to the development of a culture of research-minded practice, often in the form of action research. Not all those who contribute new knowledge and extend understanding are 'experts' or professional researchers. Many support staff who actively research their own practice would not claim to be so and are often not active in writing up their findings for publication. This kind of practitioner research can have limited visibility outside an institution but considerable influence within it.

Within large institutions, practitioners' work can be unknown or ignored by 'professional' researchers who may in any case work within a different research paradigm. The opposite is the case, too. Researchers' work may not easily reach practitioners, even within the same institution (the case studies in Schüemer (1991) illustrate the difficulties that researchers and evaluators have in disseminating their findings and influencing decision-making); this is yet another dimension in which separate worlds can exist within one institution (see Costello, 1993). One result of this lack of connection or dialectic between practitioners and researchers is missed opportunities: to build productive partnerships, to democratise evaluation, and to make use of a broader range of research approaches, particularly qualitative and participative ones. Some forms of research are more difficult for centrally

228

based research staff to do and, because of this, the range of approaches and methodology may become narrowly focused. For example, survey research is more easily managed by centrally based researchers than some qualitative forms of enquiry with distant learners.

Whether 'pure' or applied, any piece of educational research is shaped by some underlying assumptions and researchers of all kinds adopt procedures which follow from them. It is vital for practitioners and researchers alike to know what these are in order to carry out investigations or to assess in any meaningful way the products of such research. This understanding is neither the concern solely of professional researchers nor irrelevant to distance education. This belief leads me to disagree with Coldeway's view that:

> The debate over qualitative versus quantitative research in education is best left to those with a keen interest in the philosophy of science. The distinction appears to be far from the needs of distance education research at this time.
>
> (Coldeway, 1988, p. 48)

Research in distance education should not be divorced from the concerns of mainstream educational research, where there is currently lively debate and practical engagement with issues surrounding the use of qualitative and quantitative approaches and their effective combination (Bryman, 1988). To disengage from this kind of debate is to weaken the quality of research in open and distance education.

CONCLUSIONS

Clear conclusions are difficult to draw from the research on learner support. Some of the most basic questions about learner support – for example, the kind of questions Perraton poses (in Chapter 2 of this volume) about face-to-face study: 'what kind, how much and for what purpose?' – cannot easily be answered by present research findings, at least without so much qualification as to be unhelpful for practical purposes. Answers to questions such as these most often begin with the words 'it depends'. Decision-making in response to them has to take account of a number of different kinds of factors, and trade-off one set of benefits or losses against another. While research can (and should) inform practice, providing services for learners is most often a pragmatic, problem-solving activity enacted in a particular context.

But this is not an argument for abandoning attempts to do research on learner support. Useful development can be generated from within an organisation which actively researches its own practice and which ensures that it knows enough about itself in order to do this. The move from this to generalising across settings is a large one. Building theory would need stronger conceptualisation, more repeated testing of concepts and the creation of organising frameworks or theories. And some speculation: what might a theory of learner support look like? In the meantime, research-minded practice is the route to improving learner support.

REFERENCES

Boondao, S. and Rowley, G. (1991) 'Does the use of assignments in distance education courses improve their quality?' in Atkinson, R., McBeath, C. and Meacham, D. (eds) *Quality in Distance Education,* ASPESA Forum Papers, ASPESA, Australia, pp. 63–71.

Bryman, A. (1988) *Quantity and Quality in Social Research,* London, Unwin Hyman.

Calder, J. (1994) *Programme Evaluation and Quality,* London, Kogan Page.

Chan Shui Kin (1994) 'Student attitudes to text design and face-to-face contact at the OLI Hong Kong', *Open Learning,* 9(2), pp. 51–3.

Coldeway, D. (1988) 'Methodological issues in distance educational research', *The American Journal of Distance Education,* 2(3), pp. 4–54.

Cookson, P. S. (1989) 'Research on learners and learning in distance education: a review', *The American Journal of Distance Education,* 3(2), pp. 22–34.

Costello, N. (1993) 'Organizational cultures and distance learning', *Open Learning,* 8(2), pp. 3–11.

Dey, I. (1993) *Qualitative Data Analysis,* London, Routledge.

Evans, T. (1994) *Understanding Learners in Open and Distance Education,* London, Kogan Page.

Forbes, A. and Wood, M. (1994) 'From three to eight years – the foundations of literacy', *Conference Proceedings: Distance Education: Windows on the Future,* Wellington Correspondence School, New Zealand, pp. 81–6.

Garland, M. R. (1993) 'Ethnography penetrates the "I didn't have time" rationale to elucidate higher order reasons for distance education withdrawal', *Research in Distance Education,* 5(2), pp. 6–10.

Geissinger, H. and Kaman, J. (1994) 'Student needs in Papua New Guinea', *Conference Proceedings: Distance Education: Windows on the Future,* Wellington Correspondence School, New Zealand, pp. 87–95.

Gibson, C. C. (1990) 'Learners and learning: a discussion of selected research' in Moore, M. G. (ed.) *Contemporary Issues in American Distance Education,* Oxford, Pergamon Press, pp. 121–35.

Hui, H. W. (1989) 'Support for students in a distance learning programme – an experience with a course in Fashion and Clothing Manufacture' in Tait, A. (ed.) *Conference Papers: Interaction and Independence: Student Support in Distance Education and Open Learning,* Cambridge, The Open University, pp. 129–41.

Lewin, K. (1936) *Principles of Topological Psychology,* New York, McGraw-Hill.

Nonyongo, E. and Ngengebule, T. (1993) 'The SACHED Distance Education Students' Support Programme', *Open Learning,* 8(2), pp. 40–4.

Priyadarshini, A. (1994) 'Support systems for a distance learning institute in a developing country' in *Conference Proceedings: Distance Education: Windows on the Future,* Wellington Correspondence School, New Zealand, pp. 456–63.

Rashid, M. R. *et al.* (1994) 'Supporting student learning and developing self-directed learning at the Universiti Sains Malaysia' in Evans, T. and Murphy, D. (eds) *Research in Distance Education 3,* Geelong, Deakin University Press, pp. 70–7.

Schüemer, R. (1991) *Evaluation Concepts and Practice in Selected Distance Education Institutions,* Hagen, ZIFF.

Sweet, R. (ed.) (1993) *Perspectives on Distance Education, Student Support Services: Towards More Responsive Systems,* report of a Symposium on Student Support Services in Distance Education, Vancouver, The Commonwealth of Learning.

Taylor, J. C. *et al.* (1993) 'Student persistence in distance education: a cross-cultural multi-institutional perspective' in Harry, K., John, M. and Keegan, D. (eds) *Distance Education: New Perspectives*, London, Routledge, pp. 77–93.

Thorpe, M. (1988) Open Learning, Module 2 of the *Post-Compulsory Diploma in Education*, Milton Keynes, The Open University.

Warr, D. (1992) *Distance Teaching in the Village*, Cambridge, International Extension College.

Wright, S. J. (1991) 'Research on selected aspects of learner support in distance education programming: a review', selected papers, Part 1, *The Second American Symposium on Research in Distance Education*, Pennsylvania State University, pp. 59–71.

22

STUDENT SUPPORT IN OPEN AND DISTANCE LEARNING

Alan Tait

This chapter will address the principles of student support in Open and Distance Learning (ODL), aiming to identify the central concepts which underpin this area of activity, and how from the practitioner perspective these concepts are realised.

The term student support means the range of activities which complement the mass-produced materials which make up the most well-known element in ODL. It is, of course, true that printed course units, television and radio programmes, computer programs etc., which replace the lecture as a means of delivery, and offer so much both in terms of social and geographical access, and in terms of cost-effectiveness, support students in central ways. But the elements of ODL which are commonly referred to as student support are made up of: tutoring, whether face-to-face, by correspondence, telephone or electronically; counselling; the organisation of study centres; interactive teaching through TV and radio, and other activities. These activities have as key conceptual components the notion of supporting the individual learning of the student whether alone or in groups, while in contrast the mass-produced elements are identical for all learners. It will be argued that both elements are essential – and integral.

The rationale for student support in ODL has been weakly conceived over the last twenty years, and, not surprisingly, in many ODL systems, weakly realised, and subject to wild fluctuations in terms of financial support (Paul, 1988; Brindley and Fage, 1992). This author is surely not alone in having visited study centres where students never seem to be present, or observing tutorials where lectures are given that repeat or replace the content of course materials. On the other hand, there has been an enormous growth in interest, and indeed institutional commitment even in times of financial constraint, to student support in ODL, and many examples in different countries of excellent practice, although in some cases this is born out of educational instinct rather than theoretical understanding . The objective of this chapter is to consolidate the basis on which this area is established, moving from concrete to conceptual considerations. The structure of the chapter is one which has been developed as a model for planning student support in distance education, and can be represented as in Figure 22.1:

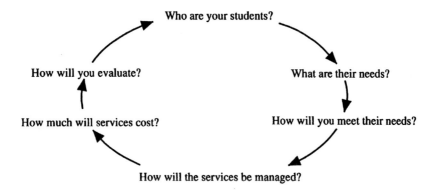

Figure 22.1 A model for planning and managing student services

WHO ARE YOUR STUDENTS?

Who are your students? This central question lies at the heart of the issue, and yet is often ignored. The question, though short and to the point, is one of considerable depth and complexity. It is not an original observation to say that education has represented a provider-led rather than a client- or consumer-led activity. ODL systems that start with the production of course materials in whatever medium can also ignore in important ways the consideration as to who their students are. There are very significant examples of alternatives, such as the learner-centred curriculum at Empire State College, State University of New York (Granger, 1990), but this by its unusualness reinforces the point. There are also very significant processes of social change which affect this. Market forces and consumerism are now near-dominant factors governing the educational system in many societies in ways that are very ambiguous at this stage of development (Field, 1994).

The question as to who your students are can be unpacked according to a number of dimensions:

- age
- gender
- geography
- social class
- cultural and belief systems
- income
- ethnic and racial identity
- educational background
- employment and unemployment

- language
- housing
- access to communications and technology
- physical disability.

This range of factors, which far from being exhaustive, represents a crude set of parameters which will need refining and expansion in particular contexts, contains the elements that begin to make it possible to know who your students really are. When articulated together they create the infinite number of individual lives represented in our student bodies. Of course, many educational institutions collect statistics on some of the elements identified above. However, what is more challenging is to use the information in practical ways in the planning and organisation of student support services (this is equally true of the construction of the curriculum, of course). It is asserted here that in constructing student support services the key task is to acknowledge the identity of the learner, complementing the mass-produced teaching materials which by virtue of their nature, and as a condition of their effectiveness, are unable to do so. Feminist analyses within ODL have been particularly educative about the principles of acknowledging the identity of learners (Tait, 1994, pp. 33–4). This is demanding for an educational institution. It may result in challenging social inequities that bring the institution into conflict with influential elements in a society, including the government. It certainly means vigilance and flexibility in organisational terms rather than continuity and hard structures. It means differentiation rather than uniformity and consistency. In organisational terms it represents moving from product to service, and in information technology terms it is paralleled by the move from mainframe to networking. In quality assurance terms it represents the centrality of the customer. In a whole range of different settings, similar ideas are at work which turn organisational thinking upside down. The function of student support services in ODL lies at the nexus of change.

Evans has provided the most interesting ethnographic accounts of student lives in ODL, and suggests:

> The challenge is to develop and maintain approaches which enable students to have their voices heard and for the open and distance educators and their institutions to be able to listen and understand the practical implications of what is being said. Learners should also recognise that they are a part of a diverse body of people whose interests need to be voiced, and whose stories need to be told.
>
> (Evans, 1994, p. 128)

WHAT DO YOUR STUDENTS NEED AND
HOW WILL YOU PROVIDE IT?

Debate within an institution about who its students are, or will be, provides the platform on which to analyse what they need in terms of student support services. However, although this may sound obvious, it is surprising how quickly one can find in one's own and other ODL systems, examples of practice which represent past rather than current needs, or top-down provision which has not resulted from analysis of who and where students actually are. Examples include study centres in places which students find inaccessible; home-based study systems for groups which are inadequately housed and who need library or study space; tutorials taking place where only 20 per cent of the students are able or want to attend; services priced at levels which exclude certain groups on a permanent basis. Other examples will surely be known to readers. Working within student support services, it is essential to have the courage to challenge such practice, but it has to be acknowledged that it can be dangerous. Often, student support services are seen as the poor and marginal relation of the course production side, and to offer up criticism is to take a risk. To challenge current practice can seem offensive within a professional framework to other colleagues, especially if student wishes are taken as very significant elements in the design of provision, which of course they should be.

The range of services are provided through activities such as:

- advice/counselling
- tutoring individually and in groups
- the learning of study skills, including examination skills
- peer group support
- feedback concerning assessment and progress
- language support
- careers guidance
- administrative problem-solving.

(See Rumble, 1992, pp. 62–74 for further elaboration of these activities.)

Media such as correspondence, face-to-face, telephone, electronic communications etc. provide a range of means which differ widely in their effectiveness for individuals and groups in ways that are as yet inadequately understood, and need constant monitoring if provision is not to replace service. Crucial elements in the design of services also include the extent to which they can be provided on a local basis, and in groups. There has been published a considerable range of accounts of tutoring, but less in the field of counselling (the journals *Teaching at a Distance* and *Open Learning* have carried the richest seam of articles). Major issues in the design of counselling systems in the UK Open University have included the tension between a number of desirable characteristics. These include the desire to have the counsellor as local as possible to the student, but also to have specific knowledge of the programme of study; and to have a link with the tutorial role but also to have continuity of concern for the student on a longer than course-by-course basis. The tensions can be represented as in Figure 22.2:

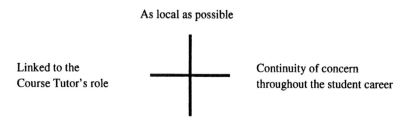

Figure 22.2   Desirable characteristics in tension in the counselling system of the UK OU

Social, cultural, economic and technological issues provide a range of factors in planning student support which ensure that each institution has a unique task, and no general schemes can be drawn up on an international or even national basis. Some of the issues can be considered schematically as shown in Figure 22.3:

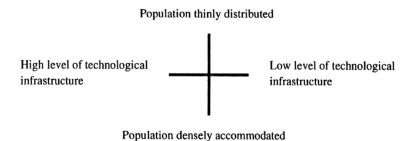

Figure 22.3 A framework of factors which affect the organisation of student support services

Thus both Norway and Sudan have low populations thinly distributed, but very different technological infrastructures which will demand differently organised student support. Equally, both London, UK, and Soweto, South Africa, have high populations densely accommodated, but again different access to technological infrastructure will demand different solutions. Economic and social factors provide further related diversity.

Study centres

Study centres form an established part of the great majority of modern ODL systems, providing the physical space for a range of activities to take place on a face-to-face basis, including variously in different systems:

- enquiry services
- pre-study advice
- application
- tutoring
- counselling
- interactive radio and TV
- telephone teaching
- audio-visual playback facilities
- library
- tutor training
- independent study spaces
- laboratories
- examination facilities
- student peer meetings
- publicity and marketing
- storage and collection point for study materials
- decentralised office accommodation.

There are also examples of 'electronic classrooms', or 'virtual study centres', which form part of the broad picture. There is not a clear terminological distinction between study centres and regional offices in different systems around the world, and it depends partly on usage, the range of the above activities which take place, and the centre–periphery organisational model that obtains, which term is employed. Sewart has examined the integrated role of study centres, rejecting the notion that they represent the 'dustbin' of distance education, i.e. where everything is put which cannot be fitted in in any other way (Sewart, 1983, p. 57).

COSTS AND MANAGEMENT OF STUDENT SUPPORT SERVICES

There are relatively few sources of reference for the issues of costs and more generally management of student support services in ODL, although Wagner (1983), Snowden and Daniel (1983), Rumble (1992, 1993), Paul (1990a, b) and Sewart (1983, 1993) all address the issues. Rumble (1993, p. 103) comments that, 'The cost of tuition and counselling is either a direct (variable) student cost or a semi-variable cost related to the numbers of students taken on by tutors and counsellors. Clearly the provision of such services represents a reversion to the labour-intensive methods found in traditional education.' It is also the case that in ODL the creation of course materials in many of the systems is more expensive than the costs of the creation of a course in traditional systems. However, by their nature student support services, which so closely relate to student numbers, and which represent the individualising rather than the mass production side of the total operation, work in reverse to the cost ratio of course materials which become cheaper per student the more students who are admitted.

Where, as is frequently the case, tutorial staff are hired on a part-time basis, the ratios in terms of costs can be seen as follows:

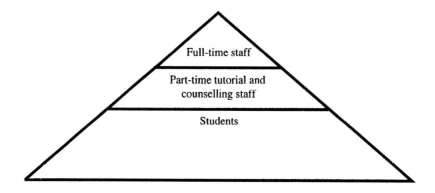

Figure 22.4 The pyramid structure of staffing and student ratios

Clearly, the varying of the ratios – how much bigger the base is than the other two levels – will be a significant element in the cost structures of student support services in many ODL systems.

In terms of management, Paul (1990a) identifies two principal areas specific to the management of student support services in ODL, namely the management of structures which are devolved from the institution's headquarters, and which involve centre–periphery relations, and the management of part-time off-campus tutors and counsellors. He also notes the crucial importance of information technology and communications (Paul, 1990b). None of these is specific organisationally to ODL systems, nor does ODL appear to have been more successful than other kinds of organisations in managing these issues. A major conclusion that emerges from Paul's work is the importance of staff development and training, in order to diminish the gap between perceptions of the range of individuals, whether based at headquarters, a regional location or part-time working at home. Sewart examines student support services from management perspectives, and notes that in the last part of this century the most relevant management theories are those which are systems-based, using the analogy of the brain or the organism, rather than the machine (Sewart, 1993, p. 8). Sewart also notes the importance of service industry rather than production approaches; 'the complex interrelationship between student volumes, course production costs, and student support costs' (Sewart, 1993, p. 10); and 'the management of student support needs to take account of the needs of students as expressed by themselves or by the intermediaries' (Sewart, 1993, p. 11).

In conclusion it is clear that costing and management of student services has to engage with at least the following key issues:

- distribution and remoteness of staff and services
- the contribution to the reduction of student attrition
- the relationship of costs with volume of students and intermediaries (i.e. tutors, counsellors, and others)
- quality issues where service rather than production is the key activity.

EVALUATION AND QUALITY ASSURANCE

Evaluation and quality assurance have come together as terms in the last six or seven years in the UK. The first edition of the major work on evaluation in ODL by Thorpe in 1988 mentioned the term quality control only, pointing out the areas of concern that such a term omitted (Thorpe, 1988, p. 199). The term quality assurance allows concerns to be addressed not only about whether standards have been reached, but also about continuous improvement and the centrality of the student experience (the 'customer-centred approach'). Thorpe's work is also notable in that it deals substantially with evaluation in ODL in the field of student support services, in particular providing case-studies of evaluation of tuition and counselling. Major conclusions reached by Thorpe include the need for 'tutor self-evaluation as well as system evaluation', in order to improve tutor responsiveness to the learner (Thorpe, 1988, p. 86), and the need for documenting the counselling process, in order to diminish the perception which may be influential in the institution 'to see the counselling interaction as a minority concern for "problem learners" or a peripheral issue' (Thorpe, 1988, p. 118).

Major difficulties in establishing quality assurance work in student support services in ODL include the fact that many tutorial and counselling staff work on a part-time basis for the institution, and their time therefore is very limited; they work remotely in a range of dispersed locations away from more than occasional visits; there are so many variables in the factors that lead to student success or failure that the demonstrability of value of student support services has hitherto eluded researchers. On the other hand, monitoring systems for quality in correspondence teaching are well established (Tait, 1993). The arrival and establishment of the quality assurance movement in education should ensure that quality assurance will gain ground in ODL, as is already in evidence internationally (Deshpande and Mugridge, 1994).

CONCLUSION

This chapter should conclude by returning to the task which it set itself, namely addressing the principles of student support in ODL. Student support systems, it has been argued, must address the question as for whom they are designed, and what is therefore needed by the learners. In turn this should lead to determination as to how those needs can be met, within the constraints of costs, technologies and geography. The management and evaluation of student support, largely influenced by notions of quality assurance, mean that student support has to be examined, documented and reflected upon. Finally, the necessary pragmatism, flexibility and openness to change does not remove the necessity to work within and contribute to conceptualisation and theorising. Research and development for student support in ODL are therefore mutually reinforcing and interactive activities.

Serving the client has become the dominant theme in many spheres as opposed to the earlier product-driven approaches; ODL is no different. Those who work in student support in ODL now find themselves at the centre of things and not at the periphery.

I would like to acknowledge that many of the ideas in this chapter have been developed through discussion and joint work with my long-standing colleague, Roger Mills.

REFERENCES

Brindley, J. and Fage, J. (1992) 'Counselling in open learning', *Open Learning*, 7(3), pp. 12–19.

Deshpande, P. and Mugridge, I. (eds) (1994) *Quality Assurance in Higher Education: Perspectives on Distance Education*, Vancouver, BC, Commonwealth of Learning.

Evans, T. (1994) *Understanding Learners in Open and Distance Education*, London, Kogan Page.

Field, J. (1994) 'Open learning and consumer culture', *Open Learning*, 9(2), pp. 3–11.

Granger, D. (1990) 'Open learning and individualised distance learning at Empire State College', *Open Learning*, 5(1), pp. 24–30.

Paul, R. (1988) 'If student services are so important why are we cutting them back?' in Sewart, D. and Daniel, J. S. (eds) *Developing Distance Education*, Oslo, International Council for Distance Education.

Paul, R. (1990a) *Open Learning and Open Management: Leadership and Integrity in Distance Education*, London, Kogan Page.

Paul, R. (1990b) 'The interaction and management of information technology in distance education' in Croft, M., Mugridge, I., Daniels, J. S. and Hershfield, A. (eds) *Distance Education and Development and Access*, pp. 289–91, Caracas, International Council for Distance Education, UNA.

Rumble, G. (1992) *The Management of Distance Learning Systems*, Paris, Unesco, International Institute for Educational Planning.

Rumble, G. (1993) 'The economics of open distance education' in Harry, K., John, M. and Keegan, D. (eds) *Distance Education: New Perspectives*, pp. 94–110, London, Routledge.

Sewart, D. (1983) 'Distance teaching: a contradiction in terms?' in Sewart, D., Keegan, D. and Holmberg, B. (eds).

Sewart, D., Keegan, D. and Holmberg, B. (eds) (1983) *Distance Education: International Perspectives*, Beckenham, Croom Helm.

Sewart, D. (1993) 'Student support systems in distance education', *Open Learning*, 8(3), pp. 3–12

Snowdon, B. and Daniel, J. (1983) 'The economics and management of small post-secondary distance education systems' in Sewart, D., Keegan, D. and Holmberg, B. (eds), pp. 398-424.

Sweet, R. (ed.) (1994) 'Student support services: towards more responsive systems', *Perspectives on Distance Education*, Vancouver, BC, Commonwealth of Learning.

Tait, A. (1993) 'Systems, values and dissent: quality assurance for open and distance learning', *Distance Education*, 14(2), pp. 303–14.

Tait, A. (1994) 'The end of innocence: critical issues in open and distance learning', *Open Learning*, 9(3), pp. 27–37

Thorpe, M. (1988) *Evaluating Open and Distance Learning*, Harlow, Longman.

Wagner, L. (1983) 'The economics of the Open University revisited' in Sewart, D., Keegan, D. and Holmberg, B. (eds).

23

SUPPORT FOR THE IN-COMPANY LEARNER

Roger Lewis

Since the early 1980s open learning has been increasingly used within employing organisations, both public and private. Yet this has rarely attracted the interest of researchers. This chapter explores one particular aspect of in-company provision: support for employees' learning. It begins by describing the learner studying within what can be termed more 'conventional' open learning schemes, such as correspondence education and open universities: what needs have been established for such students and how are these typically met? A similar analysis is then provided for the workplace learner. The support roles potentially available within the employment context are explored and the chapter concludes with an outline of issues for research and development.

DEFINITION OF THE 'CONVENTIONAL' OPEN LEARNING STUDENT

The literature typically describes a student enrolled with an educational institution, using open learning mainly for non-vocational purposes. Examples include individuals:

- learning at a distance in an open university (of which the UK Open University is a prototype)
- studying by correspondence for a public award below degree level such as (in the UK) for GCSE or 'A' level
- studying at a local college, mainly at a distance but with some face-to-face tutorial provision.

In such examples the following combination of factors normally applies:

- the curriculum is largely non-vocational
- courses extend over a substantial period of time (one or more years)
- the student learns mainly at home
- support is for the most part provided across a geographical distance.

NEEDS OF OPEN LEARNING STUDENTS

The needs of such students are now well established, not necessarily through detailed research, more through rules of thumb resulting from the experience of institutions such as The Open University, the National Extension College and their overseas equivalents. In the 1980s the then Council for Educational Technology Open Learning Systems project commissioned Graham Gibbs, of The Open University, to produce a report setting out the key stages in an open learning student's career. This, together with experience current at the time, led to the framework set out in *How to Tutor and Support Learners* (Lewis, 1984). The key stages were identified as:

- before the course
- entry to the course
- early days on the course
- mid-course
- examination/leaving point
- after the course.

Table 23.1 is an example of the subsequent elaboration. It summarises likely student reactions and consequent needs at three of the stages. Readers are referred to the source – Lewis (1984) – for further details.

Table 23.1 Reactions and consequent needs at three stages in
an open learning student's career

Reactions	Needs
Before the course	
I want to find out more about computers	A more exact identification of learning need: what aspects of computers does the student need to know more about: how they work?; how to use them?; how to program?
Is the course suitable for me?	Knowledge of what the course on offer contains and whether its objectives meet the student's own aspirations
Am I up to this? Have I got the right background?	An assessment of the student's own existing relevant skills, knowledge and experience
I don't want the whole course. Just the bits in the middle dealing with how to set up a database	Flexible administrative arrangements

Table 23.1 continued

Reactions	Needs
Early days on the course	
How do I deal with all this paperwork/teaching material/ complicated system?	Explanation of the system
Mid-course	
This is going well. I'm going to finish more quickly than I planned	
I seem to be getting very behind now	Revision of goals; flexibility over completion of work/course; provision of extra packages
I don't think this is for me after all	Renegotiation of learning goals; flexible exit arrangements without loss of face

RESPONSE TO THE NEEDS OF THE CONVENTIONAL OPEN LEARNER

Providers respond to these needs in a variety of ways, including:

- support within the materials themselves, for example via questions and activities of various kinds, with feedback
- technology, for example computer-marked assignments
- central advice and student service departments.

But the major source of support is the tutor, an academic operating in a broad role. The flavour of this is caught in two definitions from major UK providers:

> Your role as tutor is to *complement* the learning materials and extend the learner's understanding of them through marking and grading assignments and to help with general study problems. You are the first port of call if the learner cannot make sense of the material, and you act as the link between the course material and the learner, initiating and taking part in a dialogue with them.
>
> (National Extension College, no date)

> The University places a strong emphasis on students as individual learners, and they need to be able to draw on an array of teaching resources. Among these, group teaching at the study centre is an important element, but students are not obliged or may be unable to attend, and those who miss tutorials must be supported effectively.

Correspondence is an essential part of the University's teaching, and the written comments made by tutorial and counselling staff have a particularly important educational role.

(The Open University, 1993, p. 4)

To meet the requirements of this role the tutor in open learning needs:

- some knowledge of the subject the student is studying, though not necessarily expertise in all areas
- a willingness to work supportively alongside open learning materials
- an understanding of adult learning and how to facilitate it
- ability to communicate with the learner mainly at a distance, for example by post and telephone
- the ability to give feedback on the student's progress, usually through marking assignments.

In some schemes the role is extended to that of an educational counsellor (or 'tutor counsellor'), covering areas such as study skills, careers guidance and acting as friend and advocate for the student within the open learning system.

The tutor is thus the main source of support for the student beyond the course materials. Students may be encouraged to use informal sources of support, such as other students (perhaps via a self-help group) or a mentor. But these seem not to be used as frequently as might be expected, or valued particularly highly by students, who may need more encouragement than is usually given in realising the benefits of 'non-professional' support. The main source of help, and the only source formally provided, is thus usually the tutor.

DEFINITION OF THE WORKPLACE LEARNER

Even before the 1980s open learning had been used for vocational training. Tens of thousands of employees studied for banking, accountancy and other professional qualifications through the correspondence route. Many would have been partly sponsored by their employers. They worked as individuals, studying from home in their own time. Little or no support would be provided by the employer, beyond sponsorship and release to attend examinations.

In the 1980s, spurred on by government initiatives, some companies began to make innovative provision for their employees' educational development. Through company sponsorship, employees could study at college or by borrowing open learning materials, which they would study largely in their own time. Examples included Texaco (the ASSET scheme), Austin Rover, ICI and Jaguar. This strand has continued, for example Lucas's continuing education provision (Temple, 1991, Chapter 2). Though offered in and through the workplace, such provision is not 'vocational' as the term is usually defined. It is often related only indirectly to the employee's work-role, underpinning programmes such as Total Quality Management, which require employees capable of seeking – and acting upon – feedback, rather than passively waiting for direction. General open learning provision is also seen as a motivator, and a way of retaining staff.

The subject of this chapter is neither the correspondence student who happens to be in employment nor the employee studying non-vocational courses through company sponsorship. Instead the focus of interest is on a growing group of learners who share most of the following characteristics and context:

- They study by recognisably 'open' schemes as I have defined the term 'open' (Lewis, 1986).
- They study mainly to improve their performance in their current job role. The improvement may be immediate (as, for example, in a supermarket training programme on stocktaking) or less direct (as, for example, in a management development programme). They may also be preparing for progression, for example for promotion to supervisor.
- The employer expects enhanced individual performance to result in improved organisational performance, though the links between these may be hard to identify or measure.
- The learners are sponsored by their employer; in some cases the course may be taken largely at the employer's instigation rather than on the employee's initiative.
- Courses may be very short, extended over several years, or anywhere in between.
- Employers allow at least some time during the working day for study, or application of learning. Facilities, such as a quiet room or learning centre, may be available.
- The course requires employees to apply what they learn; the workplace thus becomes an arena for learning.
- Learners use workplace resources, equipment and experience as an integral part of their course; assignments and projects may require evidence of this. Thus the employer has to facilitate access to such resources.

One of the earliest documented open courses to meet most of these criteria was the National Extension College's zoo animal management course, described by Everiss (1984).

NEEDS OF THE WORKPLACE LEARNER

The needs of the workplace learner have already been touched on. They include:

- induction into this open mode of learning, including the various course components, the purpose of each and how to use them to the full

- clarity over their own responsibilities and the responsibilities of others
- suitable arrangements in which to study (space and quiet)
- access to facilities, equipment and experience
- help in identifying how learning can be applied at work, for example via the selection of appropriate projects
- feedback on progress
- acknowledgement of achievement
- encouragement
- guidance on any difficulties experienced with the learning material.

This list includes some items shared with the conventional open learner: the last two items on the list, for example. Others, though they may seem similar, are different in emphasis: feedback on progress, for example, may include not only comments on theoretical assignments but also on projects and other activity occurring largely within the workplace.

RESPONSES TO THE NEEDS OF THE WORKPLACE LEARNER

The same options are available as for non-vocational provision. Workplace learners can be helped:

- directly by the materials themselves
- through the use of technology
- by formally provided support from a tutor and others
- by encouragement to identify and orchestrate their own informal means of support.

To make materials, it is possible to design:

- project guides
- task books
- assignment booklets
- assessment guides, including how to prepare a portfolio of evidence.

In addition, activities can be specified within the main learning texts, or their equivalent in other media.

Assignments are likely to be practical rather than theoretical, and increasingly likely to be linked to statements of competence – either national, or specific to the organisation. Such assignments may be orientated towards issues the organisation is currently facing, even problems that need solution. Assignments could, for example, involve the analysis of a range of software options and a reasoned recommendation of which to purchase, or the redesign of an appraisal system. Assignments may require team working and assessment of the contributions of each individual.

It is in the third item on the list: 'formally provided support from a tutor and others' that we are likely to see the most significant differences from the conventional open learning context. A tutor, operating largely at a distance, may be able to comment on theoretical assignments but ill-placed to give feedback on workplace performance and unable to offer much help to the student in setting up the necessary arrangements for such assignments. Additionally, the environment for the workplace learner is potentially richer and more complex than that for the conventional open learner. The following roles may be present:

- a tutor from outside the company
- an assessor or assessors within the workplace
- a coach
- a mentor.

Not all roles will be in evidence. Sometimes one person may play several roles. The roles will not necessarily be described by the above terms, or recognised as such by the staff playing them. The terms will probably not appear in job titles or on job descriptions. Also, definitions differ: what is known as a 'mentor' in one organisation could be called a 'coach' in another.

So what we need to do is to tease out more fully just what is entailed in each role. Only if the complexity is untangled can workplace support be properly woven, with each role making its unique and powerful contribution to learning, focused at the point of greatest potential.

DIFFERENT ROLES IN SUPPORTING WORKPLACE LEARNING

The tutor

The essence of the tutor's role is perhaps to ensure that students absorb, and understand, the knowledge and theory components of the course. This may involve assessing assignments and giving feedback, clarifying points in the learning material, and running occasional tutorials, probably within the organisation.

An additional tool is now available to help define the contribution the tutor can make: relevant units within the UK national standards for training and development (Training and Development Lead Body, 1993). Nine units comprise an award for Supporting Learners as Tutor, Counsellor and Assessor. These are:

- agree individual and group priorities for learning
- agree learning strategies that match the needs of learners and organisational requirements
- agree learning plans and processes to monitor outcomes
- specify learner requirements for materials
- select and provide flexible learner support materials
- monitor, and advise on, the progress of learners (*)

- support the achievement of individual learner objectives (*)
- evaluate the achievement of outcomes against objectives (*)
- modify and adapt learning programmes.

The three asterisked units are particularly relevant to this chapter. The elements that comprise each of these are set out in the full national standards; each element is further amplified by performance criteria and range statements. Tutors who do not wish to take the full qualification can gain credit at the unit level. These standards can be adapted to suit the requirements of a particular scheme. They can be used as a tool for sharpening the role of the tutor in workplace open learning.

The workplace assessor

I made the point earlier that workplace open learning is closely related to specific circumstances within the employing organisation. Use of another employee as workplace assessor meets three important assessment criteria: validity, flexibility and cost-effectiveness. A distant tutor is unlikely to meet these requirements.

As with tutoring, national standards exist for workplace assessment. One unit covers assessment through direct observation; a further unit covers assessment based on a more diverse collection of evidence, usually assembled by the employee in a portfolio. Some organisations in the UK are helping their staff to gain credit in these units. Some schemes offer the employee dual accreditation, for example a university degree and a national vocational qualification issued by a different awarding body. In such cases the assessment role may be split between a tutor (assessment of knowledge and understanding) and a workplace assessor (assessment of application).

The coach

Coaching is familiar most immediately through sport. But it is also extensively used in the workplace. Analysis of a number of sources (Distributive Industry Training Board, no date; Megginson and Boydell, 1979; Open College, 1991) suggests it has the following characteristics:

- Coaching is the planned development of a skill or competence, through practice, informed and guided by demonstration and feedback from a skilled performer within the workplace (the 'coach').
- Coaching consciously uses day-to-day work, and its challenges, as a learning vehicle.
- Coaching focuses on improving the performance of an individual and/or a team.
- Coaching involves the development of learning strategies, enabling the employee to transfer skills to other contexts.

In successful coaching the coach's role reduces as the learner gains confidence and takes increasing responsibility for his or her learning. The process might develop along a continuum as follows.

- The coach performs the skill and the employee observes.
- The employee performs the skill stage by stage, with help from the coach.
- The employee performs the skill stage by stage, without help but with verbal prompting from the coach.
- The employee performs the skill as a whole, and identifies what went wrong and how this could have been avoided.
- The employee performs the skill as a whole and answers questions on why various actions were carried out.
- The employee describes more generally what has been learned and how this will help them tackle other tasks in future.

The coach thus needs a range of skills. These include:

- planning and negotiating with the learner, including the identification of specific outcomes
- provision of encouragement and support
- modelling expert behaviour
- questioning, and listening to, the learner
- assessing the learner's performance (often informally)
- offering helpful feedback, feedback that is specific, detailed and timely
- receiving feedback on their own performance from the employee, and learning from this.

The mentor

Mentoring is now widespread both in the public and private sectors. Mentors are explicitly used in nurse education and teacher training, in induction, and in continuing professional development. An Industrial Society survey showed that 40 per cent of organisations contacted had a mentoring programme in 1992, an increase of 10 per cent since 1989 (Temple, 1994).

The term 'mentor' is derived from the name of the wise old man to whom Ulysses entrusted the guardianship of his son Telemachus, during his ten-year odyssey fighting the Trojan wars. Mentor had to play many roles during this time, including tutor, guide, sponsor, patron, adviser and exemplar. Perhaps not surprisingly given this history, the term 'mentor' is often not defined explicitly; or only one aspect of the mentor's role is developed.

Mentoring can mean:

- support for a young professional during apprenticeship (as, for example, during a qualificatory period for membership of a professional body)
- induction on joining a large and complex organisation, such as a multinational company

- a means of ensuring promising new employees adopt 'correct' practices and styles, thereby rising rapidly through an organisation; in this case, the mentor sets the agenda and acts as a role model (Clutterbuck, 1985)
- support informally available during a learning process, which itself may be formal or informal.

Mentoring can thus be:

- varied in duration
- structured or unstructured
- specific or general
- monitored or unmonitored.

The mentor may be selected by the learner or provided by the organisation; a learner may choose the mentoring option or have it chosen for them. See Open College (1992) for coverage of these options.

In educational contexts the phrase normally implies that the mentor:

- facilitates learning as a key purpose
- offers general rather than skill- or subject-specific support
- works on an agenda set largely by the learner
- helps learners gain increasing independence, for example by encouraging them to reflect on their experience to identify what has been learned and how this can subsequently be applied.

ISSUES FOR RESEARCH AND DEVELOPMENT

Thus a variety of support roles may be necessary in workplace open learning. A number of different people are potentially in a position to meet learner needs. One issue is who should play which role? Staff within the organisation in regular contact with the learner include the learner's line manager, colleagues, and members of the personnel and training function. Yet care has to be exercised: the essentially hierarchical relationship between line-manager and subordinate, for example, may make it difficult for the former to play the role of mentor, even if he or she is temperamentally suited; a trainer may not be close enough to the day-to-day detail of the learner's job to act as coach. Sometimes the culture within an organisation may discourage staff from playing facilitating roles, though increasingly organisations are moving towards the creation of learning cultures (Pedler *et al.*, 1991).

Another issue is how the various roles can best complement each other. What contribution, for example, can an external tutor make that an internal coach cannot? This chapter has suggested that one necessary precondition to decision-making is greater sharpness in defining the contribution of each helper, together with an analysis of the competences needed to play each role. Careful design of learner support is also necessary to ensure complementarity of the various contributions.

Research into existing workplace open learning schemes would be helpful to ascertain:

- what roles are in evidence
- how these are defined
- how roles complement each other
- what competences are judged necessary
- how selection is managed
- what briefing and training takes place
- how effectiveness is monitored.

Understanding of what learning is, and how to facilitate it, seems common to all roles. One model for learning, described by Kolb (1984), is set out in Figure 23.1.

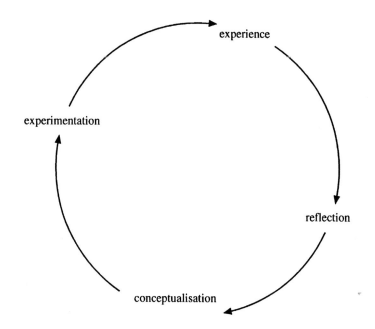

Figure 23.1 The Kolb cycle

A less abstract, equally cyclical model is shown in Figure 23.2.

What contribution can each helper make at each stage in the learning process? What are the overlaps? To what extent, for example, does the tutor also need the skills set out above for coaches? Such questions are part of the research agenda in what is still a largely uncharted area of open learning.

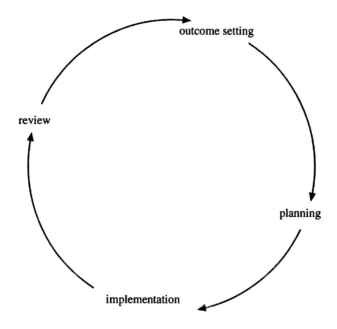

Figure 23.2 The learning cycle

The author would like to thank David Lippiatt, Fred Lockwood and Hilary Temple for their comments on an earlier draft of this chapter.

REFERENCES

Clutterbuck, D. (1985) *Everyone Needs a Mentor*, London, Institute of Personnel Management.

Distributive Industry Training Board (no date) *Coach to Succeed*, Distributive Industry Training Board.

Everiss, S. (1984) 'Zoo animal management open-learning scheme' in Lewis R. (ed.) *Open Learning in Action*, Council for Educational Technology.

Kolb, D.A. (1984) *Experiential Learning: Experience as the Source of Learning and Development*, Englewood Cliffs, NJ, Prentice-Hall.

Lewis, R. (1984) *How to Tutor and Support Learners*, Open Learning Guide 3, Council for Educational Technology.

Lewis, R. (1986) 'What is open learning?', *Open Learning*, 1(2), pp. 5–10.

Megginson, D. and Boydell, T. A. (1979) *A Manager's Guide to Coaching*, British Association for Commercial and Industrial Education.

National Extension College (no date) *NEC Tutor Pack*, Cambridge, National Extension College.

Open College (1991) *Effective Coaching*, Manchester, Open College.

Open College (1992) *Effective Mentoring*, Manchester, Open College.

Open University (1993) *Tuition and Counselling in the Open University: Information for 1994 Appointments*, Milton Keynes, The Open University.

Pedler, M., Burgoyne, J. and Boydell, T. (1991) *The Learning Company: A Strategy for Sustainable Development,* New York, McGraw-Hill.

Temple, H. (1991) *Open Learning in Industry*, Harlow, Longman.

Temple, H. (1994) 'Workplace learners: learners learning in "unconventional" settings' in Lockwood, F. (ed.) *Materials Production in Open and Distance Learning,* pp 155–63, London, Paul Chapman Publishing Ltd.

Training and Development Lead Body (1993) *Training and Development (Flexible and Open Learning) Scheme Booklet*, RSA Examinations Board.

24

IMPLEMENTING EXPERIENCES FROM SMALL-SCALE COURSES TO LARGE EDUCATION SYSTEMS

Pirkko Aalto and Merja Jalava

Learning is an extremely complex mental process which takes place under various conditions and which can be achieved in a number of different ways. Depending on the individual student's situation and on her/his learning objectives, very different learning arrangements may produce the desired result. In addition, the number of students, together with the economic resources available, are factors that affect the nature of the learning environment.

In this chapter we will discuss changes in the culture of learning from the point of view of the changing role of the teacher. What strategies should we adopt in order to construct a learning environment which allows for high-quality and deeper learning? How should the teacher act, and how is it possible to create an environment where the focus is not on the distribution of information, but on the effective guidance of learning?

APPROACH TO LEARNING AS THE KEY FACTOR

We are presently going through a phase of transition where one tradition of teaching is giving way to another (cf. Glaser, 1988; Glaser and Bassok, 1989; von Wright, 1994). The long-established traditional approach to teaching was characterised by teacher control: it was the teacher who defined the student's objectives and planned a pre-programmed learning event which (hopefully) led to the attainment of the objectives. This so-called empiricist approach still provides the teacher with a simple and safe method of curriculum planning and teaching in practice. It is also in conformity with many students' conception of teaching and studying as passive reception of information.

The new culture challenges the teacher to create learning environments which offer problems, solutions, guidance and support for the learner. This so-called constructivist approach to learning emphasises the relevance of the learner's own cognitive processes whereby new knowledge and concepts are incorporated into already existing schemata (Minsky, 1975). The nature of this process as it manifests itself in the learner's learning processes and strategies largely determines what is learnt.

In this chapter we will ask ourselves the following questions through which we will attempt to characterise the basic dimensions of the new approach to teaching:

1 How should the fact that each student makes use of their pre-existing schemata in the course of their learning and has individual learning objectives, be taken into account when providing student support?
2 How can we as teachers move away from the role of distributor of information towards adopting one which is supportive of learning and involves a real dialogue with the student?

From a theoretical approach to learning to practical solutions: situation as the determining factor

The Section for Distance Education, where we work, organises both continuing education for professionals and Open University courses.

Continuing education for professionals is organised for people involved in educational planning and for adult educators in various organisations, in both the public and the private sector. In this type of education, educational objectives are closely related to the development of the students' professional skills and to the development of distance education in the organisations concerned. The student groups are small, with approximately 20–40 students in each. In this sector our tasks include educational planning, together with the planning of teaching arrangements, the preparation of course material, face-to-face teaching and audioconferencing, project management, the preparation and assessment of assignments, and the reception and provision of feedback.

An Open University course has approximately 500 students, who work in study groups of twenty people in local Adult Education Centres throughout Finland. The study group is led by a part-time local counsellor, a tutor whose task is to provide personal guidance and who works in close cooperation with the staff at the university. The university staff is responsible for course planning, for the production of course material, for audioconferencing, for the assessment of assigments and for written feedback, for tutor counselling, and for the overall management of the activities. Teaching is carried out by the course leader, together with full-time or part-time distance teachers.

Although continuing education courses for professionals and Open University courses differ from each other in many respects, both aim at creating a learning environment which builds on the same theoretical considerations. There are, however, essential differences between the two. Compared to Open University courses, small-scale courses for professionals have the following distinctive characteristics:

- the input in terms of work and economic resources per student is considerably larger
- educational planning and practice is strictly in the hands of the same people
- directing the education towards the goals, needs and learning processes of the individual learner is considerably easier.

On the basis of these considerations, courses for professionals would seem to provide an ideal context for applying teaching practice which builds on the constructivist approach. Changing the role of the teacher from a distributor of information to one where the focus is on guiding the learning process is relatively easy in the context of professional continuing education.

Large-scale implementations require administrative structures, extensive cooperation and networks, together with long-term material production and long-term planning. Another essential characteristic of these larger systems is that the various tasks of the teacher are divided among several persons. These factors in turn generate pressures to develop teaching practices which are based on the empiricist approach. Controllable, structured systems and clearly defined large-scale objectives are familiar notions which are easy to achieve, and which provide a feeling of security as far as the achievement of academic standards is concerned. So is it at all sensible to think that continuing education courses could function as laboratories for testing ideas and that the results obtained could be applied to Open University courses which are different in many respects? Our answer to this question is yes, although the practical applications have not yet been completed and there are still a number of interesting problems to be solved.

SCHEMES AND GOALS

When we have a course for professionals ...

In continuing education for professionals the traditional notion of teaching now plays a subsidiary role in the overall implementation of courses. The role of the teacher has changed: she/he is no longer simply a distributor of information, but her/his functions include the construction of learning environments, the creation of learning situations and the provision of support and guidance for the learning process.

The course starts with an initial planning phase which is carried out in cooperation with the client, i.e. the organisation for which the course has been designed, and the students involved. This stage involves the analysis of the potential students' pre-existing schemata, their present goals and learning needs, and their study skills and learning potential (Rowntree, 1992, pp. 37–69). The starting-point for the planning is therefore not in what the educator knows or can do or what she/he is able to transmit to others, but it lies in her/his ability to understand her/his students and to adapt to the individual student's situation. In an ideal situation it is possible to carry out the analysis in cooperation with the students. This can be done in the form of individual or group assignments or in the form of a preliminary seminar. In connection with this type of analysis it is also possible to activate relevant subject-related schemata that the students possess, and to gather information about the students' attitudes and opinions which can then provide the basis for further planning.

The initial stage also involves the preparation of learning material and related learning assignments. A thorough student analysis makes it possible to construct study guides and learning assignments in such a way that they support the student's learning objectives and cognitive processes. This is a challenging task. Can an expert (i.e. a content expert) consider the object of learning from the point of view of a novice (i.e. the student), and if she/he can, how well is she/he likely to succeed in this task?

The planning continues during course work. The curriculum, together with its implementation in practice, are flexible, and this allows for changes in cases where feedback from the learners indicates they are necessary. For instance, assignments and project work are designed in such a way that both the student themself and the teacher can follow the construction and development of schemata. At their best the assignments effectively direct each individual student in their own personal development process.

But having an Open University course ...

In the context of continuing education for professionals, the students' pre-existing schemata and objectives vary considerably, although the students usually share the same professional and organisational backgound. This heterogeneity is multiplied in the case of Open University students. They come from very different situations with very different expectations. It is impossible for the course organiser to respond to the individual needs of each student. In addition, most courses are degree courses where the study content and goals must meet the standards set by the university's faculties. At first sight the situation might seem hopeless as far as implementing the constructivist approach is concerned. Real-life situations, however, offer a number of opportunities. Constructivist learning as a psychological concept involves the idea that learning is achieved through an individual mental construction process. Learning materials and teaching arrangements and distance assignments in particular can be designed in such a way that they require and support reflection and deep learning. To achieve this type of learning, the students require different types of scaffolding (cf. Vygotsky, 1975). For most students, feedback, group work and group discussions appear to be the most important forms of support. Task-oriented study groups will search for meanings and attempt to understand the phenomena underlying the abstract concepts and theories. Each member of the group will make use of this discussion in a way that is appropriate to him. The effectiveness of the groups in promoting and supporting the learning process varies considerably according to human factors which affect the capacity and atmosphere of the group and give each group its peculiar nature.

Individual feedback directs the learner to consider their own thinking processes from outside, at the same time developing the learner's metacognitive skills. There is always, however, the danger of external control: for example, when writing an essay the student's focus is on pleasing the teacher. But even these papers cannot be produced without mental construction and reasoning if the nature of the assignments concerned requires personal involvement, together with the ability to understand and apply. In other words, the student is required to reflect on her/his personal experiences as part of the task.

It is important to remember that Open University students have highly individual objectives which are closely related to their own personal development and to their own competencies and professional activities. Academic achievement and the attainment of the objectives set by the university are a kind of by-product, and the student can decide to what extent she/he will pursue them. Yet, if we take a thorough target group analysis as the starting-point in the context of Open University courses, we will be able to recognise certain schemata and objectives that are characteristic of the students. This type of analysis is especially important because it will give us an opportunity to meet the individual needs of the students by, for example, building a flexible student support system.

LEARNING AS AN INTERACTIVE EVENT

When we have a course for professionals ...

The task of the teacher is to support and to actively follow the student's learning process. The key word is dialogue, i.e. the interaction which takes place in the learning environment. The teacher and the students are constructing a shared reality and at the end of the course the teacher has learned a lot about her/his students' situations and mental realities. The dialogue has several aims. An essential aim is to promote understanding, to help the student to adapt new concepts and approaches to his personal framework of experience. It is difficult for us to depart from pre-existing modes of explanation, and helping the student in this process is an important task of the teacher.

In this dialogue the teacher also encounters the student's approach to learning and her/his personal learning style. It is often empiricist and contains the desire to be taught. If the teacher does not respond to this need they must be able to cope with frustration and resistance on the part of their students (Carey, 1986) The ability to cope with these phenomena is one of the central skills required of the 'new teacher' at least in the present stage of transition within the field of education. The teacher is required to possess communication skills, self-confidence and confidence in the individual student's processes and they must be able to preserve their own identity. In addition to being able to guide and support the individual student, the teacher must also have the knowledge and practical skills required in group management.

In professional continuing education, learning constitutes a process which is closely linked to the learner's work. The students are required to adopt a new way of thinking which involves the idea that learning is not a separate event bound to a particular time and place (cf. workshops or face-to-face seminars), but that it occurs flexibly during working hours and free-time alike and involves several different study and learning arrangements including reading, listening, writing, reasoning, drawing, discussing in groups, working in practice, etc. Teaching cannot, therefore, be regarded as simply consisting of knowledge transfer, but it involves a variety of activities such as motivating, structuring, activating, promoting linkages between new and pre-existing knowledge, developing application skills, correcting mistakes, explaining, promoting retrieval from memory and giving feedback. Both the student and the teacher must internalise the new culture, so that the students will not feel that they are being left to manage on their own, and the teacher will not feel useless, even though teaching and learning do not take place contiguously, at a particular time or in a particular place. This does not, however, mean that the interaction between the student and the teacher would decrease as a result. On the contrary, in some cases it may even increase through an appropriate use of the various media.

During the learning process, the dialogue occurs in written and in oral form, in connection with written assignments, face-to-face seminars, audio-conferences and computer-conferences. The written dialogue between the teacher and the individual student is meaningful and it often has a strong personal flavour. The correspondence takes on the function of a learning conversation where both participants influence the construction of knowledge structures through asking questions and presenting personal views and ideas and reflecting on those presented by the other party.

Each study unit also includes written guidance of self-study either in the form of a study letter or a study guide. The stimulating assignments contained in the guides and the feedback from them form an essential part of the learning guidance. The material could be described as a reflective action guide rather than as a tutorial-in-print (Rowntree, 1992, pp. 134–5). Both the dialogue and the assignments are based on experiental learning, i.e. they make use of the students' own experiences as learning resources (Kolb, 1984). This type of approach is often new to students and it teaches them to appreciate their own experiences and understanding as resources for further learning.

Guidance in face-to-face situations usually involves activating a group of students or smaller subgroups to cooperation, in other words, helping them learn from each other. Also in these situations the role of the teacher is one of a designer, generator and maintainer of situations. She/he can naturally place her/his own expertise at the disposal of her/his students as a learning resource. Active and cooperative learning helps the student to gain deeper insight into the issues under consideration and to find new perspectives (Johnson and Johnson, 1988). These learning situations are, however, also affected by the traditional trust in expertise. One of the teacher's task is, therefore, to support the members of the group in their appreciation of each others' thoughts and opinions.

Audio- and computer-conferences also offer the students an opportunity for group conversation during periods of distance and self-study. Their function is to maintain group activities and affinity and allow for cooperative learning to take place. Audioconferencing is carried out via individual participation techniques. Methods of work include student reports, individual case studies, discussions after presentations, question and answering periods and feedback (Parker, 1984, p. 48). Computer-conferences function as channels for discussing particular themes or questions which have come up during the course. They offer the participants a collective communication environment which promotes interaction. It is, however, often the case that the threshold to active and creative use of the computer is high. And this applies even to organisations where the computer is an everyday tool.

But having an Open University course ...

An Open University student is involved in a dialogue with several persons. This can be an enriching factor, but it may also be a source of distress. In most cases, however, discussions with fellow students provide important support for the learner. Furthermore, an Open University student is also involved in several monologues. These monologues can usually be transformed into dialogues depending on the teacher's professional skills and on the student's own involvement.

A written dialogue?

Learning materials and study guides have a special role in the case of Open University courses. Since the teacher has very few direct contacts with her/his students, she/he frequently communicates with them in writing, through the study guide. The guide is in the form of a monologue, but it may take on a conversation-like nature by giving the student an opportunity to contribute to the interaction through the assignments. In addition, relying on our experiences and feedback received from the students, we can largely anticipate potential problems and required interventions which are all part of the learning process of the average student, particularly during periods of self-study. The problem is, however, that no such thing as the average student exists! Writing the study guides in such a way that the student can recognise the teacher's voice and the conversational tone of the text, and so that the guides give impulses and suggestions rather than exact instructions, is extremely difficult. We need skilled and enthusiastic teachers who are willing to develop these new teaching skills over the long term. The teacher can no longer rely on formal academic writing, but she/he must be capable of a flexible and conversation-like style which takes the recipient into account.

The role of the tutor in the dialogue

The key person in the whole system is the tutor, the leader of the local study group. A considerable amount of the university's input reaches the student via the tutor. She/he carries most of the burden of interpersonal interaction, guidance, management of group processes and provision of feedback. She/he also acts as the content expert. It is crucially important that the individual and group-based activities offered to the student support her/his cognitive construction processes at the level of deeper understanding. Modifying Vygotsky's (1975) view, it can be said that tutoring is like scaffolding which gradually loses importance as the building work progresses. The individual nature of the learning process can also be described in terms of the above simile. If the student's study and conceptualisation skills are not well developed to begin with, the building process must be started from the very beginning, and this means, accordingly, that support is required for a longer time. Therefore, an important part of the tutor's task is to be able to meet the personal needs of individual students, which change as the learning process progresses.

In spite of all these tasks the tutor works part-time. Even a thorough and self-reflective training will not be enough to ensure high-quality tutoring. Tutors need continuous counselling support which will reinforce their identity as the key figures in the supportive network. The counselling can be carried out as audioconferences or as face-to-face tutorials. The need for this support is considerable particularly because of the danger of excessive emotional involvement and emotional confusion generated by group processes. Especially in the early stages of the course when the role of the tutor is taking shape, the situation is very unstable. The students' opposition towards a new kind of self-managed active learning, in other words, their desire to be taught, often causes problems for the tutor. It causes the tutor to adopt a counter-role as a teacher responsible for the learning of others. It is easier to respond to the group's need to depend than to cope with the group's dissatisfaction. However, trained tutors seldom become deeply engaged in this role. Nevertheless, they may feel confused which may in turn prevent them from providing full support for the individuals and the group. On the other hand, being a tutor is socially rewarding. Tutors feel that they learn a lot about communication and are able to improve their content expertise in their own field.

Because we have recognised the fact that the tutor's role is demanding and involves a number of possible traps, we direct considerable resources to tutor counselling. This, however, involves another danger: we may end up imposing excessive guidance and control on the tutor. How can tutors promote self-management in their students if they receive and require direct guidance themselves? The answer lies in the quality of the counselling. Are we able to design the guidance in such a way that it will support the tutor in the same way as the tutor's guidance is supposed to support the students?

The role of the distance teacher in the dialogue

The distance teacher's dialogue involves giving written feedback to the students on their distance assignments. But can this be considered dialogue? Practical experiences have shown that with some students the dialogue develops into a meaningful interaction to which the students contribute by expressing their views and opinions in writing and on the telephone. This type of interaction has relevance for both the student and the teacher.

Audioconferencing is an important part of the communication between the teacher at the university and the student groups. It does not, however, allow for a direct dialogue as in the case of small-scale courses, and the student-centred approach must be realised through other means. Whereas in professional continuing education, audioconferencing manifests itself as a dialogue between the teacher and the individual students, in the case of Open University courses the teacher interacts with the groups. Approximately four to six groups participate in a teleconference at any one time. In this situation the teacher creates a teaching event which builds on the students' questions and themes and group work. In reality, however, the system does not always function as perfectly as it should. Lecturing and departing from a personal framework come automatically to most teachers. In addition, students crave for the university to give them 'real knowledge'. And there may be a hundred students on the line at the same time. An experienced audio teacher is able to make use of the feedback they receive from their students even in a situation like this, although this feedback is different and more difficult to process than that which is received in face-to-face situations. It requires experience and good social skills, together with an ability to put oneself in the student's situation.

CONCLUSION

This chapter is a description of the real situation in which we work. The elements which may appear as fundamentally contradictory in the examples we have given, may simply represent the different aspects of the complex reality in which we operate. Creative and controlled teaching arrangements are produced through recognising the multidimensional nature of reality: flexibility and structure, open and closed, teachers' and students' objectives, external control and self-management, objective and subjective in their different forms are always present in the learning event and the focus shifts according to the situation. Particularly if we take the practical application of the constructivist approach to learning as our starting-point, we cannot present ready-made models for action. The mere notion of constructivist learning implies the rejection of the kind of thinking which does not take the learner into consideration. The student always anchors what they learn into their own life history. The educator has power and responsibilities, but the real power is vested in the student who is constructing their unique interpretation of the world with their own personal framework as the point of departure.

REFERENCES

Carey, S. (1986) 'Cognitive science and science education', *American Psychologist*, 41, pp. 1123–30.
Glaser, R. (1988) 'Cognitive science and education', *International Social Science Journal*, 40 (1), pp. 21–44.
Glaser, R. and Bassok, M. (1989) 'Learning theory and the study of instruction', *Annual Review of Psychology*, 40, pp. 631–66.
Johnson, D. W. and Johnson, R. T. (1988) *Cooperation in Classroom*, Exina MN, Interaction Book Company.
Kolb, D. A. (1984) *Experiential Learning:Experience as a Source of Learning and Development*, Englewood Cliffs, NJ, Prentice-Hall.
Minsky, M. (1975) 'A framework for representing knowledge' in Winston, P. H. (ed.) *The Psychology of Computer Vision*, New York, McGraw Hill.
Parker, L.A. (1984) *Teletraining means Business*, Madison, WI, Centre for Interactive Programs, University of Wisconsin-Extension.
Rowntree, D. (1992) *Exploring Open and Distance Learning*, London, Kogan Page.
von Wright, J. (1994) *Oppimiskäsitysten Historiaa ja Pedagogisia Seurauksia*, Helsinki, Opetushallitus.
Vygotsky, L. S. (1975) *Thought and Language*, Cambridge, MA, MIT Press.

25

MANAGING LEARNING SUPPORT

Jay Reid

INTRODUCTION

The student support model outlined in Figure 25.1 was developed by Jane Brindley (1993) and later modified in an attempt to address student support needs in an institution that had a strongly centralised student support service, but that had moved rapidly towards developing a number of regional open learning centres. The emphasis is on learning support and developing a total service to students.

The model is based on a broad definition of student support and suits an institution that views support as an holistic function and that is prepared to provide an integrated approach. It takes a student perspective, and assumes that support is best provided by multi-skilled professionals with a broad base of experience who can call on specialist advice when and if it is needed, and that students prefer a single 'gateway' for contact. It rests, however, on a high degree of staff training and good organisation and coordination.

EXPLANATION

The model is inclusive, acknowledging the importance of providing quality information, advice and guidance at pre-enrolment and early post-enrolment stages (McInnis-Rankin and Brindley, 1986; Zajkowski, 1993). Support provided at these stages (under 'Institutional Information' in the model) is essential for many students to permit them to successfully plan and develop a course of study; increasingly, too, greater institutional resources need to be allocated to aspects of career counselling and academic planning rather than just providing course or programme information. It is at this pre-enrolment stage that enquiries into the recognition and accreditation of prior learning must be addressed – later is too late!

These initial enquiries for institutional information and advice will often be made to the central organisation, but increasingly there is evidence to support the flexibility of local or regional responses to enquiries – many students need ready personal contact and interaction at this stage (Reid, 1994a) and a centralised distance teaching institution may not be able to respond in time.

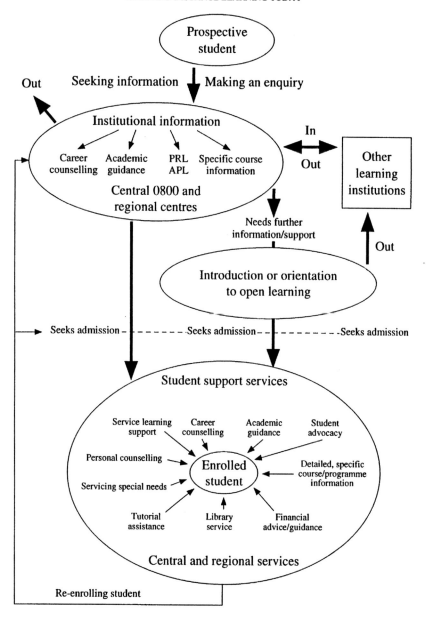

Figure 25.1 Student support services
(*Source*: Brindley (1993), modified by Burton and Reid,
The Open Polytechnic of New Zealand, Auckland, 1994)

Some prospective students will make the decision not to enrol while others may be guided by staff towards other learning institutions that better meet their needs. A small number of prospective students will need an introduction or orientation to open and distance learning, either to assist them to decide whether these forms of learning are the most suitable for them as learners, or to provide a safe and structured introduction or return to tertiary learning (Brookfield *et al.*, 1991).

In the next section of the model ('Student Support Services'), those who seek admission to courses and programmes are able to access a wide range of administrative and learning support. In the particular case of The Open Polytechnic of New Zealand (TOPNZ), where the model was developed, students have the option of a central 0800 freephone service which acts as a gateway to all available services, or regional phone or face-to-face contact. Recent research (Reid, 1994b) shows an even split between central and regional use by students, dependent on the context of student need.

In the model the following services are available through a variety of sources:

- career counselling
- academic guidance
- student advocacy
- learning support (including study and exam skills seminars, access to formal study groups and informal buddy networks, 1:1 assistance ...)
- personal counselling
- support for special needs
- specific course and programme information
- financial advice
- a library service
- specific one-to-one tutorial assistance.

No distinction is made between learning and administrative support, and freephone telephone operators and regional staff refer to the most appropriate person who is best placed to deal with a learner's needs.

ISSUES RELATED TO THE MANAGEMENT OF LEARNING SUPPORT

There are many issues impacting on learning support. I have selected four broad themes and will comment on each in some depth, drawing upon theory and relating each to published comment. While the themes and issues raised relate to the model of support outlined, they are common issues and tensions faced by all those who work in learning support.

Ownership: institutional and learner perspectives

Institutional perspectives of learner support will lie within one of two positions. The first position is complementary, viewing student support as an essential integral component of the teaching/learning process, one that has the learner as the central focus. The second position is compensatory, regarding students as having deficits in learning that need to be fixed, advocating specialists to relieve tutors of their responsibilities for meeting individual needs. Nunan (1993) charitably describes support in these circumstances as being applied in a 'reactive' fashion. The institutional perspective will dramatically constrain or liberate what is determined to be learning support, as well as affect the organisation and coordination of the service.

But the institutional perspective is equally a pragmatic one. While Earwaker (1992) writes of the challenge and risk of higher education on the one hand, and the security and safety of student support on the other, Carter and Clilverd (1993, p. 388) put the issue more bluntly: 'The cost of making a choice of goal and failing to achieve it, for the student and the organisation, is large in financial terms but enormous in human terms.'

The Open Training and Education Network, with which they are associated, takes a problem-solving approach using an integrated student support system, putting together a range of specialist options at the phase of enrolment or learning where problems occur. Learners without support are likely to delay completion of a programme or drop out altogether (Rowntree, 1992; Dallas and Lynch, 1992), and that support is most needed early in the first year of study of a programme (Roberts, 1984). Carter and Clilverd's approach relates well to the model of student support presented.

But whatever their position, all institutions *are* preoccupied with attrition rates (Roberts, 1984; Garland, 1993). Even where a few institutions appear to lack real commitment to learners as individuals, withdrawals of learners inevitably in turn mean some degree of withdrawal of Government funding. Increasingly learners who withdraw either complain because they feel they have not had quality service for the fee paid, or tell other learners of their dissatisfaction. Good news about an institution may well be slow to spread, but bad news spreads like a rash! In this case, in a competitive environment, the bad news can equally affect the institution's financial viability as enrolments decrease.

The student perspective may well be necessarily different from the institutional perspective. Learners probably require more individual personal support than general support (Rowntree, 1992), demanding that what is provided relates to their specific and unique concerns and needs. Rowntree, for example, cites evidence to support the view that institutional use of technology is mechanical and impersonal, and therefore often not always viewed positively by students. Dekkers and Cuskelly (date unknown) stress that distance learners are not generally not isolated by choice, and that open learning centres have an important role to play in providing for and facilitating interaction with staff and students, rather than taking on the mere supplementary role sometimes ascribed by institutions. They identify four important areas associated with a student perspective:

- access to academic support and other students – preferably through direct contact
- student learning characteristics – accommodation of a range of learning styles, rather than mere emphasis on study packages
- access to library and other resources to learning – especially for independent study materials
- understanding of the student learning environment and background – awareness of the family and work commitments of students.

There is ample evidence to confirm what students want and a high degree of commonality, whatever the institution and whatever the country. There is common agreement between both learner and institutional perspectives that there is a need for a place for learner/learner and learner/teacher interaction, for access to library and other resources, and (cautiously) a place for the introduction and test-running of new technology applications, particularly telecommunications (Kember and Dekkers, 1987; Harrison, c1991; Livingston, 1994).

Learning support, therefore, is not an 'add on' but 'an all pervasive component of educational processes which ensures that learning and teaching are approached from a learner centred vision of education' (Nunan, 1993, p. 1).

Learning support *is* as important as teaching; it *is* teaching; it is central to all we do as professionals.

Open vs traditional education and learning

The learning support offered by different institutions may be very similar, but there are differences between traditional learning institutions and the open learning institutions. Open learning, for example, has certain traditions: an emancipatory tradition, a liberal tradition and an industrial tradition (Reid, 1994b) and these traditions require a different orientation for learning support.

Through its emancipatory tradition, open learning is linked not only with the opening up of opportunities, but also with the breaking down of barriers. In this sense it is associated with learners previously denied access to education. While this can be construed as operating in a personal sense, it is linked, too, with the breaking down of structural constraints – institutional, social, cultural and political/economic. The management of open learning would seem to bring institutional responsibilities for access and ultimately, for equity. In this respect there is a very delicate balance between the responsibility of the institution to give career and academic counselling, and provide pathways through bureaucracy, acting as an advocate for learners, while also preserving its own integrity and maintaining an academic function. It is enormously difficult and challenging for any institution to act on the one hand as an adviser and advocate for particular learners, and on the other to concern itself with issues of quality, academic performance and public accountability. These are complementary and conflicting roles.

The liberal tradition of open learning is linked to its emancipatory tradition. There is a general recognition of the merit or ideal of universal access to education, lifelong learning and 'second chance' learning, and the belief that for a variety of reasons these are not achieved by a considerable number of people within the conventional secondary or tertiary education system, and agreement that historically what an institution has offered has not always been matched by individual learner expectations. A key message here to those involved in providing learning support is that many learners will have quite mixed feelings about their learning, requiring a sensitivity in support perhaps not matched by other groups.

Open learning also has an industrial tradition. This tradition is training-based and justified by cost-effectiveness and efficiencies, flexibility and more accurate targeting of specific skills for employees. Furthermore, it allows industry to assume responsibility and control for its own training, strengthening individual autonomy, adaptability and individual independence which are seen as key business skills. In addition, open learning is often seen as the most flexible and the only really equitable response to upskilling, training or retraining large numbers in the workforce. It is attractive to employers because of the stake they have in it, the control employers can exercise and the minimum disruption to normal work (Department of Employment, 1993). Therefore, learning support's relationship with its local business community is critical, as is its ability to work flexibly on business sites and assess employer and employee needs. There is no reason to contextualise learning support as remaining within the confines of institutions.

Meeting learner need

The provision of traditional education need not necessarily require much information about individual learners because learning outcomes tend to be determined in advance, and historically learners have had to buy what providers have produced in whatever form it has been 'sold', rather than providers market their materials based on what learners want and need (Rowntree, 1992).

Whether terms such as 'customer' or 'client' are used, there is no doubt that learners are more discerning and demanding than they have been in the past – more and more, they demand to be satisfied. In meeting this learner satisfaction, those involved in providing and supporting open learning take on responsibilities towards the learner. One of these responsibilities is to gather information about learners and use it in a way to enhance learning. The variety of information gathered could include:

- characteristics of learners as a group (e.g., full-time work, aged between 25 and 50, goal-oriented, etc.)
- why individuals are studying, with a view to promoting intrinsic benefits which learners can apply to their jobs and lives
- assisting learners to identify their own unique learning beliefs (and possibly match these to others')
- assessing their learning styles, towards a view of incorporating them into the learning material or using them as part of the learning process
- assisting learners to assess their own skill-base in terms of strengths and weaknesses.

Providers are faced with the practicalities of personalising learning: with assisting learners to incorporate their own views and experiences into their learning, in aiding learners to set personal goals and objectives, and in fostering the ability to monitor personal progress.

Two major emphases are apparent in the relationship of open learning to learning: transmitting knowledge and developing the whole person. Providers may well be faced with what can be the dilemma of developing the whole person, while at the same time having the responsibility and expectation of transmitting substantial amounts of knowledge in some form. This latter is the easier to achieve, with an emphasis on opening up access to knowledge which is seen as a commodity and assessed through recognition of competencies, and provided by packaging material and distributing it through distance education. The former, however, is far more difficult to achieve because it assumes the role of facilitation, of using the strength and experience of the tutor and learning support staff to assist the learner build upon experience, competence and interest. The model of student support outlined in this chapter is firmly based on a development model of learning support.

Through a development model it is theoretically possible and obviously desirable to increase learner autonomy (Ross, 1990) by increasing learner choice in areas of outcomes, content, learning resources and assessment. It ties in with general institutional expectations for adult learners (Hodgson, 1989). Yet, as has been pointed out (Candy, 1991; Paul, 1990a; Robinson, 1992), one should not assume that the products (students) of open learning institutions are more autonomous, independent or self-directed than when they entered! However, irrespective of this argument, with learner choice comes learner responsibility for the outcomes of the choice, and provider responsibility for supplying detail and support that enables the learner to make effective choices.

Autonomy, accountability, support and control

The student support model outlined earlier in this chapter combines central and regional services in a seamless integrated service to students, taking student enquiry as the focus.

Yet inevitably in any model based on these premises there are central and regional tensions. Ross Paul (1990b) ably outlines the classic tensions between the need for regional advocacy and flexibility on the one hand, and central policy and control on the other. Regional presences introduce management difficulties for any organisation, for the primary issues are balances between power, control and support on the one hand, and flexibility and regional need on the other. Any natural and expected differences in central and regional perspectives are complicated by the values and management style of the institution, yet there are basic understandings which if assimilated can reduce the hazards of potential conflict, especially for those working directly with students. Paul makes five excellent points. Each of these has been restated in terms of the focus of this chapter and the model of student support used.

- 'Jurisdictions and responsibilities must be very clearly defined ... and reviewed regularly by both parties on the basis of their effectiveness in carrying out established policies and procedures' (Paul, 1990b, pp. 109– 10).
- *All* staff must be subject to institutional policy, but regional staff must have the latitude to respond to local need without requesting permission for every deviation from policy. Parameters must be agreed, set and made explicit.
- The value of direct feedback from 'real' students must be appreciated by the central organisation, as well as the genuine difficulty in dealing with problems face to face. Regional staff need to adhere to policy, but have latitude on detail.
- The central organisation should have an emphasis on quality and client liaison that encourages regional reflection and suggestion. It needs to be particularly sensitive to the needs, expectations and vulnerabilities associated with open learners. A Regional Centre can offer a good-quality assurance programme by 'auditing' central policy according to its effectiveness.
- Staff development and training are crucial issues, but these relate to understanding the problems and issues of both the central and regional perspective. Appointments to regional positions require staff with exceptional skills – professionals who are generalists, highly motivated and very flexible.

IMPLICATIONS

A model of student support has been outlined. Broad themes which include classic tensions and which relate to the model have been described. What, then, are some implications for those who work in the learning support area?

- Institutional ethos should be made explicit – it will affect the model of learning support offered.
- There is a need to know much more about the students who are enrolled, not only to respond to what they want and need within the constraints of an institution's operating environment, but also to personalise learning support so that it incorporates individuals' own experiences and allows them to set their own learning objectives.
- Developing learner choice and control is a major goal of learning support.
- There must be an absolute concern for a quality service – educational institutions have not always in the past had this preoccupation.
- Particularly for institutions operating central and regional services, there must either be a single gateway as entry to students making enquiries, or very well understood multiple gateways.
- Roles change and blur. These days with an emphasis on facilitation traditional roles which separate academic and support staff are fuzzy. All staff must be valued and seen as professionals working towards a common end.
- Technology is wonderful when it enhances learning; when it doesn't, it can turn a learner off for life. Careful choices must be made about what technology is implemented, how it will be introduced to learners, and what part it will play in instruction or support.
- Irrespective of this, students do want access to independent learning materials and immediate access to the institution's library.
- Learning support is not just a liberal notion; there are contractual elements to it which bring certain responsibilities for both provider and learner. These should be made explicit.
- There is increasing evidence that within distance and open learning institutions students are eager for those providing learning support to take a more pro-active stance (Reid, 1994b).
- Part of a pro-active stance means making initial contact with target groups and individuals, having established community networks and relating to business and industry.
- We need to be aware of the assumptions that are associated with logistical independence and as learning support providers realise that these 'freedoms' may constrain and bind as much as any others.
- Learning support staff must have flexibility within institutional policy to respond directly to learner need.

- The selection and training of support staff is critical, requiring multi-skilled staff who have a broad base of experience, and highly developed interpersonal and communication skills.
- As a payback, learning support has much to offer the institution. It is one of the best sources of feedback reporting on what is successful and what is not, assisting the whole institution with course planning, the development of resources, teaching strategies ...

Finally, managing learning support will bring many challenges, but its success in any institution will be underpinned by the sharing of a common vision and model of support which places the learner firmly at the centre of *everyone's* efforts. The model of student support suggested earlier in this chapter is one means of achieving this.

REFERENCES

Brindley, J. (1993) 'Student support', an unpublished seminar given to staff of The Open Polytechnic of New Zealand.

Brookfield, B., Thompson, J. and McIlroy, A. (1991) 'Assisting extra-mural students to develop effective and efficient study and examination techniques' in Hornblow, D. and Stevens, K., Proceedings of the 7th Annual DEANZ Conference of New Zealand, Wellington.

Candy, P. (1991) 'Evolution, revolution or devolution: increasing learner control in the instructional setting' in Boud, D. and Griffin, V. (eds) *Appreciating Adults Learning: From the Learners' Perspective*, London, Kogan Page.

Carter, C. and Clilverd, S. (1993) 'Student support: the integrated OTEN model' in Nunan, T. (ed.) *Distance Education Futures*, Australian and South Pacific External Studies Association.

Dallas, D. and Lynch, J. (1992) *Evaluation of Four Regional Support Centres for Students of The Open Polytechnic of New Zealand*, December, Lower Hutt, Open Polytechnic of New Zealand.

Dekkers, J. and Cuskelly, E. (date unknown) *The Establishment and Use of Electronic Mail for Distance Education*, source unknown.

Department of Employment (1993) 'Opening employers' eyes to flexible learning', *Skills and Enterprise Briefing*, Nottingham, Issue 19/93, August.

Earwaker, J. (1992) *Helping and Supporting Students*, Buckingham, SRHE and Open University Press.

Garland, M. (1993) 'Student perceptions of the situational, institutional, dispositional and epistemological barriers to persistence', *Distance Education*, 14(2).

Harrison, C. M. (c1991) *Open All Hours: The TAFE Learning Resource Centre – Its Roles in Open Learning*, source unknown.

Hodgson, V. (1989) 'Open learning and technology-based learning materials', *Distance Education*, 10(1).

Kember, D. and Dekkers, J. (1987) 'The role of study centres for academic support in distance education', *Distance Education*, 8(1).

Livingston, K. (1994) *Student Support Direction Paper*, May, Lower Hutt, Open Polytechnic of New Zealand.

McInnis-Rankin, E. and Brindley, J. (1986) 'Student support services' in Mugridge, I. and Kaulman, D. (eds) *Distance Education in Canada*, London, Croom Helm.

Nunan, T. (1993) 'The role of stakeholders in achieving or improving quality: exploring some issues in the context of Australian Higher Education' in *Quality Assurance in Open and Distance Learning: European and International Perspectives*, Cambridge, Downing College.

Paul, R. H. (1990a) 'Towards a new measure of success: developing independent learners', *Open Learning*, February.

Paul, R. H. (1990b) *Open Learning and Open Management: Leadership and Integrity in Distance Education*, London, Kogan Page.

Reid, J. (1994a) 'The potential of open learning', addresses given to The New Zealand Qualifications Authority Conferences, *New Ways to Learn*, Auckland and Christchurch, March.

Reid, J. (1994b) 'Open learning centres: theory and reality', unpublished preliminary data from a thesis.

Roberts, D. (1984) 'Ways and means of reducing early student drop-out rates', *Distance Education*, 5(1).

Robinson, R. (1992) 'Andragogy applied to the Open College learner', *Research in Distance Education*, 4(1), January.

Ross, B. (1990) 'Distance education centres and open education' in *Distance Education for Training in Business and Industry: Forum Papers*, Tenth Biennial Forum, 10–14 July 1989, Gippsland Institute of Advanced Education, Churchill, Victoria, Centre for Distance Learning.

Rowntree, D. (1992) *Exploring Open and Distance Learning*, London, Kogan Page.

Zajkowski, M. (1993) 'Business students learning at a distance: one form of pre-enrolment counselling and its effects on retention', *Distance Education*, 14(2).

Part VII

TEXTUAL MATERIALS

26

THE LAYOUT AND DESIGN OF TEXTUAL MATERIALS FOR DISTANCE LEARNING

James Hartley

Most materials provided for distance learning come in the form of print. However, there is wide variety. The UK Open University's module for *Design and Technology in the Secondary School Curriculum,* for instance, contains the following printed materials:

- a study guide
- a book of readings
- materials from different curriculum projects and programmes
- additional texts on design, quality assurance and curriculum planning (drawn from existing UK Open University material and other sources)

and

- an assessment guide.

Thus, with distance learning, students receive *packages* of materials, many of which will vary in their presentation and level of difficulty.

Clearly, in a chapter of this length, it is not possible for me to comment on the individual design of these various bits and pieces. What I want to suggest is that there are three broad issues which can be considered with respect to most of them. These issues are:

1 What do these documents look like?
2 How easy are they to read, use and understand?
3 How can the authors of these documents find this out?

Accordingly, this chapter will be divided into three sections to cover:

- text layout and design;
- readability, use and comprehension; and
- techniques of evaluation.

There are a number of useful reference works that discuss these issues in more detail than I can here, and I have listed these in the bibliography at the end of the chapter.

TEXT LAYOUT AND DESIGN

There are two overriding considerations that must be borne in mind when designing textual materials for instruction. The first of these is that the layout should always be clear and simple, and not confusing. The second is that the detailing of the typography should always be consistent from page to page. These considerations will affect most of the decisions made by a designer or a design team producing a text for instruction (Hartley, 1994).

One of the first of these decisions concerns what size page to employ. This choice is constrained by many factors, particularly how the text is to be used, and the array of standard paper sizes (A4, A5 etc.) available. Most designers of distance learning materials opt for A4 but, as many learners will testify, A4 has many disadvantages. A4 documents are hard to shelve, hard to find desk space for, and hard to keep open and flat without a ring binding. A4 documents do have the advantage, however, that they can be used in various formats (with two, three or even four columns), and that it is easier to provide full-size illustrations.

Clearly this first decision about the size – and the orientation – of the page affects a host of other decisions about, for example, margins, column widths, the choice of type-sizes, the interline spacing, and the positioning of illustrations, diagrams, tables and graphs. Some observations (adapted from Hartley, 1994) are:

- It is important when considering the width of margins to remember that text is often photocopied and placed in a file or folder. This means, if the text is printed on both sides, that both the outer and the inner margin need to be wider than they often are. Otherwise, the edge of the text can be obscured by the binding procedure used. A margin of 2.5cm is recommended.
- It is probably wise to think in terms of only one or two columns at most, or only to use a third column for specialised comments. Remember, the aim is to keep the typography simple. Finding one's way around multiple columns can be confusing, especially if there are other textual features to navigate.
- Larger type-sizes can lead to longer lines of text, as well as fewer lines per page. With A4, of course, one might comfortably use a slighter larger size than normal. But, with most texts, type-sizes seem to err on the small side. (This text, for example, is printed in 10 point.) The Royal National Institute for the Blind suggests that 12 point is more appropriate for most texts – although rarely used – because most people can read 12 point type, even when they are slightly visually impaired. Older readers, too, might profit from more concern in this respect.
- It is important to keep clear and consistent the relationship between the text and the illustrative materials. Diagrams or tables, for example, should not be slotted in, reduced or enlarged, just to fit the space

available. These materials should appear in a sensible size, as soon possible after their first textual reference.

- One way of achieving this is to plan in advance the vertical spacing of the text. If decisions are made in advance about the amount of space above and below headings, between the paragraphs, and above and below the captions as well as above and below the illustrative materials themselves – and these decisions are rigidly adhered to – then this will ensure the clarity of the text.
- Finally, let me make a few points about the use of typography to cue points of emphasis. Readers will be familiar with the typographic devices one can use in this respect – italic, bold, capital letters, larger type-sizes and colour. Again, in keeping with my emphasis on simplicity, I think it important not to overdo this use of typographic cues. A simple rule of thumb is to use only one cue at a time and, of course, to use this cue consistently throughout the text.

Figures 26.1 and 26.2 provide a 'before and after' illustration. Here changes are mainly made to the text, although I have increased the type-size from 10 to 12 point type. Figure 26.1 shows a piece of text as it was originally produced; Figure 26.2 shows the same text revised in terms of its readability and layout.

READABILITY, USE AND COMPREHENSION

There are several guidelines on how to write clear prose, and how to revise existing documents in order to make them easier to understand (see, for example, Britton *et al.,* 1993). However, there are no firm rules, accepted by all, that are routinely applicable. None the less, it is possible to make useful suggestions that writers can consider with reference to their own work.

Certain tools can be used to evaluate the suitability of an intended text for its audience. They can be used by *authors* when they are producing text, and they can be used by *readers* or *judges* when they are assessing the suitability of published texts for others. Let me consider just two such measures here – readability formulae and readers' judgements.

Readability formulae aim to predict the suitability of text, mainly for children of different reading ages, thus their scope for distance learning materials is limited. Typically a readability formula contains two main measures combined with a constant to predict a reading age. These two main measures are: (a) the average length of the sentences in samples of the text; and (b) the average length of the words (usually measured in terms of the number of syllables) within these sentences. Clearly the underlying notion is that the longer the sentences, and the more complex the vocabulary, the more difficult the text will be to read. Such a notion is obviously sensible but, of course, it has limitations. So readability formulae can only provide a rough guide to difficulty (Davison and Green, 1987).

The Patient's Charter

The rights and standards set out in this leaflet form *The Patient's Charter.*

The Charter is a central part of the programme to improve and modernise the delivery of the National Health Service to the public, while continuing to reaffirm its fundamental principles.

The Patient's Charter puts the Government's *Citizen's Charter* initiative into practice in the health service.

Every citizen already has the following National Health Service rights:

- to receive health care on the basis of clinical need, regardless of ability to pay;
- to be registered with a GP;
- to receive emergency medical care at any time, through your GP or the emergency ambulance service and hospital accident and emergency departments;
- to be referred to a consultant, acceptable to you, when your GP thinks it necessary and to be referred for a second opinion if you and your GP agree this is desirable;
- to be given a clear explanation of any treatment proposed, including any risks and any alternatives, before you decide whether you will agree to the treatment;
- to have access to your health records, and to know that those working for the NHS will, by law, keep their contents confidential;
- to choose whether or not you wish to take part in medical research or medical student training.

Figure 26.1 The 'before' illustration
(Readability level = 17.3 years)

Today, with the advent of word-processing systems, it is easy to apply some fairly complex readability formulae. For example, my word processor currently provides me with two measures of readability derived from two different formulae. When these measures were applied to this text the following results emerged:

Formula	Suggested reading age
1	18 years
2	15–17 years

The Patient's Charter

This leaflet describes your rights as a patient in the National Health Service.

Our aim is to let you know what you can expect from the National Health Service in our efforts to improve it.

The Patient's Charter says:

- You have the right to medical attention, whether or not you are able to pay for it.
- You have the right to any emergency treatment. This may be given by your doctor, the emergency ambulance service, or a hospital.
- You have the right to have your own doctor.
- Your doctor can, if necessary, send you to a consultant, but this consultant must be acceptable to you.
- You have the right to receive a clear account of what will happen to you before you decide whether or not to have any treatment. This account must describe the risks involved and outline any other possible treatments.
- You have the right to see another doctor or consultant for a second opinion, if you and your doctor agree.
- You have the right to choose whether or not you wish to take part in medical research, or in the teaching of medical students.
- You have the right to see your own medical records, and to know that they are confidential.

Figure 26.2 The 'after' illustration
(Readability level = 14.3 years)

My program also gave me some more statistics. It told me, among other things, that:

- the average sentence length was 14.8 words, and that most readers could easily comprehend sentences of this length;

- the average word length was 1.64 syllables, and that most readers could comprehend the vocabulary used in this chapter; and
- the average paragraph length was 2.1 sentences, and that most readers would easily follow paragraphs of this length! (I actually doubt this last statistic – which implies that computer-based data need careful watching. I suspect the program is counting listed points as separate paragraphs.)

As far as Figures 26.1 and 26.2 are concerned, the readability formulae indicate that the average reading age required for Figure 26.1 is 17.3 years, and for Figure 26.2 it is 14.3 years. This change was achieved by deleting some text that did not seem important, by changing one long list into a series of separate sentences, and by simplifying these sentences and their wording.

Many academic texts are harder to read than this chapter, and it is not always easy to write clearly and simply. Authors of distance learning materials, however, are advised to check their materials from time to time, and especially those additional materials that they do not write themselves. Learners may be discouraged if the writing is too 'academic'.

Readers' judgements may help in this respect. One of the standard procedures that writers can use to assess the difficulty of their documents is to try them out with appropriate samples of readers. One tip that I find particularly helpful in this respect is to ask such readers to mark or circle on the text any parts that they think that readers *less able than themselves* will find difficult. In my experience readers are much more likely to comply with this request than with one which asks them to mark any sections that *they themselves* find difficult!

One problem that I suspect is particularly acute for distance learners is finding their way around – and cross-referring between – the different materials that they are sent. The term *access structures* has evolved to describe the various techniques that writers use to help learners in this respect. Access structures include the following:

- tables of contents
- chapter titles
- summaries – beginning, interim, concluding
- running headings
- sub-headings
- page, section, and paragraph numbers
- glossaries
- indexes
- in-text questions
- study guides.

Such items are designed to help the learner, but some of them can be overdone, especially numbering systems (see Waller, 1980). Furthermore, what little research there is, suggests that students often avoid items like tables and in-text questions and make limited uses of such devices (Marland *et al.*, 1990). Indeed, some writers remind us that it is quality that is important in distance learning materials: loading up the text with trivial in-text questions may be counter-productive.

These issues are important to bear in mind when we think of assessing learners' *comprehension*. Many distance learning materials are academic rather than practical: thus they do not ask readers to do things, or check their ability to do so. Consequently, it is difficult to measure their effectiveness. We shall come to this issue again shortly, but here I want simply to draw attention to a distinction frequently being drawn these days between 'deep' and 'surface' learning (see Marland *et al.*, 1984). Presumably most authors of distance learning materials want their readers to think meaningfully about what it is they are reading, and not simply to be able to regurgitate it in examinations – and then forget it. For texts to be meaningful they need to use language with which their readers are familiar, to include experiences which their readers share, to provide meaningful examples, and possibly to provide examples and problems which readers have to work through in order to follow the subsequent exposition. Naturally, all this is difficult to achieve when the readership is varied, as it usually is in distance learning. Thus the text has to be evaluated to ensure that misconceptions do not occur.

TECHNIQUES OF EVALUATION

It is comforting to think that, because you have written something, and have applied all the expertise that you have, there is nothing more to do. Unfortunately, as psychologists often remind us, it is wiser to obtain some data to see if our suppositions are upheld. Data can be obtained for two purposes: (a) to see if the text does what we say it does; and (b) to see how the text can be improved in the light of the data obtained.

Distance learning materials can be evaluated in many different ways. One three-fold distinction developed by Schriver (1989) that I find useful is that between:

- text-focused studies
- expert-focused studies, and
- reader-focused studies.

Text-focused studies measure the characteristics of the text. Readability formulae are good examples, and so too is the use of computer-based grammar checkers to compile data of the sort discussed above. These measures have the advantage that you don't have to consult the readers – or anyone else – and they can be quite helpful. But I don't think I would wish to rely on them alone.

Expert-focused studies rely on the opinions of others – for example, colleagues, members of the design team, and outside subject-matter experts.

The opinions of experts are valuable but, again, they may not be sufficient on their own. Experts tend to tell you different things from learners.

Reader-focused studies, as their name implies, collect information from relevant readers. This information may be simple – such as preference judgements – or it may be more complicated – involving observing and questioning what readers do, where they go, and why, while they are reading a particular text.

These three kinds of studies complement each other. Doubtless few writers of distance learning materials will want to bother making experimental comparisons between different versions of the same piece of text, or between different instructional procedures. However, sampling from each of these three approaches to evaluation may be helpful. Furthermore, writers may find it useful to employ the tool of re-iteration to evaluate how well their text is performing. Here the notion is that first of all one can develop a piece of text designed to achieve a particular job. Then one can select appropriate tools from one's 'evaluation toolbox' to test how well the text does achieve its objectives. The results obtained will tell you how well – or how badly – the text is doing. The text can then be revised in the light of these results, and then re-tested again. This procedure – write, test, revise, test, revise – can be re-iterated until the writer is sure that the text is achieving its stated objectives.

BIBLIOGRAPHY

In this chapter I have discussed briefly a number of different issues concerning the design and layout of distance learning materials. However, fuller discussions – with illustrations – can be found in the following references.

Learning from instructional text
Baath, J. A. (1986) 'Learning by written material', *European Journal of Distance Education*, 2, pp. 8–23.
Britton, B. K., Woodward, A. and Binkley, M. (eds) (1993) *Learning from Textbooks*, Hillsdale, NJ, Erlbaum.
Lockwood, F. (1992) *Activities in Self-Instructional Texts*, London, Kogan Page.
Marland, P., Patching, W. and Putt, I. (1992) *Learning From Text: Glimpses Inside the Minds of Distance Learners*, Townsville, Australia, James Cook University of North Queensland.
Marland, P., Patching, W., Putt, I. and Putt, R. (1990) 'Distance learners' interactions with text while studying', *Distance Education*, 11(1), pp. 71–91.
Marland, P., Patching, W., Putt, I. and Store, R. (1984) 'Learning from distance-teaching materials: a study of students' mediating responses', *Distance Education*, 5(2), pp. 215–36.
Marland, P. and Store, R. E. (1982) 'Some instructional strategies for improving learning from distance teaching materials', *Distance Education*, 3(1), pp. 72–106.

Designing instructional text

Dekkers, J., Kemp, N., Nourens, F. and Towers, S. (1991) *Course Materials Development for Distance Education*, Rockhampton, Queensland, Division of Distance and Continuing Education, University College of Central Queensland.

Hartley, J. (1994) *Designing Instructional Text*, 3rd edn, London, Kogan Page.

Misanchuk, E. R. (1992) *Preparing Instructional Text: Document Design Using Desktop Publishing*, Englewood Cliffs, NJ, Educational Tech-nology Publications.

Rowntree, D. (1994) *Preparing Materials for Open, Distance and Flexible Learning*, London, Kogan Page.

Waller, R. (1980) 'Notes on transforming No. 4: numbering systems in text' in Hartley, J. (ed.) *The Psychology of Written Communication*, London, Kogan Page.

Readability and clear writing

Britton, B. K., Gulgoz, S. and Glynn, S. (1993) 'Impact of good and poor writing on learners: research and theory' in Britton, B. K. *et al.* (eds) *Learning from Textbooks: Theory and Practice*, Hillsdale, NJ, Erlbaum.

Davison, A. and Green, G. (eds) (1987) *Linguistic Complexity and Text Comprehension: A Re-examination of Readability with Alternative Views*, Hillsdale, NJ, Erlbaum.

Race, P. (1992) *53 Interesting Ways to Write Open Learning Materials*, Bristol, Technical and Educational Services.

Steinberg, E. R. (ed.) (1991) *Plain Language: Principles and Practice*, Detroit, Wayne State University Press.

Evaluating instructional text

Hartley, J. (1995) 'Is this chapter any use? Methods for evaluating text' in Wilson, J. R. and Corlett, E. N. (eds) *Evaluation of Human Work*, (2nd edn), London, Taylor & Francis.

Schriver, K. A. (1989) 'Evaluating text quality: the continuum from text-focused to reader-focused methods', *IEEE Transactions on Professional Communication*, 32(4), pp. 238–55.

27

USING INSTRUCTIONAL ILLUSTRATIONS FOR DISTANCE EDUCATION

Richard Lowe

It is widely accepted that, compared with materials for classroom instruction, the textual components in distance education materials need to be both more explicit with respect to the presented content and more supportive with respect to the instructional guidance that is provided for the learner. A similar expectation is typically not held for the illustrations in such materials. This may be a consequence of the secondary role that illustrations have traditionally served while text carried most of the responsibility for presentation of content. However, in our increasingly visually oriented society, such a role for illustrations seems inappropriate. This chapter is based on the assumption that the illustrations used in distance education materials should also be more explicit and supportive than would be considered appropriate for other modes of instruction.

It is still comparatively rare for illustrations to be treated as a fully integrated part of the instructional design and development process. The reliance on text as the primary means of communicating is deeply embedded in academic discourse and tends to be reflected in the way in which learning materials of all types have been produced. In the past, the primacy of text over illustrations was partly due to the specialist skills needed to produce illustrations and their high cost of production relative to text. However, recent developments in computer technology have made the production and presentation of graphic materials both easier and less expensive. With fewer barriers to the inclusion of illustrations in distance education materials, they can be expected to make up an increasing proportion of these materials in the future. It is therefore appropriate to consider what is required to make use of these illustrations in an instructionally effective manner.

In addressing the topic of this chapter, I have chosen not to present a range of examples of instructional illustrations from a variety of specialist subject areas. Instead, I have 'invented' a hypothetical example involving a familiar object (a videocassette) so that no specialist knowledge is required of you, the reader. We will assume that the purpose of the illustrations presented in this chapter is to help the distance learner understand the cassette's internal structure and function.

PURPOSES OF ILLUSTRATIONS IN DISTANCE EDUCATION MATERIALS

There are two widely accepted broad categories of use for illustrations within instructional materials (Peeck, 1987):

(a) motivational-affective purposes, in which the intention is for illustrations to perform functions such as eliciting and maintaining the learner's engagement with the material or provoking particular affective responses to the subject matter;

(b) cognitive purpose, in which the ultimate goals include helping the learner to understand and remember the subject matter or to perform tasks such as problem-solving.

Both of these uses are undoubtedly important in distance education. Capturing and sustaining the attention and interest of distance education students is a necessary precondition for any cognitive purposes of the materials. However, an author needs to be clear about what the illustration is intended to do and the limitations of the motivational-affective effect. Unfortunately, far too much faith often seems to be placed in this effect, almost as if it will make up for any difficulties that exist in the subject matter. The content and treatment of the illustrations themselves may stimulate the learner to engage with the text. Further, illustrations can be a valuable graphic design element that make instructional materials initially more inviting to the learner. For example, it is considered effective to use illustrations to break up what may otherwise be dauntingly large blocks of text (Evans *et al.*, 1987). However, care must be taken that precedence of graphic design considerations (such as the aesthetic qualities of a page-spread) over cognitive-processing demands does not actually make it more difficult for the learner to work through the subject matter being presented (see Goldsmith, 1986).

With regard to cognitive purposes, the mere presence of an illustration in an instructional segment appears to be of little ongoing value in facilitating the learning of material in that segment unless it is appropriately related to the segment's subject matter. Purnell and Solman (1991) suggest that instructional illustrations should be given a degree of consideration comparable to that given to instructional text. This would mean treating illustrations as an 'equal partner' with other forms of representation right from the very beginning of the instruction design process (Lowe, 1993). By dividing up the information to be covered between illustrations and other forms of representation, each can address those aspects of the content to which it is most suited. This requires that the content analysis includes a

289

consideration of the nature of the subject matter that is sufficiently detailed to permit this partitioning of instructional responsibility (see Guri-Rozenblit, 1988).

SPECIAL CHALLENGES FOR ILLUSTRATIONS IN DISTANCE EDUCATION

If the illustrations included in distance education materials are to carry a substantial proportion of the instructional responsibility, the aim should be for the learner to treat the pictorial component as seriously as the text component. An illustration may therefore require more than a cursory glance. This is not necessarily the way that many people are accustomed to dealing with pictures, especially in a society that is used to dealing in a superficial, intuitive way with the barrage of images that are encountered in the media. Let's see what this means for our hypothetical example. A glance at Figure 27.1 is all that is needed to recognise it as a partly disassembled videocassete. However, it requires more careful, thoughtful inspection to realise that the curved strip between the cassette's 'windows' is a spring that bears on the tape spools in the assembled cassette.

There is evidence that even if appropriate visual aids are provided, students do not necessarily use them to the greatest instructional advantage (Moore, 1993). Without the physical presence of an instructor to guide the learner through an illustration that forms part of a distance education resource, responsibility for guidance falls mainly on the accompanying text. Not only should the text make explicit directive references to the illustrations ('Now study Figure 27.1'), it should also make clear what aspects of the illustration should be attended to and why. In Figure 27.1, the text could specifically draw learners' attention to the spring, ask learners to consider where the spring would be located in the assembled cassette, and challenge them to work out its function. A supplementary line drawing could also be provided to clarify the relationship between the spring and tape spools. This form of highly detailed guidance is rarely found in conventional textbooks. Thus, if distance education materials are to accompany a conventional textbook, they should include guidance through the textbook's illustrations.

It is usually helpful to give an overview of the purpose and global layout of illustrations before going into detail ('Figure 27.2 is a top view of the inside of a videocassette. The shading highlights three main aspects: the tape path, the tape guidance system, and the spool locking/release mechanism'). It may also be useful to indicate the overall structure with a simplified supplementary graphic that omits or suppresses the detail. In a classroom situation, students can be encouraged towards a deeper consideration of an illustration by thought-provoking questions from the teacher. In a distance education setting, the learner can be helped to engage with an illustration more deeply if some of the accompanying text is in the form of questions,

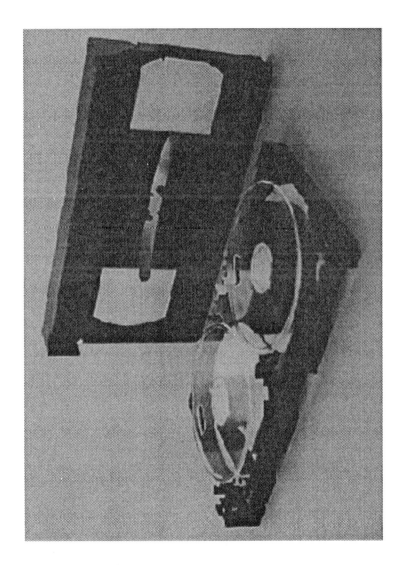

Figure 27.1 Videocassette with top cover removed

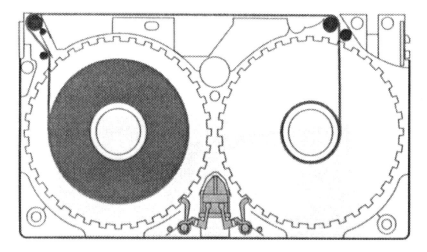

Figure 27.2 Internal structure of videocassette

rather than being the straight description or explanation that is usually found in a textbook. These questions should encourage the learner to interrogate the illustration to uncover key aspects of what is depicted and how these aspects are related within the picture. This is particularly important where these key aspects are not visually obvious in the illustration ('Examine the spool locking mechanism in the bottom centre of Figure 27.2. Are the spools currently locked or unlocked?').

TEXT AND/OR ILLUSTRATIONS?

The effective use of illustrations and text within distance education materials should use each of these representations in a way that takes best advantage of their distinctive strengths. Anyone who has tried to follow a set of purely pictorial instructions for an unfamiliar task of even moderate complexity rapidly realises the limitations of illustrations that are not supported by at least some text (see Gombrich, 1990). Similarly, there are plenty of examples of impenetrable text-based explanations that would be helped by a few well-considered illustrations.

While text is an effective way to present information that is suited to a sequential exposition, its serial structure can be an impediment for types of information that are best dealt with via the typically more parallel structure of illustrations. For example, by presenting 'all the information at once', illustrations can convey a more accessible and immediate sense of overall arrangement than is possible with extended text (in which this arrangement typically becomes apparent only after it has been read through completely). In addition, ideas presented in the early part of a text passage need to be retained in the memory if they are to be compared to later ideas, whereas with an illustration's non-sequential presentation, no corresponding memory load is imposed. Illustrations can also allow the user to access different parts of the subject matter by simple inspection instead of requiring the more deliberate and systematic search processes that are typically involved in locating particular items within a body of text (Larkin and Simon, 1987). At the same time, the relations between individual informational elements in a well-designed illustration are more readily accessible because the related items are arranged in close proximity or are coded by characteristics such as shape, size, colour or texture. These visual advantages are used to good effect in pictorial representations such as tree structures, flow-charts and life-cycle diagrams.

The decision to use illustrations is usually straightforward when the subject matter is intrinsically visual or spatial. In such cases, an attempt to give a textual representation often requires elaborate explanation and may well be confusing. However, there are many types of subject matter which are not predominantly visual or spatial in nature and yet are often represented in the form of an illustration – such as the simple two-dimensional line graph in which both the spatial arrangements of graphic objects and the physical form of those objects bear no direct relationship to their referents. Consider, for example, a graph that plots the educational expenditure of different countries over the past twenty years. Financial and temporal dimensions are depicted via spatial dimensions while national identities are represented by arbitrary shapes such as crosses, circles and squares. An alternative way of representing these data would be to arrange them in a numerical table, a much less satisfactory form for appreciating trends because it does not make best use of the powerful pattern-recognition capacities of our human information-processing system. However, if our interest was in specific values rather than trends, a table would probably be the more appropriate form of representation.

STYLE OF ILLUSTRATION

A common way to categorise illustrations is according to their degree of realism, which can range from highly realistic depictions such as photographs to quite non-realistic 'arbitrary' depictions such as abstract diagrams (Alesandrini, 1984). In a distance education context, learners frequently have no personal access to the specialised equipment, teaching aids or physical examples that are used in classroom teaching on campus. It is therefore often appropriate to provide photographs or realistic drawings of such resources in distance education materials to give a more rounded educational experience. However, these illustrations may need to include several different views or aspects of each item to make up for the fact that the student is not able to explore the items in detail. Where learners are required to assemble equipment or perform processes, it is important to picture the operations from the student's point of view, rather than from the view of an outside observer.

It is sometimes thought that the more realistic the illustration, the better it will be from an instructional point of view. A possible justification for this view occurs when the learner has no prior knowledge of the subject matter and so needs to be introduced to the appearance of the objects under consideration. However, the detail of a photograph may also overwhelm the learner with irrelevant information so that instructionally salient features are difficult to discern. Alternatively, the 'intact' view of the subject matter given by a simple photograph may not reveal critical information. For example, Figure 27.3 would probably have very limited instructional value because it shows only the overall appearance of a videocassette; far more valuable information could be shown if transparent, cross-sectional or exploded views were used.

It can be helpful to learners to include a number of versions of the subject matter, each produced in a different style and emphasising different aspects. However, the coupling of (say) a photograph of the subject matter with a diagram needs to be done with care so that the learner has no difficulty in moving between these multiple representations. The relations between the different representations may need to be made clear using graphic devices (such as arrows) or accompanying text to specify the links between relevant features. For example, although Figures 27.1 and 27.2 discussed earlier have much in common as far as the information they depict is concerned, the learner may need support in integrating these two representations because of the differences in viewpoint and pictorial treatment.

Another consideration that should influence the choice of style of an illustration to be used within distance education materials is the likely capacity of the learner to process the chosen depiction effectively (see Hegarty, 1993; Winn, 1993). For example, although abstract diagrams and specialist images such as electron micrographs have the virtues of presenting the subject matter with great clarity, economy and explanatory power, they can place considerable demands on the viewer in terms of interpretation (Lowe, in press). While the identity, location and significance of salient features within such displays are obvious to a subject matter expert, these displays may have much less meaning to students unless they are given considerable support in how to interpret them effectively.

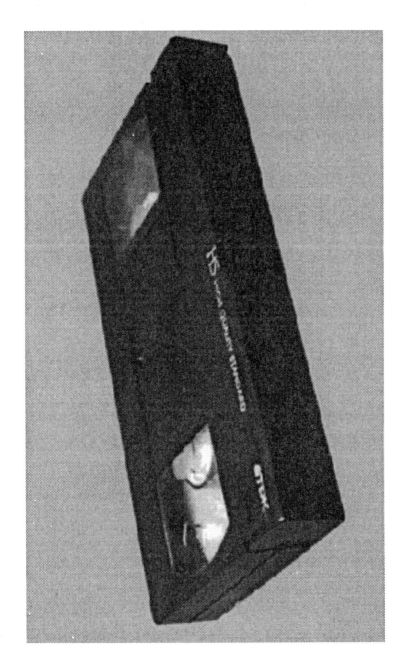

Figure 27.3 External appearance of videocassette

PHYSICAL INTEGRATION OF ILLUSTRATIONS

As a general rule, illustrations should be as close as is practicably possible to their associated text. In many circumstances within print materials, this means having the text and illustrations at least on facing pages (if not on the same page). Even when this coordination has been achieved, care should be taken to sequence multiple illustrations on a page so that they are arranged in the same order as the textual material to which they are related. In some cases, this may lead to a less elegant product from a graphic design point of view but the first concern should be to minimise extraneous information-processing demands on the learner.

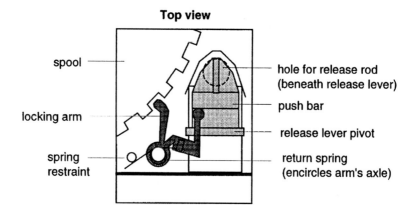

Top view

spool — hole for release rod (beneath release lever)

push bar

locking arm

release lever pivot

spring restraint

return spring (encircles arm's axle)

Parts of spool locking mechanism
(Note: release lever indicated by light grey shaded area)

Figure 27.4   Identification of components in illustration
(*Note*: (i) title denoting view, (ii) regular arrangement of labels that does not clutter illustration, and (iii) caption to specify function of the illustration)

Careful consideration should be given to the different possibilities for combining text and illustration by effective use of picture titles, captions and labels (Figure 27.4). The principle of minimising the extraneous processing load for the learner can even be taken as far as moving the relevant text out of its conventional place in a column and attaching chunks of text directly to the region of the illustration to which it refers (Chandler and Sweller, 1991). Where physical space constraints make this impracticable, a clear, systematic keying system of numbers and letters should be used in both text and illustration to facilitate cross-referencing of these two representational systems. The aim should be to minimise the amount of unproductive search activity that is required so that most of the learner's effort is directed towards comprehending and integrating the different parts of the information that are represented in the text and illustration.

READING ILLUSTRATIONS AS A LEARNED SKILL

A common misconception is that the meaning of an illustration is 'transparent'. In other words, simply by looking at an illustration the viewer effortlessly sees straight through to the situation that the illustration represents. This contrasts greatly with the way that the reading of text is regarded. It is becoming increasingly apparent that the 'reading' of an illustration is often not the transparent process that it has been assumed to be. Compared with the processes involved in reading text, much less is known about the details of the way we process illustrations (Winn, 1993). However, research indicates that many aspects of reading illustrations can also be regarded as learned skills; for such reading to be effective, prolonged strategic exploration of an illustration may be required. This is particularly likely to be the case where the illustration's subject matter and representational conventions are new to the learner, a situation that frequently applies with instructional materials. As a result, the casual, everyday picture-reading habits that a learner brings to the specialist illustrations found in instructional materials may not be sufficient to process those illustrations effectively. For example, Figure 27.5 assumes that the learner will systematically go back and forth between the two boxed illustrations to discover their relevant differences. It also assumes that the learner is able to relate these differences to the wider context of the videocassette's operation. Treating illustrations in distance education materials as if they are an intrinsically easier road to understanding than text is to misjudge seriously the demands that illustrations can make on the learner. Part of the distance educator's role may well be to instruct the learner in how to read the provided illustrations effectively, rather than assuming that the pictures will be the least of the learner's worries.

The rules for reading text are far better established and more regular than any 'rules' that may be suggested for reading illustrations. At a mechanical level, we know that if we read from left to right and top to bottom through columns of well-structured text, the subject matter will be presented to us in a more-or-less sequential manner. This means that by working through a text passage in this fashion, we can be fairly sure of building up a coherent meaning from the passage. As we read, we expect that various signposts (such as headings, sub-headings and standard conventions of layout) will help us to judge the relative importance of different aspects of the subject matter and understand how that subject matter hangs together. In contrast, the conventions used in representing subject matter via illustrations are much looser than the rules that apply to text (Salomon, 1979) and there is typically

Compare the positions of the locking arms and release lever in these illustrations

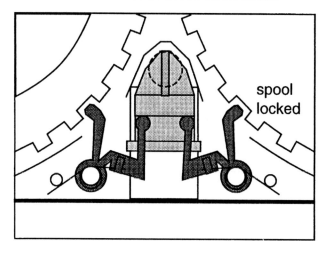

a. Tape not in VCR
   (release lever not raised)

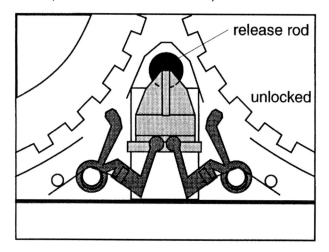

b. Tape in VCR ready to play or record
   (release rod has raised release lever)

Figure 27.5 Illustration to show change of state in spool
locking/release mechanism
(*Note*: (i) instructive title to direct processing, (ii) minimum use of labels since
components already identified in Figure 27.4, and (iii) captions draw attention to
salient features and relevant contextual information)

far less certainty about what are appropriate procedures to uncover the meaning of a particular illustration. Illustrations do not have strict, widely applicable rules about where to start and finish an exploration of their contents. There is no standardised sequence in which the material they contain should be processed in order to build up a coherent meaning. The cues as to the relative importance and semantic status of different parts of an illustration are much less formalised than they are for different parts of a passage of text. These differences mean that 'free' exploration of an illustration by a learner will not necessarily result in the desired instructional results. It has been shown that the way in which a particular illustration is explored can be highly variable, depending upon a range of factors such as the viewer's background knowledge, expectations and purposes (see, for example, Lowe, 1989; Yarbus, 1967). Different types of pictures can also elicit different depths of processing and patterns of exploration. If the illustrations that are provided in distance education materials are to be used in a manner that is appropriate to the learning task in hand, the student will often need guidance about how to process the illustration most effectively. This support may be provided in various forms including the use of supplementary illustrations that act as processing aids revealing the way the illustration 'works', elaborative text that sets the context of the pictorial material being processed, and audio commentaries that direct the learner on an instructionally productive path through the illustration.

REFERENCES

Alesandrini, K. L. (1984) 'Pictures and adult learning', *Instructional Science*, 13, pp. 63–77.

Chandler, P. and Sweller, J. (1991) 'Cognitive load theory and the format of instruction', *Cognition and Instruction*, 8, pp. 293–332.

Evans, M. A., Watson, C. and Willows, D. M. (1987) 'A naturalistic inquiry into illustration in instructional textbooks' in Willows, D. M. and Houghton, H. A. (eds) *The Psychology of Illustration, Vol. 2*, New York, Springer-Verlag.

Goldsmith, E. (1986) 'Learning from illustrations: factors in the design of illustrated educational books for middle school children', *Word and Image*, 2, pp. 111–21.

Gombrich, E. (1990) 'Pictorial instructions' in Miller, J. (ed.) *Images and Understanding*, Cambridge, Cambridge University Press.

Guri-Rozenblit, S. (1988) 'Impact of diagrams on recalling sequential elements in expository texts', *Reading Psychology*, 9, pp. 121–39.

Hegarty, M. (1993) 'Constructing mental models of machines from text and diagrams', *Journal of Memory and Language*, 32, pp. 717–42.

Larkin, J. H. and Simon, H. A. (1987) 'Why is a diagram (sometimes) worth a thousand words?', *Cognitive Science*, 11, pp. 65–99.

Lowe, R. K. (1989) 'Search strategies and inference in the exploration of scientific diagrams', *Educational Psychology*, 9, pp. 27–44.

Lowe, R. K. (1993) *Successful Instructional Diagrams*, London, Kogan Page.

Lowe, R. K. (in press) 'Selectivity in diagrams: reading beyond the lines', *Educational Psychology*.

Moore, P. J. (1993) 'Metacognitive processing of diagrams, maps and graphs', *Learning and Instruction*, 3, pp. 215–26.

Peeck, J. (1987) 'The role of illustrations in processing and remembering illustrated text' in Willows, D. M. and Houghton, H. A. (eds), *The Psychology of Illustration, Vol. 1*, New York, Springer-Verlag.

Purnell, K. N. and Solman, R. T. (1991) 'The influence of technical illustrations on students' comprehension in geography', *Reading Research Quarterly*, 3, pp. 277–97.

Salomon, G. (1979) *Interaction of Media, Cognition and Learning*, San Francisco, CA, Jossey Bass.

Winn, W. (1993) 'An account of how readers search for information in diagrams', *Contemporary Educational Psychology*, 18, pp. 162–85.

Yarbus, A. L. (1967) *Eye Movements and Vision*, New York, Plenum Press.

28

THE DEVELOPMENT OF PRINTED MATERIALS

A view of print production for distance learning in the light of recent developments

Michael Macdonald-Ross

STAGES OF PRINT PRODUCTION

The process of producing material in print has three stages: authorship, transforming and realisation.

Authorship

In 1969 The Open University, UK, put responsibility for managing the writing process with course teams instead of individual academics. This was a key innovation. Of course, there are precedents, for instance in the production of newspapers and magazines, where the staff work as members of a team.

The course team includes all who take part in planning, writing, commenting and initial revision of the teaching material. It may include academics, educational technologists, editors, TV producers, tutors, consultants – in fact, any who may influence the content of the work, or who are key to the stages described below as *transforming*.

Our course team method has proved greatly superior to the traditional university approach – at any rate for producing teaching materials in print and other media. For one thing, it is possible for us to bring to bear a wide range of skills; for another, it is possible for us to help staff who are newcomers or who need extra help; finally, we can achieve good coordination of content between levels, and between neighbouring courses.

At the end of the authorship stage the prose is captured in some kind of word-processing software. Like much of higher education, our courses do tend to be led by words, with graphics added later – a bias that goes back to the roots of our culture (see Richard Lowe, Chapter 27 in this volume).

Transforming

Transforming is the process of turning a rough draft into a finished product. It covers those creative activities which help to change a draft into a form suitable for the reader.

Thus transforming includes all the work associated with layout planning, text editing, typographic design, illustration, photography, picture searching and pagination. The work of transforming needs to be organised around a leader with authority to take decisions and deploy resources. Such a person is, so to speak, the chief transformer. There are many parallels for this role in media work outside education. In newspapers there is the chief sub, in book publishing and magazine work the editor, in television the producer, in films the director.

For distance learning texts the transforming of text material may be co-ordinated by an educational technologist, whose art is to anticipate the needs of the learner as he or she works with the learning material in a course. Equally good might be the choice of an academic with experience in education and in print production; or a designer or editor who has adequate credibility in academic and educational terms. To lead a team engaged in transforming requires *credibility* with both the managerial and the subject-matter interests.

In all these settings – newspapers, magazines, open learning material – the production involves a high degree of teamwork and co-operation between staff with a variety of specialist skills. Since the finished text is an organic whole in which every part may affect other parts, the working methods must produce integration in the final product. Such integration cannot be so well achieved if the different specialists work separately in departments. They should work together as members of a team, and owe their allegiance to the team task.

This leads me to suggest a large room, or suite of rooms, in which educational, content, design, editing and other skills are brought together in one place and at one time, to achieve an ideal integration in the product.

The end-product of the process of transforming is made-up text, including illustrations and graphics, in digital form, usually in pagination and graphics software.

Realisation

Realisation is a term which covers the manufacturing process. It ends with print products which can be used by learners.

TYPOGRAPHIC DESIGN

A key task of transforming is to achieve a typographic organisation that matches the structure of the content and helps the reader to work with the text.

Discourse and typography

The discourse of educational texts falls into a pattern:

1 First there is discourse about the subject-matter. This is presented in language, in mathematical or other special notations, and in graphical form such as tables, graphs and diagrams.
2 Next, there is discourse about the process of learning. This will include all the apparatus of study guides, objectives, questions, feedback, practice examples and so on. These ideas came mainly from programmed learning, and from the common sense of teachers, textbook writers and editors.
3 Lastly, there is discourse which helps readers to find their way around the text. It also signals where the reader is and signals the status of the material being read. These devices include the paragraph, the title page, running heads, the index, page numbers, chapters, and so on. There are also ways of signalling voice, discourse type, dialogue, in-text questions and places for readers to respond.

Some authors use the term *typographic signalling* (or cueing) for this kind of discourse, but thinking those terms too narrow, Macdonald-Ross and Waller coined the term *access structure* for this discourse.

Reading strategy and typography

Reading is selective, and most text is not read sequentially from beginning to end. This is obvious with newspapers and magazines, and it is also true for educational material.

Reading may take place for different purposes, and the same reader may work on a text in a different way at different times. The performance required of the learner after reading may vary greatly. In education, where rote recall is now outmoded, activities and projects may follow reading.

Since typographic design has to cope with this variety, it tends to be complex, though the complexity may be largely invisible to the reader. (There is more about typography in Chapter 26 in this volume, by James Hartley.) Educational texts are structurally complex when compared to prose works such as novels, though they do not use such a wide range of graphic tools as do mass circulation magazines.

THE EDUCATIONAL PUBLISHER

What role does the educational publisher play in all this? Partnerships and agreements between traditional publishers and distance learning institutions are possible and often desirable. There is now growing cooperation between book publishers and educational institutions. Publishers of educational material also play an active role in generating the content, and are innovative in marketing.

1 There has been much use made of market research by the big textbook publishers in the United States. Their extensive research into college syllabuses, their field trials and their use of critiques by experienced and influential teachers, allow them to design books which can be guaranteed in advance to meet the requirements as course-books for leading institutions.

Much of the writing and transforming work for such books are done in-house by the publishers themselves, thus achieving a closer fit between writing, production and marketing.

Related to this is the 'mix-'n-match' idea, where a range of chapters is kept on computer, and a selection made, together with some of the instructor's own notes, for each institution that chooses the work as a course-book. This tailor-makes the book for the instructor. Course-books also carry satellites along with them, such as instructors' manuals. (See Chapter 18 by Martin Valcke and Guillaume Vuist.)

2 The UK Open University has introduced a system of *collaborative publishing* after twenty years of publishing its own materials. In this new mode, we write and transform the teaching material as before, then offer publishers the chance of adding the material to their lists as books available for open sale in bookshops.

Once a deal is struck the University gets shared costs, economies of scale and some enhanced quality (for example, a more frequent use of second or four colour printing). As copyright holder, the University earns royalties, and arranges buy-back of copies for its own students.

3 Much publishing is done on topics that are truly educational, but are not offered in formal educational establishments.

CONTINUOUS IMPROVEMENT

It has always been an ideal of educational technology that instruction should be modified as data on learner performance becomes available, until courses deliver in practice the objectives that have been promised in theory. This *systematic approach* puts emphasis on the revision of courses based on the actual performance of learners, as well as any content improvements that the passage of time may bring to light.

New electronic production leads to *printing on demand,* and makes continuous improvement simple and economic:

1 the process of revision and reprinting is now almost entirely under the direct control of the institution.
2 revisions can be made online as regularly as information about the course becomes available.
3 the manufacturing process is now often much faster and cheaper than it was with the old technology. If a modern in-house document copier is used, the increase in speed and reduction in costs can be dramatic.
4 to take advantage of the technology, the process of course maintenance must be changed to course improvement, so that each year the course is a subtly new creature, constantly improving and adapting and growing, rather than being static, gradually getting stale.

With all this in mind, how should continuous improvement be applied to distance learning systems?

• One way would be to use a modern document copier for production. This gives printing on demand, and allows changes to be made throughout the life of a course.
• Another option is to sign 'just-in-time' contracts with printers, who deliver exact numbers of copies for mailing at the time needed. This method eliminates the need for warehousing.
• Less satisfactory is the use of ring binders and loose-leaf printing. This does allow revisions to be inserted as required, but for the user there are ergonomic penalties.
• Another way is collaborative publishing in a series of volumes. Volumes can be revised as the need arises, or when staff can cope. This allows the life-span of a course to be extended indefinitely.

All these methods are preferable to the old way, when a course with known deficiencies could be kept on the market for up to a decade. The ability to change the course each year will prompt us to do more, no doubt. It is necessary to get the micro-structure of a course working properly, and for the course to improve. This is exactly what the new technology facilitates.

ERGONOMICS OF USE

There are a number of questions which make up the practical ergonomics of use by the learner. The size and weight of texts, the format, binding and choice of paper are some of these factors. Perhaps the most under-rated of all print topics is the way in which books are handled and used by the reader.

Legibility

The past decade or two has seen a tendency for some educational material to be published with inferior typography, leading to reduction in legibility. This may be caused by sheer ignorance, or it may be a by-product of technological change; but perhaps more often it is due to false economy by publishers, many of whom do not employ professional typographers as they once might have done.

It cannot be said too often that the most important single requisite of book production is now, as always, good legibility.

Ease of handling

Weight, size, and ability to open flat are important. Heavy books affect portability and handling quality; this in turn reduces the readers' options as to where study takes place. The UK Open University's course book for *Evolution* (S365) weighs 2.5 kilograms, with more than a thousand pages! This is awkward in the hand and difficult to carry about – not a sensible weight from the user's point of view. When faced with huge and weighty course texts, students might be well advised to take a tip from Charles Darwin. He used to take a binder's knife to the spine of large books and separate them into three or four sections of modest size, then wrote notes on them.

In general, educational material bound in one volume should not weigh more than 750 grams. The application of this guideline can be flexible, so that 1 kilogram might be tolerated on occasion, but 1` kilograms never. The choice of paper is critical: there is often a tension between the need for lighter paper and the need for opacity to reduce show-through. In collaborative publishing we may need to balance the needs of the publisher with the needs of our students. If a publisher wishes to produce a huge tome we may need to arrange for our students' texts to be bound differently from the publisher's version.

Ease of opening is a factor. *Binding* affects ease of opening: where books don't open flat two hands must be used to hold it open, or alternatively the spine must be savagely handled to enforce its opening. Ring binders are awkward to handle, and are a poor choice.

Format

One thing that separates us from traditional publishing is the format. Overwhelmingly, in-house publishing uses international page sizes, especially A4. This choice is rather awkward from the point of view of the reader. The measure of type across an A4 page is rather too long for good legibility if a single column layout is used. Also, the size is not convenient in the hand, which indirectly affects frequency of use.

In a bookshop, A4 often needs shelving apart from the usual book sizes; it does not sit comfortably on the standard shelf size – indeed A4 books often cannot stand up unaided on a shelf. These things can be important for a bookshop. Commercial publishers generally choose a smaller format except for highly illustrated works.

However, a two- or three-column layout can work well on A4 (it shortens the measure to acceptable dimensions). There are even some advantages to A4; for example, it is good for highly illustrated works; and in production most machines have an A4 setting.

In general, the ergonomics of use are more important than the convenience of the producer, and from that point of view A4 should not be the first choice. The international range of paper sizes does offer more acceptable options. A5, half the size of A4, is excellent ergonomically, rather similar to demy 8vo in size. Also there is the international B series, which offers B5, a size somewhat larger than A5. In commercial book publishing, the traditional page sizes are more usual.

In general, *large size* may cause problems on a desk when room is needed for other sources and notebooks; in particular, landscape format is always apt to cause difficulties on a crowded desk. Large size also affects portability and ease of handling away from the desk. There is a tendency nowadays for page size to get larger, perhaps to accommodate more illustrations, but often for no good reason.

Durability

It is famously true that learning material is hard used, often *very* hard used. Yet, for relatively minor savings in production cost, educational material is all too often given the least durable binding. The main choice in binding a book lies in the way in which pages are joined together.

What should be avoided is the kind of 'perfect binding' which tends to result in a shower of pages onto the floor after hard usage. This method, in which separate pages are attached by little more than PVA (poly-vinyl adhesive) is not sound for learning material.

Much superior is the traditional method of sewn sections, which allow ease of opening, yet are so durable. For special purposes other types of binding may be preferred: there is a widespread use of spiral and ring binding for computer manuals (though softback books with sewn sections do lie flat and are durable). Advanced document copiers offer taped hot-melt binding as an option; a much improved type of perfect binding, though still not so durable as sewn sections.

Other factors in durability are the cover – soft covers, if chosen, must be able to stand up to wear and tear – and the paper. Popular paperback publishing tends to use small type on paper that browns and becomes friable, and perfect binding; obviously such books are less legible and durable than we might wish.

On the other hand, expensive reference works may now be printed on acid-free paper, and sewn and bound securely, thus enhancing their potential life. Some reference works are available as compact discs, satisfactory so long as the amount of reading required on each occasion is minimal.

Packaging

The options available for binding and packaging are increasing. Much educational material is marketed as packs, which in effect means boxes, slip cases, folders, ring binders and other types of packaging. Inside the pack may be separate sheets, books, video- and audio-tapes, records, even computer disks. In the world of adult seminars and workshops almost all the material is like this. However, the traditional book is still a marvellously flexible teaching machine, and for the publisher still the most convenient vehicle for marketing.

As mentioned earlier, printing on demand makes use of a kind of binding by document copier of which we have at present limited experience (taped hot-melt binding). Yet it is fast and economical, and so for some purposes it will be ideal.

In summary, poor decisions in the ergonomics of book design and production are a frequent source of problems for the reader.

NEW MEDIA

We are all aware that text nowadays can be presented on-screen rather than printed. This has the virtue that the text might be linked to other modalities. Prose can join with film, cartoon, or simulation at a personal work station. Links with databases and telecommunication facilities can also be made.

However, text on computer screen does have some serious deficiencies. Computer-based presentation of text will not get used regularly in education without solutions being found to at least two critical problems:

1 The ergonomics of reading screen text is a poor second-best to printed text. Text on screen lacks legibility and is hard to access at speed. Also, screens are less portable than books.
2 Multimedia screen-based systems are expensive to produce and to make available to the learner.

Both these factors have been seriously underestimated by computer technologists, who are not expert on typography and the reading process, and whose appreciation of the practical economics of mass education at a distance is usually negligible.

Educational planners should be sceptical about claims that the bulk of distance education can be delivered on non-text media. Print is still the central medium of education, and will for a long time to come be the most cost-effective and appropriate way of delivering education to large numbers of people at a distance.

The reasons for the centrality of print in education lie in the way knowledge is represented and communicated (at any rate, the kind of knowledge usually involved in formal learning), in the economics of print as compared with other media, and in the psychology and ergonomics of learning from print as compared with other media.

Having said that, other media can and should be used as partners to print. Even the older audio and televisual media can make dramatic and valuable contributions, and no doubt some of the promise of new computer media will eventually be realised. Many courses do require experimental work, or projects or work on computers. But claims to the effect that 'the day of the book is over' are seriously wrong; anyone tempted to believe this sort of thing should remember what happened to the 'paper-free office'!

Even though the computer revolution has dramatically changed the way in which print is produced, and has created new media, and new combinations of media, the printed text is *still* the key medium for distance education, and will remain so for the foreseeable future.

MOTIVATION OF THE READER

It is a sad but true observation that much printed educational material is rather unappealing to all but the dedicated. It often fails in one of the basic aims of communication: to arrest the subject's attention, to arouse his or her interest, and to encourage the subject to read on. So it must be a major aim of text development and production to use all means available to help produce material that motivates the reader.

- The choice of topic: here relevance to the reader's interest is crucial.
- The writing process: the effort to produce vivid, clear prose is vital.
- The discourse about the subject-matter should be aimed at the appropriate level of difficulty, up-to-date and illustrated by imaginative activities and examples.
- The discourse about the learning process should do its work in helping the student learn the material and achieve the course objectives.
- The typography should achieve its aims of signalling the structure of the text and enabling the reader to access the content. The text must be highly legible, but at the same time economical in its use of space. Reading should be a pleasure.

  Since educational texts do tend to be complex, the overall page design, and the detailed decisions on positioning, the use of rules, screens and other devices are vital to the reader's sense of ease and ability to perform.
- Graphics are a vital component of many texts and can greatly enhance reader motivation.

- Colour: one visible result of new technology is the great increase in colour printing in recent years in magazines, newspapers and textbooks. Readers now begin to expect colour as the norm, a trend which is likely to continue, as it did in film and television.

  Second colour in educational texts is now usual in countries with easy access to the new technology. Full colour (four- or five-colour printing) is still not widespread in education except for special purposes.
- The binding should be attractive, pleasant to hold, durable, of appropriate size and weight.

Much more could be said, of course, on the subject of motivation: distance learning systems succeed as much by the motivation of their students as by the excellence of their teaching.

STAFF DEVELOPMENT

Staff development is a pressing need. Changes in technology have caused profound changes in working methods. It takes time to learn how to get the most from the software, and it takes more time to get used to the new working methods.

This is not all: the software is now often in the hands of staff who do not have enough background in editing, in the graphic arts and typography. Few organisations are able to employ in-house the kind of expertise found only in top-class publishing houses or magazines. This leads to some fundamental questions:

- How does one give staff some of the skills of editing, design and typography that once took half a lifetime to learn? Training and updating in computer software is also a permanent problem these days. In these fields short courses are only part of the solution: there is a big difference here between *acquaintance* and *mastery.*
- The next question is how should these renaissance communicators combine in work-teams to produce a quality product?

  One key idea is that teams doing the transforming should work together in one area on a linked group of terminals so as to encourage synergy and teamwork. This is a practice already followed by some highly successful production groups.
- Another problem is how to negotiate the changes in working practice in what was a highly trade-unionised setting. The adoption of in-house publishing has made it easier to evade the problem of long-standing craft and union differences.
- How best to use specialist consultants in typography, design and computer software is another issue facing management.

One cannot give pat solutions to these questions, but knowing the problems exist is itself an advance.

29

CONTEMPORARY DEVELOPMENTS IN THE TYPOGRAPHICAL DESIGN OF INSTRUCTIONAL TEXTS FOR OPEN AND DISTANCE LEARNING

John Dekkers and Neale A. Kemp

CHARACTERISTICS OF THE OPEN AND DISTANCE LEARNER

The design of quality open and distance learning materials is a considerably more complex task than for conventional on-campus learning materials as the latter tends to be solely focused on the presentation of content. In open and distance education, learning materials tend to be the primary instructional resource for learning situations requiring a high degree of independent study.

Typically, open and distance education students are adults, which means that they have full and busy lives with many responsibilities. Often they will be undertaking their studies after all other essential tasks have been completed – usually at night-time. Furthermore, adult learners will bring a wider range of expectations to their studies than conventional on-campus students. There are those who are very able and confident. These students may readily explore and develop subject ideas and take an active approach to working with course materials, enthusiastically and constructively communicating with academic staff and other students. Some may be extending their knowledge from an existing base, knowing what they want to learn and how they have successfully studied in the past. Others may lack the confidence or be studying for the first time since leaving school.

WHAT CONSTITUTES 'GOOD' LEARNING MATERIALS?

Accordingly, the development of quality instructional text for open and distance education needs to be based on the theory and practice of adult learning (Knowles, 1986); educational and psychological constructs (e.g. Ausubel, 1986; Witkin *et al.*, 1977); instructional design theory and practice (e.g. Gagné and Briggs, 1979; Reigeluth, 1983; Romiszowski, 1995; Rowntree, 1990); and research and evaluation studies on the typographical features of instructional text that facilitate its use by the independent learner (e.g. Hartley, 1994; Kemp, 1993).

Based on the foregoing and our own experiences, 'good' practice in the development of open and distance learning instructional text would suggest the incorporation of a number of features to accommodate the wide range of learning styles. Instructional text should:

- be written to satisfy learners
- focus on learners' experience
- aim to develop independent learning skills and strategies
- be intended for initial learning
- emphasise learning objectives
- be structured to the needs of the learners
- aim at a defined target audience of learners
- contain features that can motivate learners
- build on study skills attained or acquired by learners
- provide for prerequisite learning
- encourage application of knowledge and skills by learners
- ask the learner frequent questions
- provide teaching feedback
- confront and explore learner conceptions
- provide ample and progressive practice for learners
- demand reading and activities of learners
- allow the learner to check progress
- provide a layout which will facilitate and promote efficient learning
- contain manageable chunks of information for single learning sessions.

The above recommendations are central to the advice and assistance provided by staff from the Central Queensland University for its clients from other universities, government agencies, industry and commerce, seeking to use open learning for the delivery of their education and training programmes (Dekkers *et al.*, 1991).

This chapter will consider the application and findings of recent studies carried out by the authors and other researchers on the typography, and students' use, of instructional texts. Among other objectives, these studies sought to determine those instructional and typographical elements, present or not in instructional text, which might facilitate learning.

THE APPLICATION OF TYPOGRAPHICAL VARIABLES IN THE DEVELOPMENT OF INSTRUCTIONAL TEXTS

There has always been a belief among those not directly involved in the publishing process that typography is simply another art form whose qualities may be judged in purely aesthetic terms. While there is no doubt that aesthetics plays a role in sound typographical design, the major concern of the textual designer is to expedite the communication process from author to reader.

Over a considerable number of decades, the publishing industry has established well-developed conventions in typographical layout and general document design to meet the needs of reading audiences. These conventions, however, are often not appropriate for instructional applications. This situation is compounded further by the fact that many of the existing established guidelines for both general and educational publishing, often rigidly adhered to, are based upon aesthetic considerations rather than on careful research that has taken account of the learner.

Developments in computer-aided publishing, coupled with emerging instructional technologies, now provide the tools with which developers can design open and distance learning materials to suit a range of learner settings, styles and other individual requirements. Unfortunately, only too often the design of these materials is based on the developer's own beliefs about what constitutes 'good' typographical layout, with little consideration given to aspects of legibility, readability and, importantly, how the materials will be used.

A comprehensive investigation of the typographical features used in instructional texts has identified the major factors which can influence the ways in which students use these materials (Kemp, 1993). These factors, in conjunction with contemporary principles and practices of instructional design (e.g. Reigeluth, 1983), have enabled the development of a variety of alternative instructional formats for the design of distance and open learning materials.

The typographical factors identified by Kemp (1993) as influencing the learners' use of instructional texts have been classified in respect to their micro- or macro-design implications on the textual layout. The recommendations, summarised in Table 29.1, are based on over one hundred articles from the published literature in combination with a considerable amount of research work undertaken by the authors over the past three years.

In this table, the micro-typographical parameters of a publication are essentially those which govern the legibility and readability of the type, whereas the macro-typographical features are those which govern the spatial arrangement of page elements to ensure the structural cohesion of a document. You will note that some of the recommendations listed in Table 29.1 are reinforced by James Hartley's discussion on textual readability in Chapter 26 of this volume.

Table 29.1 The recommended treatment of a range of micro- and macro-typographical variables when utilised for the development of instructional texts

Typographical variable	*Recommended treatment*
Micro-typography	
textual typeface	• serif typefaces are preferred over sans serif types for readability and legibility
type-size	• 9pt to 12 pt depending upon line length, typeface and method of composition
use of italic and bold	• use italic to denote derivation of a term or accentuation of a proper noun
	• use bold as a visual cue to accentuate a concept
	• use either bold or italic in preference to all capitals for emphasis
use of capitals and lower case	• capitals should not be used in text and should be reserved for short headings
	• lower case characters are more readable than capitals in any typeface and should always be preferred for text
headings	• lower case characters preferred to all capitals except where headings are short and require specific emphasis
method of textual composition	• use unjustified/ragged right format to ensure consistent word spacing
line spacing	• provide between 20% and 30% of the textual type-size as interlinear space (between 1.2 and 1.3 line spacing)
line length	• 39 to 70 characters with preference for lengths in middle or at the bottom of this range
numbering systems	• useful for organising the access structure of a document through page and figure numbering
	• generally superfluous when used for heading and textual differentiation

Table 29.1 continued

Typographical variable	Recommended treatment
Macro-typography	
page size	• ISO (International Standards Organisation) paper sizes preferred for production reasons
	• A4 provides much flexibility in page layout
margins	• sizing must allow minimum for reproduction requirements (e.g. 25mm binding margin)
	• sizing will affect line length
columniation	• prefer single column format for textual commentary supplemented by a lesser sized column for instructional cuing
vertical spacing	• prefer a planned and consistent use of space between textual and graphic features based upon fractional or multiple increments of the textual line space
paragraph separation	• use minimal vertical spacing increment rather than indentation
page text depth	• use 'floating baseline' concept (vertically unjustified) to enable functionally related page elements to remain together
tables	• avoid vertical rules
	• use only horizontal rules above and below the table and to separate headline
	• in long tables, group information to aid retrieval
instructional icons	• must be universally interpretable
	• learners must be informed in advance of why and how icons are to be used
typographical and spatial cuing	• aim is to provide an access structure to the content
	• provide details in advance of why and how cueing system has been used

A major finding from our research is that the majority of the typographical variables listed in Table 29.1 are highly interdependent, which underscores the fact that the selection of the typographical parameters of an instructional text is a highly complex task. As an example, a singular decision by a developer to utilise 10pt Times for the textual component of an instructional text will have the following implications:

- it will determine the line length as measured by the optimum number of characters
- line length will determine the columniation of the document
- line length and the columniation will determine the margin sizes
- line spacing will be determined from the text type-size
- vertical spacing increments will be determined from the line spacing increment
- paragraph spacing will be determined from the vertical spacing increments
- variable heading sizes and font will be determined based upon the size and font of the text (10pt Times)
- the size and font of figure captions and other textual elements will be determined from the size and font of the text (10pt Times).

This decision flow chart is illustrated graphically in Figure 29.1 which exemplifies the fact that decisions regarding a singular typographical variable cannot be made without full consideration of the other interdependent typographical variables.

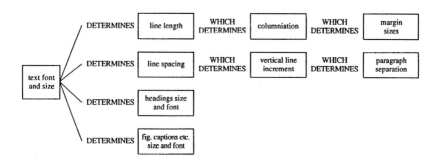

Figure 29.1 A decision flow-chart based upon determining typographical variables from the text size and font

LEARNERS' USE OF INSTRUCTIONAL TEXTS AND THEIR APPROACHES TO LEARNING

The above research findings on the application of typographical features provide sufficient information to enable the development of alternative instructional formats for a range of open and distance learning materials.

Evaluating the typographical effectiveness of these materials, however, requires examination of how distance education students interact with their study materials and if, in fact, the typographical format of the materials has any effect upon their individual study techniques.

Designers of instructional texts generally focus on mechanisms which will maximise the effectiveness of their materials in promoting student learning. The resulting instructional and typographical design of these texts is, however, often based on the writers' assumptions about the way in which students use their materials (Clyde *et al.*, 1983). However, the chapters in Part II of this volume indicate some of the factors that influence student learning and how we may improve it. In this context individual learning styles have been identified as a major contributing factor to course completion. This is underscored by the results of Cookson's (1989) research which indicated that student persistence in distance education courses is enhanced by the quality of instructional presentation in study guides and that ultimately the success of any distance education programme is highly dependent upon students' satisfaction with their learning experience.

It is clear from these studies that a learner's orientation to study (see Taylor *et al.*, 1981) may predict a particular study strategy which they will employ in the learning task. There is some argument, however, that study orientations are dynamic rather than static and that they change and develop in a continual process of refinement. This implies that, although a student may be extrinsically motivated to undertake a course of study and initially employ 'satisficing' study strategies to undertake only that which is necessary for successful completion, the student's orientation to study may be influenced by any number of factors in the teaching/learning process. This alone has profound implications for the design and presentation of open and distance education instructional texts.

The authors' own research has indicated that there are two major groups of students who adopt distinctly different routes of study through an instructional text. Our studies identify students as either:

1 'serialists' – learners who work through the instructional text in a linear, sequential fashion, undertaking all, or the majority of the tasks presented while rigidly adhering to the implied study path; or
2 'selective samplers' – learners who sought and acquired information on the basis of their own pre-determined criteria of content relevance.

This latter group can be further subdivided in respect to their reasons for adopting selective sampling strategies. Our investigations into the study techniques of this non-serialist group indicate that learners used this strategy to either:

(a) expediently satisfy only the assessment requirements of the subject; or

317

(b) enable them to direct their own study and choose a study path which enabled them to achieve their personal objectives in the subject (see Fred Lockwood, Chapter 19 in this volume).

It is clear that the level of reliance a student places upon a provided learning structure may predict a particular study pathway. Our studies have continually indicated that most of those students who exhibited a high level of reliance upon a provided learning structure within the instructional materials have adopted a 'serialist' study strategy in which they utilised most, if not all, of the instructional and typographical features of the study materials whilst adhering to the prescribed instructional sequence. In comparison, those who were less reliant tended to adopt study strategies which enabled them to 'selectively sample' the content of the instructional text.

The preparation of open and distance learning texts generally involves the development of a series of instructional sequences planned by the developer. This typically results in the development of what may be termed a 'prescriptive' approach to instruction in which the developer has expectations about the way in which the student will work through the materials – an 'implied study path'. However, as suggested above, learners will often adopt an unpredictable selective sampling strategy which will, more than likely, result in a unique study path through the material.

We should be aware that the study paths of many students are dictated by the students' focus on satisfying the assessment requirements of the subject or module of study. This 'satisficing' strategy is also often adopted by students in situations where study time is limited and they are obliged to adopt study strategies which are time-efficient.

The open/distance education mode is intended to provide students with a considerable degree of autonomy in developing their own unique approach to study. This makes it very difficult for instructional designers to predict the ways in which students will work through instructional texts. It would seem that the only reading behaviour which developers of instructional materials can confidently predict is that learners will read selectively. This concept of selective sampling suggests that, when working with instructional texts, learners seek and acquire, rather than passively process, information. This assumes that learners are active participants in the learning process and should be able to access and sample information on the basis of their own pre-determined criteria of content relevance.

The selective study strategies adopted by students can be somewhat controlled in a face-to-face learning environment. However, in open and distance education, developers should be aware that students make decisions about how they will deal with the instructional texts, and what information they believe is relevant to their own learning.

One of the factors which can influence the ways in which students focus attention within a text is the limited capacities of working memory. Because of these limitations, students organise information into hierarchical-related conceptual categories, and direct their attention differentially to ideas, with the most important ideas receiving the most attention. This finding alone indicates that the content of instructional texts should be structured in such a way that the hierarchy of information is immediately obvious to the learner.

The idea that students organise information into hierarchically related conceptual categories assumes that students possess the interpretation skills to enable them to decode an instructional text to isolate salient concepts. This decoding process can be expedited through the use of typographical and spatial cues which help learners to identify, organise and interpret the most important information. Typographical cues (e.g. use of bold, italic, differing type-sizes, spatial separation) allow writers to highlight the important concepts of a text through differentiation of the textual presentation. This variation of the presentation style can be used to help readers overview the text and locate relevant parts efficiently (i.e. provide an access structure).

The salient point here is that a sequential reading strategy is not common for users of instructional texts. Moreover, selective sampling strategies are employed by the majority of learners and an instructional text in which the main ideas are typographically or spatially signalled enables easy access for previewing, reference and revision. Text structuring, through cueing, should therefore provide the student with sufficient instructional 'clues' to enable them to construct effective decision criteria for selective sampling.

DEVELOPMENT OF A TYPOGRAPHICAL MODEL FOR THE DESIGN OF INSTRUCTIONAL MATERIALS

Clearly, by varying the micro- and macro-typographical parameters of an instructional text, the readability of the document can be significantly influenced. Moreover, it is our belief that there is a link between the study techniques which students employ and their reliance upon the typographical presentation of an instructional text to facilitate their study. Ideally, the development of a generic typographical model for instructional materials should address the range of study techniques for students who exhibit varying levels of reliance upon the instructional materials for provided learning structure.

We have found consistently the application of the typographical parameters listed in Table 29.1 to be highly successful for independent learners and these are recommended for planning the design of instructional texts. It is noteworthy however, that these recommendations provide flexibility, in micro- and macro-terms, in the specific design parameters which may be employed for different layouts. Due to the interdependence of these variables, a change in any one of the parameters will undoubtedly impact upon the other variables.

Beyond the specific formatting of the textual and graphic elements of the instructional text, it is our belief that the accessibility of textual elements is of paramount importance to all learners. Because it is evident that the majority of learners are 'selective samplers' of texts rather than passive readers who adopt a purely linear study strategy, the entire structure of an instructional text should be accessible so that learners can make informed decisions about strategies they may employ for coping with the textual content.

Our studies (Dekkers *et al.*, 1993; Kemp, 1993) have demonstrated that a lack of instructional and typographical features does hinder study progress and can have the following deleterious effects on the learner:

- increases time required for study
- the materials are seen as confusing and/or difficult to learn from
- the materials are not motivating
- the materials do not facilitate the study process.

It is therefore recommended that developers use typographical and spatial cues to ensure that instructional texts are accessible by the learner – particularly those who adopt a 'selective sampling' strategy. Cues which are particularly effective are:

- a structured hierarchy of headings
- instructional icons
- the spatial isolation of key concepts from the main text commentary
- use of bold face
- systematic and high level use of vertical space to indicate the structure of the text.

The design of the 'ideal' instructional text should provide typographical and instructional features to facilitate the study techniques of all students. The design recommendations therefore need to consider both the aspects of readability and information accessibility. From the perspective of the 'serialist' learner, as a student who builds understanding in a linear sequence, issues of text readability and content sequencing are of major concern as is the accessibility of particular textual elements upon revision. The 'selective samplers' on the other hand tend to focus on identifying particular elements of the text as a priority in their study technique. As such, they are very reliant upon visual cues in the materials to facilitate their searching strategies.

The typographical model should therefore define its parameters in respect to both textual readability and the accessibility of components of the text. In this way the typographical design of the instructional text provides benefits for the range of study techniques employed by distance and open learning students.

It is our recommendation that the provision of a typographical structure which supports the study technique of the highly reliant 'serialist' learner will provide a framework to allow those students who operate more independently to determine a unique study pathway to efficiently 'selectively sample' and thus satisfy their own objectives for learning whether they be assessment focused or course focused.

BIBLIOGRAPHY

Ausubel, D. P. (1986) *Educational Psychology: A Cognitive View*, New York, Holt, Rinehart and Wilson.

Clyde, A., Crowther, H., Patching, W., Putt, I. and Store, R. (1983) 'How students use distance education study materials: an institutional study', *Distance Education*, 4(1), pp. 4–26.

Cookson, P. (1989) 'Research on learners and learning in distance education: a review', *The American Journal of Distance Education*, 3(2), pp. 22–34.

Dekkers, J., Cuskelly, E., Kemp, N. and Phillips, J. (1993) 'Use of instructional materials by distance education by distance education students: patterns and student perceptions', Proceedings of the International Council for Distance Education 16th World Conference, Bangkok, Thailand.

Dekkers, J., Kemp, N., Nouwens, F. and Towers, S. (1991) *Course Materials Development for Distance Education*, Rockhampton, Australia, University of Central Queensland.

Gagné, R. M. and Briggs, L. J. (1979) *Principles of Instructional Design*, New York, Holt, Rinehart and Wilson.

Glynn, S., Britton, B. and Tillman, M. (1985) 'Typographical cues in text: management of the reader's attention' in Jonassen, D. (ed.).

Hartley, J. (1985) *Designing Instructional Text*, (2nd edn), London, Kogan Page.

Hartley, J. (1986) 'Planning the typographical structure of instructional text', *Educational Psychologist*, 21(4), pp. 315–32.

Hartley, J. (1991) 'Textbook design: current status and future directions' in Hartley, J. (ed.) *Instructional Media and Technology Research*, London, Kogan Page.

Hartley, J. (ed.) (1994) *Designing for Learning: Effectiveness and Efficiency*, London, Kogan Page.

Jonassen, D. (ed.) (1985) *Technology of Text II*, Englewood Cliffs, NJ, Education Technology Publications.

Kemp, N. (1993) 'Typographical features within instructional texts and their influence on the study techniques adopted by distance education students', (MSc diss.), Perth, Curtin University.

Knowles, M. S. (1986) *The Modern Practice of Adult Education*, New York, Cambridge University Press.

Marland, P., Patching, W. and Putt, I. (1992) 'Thinking while studying: a process tracing study of distance learners', *Distance Education*, 13(2), pp. 193–217.

Marland, P., Patching, W., Putt, L. and Putt, I. (1990) 'Distance learners' interactions with text while studying', *Distance Education*, 11(1), pp. 71–91.

Marland, P., Patching W., Putt, I. and Store, R. (1984) 'Learning from distance teaching materials: a study of students' mediating responses', *Distance Education*, 5(2), pp. 215–36.

Marland, P. and Store, R. (1982) 'Some instructional strategies for improved learning from distance teaching materials', *Distance Education*, 3(1), pp. 72–106.

Marton, F. and Säljö, R. (1976) 'On qualitative differences in learning outcome and process, Part 1', *British Journal Psychology*, 46, pp. 4–11.

Pask, G. (1976) 'Styles and strategies', *British Journal of Educational Psychology*, 46, pp. 128–48.

Reigeluth, C. (1983) *Instructional Design Theories and Models: An Overview of their Current Status*, New Jersey, Lawrence Erlbaum.

Romiszowski, A. J. (1995) *Designing Instructional Systems*, London, Kogan Page.

Rowntree, D. (1990) *Teaching Through Self-instruction: How to Develop Open Learning Materials*, London, Kogan Page.

Taylor, E., Morgan, A. and Gibbs, G. (1981) 'The "orientation" of Open University foundation students to their studies', *Teaching at a Distance,* 20, pp. 3–12.

Waller, R. (1985) 'Using typography to structure arguments: a critical analysis of some examples', in Jonassen, D. (ed.).

Witkin, H. A., Moore, C. A., Goodenough, D. R. and Cox, P. W. (1977) 'Field-dependent and field-independent cognitive styles and their educational implications', *Review of Educational Research*, 47, pp. 1–64.

30

ELECTRONIC LAYOUT AND DESIGN VISIONS OF THE FUTURE

Paul Lefrere

INTRODUCTION

To achieve ... quality growth, we not only have to change what we do, but also how we do it ... [hence there are] new directions for change.

1   from long to short response times

2   from complexity to simplicity

3   from provider-led to customer-centred ...

6   from quality control to quality assurance.

(Peters, 1994)

As recognised by the companion chapters in this section, students vary in their interests, in their needs and in their capabilities. Ideally, therefore, each student on an open and distance learning course would receive personalised textual materials, whose design and layout suit that student as an individual. Further, by analogy with the short product life-cycles that are now common in many industries, it should be possible for course providers to change the content of courses at short notice, to suit the needs of the moment.

Unfortunately, it is uneconomic to make even minor changes to content, design and layout, if we use today's 'supply-driven' methods of creating open learning courses. Those methods are predicated on the notion of lower unit cost through economy of scale. The goal is to minimise the 'per student' cost of courses to the supplier, by providing each student on a course with the same material as other students on that course.

Inevitably, a single version of a course will not suit every user, although its content and layout can be chosen to be as effective as possible for a notional average user. If there are sizeable subgroups of users who are very different from average, then more than one version can be justified. An obvious example is the need to cater for students who are visually impaired. If funds permit, they can be given braille versions, large print versions or audiotape versions of standard printed materials.

Many open learning institutions are not open access, so there may be little difference in the background and capabilities of their students. On the face of it, multiple versions of courses are not justified. The temptation, then, is to run courses unchanged over several years, cutting the cost per copy by printing more copies than are needed for one year. This inflexibility is unwise. It is surely far better to have a flexible way of handling changes routinely, quickly and at low cost. By 'a flexible way of handling changes', I mean either a flexible course production system or what I call a flexible 'course consumption' system.

In my view, we need to think much more about courses in terms of a *consumption* model. For example, consider the cost of 'consuming' a course. This covers more than the cost of supplying a course. In this context, the cost of consumption by students – sometimes called the total cost of ownership – includes three elements:

- the purchase price of a course (which will depend on the cost to the supplier of producing and delivering the course)
- a student's study time (which should be as short as possible)
- any direct expenses that students incur during a course and as a result of taking a course.

When we look at the total cost of ownership, we are taking a customer-driven focus. Our concern is then with producing courses that have a low total cost to an individual student, rather than a low cost to the course provider per student. We can cut the total cost if we make courses easier to learn from (thus reducing study time), and if we use faster and/or more flexible ways of creating courses (thus reducing initial cost).

In this chapter, I shall look at two ways in which course providers might cut the total cost of ownership, and point to policy issues that may arise. The two approaches I shall consider are based upon providing students with tools that contribute to the creation of a flexible course consumption system. These are:

- tools to personalise the content, design and layout of a course, *while they are studying* the course; and
- tools to assess and lay out material drawn from sources of *their* choice, either as a substitute for course material provided centrally, or for enrichment purposes.

ADDING VALUE THROUGH PERSONALISATION

In general, information gains value if it is made more timely and generally more pertinent to the user. This is taken advantage of by some publishers of business newsletters, who provide business newsletters tailored for individual users and delivered electronically or by fax.

Proponents of the so-called information superhighway want to extend the ideas of timeliness and pertinence by creating a personal newspaper, 'The Daily Me', whose contents differ for each reader. It would be delivered electronically to individual readers and either read on screen or printed out by a reader to be read when convenient. While I find that scenario rather fanciful, technology now exists, in the form of modems affordable by students, to enable open learning providers to provide daily updates to open learning material, via the Internet.

Technology exists also, in the form of 'on-demand' printing, to provide printed material that is tailored to particular subgroups of students. This development has been made use of for some time on lecture courses at Cornell, Harvard and elsewhere. It is used to a lesser extent in open learning, typically on courses that date rapidly or whose modules can be studied in more than one sequence. With on-demand printing, such courses can be supplied in loose-leaf format, and students can remove or add pages, or re-order pages, as needed.

On-demand printing can be used to save students time. A good example is its use to eliminate manual searches for articles in a library. Students often have to read material which comes from a variety of original sources (e.g., books, journals and newspapers). There is only a limited amount to be gained educationally from searching through a library catalogue, finding the source material and then photocopying it. This is why, in the UK Open University, many courses provide a course reader, containing reprints of key articles. Producing a course reader in this way is an expensive and lengthy process, one part of which is clearing copyright. Some North American publishers now produce readers via on-demand printing. They can provide compilations of material, which they then bind into a book, often for little more than the cost of photocopying; those publishers also take care of payments to the original copyright owner and other administrative details.

THE CASE FOR FACILITATING CHANGES TO OPEN LEARNING TEXTS

If you own the copyright to your open learning material, then in principle you can use your material in any way you like. For example, you could create your own compilations, changing the layout of the original source material as you wish, and selecting extracts rather than reprinting complete sections. Changes of those kinds are trivial, if textual layouts are simple. However, open learning texts can have very complex layouts. I believe, and shall argue below, that the way we currently create those complex layouts hinders the re-use of material.

In Chapter 18 of this volume, Valcke and Vuist characterise typical open learning texts as consisting of a core discourse (the basic content),

> ... enriched with embedded support devices (ESD), such as advance organisers, pre- and post-questions, tasks, content pages, indexes, margin texts, examples, schemes, etc. [which] motivate and activate the student to access the study content, to process the content and to test their own mastery of the course objectives. Embedded support devices comprise up to 40–45 per cent of the content of the printed learning materials.

According to Valcke and Vuist, the problem is that pre-printed courses are based upon a priori decisions and selections of the basic content in relation to embedded support devices. These premature commitments (a priori choices) cause problems, because students have needs that change as they study:

> ... at the start of the process, students need to be able to browse and to travel through the materials. At a later stage they may want to approach the materials from an evaluation point of view ... [and] construct study modes (... test mode, rehearsal mode, etc.) to work through the materials.

It is evident to me that no single layout and no single selection of material can satisfy each of those needs in an optimal way. This is why I believe it is essential, as soon as it is practicable, to provide students with ways of modifying their open learning material to suit their evolving needs.

THE DIFFICULTY OF CHANGING OPEN LEARNING TEXTS

Unfortunately, even though most open learning texts are prepared on computer, rather than by manual pasting up of elements, the choice of program is generally restricted to XPress, PageMaker or Word. The approach to page layout encouraged by those programs is 'make it look OK' (MILOK), rather than 'make obvious relationships explicit' (MORE). Those programs provide little or no support for treating the elements in a text in an interrelated way, automatically. Instead, designers have to follow a MILOK approach: they have to make a series of design decisions about each double page spread, involving the size, placement and juxtaposition of body text, illustrations, tables and embedded support devices.

As well as being labour-intensive, MILOK decisions are typically independent of each other. For example, in many cases it is possible to move a heading without moving an embedded support device that has a logical link with it and so should move. Further, any changes to the relative size and position of a specific embedded support device will have to be repeated for all other occurrences of that support device, if consistency is important.

This indicates an absence of explicit structural relationships between the text and embedded support devices in the laid-out document. Since those structural relationships are not explicit, it is hard to make changes quickly, even for skilled designers. This is one justification for the creation of what I have termed a flexible 'course consumption' system, based upon the MORE approach mentioned above.

TOWARDS A FLEXIBLE 'COURSE CONSUMPTION' SYSTEM

By analogy with consumer products, most open learning courses are available only as basic models. Every student receives the same books, the same software, the same level of support and the same exam. The pioneers of the UK Open University termed this an 'equal misery' approach, in which every student was assumed to have a basic level of provision, and no student was to be assumed to have a superior level of provision. This runs counter to modern trends, such as the wish by consumers to have some control over the products and services they use. Manufacturers and service organisations take advantage of this by offering 'add-ons' – additions to a product, extra facilities and so on.

Taking this into account, it seems peculiar that we provide students with software that can be tailored by them as they wish, but we do not provide them with the means to tailor their courses in any significant way. If we were to do this, we would create a flexible 'course consumption' system, in systems engineering terms, which could take a standard product (an open learning course) and alter that product to suit a user's needs.

WAYS TO PERSONALISE OPEN LEARNING TEXTS

I have suggested previously that it would be useful to have tools which make it easier to change the content, design and layout of a course. For example, imagine that you wanted to create one version of an open learning booklet in which the answers to each self-assessment exercise followed that exercise, and another version in which the answers were at the end of the booklet. With the MILOK approach described above, origination of the second version would involve a series of time-consuming manual cut-and-paste operations. By contrast, with the MORE approach, an example of which is provided by the work of Valcke and Vuist at the Dutch Ou (see Chapter 18 in this volume), all that is required is the creation of two generic templates (one for each version). The software would then use those templates to lay out each version automatically.

The MORE approach can be used by both supply-driven and customer-driven open learning institutions. Consider the response of each to a demand by students for versions of material to suit three distinct study modes – initial study, revision, and use for reference purposes after the exam.

- A supply-driven institution would create three fully laid-out versions of course material (one for each mode), then either provide them in printed form or provide a printed copy of one version, plus electronic copies of the other two versions. Those electronic copies might be supplied on a diskette or a CD-ROM, or be made available via the Internet.
- A customer-driven institution would determine which version would be used most frequently by students, and supply a fully laid-out printed copy

of it. It would also provide electronic copies of all three versions, *plus tools to enable students to create further versions quickly and easily.*

In principle, the MORE approach makes it easy to change the appearance of graphic elements, such as tables, graphs and formulae, to suit the changing needs of a student on a course.

Consider, for example, how a student's needs might change on an open learning course about chemistry. This particular subject requires students to become familiar with a range of pictorial representations of molecules. Examples of these, taken from an open learning course on Cosmetic Science, are shown in Figure 30.1.

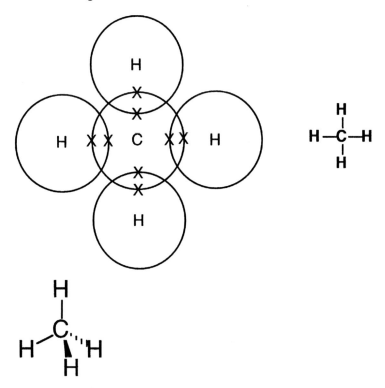

Figure 30.1 A range of pictorial representations of molecules
(Derived from illustrations in Module 1 of the open learning course *Diploma in Cosmetic Science,* produced by the Society of Cosmetic Scientists)

Typically, the novice student is supplied with a three-dimensional molecular modelling kit, containing little coloured balls (the atoms), joined by sticks (the bonds between atoms). By using the kit, the student can gain a more intimate appreciation of what kinds of molecules can be formed, and how the shapes of those molecules correspond to their abstract representations as chemical formulae. To reduce costs, most open learning courses on chemistry contain just a single representation of a given molecule. If that molecule is discussed early in the text, it is represented as a simple model (e.g., a ball-and-stick model). If it is discussed later in the text, a more sophisticated representation is used.

Students should have available all relevant representations of a molecule, from the simple ball-and-stick models they need when they start, to the less representational formulae they need for an exam, and perhaps even the highly abbreviated abstract formulae used by professional chemists. Authors of open learning texts on chemistry have available specialist tools (for example, ChemDraw) to create those multiple versions, at little or no extra cost. They could either provide compilations of those multiple versions, or they could provide access to the tools – either directly, which would require training in the use of the specialist tools, or indirectly, perhaps through the fulfilment by 'form-based' software, of requests from students, via the Internet, for a particular representation.

What is remarkable is that, although equivalent specialist tools exist in many other areas of open learning (e.g., Mathematica, in maths), we neither provide multiple representations of material, nor do we give students even indirect access to those tools. By contrast, it is increasingly common for students on traditional face-to-face courses to have access to such tools on a routine basis, as part of their professional development.

Some students on open learning courses have jobs that give them access to professional equipment and software on a par with the facilities available to authors; many others have access to facilities which are less impressive, yet still far above the minimum level that may be assumed by the course author.

For example, very many students now have access to MicroSoft Office, which enables them to create pictorial representations of tabular data. It seems strange that we do not give them guidance on visual presentation, in the context of their access to such software. Further, it is odd that we do not generally provide electronic copies of course material, which would make it easier for well-equipped students, who may form a significant proportion of the enrolment on vocational courses, to exploit the facilities available to them for reworking material.

WAYS TO AUGMENT OPEN LEARNING TEXTS

I suggested earlier that it would be helpful to provide students with tools to assess and lay out material drawn from sources of their choice, either as a substitute for course material provided centrally, or for enrichment purposes. In a sense, this is done whenever a publisher creates a course reader from electronic versions of existing material, and it is useful to remind ourselves of the steps involved, so that we can spot possible parallels with what students need.

First, a judgement is reached as to the value of a particular piece of source material, then its legal availability is determined, then it is edited and laid out to suit the new compilation.

Editing and layout are easier if both text and graphics in the source material are available in a structured form. For text, the de facto standard format tends to be that of Microsoft Word documents. In such a case, it is necessary to add special structural tags to the text, to indicate relationships between elements. SGML (Standard Generalised Markup Language) is commonly favoured for this, although it is not well suited to complex layouts. Unfortunately, there is no de facto standard for graphics; the nearest to this, CGM (Computer Graphics Metafile), does not maintain any meaningful relationships between the components of a graphic, but just facilitates the exchange of complete pictures between one program or computer and another. It is best, therefore, to deal with each graphic on a case-by-case basis, using specialist software to process and alter each class of graphic (graph, table, formula, block diagram etc.).

Just as an author is generally concerned with the final appearance of a book rather than the details of the tagging language used to mark up the book (e.g., SGML, L^AT_EX), so, in general, students will have little interest in how any structural relationships are achieved in the materials they have access to. Instead, their focus is on finding material that is relevant, removing any parts that are irrelevant, and making what is left more intelligible and useful.

Today's students have several possible sources of enrichment material that were unavailable just a few years ago. For example, many of them have access to a wide and increasing range of reference information from commercial CD-ROMs. Other students have access to the Internet, through which they can search many thousands of databases, ranging from an electronic version of the Encyclopaedia Britannica, to databases of physical and chemical properties, to commercial on-line services (e.g., news, patents, journal citations). Further resources available, often at no charge, include full-text versions of thousands of books that are out of copyright, and illustrations and multimedia material on virtually every topic one can think of.

The existence of such resources, like the existence of open learning courses now available on the Internet, should cause all open learning institutions to re-examine their activities. Perhaps we should be moving to a model of developing courses that is more like resource-based learning: give students more materials than they need, and help them to select what they need.

If we do offer resource-based courses, we must provide tools to enable learners to make good use of all available information, not only existing courses, but also new sources of information and courses. In this context, it is important to keep in sight the issue of quality in open and distance learning. Many of the new resources are of very variable quality. At the very least, we could provide the equivalent of a consumers' guide to each new resource. Further, the resources are in many different formats, few of which are immediately usable by students. Here, too, we could provide programs to convert resources into appropriate forms.

Going further, and in conclusion, we could take the more valuable of the various new resources available publicly, and add value to them, either by providing enhanced versions of them, with more effective layout and design (a kind of quality control approach), or by devising tools to enable our students to appraise and improve source material (a kind of quality assurance approach). In the latter case, we may need a sustained programme of research, to codify what is known about the design of effective documents, and make that knowledge available in an usable form to our students.

REFERENCE

Peters, G. (1994) *What is 'New Directions' all about?*, Leaflet 94/3, Milton Keynes, The Open University.

Part VIII

EVALUATION AND QUALITY

31

BUILDING GOOD QUALITY IN, RATHER THAN INSPECTING BAD QUALITY OUT

Jack Koumi

INTRODUCTION

This chapter takes a controversial view on how quality should be achieved in open and distance learning. I shall argue that resources should be concentrated more on the *creation* of high quality materials and less on the *testing* of these materials. The discussion purposely excludes other factors that undoubtedly affect quality, such as the *delivery system* and *learner support*: I restrict attention to the appropriate balance between *creation* and *testing*.

To be more specific, I will argue that quality can be virtually guaranteed by using creative, well-trained, experienced teacher-producers, who know their target audience, and who are allowed adequate time for drafting and refining both the materials and the underlying student-centred design principles. In these circumstances, I argue that empirical developmental testing is largely unnecessary. (I use the term *empirical developmental testing* to mean pre-testing of materials on a sample of the intended audience or on surrogate students with similar backgrounds.)

I accept the value of a certain amount of developmental testing for every open learning course and even the testing of every lesson for selected courses. However, I don't want the idea of developmental testing to distract attention from what I see as the central concern: striving for the highest pedagogic skills, experience and creativity of the authors of materials, and ensuring adequate time for them to exploit their expertise.

I shall argue my case for this order of priorities later, but let me first accept some of the opposing arguments concerning the risk of using untested materials.

THE CASE FOR EMPIRICAL DEVELOPMENTAL TESTING

Every teacher-producer of open learning materials has some idiosyncratic misconceptions about how best to present the subject matter to the target students. Therefore, it might be argued that every lesson should be developmentally tested on a sample of the intended audience. If any learning difficulties are exposed, the material can be modified to obviate them – or the *study guidance* can be modified, or the *learning environment*. This argument is especially strong in the case of a prototypical course, as opposed to a course that is similar to a previous one.

The risk of materials being way off the mark is reduced significantly when they are produced by a *course team,* collaborating intimately on every lesson, rather than by an individual. This is especially likely when the team knows the audience well. However, some risk does remain, because the team may still retain some *shared* misconceptions.

This view is supported by some of my experiences at The Open University, UK. One subject area at the UK OU where shared course team misconceptions are *expected* is Computing: whenever a course involves students working individually on a personal computer at home, course teams have learned from experience that unpredictable user-difficulties are inevitable. In such subjects, therefore, empirical developmental testing is carried out on most of the materials, although this testing is often superficial, due to restricted availability of suitable test-subjects and of funds to pay them. The subjects are usually surrogate students: people with similar experience to the intending students, but rarely the actual students.

The interesting phenomenon here is that courses utilising personal computers are no longer prototypical. Yet they retain their prototypical problem: teachers still fail to predict a variety of student difficulties.

THE CASE FOR A HIGHER PRIORITY FOR MATERIALS CREATION

In other UK OU subjects, such as mathematical subjects with no personal computer element, no empirical developmental testing is carried out. One reason for this omission is again the scarcity of developmental test-subjects and of funds. However, an extenuating reason is confidence that the highly experienced course team can second guess the students. This confidence is based on past experience of summative evaluations of similar courses and on substantial face-to-face contact with students of similar courses. The team sometimes seeks help in pre-empting students' difficulties from critical readers, who are part-time tutors rather than students, but even this might be considered unnecessary for the well-established type of course.

Now, is such a course team's self-confidence in its consensus views justified?

I contend that when you have a trained, high-quality team of experienced teachers who know their target audience well, then their self-confidence is rarely misplaced. For such a team, permitted sufficient thinking-time, the ensuing conception of the learning materials is based upon several lifetimes of teaching experience and mature intellectual development. I would personally place far more trust in their *untested* materials than on those produced, and modified after pre-testing on bewildered students, by an inexperienced, perplexed team. Test-students can identify material that doesn't work but they can rarely come to a consensus on how to improve it. Effective improvement needs an experienced teacher, with good judgement, or better still, a team of them.

The level of thinking that can be achieved by consensus peer-group appraisal – i.e. course team debate – is far more profound than the recommendations of a typical empirical evaluation. A discussion between peers can be so wide-ranging, building creative momentum as a result of interactivity: the interactivity stimulates a virtuous circle in which the critical analysis becomes deeper and deeper. Effectively, the team is carrying out a whole *series* of developmental evaluations and re-evaluations, as *thought experiments*, each member of the team repeatedly taking on the role of a hypothetical student.

Moreover, if the team is long established, this analysis will be *theory-led:* the team will have developed a consensus design model, even if it is rather vague and intuitive. Ideally, such unspoken design theories will be gradually refined and made more explicit during discussions of materials, although this is rare. In any event, the team will be working to some form of causal theory of why it believes its materials will work for its particular target audience. In the absence of such a theory (or set of design principles), then even if the material works, the team won't know *why* it works – so it can't guarantee success next time.

You might say, why not have the best of both worlds: a high-quality, trained, experienced, materials-creation team, which has developed explicit student-centred design principles and which is permitted plenty of thinking-time – *plus* – empirical developmental testing of the materials. I would say, *yes sometimes.* However, when the team and the conditions are really good, I contend that the risk of substantially poor materials is so reduced that pre-testing need not be universally applied.

In these circumstances, empirical developmental testing can be safely restricted to the few really deserving cases, namely:

- notoriously unpredictable subjects such as Computing
- materials for which, despite prolonged debate, the course team failed to reach a consensus
- the *occasional* random sample lesson: if the material were found wanting, the design model could be reappraised.

THE CASE AGAINST UNIVERSAL
DEVELOPMENTAL TESTING

The above arguments are *comparative:* that empirical developmental testing should get lower priority in comparison to materials creation. There are also *absolute* arguments, below, that universal developmental testing per se has some inherent disadvantages.

Spreading resources thinly jeopardises evaluators' reputations

Another argument for restricting the breadth of developmental testing is to avoid spreading resources too thinly. A successful design for the interrogation of learners (or surrogate learners) and the interpretation of results, is necessarily a complicated time-consuming endeavour. A hurried, under-resourced evaluation will not produce credible, practicable recommendations for improving the materials. This would be true in the simplest of situations, but it is doubly true for multimedia packages and those frequent media lessons whose learning objectives are difficult to evaluate: for example, long-term objectives, non-specific objectives, each medium contributing only partially towards an objective.

Most institutions do not have even one-tenth of the evaluation staff that would be required for such in-depth empirical formative evaluation of every lesson. And if evaluations are done badly because of under-staffing, the evaluators' reputations will suffer and they will lose the confidence of the teachers.

Why empirical developmental testing of
UK educational television is rare

In distance education in the UK, there is one medium – broadcast television – for which little or no empirical developmental testing is carried out. That is, the television programmes are hardly ever pre-tested on students, or even on surrogate students. This is the case with TV for both schoolchildren and adults. A major reason for the lack of testing is that a completed programme would be too expensive to modify (if the test results recommended any modification). On the other hand, a half-developed programme is not considered adequate for developmental testing: it is believed that if students are subjected to such a *rough draft* of a TV lesson, the deleterious effect on their information-processing is critical – far more so for TV than for print. This conviction derives from TV producers' occasional painful experiences of showing *rough-cut* programmes to subject experts who are not yet experienced.

Yet few of these programmes are judged to be unsuccessful (although there do exist minority negative views). I suggest that the general success is due to the *prodigious endeavour* that goes into their production. Successful educational TV screenwriting requires prolonged, deep, student-sympathetic deliberation and re-deliberation. Hence, the process of production involves *self-appraisal* by the producer/teacher scriptwriting team – essentially, formative evaluation of their own draft scripts. In the UK OU, the same degree of self- and peer-appraisal is carried out in the production of *print, audio* and *computer* materials.

Incidentally, many TV lessons for the UK OU do undergo *summative* evaluations, which have resulted in some global recommendations for future designs (Salomon, 1983; Bates, 1987; Laurillard, 1991).

Foreknowledge of empirical developmental testing encourages laziness

Let me go out on a limb with the following suggestion: foreknowledge that the TV lesson will be objectively evaluated could encourage screenwriters to *abort* the above painful mental perseverance at an embryonic stage. The same would apply to other media.

This may sound unlikely, but it certainly happens. I have occasionally been present at a discussion that ends by one protagonist declaring 'Well, we can't agree, let's choose one solution and see what the students think.' There's nothing wrong with the statement itself, but its timing is often too early in the discussion. That is, the scriptwriting team cannot agree on a certain point and, instead of persevering with the analysis and reaching a consensus, it abdicates this responsibility to the evaluation.

The danger here is that if there are two proposed solutions to the disputed section and the two proponents disagree strongly about which solution should be used, it is quite likely that both are imperfect. However, the subsequent evaluation would test only one of the solutions – the one that was adopted in the final media lesson. In contrast, further script discussion in depth, i.e. *thought experiments* conducted by the scriptwriting team, could have resulted in a third, agreed solution that was superior.

This scenario is the *word-processor syndrome*: because it's so easy to modify your typing on a word-processor, you take less care with your first attempt.

In the same vein, I have often been asked the question by new educational TV production students, 'How do I know if my programme will be effective?' One answer is: you need to work extremely hard, *evaluating the material in your mind* as you design and redesign it, until you are *almost certain* it's effective. If you have *no* opinions as to whether the programme is likely to succeed, you are not qualified to produce the programme. To qualify, you need to practise critical *self-appraisal.* This is not to say that self-appraisal is always sufficient, merely that it is necessary. But if the producer and scriptwriting team are really good, it's *often* sufficient. The same applies to all media.

Obsessive evaluation procedures will antagonise conscientious producers

Some authors recommend several levels of testing, by several categories of testers. For example, Chinien and Hlynka (1993) report that most authors recommend a three-stage evaluation with student subjects – one-to-one, small group, field test – having already carried out evaluation by experts. For this prior stage, some authors recommend extensive evaluation by numerous different experts: experts on the subject matter, delivery, media, format, pedagogy, instructional design, and even language experts.

Such obsessive testing reveals a complete lack of confidence in the creators of the materials. It's as if an experienced creative team of subject-expert teachers is being viewed as an *idiot savant* whose mindless labours are at best only *accidentally* successful – as an oversight – and must therefore be monitored carefully by so-called professional evaluators.

In truth, the typical team does not merely provide a purely top-down transmission of knowledge. Rather, it designs with student-centred intent that the learner will *develop a critical attitude towards such and such* or will *follow this argument* or will *master this technique,* etc. Typically, the team undertakes diligent, painful *self-appraisal* of its materials. The guiding philosophy behind this endeavour is *empathy with the students* – the team is continually trying to put itself inside the students' minds, trying to predict their various intellectual predicaments. So, whatever success the team's materials achieve in connecting with students' minds, this has been achieved by *insight,* not by oversight.

Such a team would not take kindly to an external evaluator, who has not shared its prodigious deliberations, has little inkling of its unspoken design principles (usually vague and intuitive, yet strongly held) and is not a subject expert. This may be bigoted, but it's understandable.

It might be argued that these difficulties could be ameliorated by extensive consultation between evaluators and materials creators. However, an objective, intelligent evaluator will still practise a good deal of independence in both designing the evaluation and interpreting the results. This is laudable but could well upset the creation team.

This conflict is most likely to occur if the teachers, who believe their techniques derive from experience and empathy with the students, cynically suspect that the evaluator *lacks the disposition to empathise with students.* There is a vicious circle that almost guarantees such suspicion. If the evaluator dismisses expert appraisal by the creators themselves and insists that only empirical evidence is trustworthy, the creators will draw the conclusion that the evaluator cannot conceive of empathising with students and pre-empting their intellectual difficulties.

CONCLUSION

In order to *assure quality* of open and distance learning materials, this chapter has recommended that the following circumstances be worked towards:

- recruitment of high-quality staff for materials creation
- training of staff
- incorporation of substantial face-to-face student contact within staff duties
- striving to retain staff so that they become experienced
- working in well-established teams
- teams permitted plenty of thinking-time to re-draft and refine materials
- teams working to a student-centred set of design principles, which are frequently reappraised.

Given the above conditions, it has been argued that *good quality can be built in, rather than bad quality being inspected out* by empirical development testing. Such empirically based control should be restricted to the few materials where the creation team fails to reach a consensus after prolonged deliberation, or to notoriously unpredictable topics, such as Computing, and to a small random sample of lessons.

For the majority of lessons, several arguments have been advanced against such empirical formative evaluation. The principal argument has been that resources should be concentrated on achieving the above circumstances for materials creation. Then the deliberations of the creators would generally constitute *more effective* formative evaluation, because the creators would repeatedly hypothesise students' intellectual predicaments. Moreover, they would address these from a position of pedagogic expertise rather than futile bewilderment.

Another argument was that foreknowledge of empirical testing might encourage premature cessation of such prodigious endeavours. The resulting imperfect materials might even be too *embryonic* to bear profitable testing.

Finally, there were arguments involving the sensitive relationship between author and critic (teaching-materials creator and evaluator). Hasty, under-resourced evaluations would lead to loss of teachers' confidence. On the other hand, obsessive over-evaluation could threaten teachers' self-esteem and insult their professionalism.

But what does one do if the above circumstances for creation do not hold? For example, when a distance teaching institution is young, most creation teams cannot be well established. Or when the institution has severe financial constraints, it cannot pay high enough salaries to recruit high-quality materials creators. If this is the situation, then until it improves, do developmentally test, with students or surrogates – but don't be obsessive about it, and use high-quality evaluators!

My earlier argument rests heavily on my final prerequisite for building quality in: the development of a student-centred set of design principles.

Table 31.1 illustrates the kind of thing I mean: it's a brief outline of the video screenwriting principles advocated in the BBC's annual *EDTV* course on educational media production (Koumi, 1991). At the level of generality given in Table 31.1, most of the principles apply equally to most media, including print.

Table 31.1 Outline of ETV screenwriting principles

A   How is the programme to be used?

By whom: target audience characteristics

Context: learning context, complementary learning

Purpose: educational objectives
(motivational, experiential, cognitive)

B   Structure each chapter of the story

Make them want to know

Tell them what you will do

Do it, with sympathy: texture, reinforce, sensitise

Tell them what you have done

Connect it – to the next chapter of the story

C   Sympathetic picture–word composition

The Producer should get into the viewer's mind

– i.e. what are they thinking/looking at?

– e.g. optimise load, pace, depth

– words reinforcing pictures and vice versa

The Producer should get out of the viewer's mind

– Rationale: don't blinker/give elbow room

– Encourage *mindful* learning by a *range* of viewers

– e.g. pause for contemplation, pose questions

REFERENCES

Bates, A. W. (1987) *Educational Television,* Units 25/26 of the OU Course EH207, Milton Keynes, The Open University.

Chinien, C. and Hlynka, D. (1993) 'Formative evaluation of prototypical products: from expert to connoisseur', *ETTI*, 30(1), pp. 60–6.

Koumi, J. (1991) 'Narrative screenwriting for educational television: a framework', *Journal of Educational Television*, 17(3), pp. 131–48.

Laurillard, D. (1991) 'Mediating the message: programme design and students' understanding', *Instructional Science*, 20, pp. 3–23.

Salomon, G. (1983) 'Using television as a unique teaching resource for OU courses', Milton Keynes, The Open University (mimeo).

32

COURSE EVALUATION AND ACADEMIC QUALITY

Ellie Chambers

INTRODUCTION

Within distance education it is axiomatic that institutions undertake course evaluation in order to assure and improve the quality of the courses they offer students. For in this context it is recognised that spatial and temporal separation of teacher from student may result in mismatch between their respective expectations; courses may fail to engage students' interest or teach them effectively. Moreover, many of these courses are expensive to produce in published form. Accordingly, comprehensive evaluation encompasses processes of course development and systems for production and delivery, as well as the quality of course materials themselves. Such evaluation has a practical purpose: to inform policy-makers and managers at various levels within the institution, including course writer-producers, enabling all of them to strive for improved quality of provision, more efficient use of resources, and increased student numbers and rates of retention (Chambers, forthcoming).

At least that is the official story. In reality, 'failure to engage students' interest and teach them effectively' is actually experienced by many of our (usually adult, part-time, fee-paying) students as a devastating personal failure, a wasted investment of time and money, or a 'con', depending on the individual. These reactions are damaging to the institution (let alone to some students) simply because these people are unlikely to buy any more of its courses. Worse, from the distance education community's point of view, they may never again 'buy into' distance education. In other words, distance education itself would tend to become discredited – increasingly seen as the second-best option or 'quick fix' that its critics always said it would be. For these reasons it is vital that distance education institutions produce courses of very high quality: not only that, they must be *seen* to be so. In universities this means investing considerable resources into producing a range of courses of high *academic* quality – the 'pearls' in Alan Woodley's string (see Chapter 33 in this volume). As he says there, an important aspect of assuring quality is discovering how people actually interact with and learn from our courses.

Here, then, we focus on issues surrounding evaluation of course materials in particular, illustrating some of the ways in which investigation of students' expectations and experiences of study may contribute to quality assurance and course improvement. In the longer term, insights gained into processes of students' learning also illuminate course designer-writers' understanding of the teaching of their discipline generally, and thus contribute to preparation of courses of high quality in the future. However, precisely what we might mean by 'quality' in this context is a prior question.

EVALUATION AND 'QUALITY'

Notoriously, what is meant by 'quality', and the judgements made about it in particular cases, depend upon who is doing the viewing and judging and from what point of view. In an overview of the work of the UK Council for National Academic Awards, Harris (1990) provides this summary:

> Perceptions of quality vary in relation to the purposes of the perceiver (for example, the academic quality of a course is not necessarily the same as its quality as a vocational preparation), they vary over time, and they vary between subject disciplines. Absolute judgements are not achievable
>
> (Harris, 1990, p. 41)

First, quality is a multi-dimensional concept: attempts to assess the quality of courses from any one perspective (such as 'fitness for purpose') can only result in a partial conception of it. Secondly, it is a dynamic concept – perceptions of quality change over time. And, third, such perceptions vary according to the subject-matter in question. Accordingly, ensuing discussion is illustrated by material drawn from a particular case – an evaluation of beginning undergraduates' study of the *Introduction to Art History*, part of the UK Open University's Arts Foundation Course.

Since the *Introduction to Art History* is part of an undergraduate course, the aim of evaluation in this case is assessment and improvement of its *academic* quality. With respect to this, Wicks (1992) has argued that, 'Standards have always been those appropriate to the current cultural context and body of knowledge of the subject' (p. 68). Further, Pring (1992) maintains that these standards are intrinsic to academic disciplines themselves, which also embody certain values. That is, academic standards are the measures of 'correctness, appropriateness, stylishness, validity, within distinctive traditions of enquiry' (p. 18). In this they differ markedly from the 'extrinsic' standards that apply to vocational study, for example, where:

> Successful learning signifies fitness for purpose; one first identifies the requirements of the job and then one specifies ... the competences that enable one to do the job. The competencies, revealed in the undertaking of ... job related tasks, constitute the standards.
>
> (Pring, 1992, p.13)

So, as regards the *Introduction to Art History*, the standards against which the academic quality of the course may be judged are those currently and widely accepted within the community of art historians. However, these standards apply at particular levels of study; in this case, at the introductory level. It follows that those best placed to make judgements about quality are not only academic peers (who usually contribute during the period of course preparation), but also evaluators – educationists whose primary role is to investigate and assess the responses of the students for whom the course is intended. Here, we focus on the evaluator's role.

In order to interpret students' responses meaningfully, to make judgements about the academic quality (appropriateness, validity etc.) of the course, and to communicate such assessment to course writer-producers in ways that engage with their concerns and carry conviction, evaluators themselves must to some extent be 'on the inside' of the discipline concerned. That is, in this case, they must have some knowledge and understanding of the distinctive purposes and objects of study that characterise art history: its major text-genres, key concepts, methods of enquiry, uses of evidence and tests for 'truth'; and the conventions that govern spoken and written discourses within it. When equipped with such knowledge and understanding the evaluator is less Jack Koumi's 'so-called professional', precariously poised outside the course team looking in (Chapter 31 of this volume), and more a team member whose particular expertise is precisely to help formulate course design principles which may be understood by and negotiated with others. While launching this kind of pedagogic discourse within an institution cannot guarantee 'success next time', it is surely a necessary condition of continued successful teaching.

On this view of the nature and purposes of course evaluation, then, the evaluator's role is to assess students' responses to a course in the light of their understanding of the standards and values that currently inhere in the discipline concerned – from which the aims of particular courses are derived – and also of the pedagogic principles that apply at particular levels of study. In what follows, teachers and evaluators in other domains will want to make appropriate substitutions for the subject-matter discussed here.

CRITERIA OF EVALUATION

The nature of the discipline and aims of the
Introduction to Art History

In common with other humanities disciplines, study of art history centrally involves analysis and interpretation of the activities, ideas, beliefs, cultural practices and products of individuals and groups within society, over time. What unites these disciplines is that the objects of study are 'texts', broadly defined and of various kinds (pictorial, historical, literary, auditory, philosophical, symbolic), representations, images and accounts of reality, of human experience and imagination. These texts must be analysed and interpreted appropriately in order to produce meanings. Textual analysis proceeds according to the quasi-technical 'formal rules' that govern the composition of different text-genres. Analysis of paintings in the landscape genre, for example, among other things focuses attention on the problems involved in representing distance, and light and shade, and involves application of analytical concepts such as perspective, mass and colour density. In addition to such understanding of form, interpretation requires knowledge of the socio-historical circumstances of a text's inception and reception and about the interplay of these contexts in which meaning is made. Students must learn how to analyse and interpret the primary and secondary texts produced by their predecessors, to make their own enquiries and produce their own texts.

In other words, in the humanities significant knowledge is socially constructed, through our discourse past and present, and introduction to these disciplines involves coming to understand and participate in certain traditions of academic discourse. A discourse is here understood as a particular way of using language and other symbolic forms communicatively, or, in ways which produce meaning and understanding. Students become participants in a discourse by entering into the relevant processes of textual analysis, interpretation and judgement, and by learning to think, speak and write within the academic conventions that apply. In the process, they come under the sway of the values and beliefs that are enshrined in the discourse, but they must also understand these things as conventional and open to challenge (Chambers, 1993).

Accordingly, in the Preface to the *Introduction to Art History* students are informed that 'art is a human activity with a history; … a social function … distinct from but related to the broader history of human societies' – a view which, if they have always thought of art as 'spontaneous self-expression', may be 'new'. The overarching aim of the course is to 'acquaint you with the premises and methods of … the history of art', a discipline which is 'constantly undergoing redefinition'; also to 'furnish you with enough raw material, examples of art, to enable you to "do art history" yourself – to think about certain products of human creativity not only with interest and pleasure, but systematically …' (Langmuir *et al.*, 1994, p. 3, adapted from Langmuir, 1986). It is assumed that students do not have any previous knowledge of the visual arts: they will address such questions as 'What is art?' and 'What does this work of art mean?', as well as studying the circumstances of its creation and reception and, more generally, ways in which art may be analysed and classified.

Pedagogic principles

As well as understanding the nature of the discipline and course writers' particular aims and purposes, evaluators must also have insight into those principles of teaching–learning that apply at the particular level of study. Some of the pedagogic principles which flow from the foregoing analysis may be discussed only briefly here.

- *The principle of engagement.* When the aim of teaching is that students come to understand and ultimately participate in the discourse, and when understanding itself is regarded as an active 'making of meaning', starting-points for study are of the first importance. In order to engage students' interest and begin to introduce the academic discourse in ways that enable them to make sense of it from the start, teachers in distance education need as much knowledge about the students as possible; their social and educational backgrounds, their aims and expectations, pre-conceptions of the subject-matter, and so forth. On this view, 'starting from where the student is' is understood as a *socio-cultural* process of engaging with the assumptions, pre-conceptions and knowledge that students *share* – by virtue of their membership of a cultural and linguistic group – rather than as a matter of attempting to cater for individuals' (psychological) preparedness for study (Chambers, 1993).
- *The principle of intelligibility.* This principle draws attention to the need for teachers to set up a framework for students' understanding of the subject from the start of study and, by providing sufficient structure and direction for their thought processes (or, by constructing a teaching 'narrative'), to help sustain strands of meaning throughout. The narrative should, of course, proceed towards 'closure' – towards some satisfying, if temporary, resolution of the issues. It is helpful if at first the range of terms in play is relatively restricted, and abstractions are few and grounded in concrete examples or illustrations which will be familiar to students; in other words, if teachers construct an 'intermediate discourse' early on, only gradually shifting the terms of discussion towards the 'full blown' academic discourse (Northedge, 1992).
- *The principle of participation.* The view of humanities undergraduate education as an introduction to academic discourses as a participant, has the advantage of giving primary place to development of discursive processes themselves: the interconnected processes of analysis–interpretation–judgement; of learning to 'read' different kinds of text appropriately and to speak and write confidently within the terms of the discourse. Moreover, on this view, such processes are understood as immanent. They are not simply means to ends – generalised study 'skills' which may be taught and learned separately from and irrespective of subject-matter. For example, at the beginning students need detailed guidance as they approach each different text-genre (within painting, the

347

genres of landscape, portraiture and still-life, for instance). And in order to become participants, students must be encouraged to use what they read, analyse and discuss to make their own interpretations and judgements, and formulate their own views, which they learn to give voice to appropriately and persuasively.

It follows from all three principles that the ground teachers aim to cover at the introductory stage needs to be suitably restricted, so that students have time to think about and assimilate what is presented to them, to explore the subject for themselves, and to apply and practise the skills involved (Chambers, 1992).

Criteria of judgement

This brief analysis of the nature of the discipline, the aims of the course, and some of the basic pedagogic principles that apply at the introductory level suggests a number of criteria for evaluation of academic courses. Three are presented here, at first in general terms. Each criterion is then illustrated with reference to evaluation of the *Introduction to Art History*. Only a very small part of the available data may be discussed here, providing an indication of the kind of enquiry that might be undertaken in relation to each criterion and of improvements that may be made to a course as a result, along with some illustration of the claims made earlier about the evaluator's role in assessment of academic quality.

1   *The criterion of appropriateness*: that the course is appropriate to the student body for which it is intended; their preparedness for study, expectations, aims and interests. We may ask, for example, whether the assumptions teachers make about students are justified. (Do students at the introductory level in fact have no knowledge of the subject? What are their backgrounds? What do they expect study to be like? What assumptions do they make? What are *their* interests and study aims?) Here we touch on two issues raised by the pedagogic 'principle of engagement'; students' initial study interests and the extent of their preparedness for study.

Broadly, writer-producers of the *Introduction to Art History* were right in their assumptions about students of the course. Only one in seven had ever studied art history before (Chambers and Tunnicliffe, 1992), yet three-quarters of them said 'I am interested in it' and over half 'I feel very enthusiastic about doing it'. However, it transpired that though students were particularly interested in painting, they were markedly less keen on studying abstract art.

As regards preparation for study, very few students had set about it in any systematic way: a third of them had not even looked at the 'Preparatory Pack', which is provided before the start of the course at no extra cost; only a third had attended a preparatory course of any kind; and a staggering 80 per cent had not seen any of the published course material before enrolling for the course. Further analysis revealed that women students were rather more likely to prepare for study than men, and that the older the students the more likely they were to take preparation seriously (Chambers *et al.*, 1993).

Of particular interest to course writers were the prejudices students display here, in favour of painting (as opposed to sculpture or architecture, for instance) and against abstract art. This is an example of the kind of belief referred to earlier; which students share, which derives from the wider culture, and which course designer-writers need to be aware of. Preconceptions such as these may be taken as pointers towards appropriate content for future courses at the introductory level. At the least, the finding suggests that if abstract art were to be included, for example, then writers would have to acknowledge and take account of the initial prejudice against it. Arts Faculty managers were particularly impressed by the low take-up of the Preparatory Pack. They are now persuaded of the need for more, and better, material at the access level, and to make more strenuous efforts to persuade those student groups most in need to prepare themselves adequately for undergraduate study. The Faculty is currently preparing a comprehensive access course.

2   *The criterion of engagement*: that the breadth and depth of treatment of the subject-matter, and the level of discourse, are manageable; that students' interest is sustained. This raises the question whether students do in fact find the courses they study interesting, pleasurable and challenging. (Has the course engaged/sustained their interest? Have teachers set up a suitable 'framework for understanding' and launched the kind of fruitful 'teaching narrative' suggested by the pedagogic 'principle of intelligibility'?) Relationships between three measures are particularly significant here: the level of students' interest in the subject during and after study, the degree of difficulty they experience, and the extent to which they feel overburdened by the demands of the course.

As regards the *Introduction to Art History*, while three-quarters of students found the work difficult to some extent, a resounding 90 per cent of them judged it 'very/fairly' interesting. This alone suggests that the level of discourse was manageable. However, half the students thought there was 'far too much' work to do in the time set down for study by the university (12–14 hours per week). Women students found the work markedly more time-consuming than men did, a significant finding because women form the majority in the Arts Faculty (at around 70 per cent of the student body). In order to understand more fully how students interacted with and learned from the course, they were asked about these three aspects of it in relation to each major section of the study material, as indicated in Figure 32.1 (Chambers *et al.*, 1993, p. 21).

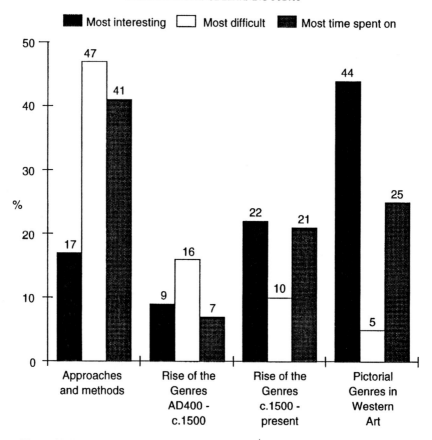

Figure 32.1 A comparison of 'most interesting/difficult/time-consuming' sections of the *Introduction to Art History*

In this comparison, section 1 ('Art History: Approaches and Methods') emerges as by far the most difficult and time-consuming. Responses to open questions revealed a reason for this. Students complained that as part of the work they were asked to read approximately one-third of a textbook – a form of study and text-genre that most students are quite unused to at the beginning. It transpired that the majority of them found the book not only time-consuming to study but also very difficult. However, students' responses may be interpreted in another way, which perhaps only an evaluator fairly familiar with the discipline might perceive. Section 1 is meta-discursive in nature: it contains talk *about* art history as a discipline. Arguably, such talk is misplaced here at the start; before students have the opportunity to 'do' some art history which would provide substance for their thoughts. As things stood, the discussion may well have seemed abstract and difficult to engage with. In contrast, students found section 4 ('Pictorial

Genres in Western Art') by far the most interesting. In this section they were asked to study a wide range of illustrations, mainly of representational painting. As we saw, students are anyway inclined to favour both painting and representational (as opposed to abstract) art.

These evaluation results reinforce the earlier finding – that teachers need to prepare students carefully for aspects of study which at the outset are unfamiliar or unwelcome. And they exemplify the kinds of insight that evaluation of a specific course may offer into students' learning processes generally, which contribute to the making of courses of high quality in the future. In this case writers were strongly urged to revise section 1 of the course. In the re-written version, only selected parts of the textbook are set for study and students are offered more guidance in how to read and use it: meta-discursive talk is much reduced and, instead, students are offered a comprehensive and practical approach to identifying the elements of painting.

3   *The criterion of performance*: that teaching of the central processes and concepts of the discipline enables students to study successfully at the level concerned. Here we may ask to what extent students have understood the nature of the discipline, and are 'on the inside' of it. (Can they engage satisfactorily in processes of analysis and interpretation? How successfully can they communicate their ideas and arguments: can they 'speak' in the conventional terms of the discourse, as suggested by the pedagogic 'principle of participation'?)

As regards communicative processes, an important measure of success is the quality of students' written work during the course and in end-of-course examination. Though these measures did indeed form part of the evaluation of the *Introduction to Art History* we cannot explore them here. Instead we focus solely on those beliefs about studying art history that may reveal the extent to which students have understood its central concerns and values (Chambers *et al.*, 1993, pp. 10, 32): see Table 32.1.

The downward trends here occur with respect to what we might call the emotional or affective aspects of study ((a), (c) and (d) above). At the same time, perceptions of the study of art as demanding and difficult have increased and statement (b) has shifted from second to first place. What this suggests is that students have indeed internalised some of the central values of the discipline, for within it emotional responses to art are undoubtedly regarded less highly than the intellectual (analytical and interpretive). Whether such values are desirable, either in themselves or in the light of students' own perceptions and desires with respect to study, is a further question – and one which evaluators are perfectly entitled to raise.

Table 32.1   A comparison of some attitudes to the study of Art History, before and after experience of the *Introduction to Art History*

Statements	Percentage agreement before study	Percentage agreement after study
(a) Art helps us enjoy our lives more	70	61
(b) Art history is important for under-standing the development of our culture	66	64
(c) Art helps us to engage with our feelings and emotions	62	48
(d) Art helps us to understand our feelings and those of others better	35	28
(e) The study of art is particularly demanding and difficult	28	39

CONCLUSION

The view of the nature and purposes of course evaluation taken here is perhaps closest to Judith Calder's 'educational psychology model' (Chapter 34 of this volume), in that the impact of such evaluation is on teaching and its principal beneficiaries are course designers and writer-producers. However, there is a crucial difference. On this view, processes of teaching–learning are regarded as *socio-cultural* in nature; a view that challenges the individualistic and inner-directed accounts of them which derive from psychology and are currently dominant. The underlying belief is that by re-conceptualising these processes of teaching–learning, along the lines outlined here, we in distance education will produce courses which engage our students and teach them more effectively. The underlying assumption is that where there is quality of provision, there is quality of education.

REFERENCES

Chambers, E. A. (1992) 'Workload and the quality of student learning', *Studies in Higher Education*, 17(2), pp. 141–53.

Chambers, E. A. (1993) 'The role of theories of discourse in course design for humanities distance education', *Media and Technology for Human Resource Development*, 5(3), pp. 177–96.

Chambers, E. A. (forthcoming) 'Information towards effective management: a case study', Proceedings of the VIII Annual AAOU Conference *Structure and Management of Open Learning Systems,* New Delhi, Asian Association of Open Universities.

Chambers, E. A., Close, J. and Tunnicliffe, T. (1993) 'Studying for a degree in the humanities: students' expectations and experiences of Art History', Humanities

Higher Education Research Group Report 12 (Internal paper), Institute of Educational Technology, Milton Keynes, The Open University.

Chambers, E. A. and Tunnicliffe, T. (1992) 'Studying for a degree in the humanities: students' motivation and commitment', Humanities Higher Education Research Group Report 6 (internal paper), Institute of Educational Technology, The Open University.

Harris, R. W. (1990) 'The CNNA, Accreditation and Quality Assurance', *Higher Education Review*, 22(3), pp. 34–54.

Langmuir, E. (1986) *An Arts Foundation Course: Introduction to Art History*, Milton Keynes, The Open University.

Langmuir, E., Fer, B. and Walsh, L. (1994) *An Arts Foundation Course: Introduction to Art History*, (3rd edn), Milton Keynes, The Open University.

Northedge, A. (1992) *Living in a Changing Society: Teaching Access*, Milton Keynes, The Open University.

Pring, R. (1992) 'Standards and quality in education', *British Journal of Educational Studies*, XXXX(1), pp. 4–22.

Wicks, S. (1992) 'Peer review and quality control in higher education', *British Journal of Educational Studies*, XXXX(1), pp. 57–68.

33

A STRING OF PEARLS?
A BROADER APPROACH TO COURSE EVALUATION

Alan Woodley

INTRODUCTION

It is perhaps inevitable that distance educators become extremely attached to their courses. Whether singly or in teams, they may well have spent several years honing the course to educational perfection. By the time it gets to students, it will probably be an integrated multimedia package which incorporates all of the design features demanded by the current pedagogic orthodoxy. During subsequent presentations the course writers will usually monitor performance indicators such as student numbers and success rates, treasuring the good ones and hoping to explain away the bad ones.

While basic course evaluation and monitoring has its place, I would contend that this must be supplemented by a much broader approach to course evaluation which takes into account the context in which the course is being studied. At the individual course level this requires research into who is taking the course and how they are studying it. Quantitative studies are needed to determine factors such as the educational and ethnic background of students and how this affects performance on the course. Qualitative and ethnographic studies of the course in action are also needed. Such studies would examine how people actually interact with and learn from the course, and how this relates to their personal, family and occupational circumstances. However, in this chapter I am going to consider course evaluation in the context of other courses.

Courses are rarely studied in complete isolation. Students have usually taken other courses previously (in the the same programme, in the same institution or elsewhere), they may be taking other courses in parallel, and they will probably go on to take further courses. While the number of pathways is infinite, once an institution has been in existence for a number of years, certain patterns emerge. Lessons can be learned both at the institutional and course development level.

Course team writers should continue to strive for perfection and to produce educational 'pearls'. However, they must be aware of how and why students are stringing these pearls together, because this affects the interpretation of evaluation data and has implications for future course design. At the institutional level, this form of analysis may well suggest ways to improve the teaching system and also cast further doubt on crude performance indicators.

THE COURSE IN CONTEXT

We begin with a simple example to underline the basic point that regardless of a course's 'quality', its impact – measured here by drop-out rates – is likely to vary depending upon factors other than inherent design features.

Figures taken from The Open University, UK, undergraduate programme showed a tendency for drop-out rates to increase over successive course presentations (Woodley and Parlett, 1983). This finding was counter-intuitive in the sense that student folklore warned people not to take a course in its first year of presentation because they rarely ran smoothly. Thus, while a course might become 'better' as the bugs are ironed out, it appears that there are countervailing factors that override this effect. Alternative hypotheses are that the first intakes consist of the keenest students who have been waiting for the course to come on stream, or that tutors are more motivated when they are teaching on new courses.

Another finding from the same research was that the closer students were to gaining their BA degree, the more likely they were to pass their current course. However, there appeared to be a fall in motivation after this point and there was a decline in success rates among students going on directly to attempt an Honours degree. Clearly, this will affect the success rate of any given course, depending upon where it occurs within typical degree profiles.

Students in the UK OU undergraduate programme have a fairly free choice of courses. However, certain courses have 'recommended prerequisite' courses which students ignore at their peril. In practice students tend to follow the recommendations or, if they do not, it is because they have acquired the relevant skills through a previous course or in their job. The point is that in an 'open' system where students can select their own route through an array of courses, there is no guarantee that they all have the prior knowledge that was assumed by the course designers.

Students frequently enrol on more than one course at the same time, then discover that the workload is too great. Some end up by failing everything, others make tactical withdrawals from some of their courses to maximise their chances of passing one. In the latter case, the choice might be random depending upon which course has an assignment due or it might be influenced by features of the course. For instance, in the case of the UK OU, a student might choose to continue with a particular course that has a residential school because they would have to pay for it even if they withdrew. Thus, when looking at the performance of a given course, it is

355

important to consider whether it tends to be studied along with other courses and, if so, which these courses are.

STRINGING THE PEARLS

When I have asked UK Open University academics what they think the graduation rate is, they typically answer something like "I don't really know – it's about 60 per cent, isn't it?" I think this is revealing on three counts. First, I believe that this reflects academics' concern with their own courses rather than the overall picture. Secondly, it reflects the difficulty in measuring graduation rates and, thirdly, it is a tribute to the University's own publicity.

The Open University, UK, has over one hundred undergraduate courses currently on offer. Each course counts as a full or half credit and can be at Foundation, Second, Third or Fourth level. Undergraduates do not enrol on a degree course of a specific duration and in a particular subject. Rather they can accumulate credits towards a degree over as many years as they wish, which presents problems when we come to calculate 'graduation rates' because the rate for a given year's intake can in theory go on increasing over a fifty-year period or more.

In its promotional literature the University likes to say that around six out of ten of its first intake have now graduated. While this is true, the unspoken implication that subsequent intakes will match this figure, given time, has not been critically examined. Instead the University has concentrated its attentions on publicising the large numbers of graduates that are produced each year, and on the very large cumulative total of graduates. However, now that the University has had twenty-four annual intakes of undergraduates, data exist for a more rigorous analysis of graduation rates. One solution has been to calculate the proportion of a given year's intake of new finally registered students who have gained a six-credit BA within a fixed time-period; when the University was being reviewed by the government in 1991 this was taken to be eight years.

When this measure is used for the first fifteen intakes it reveals that there has been a slow but steady decline in the figures from 54 per cent for the 1971 intake to 35 per cent for the 1985 group. Now this may be because later intakes are merely taking longer to graduate, or it may be because more of them are giving up their OU studies before gaining a degree. In either case the decline might be due to changes in the characteristics of new students.

If later intakes are graduating at a slower rate than earlier ones, then one would expect them eventually to begin to 'catch up' in terms of cumulative graduation rates. A simple way to examine this is to compare the cumulative graduation rates in successive years and the figures do suggest that later intakes were indeed gaining on earlier ones after eight years of study. For example, the 1985 intake added a further 3.5 per cent to their cumulative total in the eighth year compared to 1.6 per cent for the 1971 intake.

This 'catching up' is less marked in subsequent years of study and when we compared the figures for study years thirteen and twelve, there was virtually no difference between the intakes. The implication we might draw from these figures is that we should be using the twelve-year graduation rate rather than the eight-year rate when comparing intakes.

While twelve years might be the most appropriate for comparisons, it is not the end of the story. Small numbers of students continue to graduate from even the very earliest intakes. Clearly we can never calculate a 'final' graduation rate. At the moment it does seem likely that, with the possible exclusion of the 1971 intake, the twelve-year graduation rate will increase by 2 to 3 per cent over the following ten-year period.

We turn now to changes in the student population. In 1971 students with teaching certificates formed 32 per cent of the intake. By 1985 this had fallen to 11 per cent. Given the better progress made by those with high educational qualifications and with advanced standing, it was predictable that this would have an impact on overall graduation rates. However, when we looked at graduation rates within four bands of educational qualifications there was still a general tendency for graduation rates to decline within each band. This decline in graduation rates was relatively greater among those with 'Low' and 'Medium' qualifications than for those with 'High' qualifications or teachers certificates.

In Figure 33.1 we have tried to show how much of the general decline in graduation rates was due to a slowing down in student progress and how much was due to changes in the educational qualifications of students:

- The cumulative graduation rate after twelve years is markedly higher than the eight-year rate, especially for later intakes.
- We have extrapolated the twelve-year graduation rate figures for the 1982–5 intakes. (We took the graduation patterns of students from each of the four educational bands from the 1971–81 intakes and used linear regression to carry existing trends forward. In the case of the 1982 intake, for example, we plotted the twelve-year graduation rate as a percentage of the eleven-year graduation rate for each of the earlier intakes, then used linear regression to predict the result for 1982.) It appears that the twelve-year graduation rate for the 1985 intake will be around the 40 per cent mark. Over the following ten years one might expect it to rise to 42 or 43 per cent.
- The top line in the chart shows what the twelve-year graduation rate would have been if each successive intake had contained the same proportions in the four educational qualification bands as did the 1971 intake. Looking at the figures for the 1981 intake, it can be seen that approximately two-thirds of the decline in the eight-year graduation rate since 1971 could be accounted for by controlling for the slower

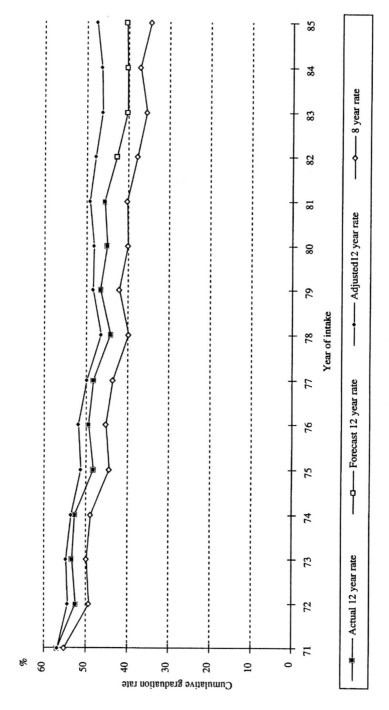

Figure 33.1 Twelve- and eight-year graduation rates at The Open University

graduation rates (i.e. by looking at the twelve-year rate) *and* the changing student population as measured by previous educational qualifications.

If, as it appears, graduation rates are getting both lower and slower to a certain extent, how can we account for it? Given that in recent years UK Open University course pass rates have remained fairly constant, is it something that can be affected by improved course design?

In attempting to answer these questions we will need to look at the patterns among the varied routes students take through the UK OU's system and we will have to ask them to tell us about the reasoning behind their choice of routes. Topics to explore include the following:

- Are UK Open University students increasingly using their course credits to transfer into full-time higher education? If so, is such a move a positive one inspired by OU studies or a negative one to escape further OU studies?
- Are people who leave without a degree satisfied with their OU experience?
- To what extent are people slowing down their studies by taking 'rest years' rather than reducing their course workload? Are they slowing their studies because of the cost of the courses or because the courses require too many hours of study? Are more of the recent students taking courses for leisure purposes and hence wishing to study at a slower pace?
- To what extent are students taking courses from within a single discipline and does this affect the way they move through and out of the system?
- How will student progress rates be influenced by changes in the student population (e.g. a possible increase in students with low educational qualifications as stated in the University's aims); in the external environment (e.g. transfers from the UK OU to higher education elsewhere becoming more or less difficult); in the OU system (e.g. the award of sub-degree qualifications, direct entry to post-foundation courses, and the six-credit Honours degree).

CONCLUSIONS

Course designers frequently complain about research that tells them that 57 per cent of students found the course 'fairly or very interesting', saying that they do not know how to use such information. The type of research that I have outlined in this chapter could well suffer the same fate because it is not course-specific and it does not offer any pat solutions. In the worst case the research results would be used to justify lack of action by course designers because they would say that poor performance indicators were probably caused by contextual factors that were out of their control.

I am arguing that, while it is necessary for the course designers to continue to produce their educational 'pearls', they will do so at their peril if they ignore the wider context in which they are studied. In the example I gave concerning graduation rates, they need to know whether people are ceasing to study because of the subject and quality of the courses on offer. If people are transferring to higher education elsewhere without taking third or fourth level courses, they need to consider whether they should be capitalising on this by offering more lower level courses.

My reasoning and my example is drawn from my experience at The Open University, UK. As such I hope that it will have direct relevance to other similar institutions around the world. However, I believe that the underlying principles hold true for smaller institutions and for designers of 'one-off' courses. They, too, must remember that their 'perfect' courses will be studied by mere mortals, each with their own personal agenda and each studying within an individual and social context.

REFERENCE

Woodley, A. and Parlett, M. (1983) 'Student drop-out', *Teaching at a Distance*, No. 24, pp. 2–23, Autumn.

34

EVALUATION AND SELF-IMPROVING SYSTEMS

Judith Calder

Decision-makers within open and distance education see the role of institutional research and evaluation in a variety of different ways. Among the models most commonly drawn upon are the Quality Assurance, Market Research, Institutional Planning and Educational Psychology models. Each of these perspectives has rather different implications for the type of research and evaluation which an institution undertakes. This chapter will discuss the effects of these different perspectives on the likelihood of an institution achieving the status of a self-improving organisation.

INTRODUCTION

In education, as in most other fields, economic, social, technological and political changes mean that there are no certainties and few predictabilities in the external environment within which organisations have to operate. For example, changes in the political climate, or in funding levels and mechanisms, or the further development of new information or communication technologies can present considerable challenges to distance teaching institutions as organisations if they are to respond to the opportunities and threats which these present. The necessity of being able to cope with changes in the external environment is therefore now accepted by most distance teaching organisations.

One of the major problems is that open and distance teaching organisations are usually either part of a large and complex organisation or are themselves large and complex. They usually have to deal with the recruitment, teaching, support and assessment of a body of students who are dispersed over large distances, as well as with the provision of course materials using a variety of media, either bought in or produced internally. Whether their concern is to maintain the quality of their provision or to improve it, there is a need for constant change within the organisation in order to compensate for and adapt to changes in the external environment. For example, modifications may need to be made to the curriculum to reflect the changing interests of key funding bodies, or of sponsors of students, or of potential students, or of existing students who have particular vocational needs or career aims; or student recruitment and support practices may need to be reviewed because student non-completion rates are seen as unacceptably high.

ORGANISATIONAL LEARNING

Thus, organisations need to be able to identify where the key problems are occurring and to devise solutions for them. In other words, they need the sort of information which can be provided by institutional research and evaluation (see Calder, 1994). When the results of the evaluation are internalised by the institution as an institution and when the organisation can generalise from those results, then it can be said that organisational learning has occurred (Argyris and Schon, 1978). Such learning may be accidental, random or ad hoc, or it can be deliberate, systematic and sustained.

The concept of an *organisation* which learns – as opposed to the learning by the individuals within it – is essential to the idea of a self-improving system. A number of authorities have already identified the necessity to include both the 'hidden' learning or tacit knowledge which an institution acquires and its more open, overt learning, predicated on ideas such as error detection and correction, and necessary major changes in priorities and objectives. As Jones and Hendry point out,

> The organisation's capability is the sum total of its learning activities, both hidden and revealed ... Organisational capability is not just the sum total of the organisation working in unison and changing values and mental models. Capability also means expanding and building on that which remains undeveloped and this is the focus of the learning organisation concept.
>
> (Jones and Hendry, 1994)

The idea of a learning organisation as one which 'continuously transforms itself' (Pedler *et al.*, 1988, p. 3) provides the informing perspective for any review of the function and purpose of institutional research and evaluation within an organisation.

SOME MODELS OF RESEARCH AND EVALUATION IN DISTANCE EDUCATION

There are a variety of different models used within distance teaching organisations (see, for example, Woodley, 1993). The ones examined in this chapter are among the most common.

Market research

One way of defining market research is to describe it as the bringing together of any data which inform marketing decisions. In distance teaching organisations, it is typically concerned with the improvement of student recruitment and the retention of students. Where sponsorship is an important factor, then the collection of data about sponsors' curriculum preferences may be included. Within what might at first glance appear to be a relatively modest remit lies a wide range of potential studies: for example, research into the public perception of the qualifications awarded by the organisation; employers' attitudes to the quality of the graduates and successful students; the features that attract those who apply to register for a course or programme of study; what turns people away from applying after the enquiry stage. All these studies will inform and guide the decisions which are made about how best to present information about the organisation and its courses. At the same time, information can be gathered about what are perceived as the less desirable traits of the organisation and its courses. In particular, the views of those groups can be sought from which both current and future students might be drawn.

Institutional planning

By the same argument, institutional planning studies could be described as those studies which collect data which inform planning decisions within an organisation. For example, problems concerning the extent and nature of the competition from other organisations, student throughput and demand, student success rates, demand prediction, trends in course take-up – all will need essential planning data derived, in the main, from databases holding detailed records of students on an individual basis. The analysis of student registration data plays an important role here, but this can be usefully supplemented by other data collection exercises, usually of a quantitative nature.

Educational psychology

This is perhaps one of the earliest models in use for institutional research and evaluation purposes. Hilgard pointed out in 1956 that, 'Professional educators have welcomed educational psychology as a foundation science upon which to build their practices'. However, it has been argued that the emphasis on developing the study of psychology as if it were a traditional science very much limited education's view of learning in that it threw emphasis on experimental approaches to research and therefore on ways of learning which could be relatively easily controlled (e.g. memory), rather than on such anthropological-type approaches as participant observation which take in contextual and cultural influences (Smith, 1984). Nevertheless, the knowledge provided by experimental psychology has in more recent years been supplemented by new areas of knowledge through the use of cognitive psychology, by data from classic work carried out by developmental psychologists such as Piaget, and by anthropological-type approaches. The educational psychology model therefore primarily informs a range of views of learning from the simplest behaviourist model to the most complex multiple-perspective model, which are used by the course designer or the course developer in the development of the course materials.

Quality assessment

In contrast, 'quality assessment' is perhaps one of the newest models of research and evaluation which are used in distance teaching organisations. In the UK, the term quality assessment is used separately from terms such as quality assurance, quality control and quality audit. Quality assessment is 'the process of external evaluation of the actual provision of education' (SHEFC, 1992). The two key distinguishing features of this model are that the focus of attention is the courses themselves and the student work which is achieved, together with the methodology which is employed to evaluate the provision. The methodology is based on an initial self-evaluation carried out by the course-providers; this is then subject to external assessment by peers who scrutinise institutional documentation and student work, who observe the teaching process where feasible, and who interview staff and students. This exercise is designed to provide evidence of the quality of the teaching in specific subject areas. For organisations involved in distance education, therefore, there can be both pluses and minuses in a situation where colleagues who may not be familiar with distance education techniques have to assess the teaching quality of what, in a conventional institution, is normally a simultaneous event, i.e. teaching and learning.

PREDOMINATING VIEWS OF RESEARCH AND EVALUATION IN DISTANCE EDUCATION

Each of these models provides a distinct and different view of the work and the quality of the provision of a distance teaching organisation. In one sense, the model which is most familiar to an organisation will help determine their perceptions of where problems lie. For example, a pharmacist will turn first to pharmaceutical remedies when treating someone who is ill, while a psychiatrist will want to examine the patient's emotional state; the physiotherapist would first examine the patient's anatomy while the reflexologist would initially examine a patient's feet. Thus an organisation which had been particularly concerned about generating and sustaining a good level of demand for its courses would be likely to develop a view of research which focused particularly upon market research activities. Having acquired some knowledge of and competence in using market research methodologies, it would then tend to view research and evaluation as a market-research-type activity and would interpret its data needs in the terms most susceptible to those kinds of approaches.

In part, this situation is reinforced by the system of utilisation which will have established itself within the institution. In the case of the institutional planning model, for example, the principal users will be senior managers with a planning responsibility within the organisation. These may include heads of programmes of study, heads of service units, planning officers with a cross-organisational responsibility and the most senior managers of the institution itself. The emphasis on quantitative data and on the analysis of trends do allow for survey-based work on topics such as future study plans, or student access to media resources or communication networks where data are needed for planning purposes; but the predominant methodology will be on statistical data using databases which allow for information on individual cases to be collected over time, and which include as wide a range of routinely collected data as possible about those cases on an individual basis. In contrast, if the educational psychology model is being used, the principal beneficiaries will be course designers, contributors to course materials and staff involved in student support. The impact, in other words, will be primarily on teaching and support-related issues, but with some possible subsequent secondary impact on finance and planning. The diversity of methodological approaches which can be used – testing, completion of inventories, student diaries, observation, in-depth interviews – does also provide an opportunity for investigating those other issues where an understanding of complex situations or processes is needed. For example, research into the factors affecting course choice, students' approaches to study, or students' organisation of their study might be expected to be linked closely with the educational psychology model.

The two remaining models provide contrasting examples of the aspects of the operation of a distance teaching organisation which are highlighted through their use. The market research model and the quality assessment model both involve a broad spectrum of staff with academic and planning responsibilities in the specification of the research problem and thus of the data needed and in the utilisation of that data. The difference occurs in that, where the market research model predominates, the focus is on establishing an understanding of the environment within which the organisation operates: who the potential students and sponsors are; what sort of teaching provision they perceive themselves as needing; what features of the provision potential students and sponsors respond to positively and which negatively. In contrast, the quality assessment model focuses on the final product, on the quality of the courses which have been produced, and the teaching which is offered by the institution. The methodologies which are employed do overlap: while the market research work will employ the full range of social research methodologies – quantitative and qualitative, such as small group, large group, and survey work – the quality assessment data will normally be more dependent on quantitative data drawn from formal surveys and student records although qualitative work is by no means excluded.

EFFECTS ON RESEARCH AND EVALUATION ACTIVITIES

Although the boundaries between the different models are not as distinct as the discussion so far might suggest, nevertheless what is revealed are the major areas of commonality and difference between the models in so far as they affect the research and evaluation emphasis within the institution.

Table 34.1 Aspects of the organisational system, in relation to the interests of specific models of research and evaluation

Evaluation issues	Research model	
	Primary model	*Secondary model*
Context	Market research	Institutional planning
Input	Institutional planning	Market research
Process	Educational psychology	Quality assessment
Product	Quality assessment	Educational psychology

Consider the distance teaching institution in terms of its context, input, process and product (shown in Table 34.1). It can be seen that where the market research model is operated as either the primary or the secondary research model, issues relating to context and, to a lesser extent, input are covered. However, there is likely to be little learned which sheds light on the teaching and learning process in a way which assists process-related or product-related issues such as the course development process, student retention problems or the quality of the student learning experience. Conversely, if the institutional planning model is the predominant model, then issues related to institutional and programme strategy such as recruitment figures, demographic data on applicants and on registered students, information on geographic spread, study intentions, sponsorship data, fee payment data and so on which could be classified as Input issues will be the primary focus, with context issues, such as information about new developments and changes in the target population, provision available from other organisations, as the secondary focus.

Similarly, the educational psychology model and the quality assessment model may be seen as a pair. The work on learning and motivation which is carried out within this model contributes primarily to process-related institutional problems, but can also be seen as contributing to other issues such as the acquisition of study skills (for example) which would be seen more as product-related issues. Finally, the primary focus of the quality assessment model is the product itself. In distance teaching terms, this can be seen as the course which is offered to students, the support provided for students, and as the knowledge and skills acquired by the student from the course. The quality assessment model is not an exclusively summative model, however, but can be used formatively to contribute to the improvement of the courses and the supporting systems during the Process stage.

IMPLICATIONS FOR QUALITY AND SELF-IMPROVEMENT

It is important to identify the dominant research and evaluation model(s) in operation within an organisation in order to understand the strengths and limitations which this will impose on the organisation's capacity to investigate problem areas. In other words, its capacity to identify those areas where standards are not being met, or where priorities and goals may need adapting to meet changed external conditions. Argyris and Schon (1978) have drawn attention to the struggles and internal conflicts which can accompany the practice of 'self-improvement'. Given that battles over the need for, and nature of, internal change appear to be a normal feature of organisational life, access to research and evaluation facilities and the information which they can provide is obviously important for individuals within an organisation, as well as for the organisation itself. If there is a dominant model rather than a mix of models, then certain parts of the organisation will be unable to learn and develop to the same extent as other parts. Like the body-builder who concentrates on developing one part of his body to the exclusion of other parts, deformity will become a real danger.

The need, then, for an organisation which aims to be self-improving is to aim for all-round development. Once the research and evaluation models being drawn on have been identified and their relative influence assessed, the aim will be to achieve a balance in the type of models which informs the institution's thinking. This may well involve 'perspective transformation' among key managers in the way in which they perceive the role and function of research and evaluation within the institution, but the fact that this process does not necessarily have to involve additional resources may make the task easier.

The same data may be used in a variety of different ways in order to shed light on very different problems (see Figure 34.1). The key is in the fact that under the institutional planning model, for example, we do not talk about 'planning data' as if the data were exclusive to that one aspect of institutional operation, but of 'data which is used for planning purposes'. This releases

Market research data

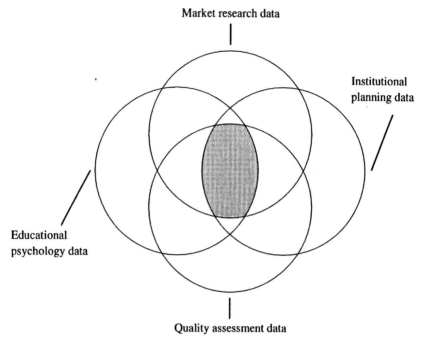

Institutional
planning data

Educational
psychology data

Quality assessment data

Figure 34.1 Multiple utilisation of institutional research and evaluation data

any particular set of data from the constraints of one model, and makes it available for use for other purposes. So, for example, data from a study which is investigating students' use of and reaction to different course components may be used for market research purposes (identifying components which students appear to particularly enjoy/dislike using); institutional planning purposes (contributing to the institution's understanding of students' course preferences and progress, perceived cost-effectiveness of different media); pedagogical purposes (teaching effectiveness of different components on different types of courses/with different types of students); and for quality assessment (as a quantitative measure of the quality of one aspect of the teaching/learning experience as experienced by the students). Any set of data, whatever the purpose behind its initial collection, can be regarded as a resource for research and evaluation. The opening up of perceptions of the role and function of research and evaluation within an organisation is a key initial step in enabling that organisation to operate effectively as a learning organisation.

REFERENCES

Argyris, C. and Schon, D. (1978) *Organisational Learning: A Theory of Action Perspectives*, Reading, MA, Addison-Wesley.

Calder, J. (1994) *Programme Evaluation and Quality: A Comprehensive Guide to Setting up an Evaluation System*, London, Kogan Page.

Hilgard, E. *et al.* (1956) *Theories of Learning,* (4th edn, 1975) London, Prentice-Hall.

Jones, A. M. and Hendry, C. (1994) 'The learning organisation: adult learning and organisational transformation', *British Journal of Management*, Vol. 5, pp. 153–62.

Pedler, M. *et al.* (1988) *Learning Company Project: A Report on Work undertaken October 1987 to April 1988*, Sheffield, The Training Agency.

SHEFC (1992) *Quality Framework*, Scottish Higher Education Funding Council.

Smith, F. (1984) *Joining the Literacy Club*, Victoria, BC, Centre for the Teaching of Reading in conjunction with Abel Press.

Woodley, A. (1993) *Improving Distance Education Universities through Institutional Research: A Consideration of the Roles and Functions of the Institutional Researcher*, SRC Report No. 79, Institute of Educational Technology, Milton Keynes, The Open University.

INDEX

action research, *see* ethnographic
approach
active learning, 136
activities, 16, 175, 201–6: benefits of,
202–3; cost–benefit analysis model of,
205–6; costs, 203–5; non-completion,
203–4; selectivity 205; time, 203; *see
also* assessment, embedded support
devices, students' use of activities
adult learning, 156
alternative media to print, 89
approach to learning, 55–6, 255–7:
active, 59; cognitive, 157;
constructivist, 155–6, 255–6, 257,
258–9; context, 55, 61, 79–80; deep,
55–8, 59, 60, 79, 80, 81, 181, 283;
empiricist, 255; holism, 61–3, 79, 80,
82, 160; influence of assessment
system on, 57, 61; interactive, 259–63;
model of student learning, 61–3; and
relation to people's lives, 63; strategic,
64; surface, 55–7, 61, 79, 80, 81, 181,
283
art history: evaluation of course, 345–52;
nature of the discipline, 345;
pedagogic principles, 347–8
assessment: effect of on study, 197–9;
student response to, 197–206; TMA
Consciousness, 198; TMA Dominated,
198–9, 199–200; TMA Aware, 198–9,
200–1; using electronic networking
for, 167, 208–16; in workplace
learning, 245–6
assessment, electronic, 208–16:
advantages of, 209, 212, 216;
applications, 211; collaborative, 214–
5; disadvantages of, 209–10, 212;
innovations made possible by, 212–5;

online assignments, 213–4; staged
assignments, 213
assignments, *see* assessment
audience research, 77–83
audience response, implosion of distance
between message and, 76–7
audiocassettes, 131, 136: use by disabled
students, 88
audioconferencing, 155, 157–8, 159,
260, 261, 262, 263
audio-graphics, 35, 159

Bangkok Project, 34
Baudrillard, J., 76–7, 83
Behavioural Objectives Approach, 16–7
behaviourism, 364: limitations of, for
conceptual learning, 175
Big Bang in distance education, 3, 4, 5–
6: costs 9
broadcasting, 78, 133–4: lack of
developmental testing, 338;
programme creation, 338–9, 341–2;
student interpretation of, 78, 136;
summative evaluation of, 339; use in
teaching, 78, 135; *see also* satellite
network

cable networks, 5, 33, 34
CD-ROM, 49, 130, 176, 327, 330: use by
disabled students, 89, 90, 91; *see also*
image types, dimension of;
multimedia
change in distance education: cost-
effectiveness, 43–4; managing, 29, 48;
strategy for, 43
class, effect on context of learning, 81
client-led provision, 235, 240, 271, 272,
324–5

Printed in the United Kingdom
by Lightning Source UK Ltd.
107457UKS00004B/69-124